# POLITICS

## *Individual and State*

ROBERT WESSON

*Hoover Institution*

PRENTICE HALL, *Englewood Cliffs, New Jersey 07632*

**Library of Congress Cataloging-in-Publication Data**

Wesson, Robert G.
  Politics: individual and state.

  Includes bibliographies and index.
  1. State, The.   2. Authoritarianism.   3. Democracy.
I. Title.
JC325.W487    1988         320      87–12582
ISBN 0–13–684309–3

Editorial/production supervision: **Susan E. Rowan**
Cover design: **Wanda Lubelska**
Manufacturing buyer: **Carol Bystrom**

*To the multitudes
cheated by the inhumanity of power*

Printed in the United States of America

10   9   8   7   6   5   4   3   2   1

ISBN 0-13-684309-3

PRENTICE-HALL INTERNATIONAL (UK) LIMITED, *London*
PRENTICE-HALL OF AUSTRALIA PTY. LIMITED, *Sydney*
PRENTICE-HALL CANADA INC., *Toronto*
PRENTICE-HALL HISPANOAMERICANA, S.A., *Mexico*
PRENTICE-HALL OF INDIA PRIVATE LIMITED, *New Delhi*
PRENTICE-HALL OF JAPAN, INC., *Tokyo*
PRENTICE-HALL OF SOUTHEAST ASIA PTE. LTD., *Singapore*
EDITORA PRENTICE-HALL DO BRASIL, LTDA., *Rio de Janeiro*

# Contents

# Preface

    This book is entitled *Politics* (with a bow to Aristotle and Harold Laski) because its subject is the span of political affairs from democracy to authoritarianism to the interactions of the superpowers—a scope broader than is ordinarily considered proper for works of political science. It is not the kind of book that one researches and then writes; rather, it is the result of many years of varied reading and thinking. In a sense it was begun fifty years ago, when world war was on the horizon and a boy realized that an abundance of good minds was dedicated to natural science but there was a shortage of problem solvers in the most critical matters for humanity, the problems of political conflict.

    The study of politics is less elegant than devising theorems of finite groups or grand unified theories of physics, but it is equally difficult and more frustrating. It requires weighing crucial questions for which there are no good scales and concerning which the best observers often err. Yet the deepest theories of the physical universe and the most marvelous robots will go for nothing unless the political universe can be managed. If civilization comes to grief, it will be for lack, not of scientific-technical knowledge, but of political wisdom.

    Because truth in political affairs is so complex and shadowy, the journey to some sort of synthesis has been long. First came an interest in foreign countries and international affairs. Study of Soviet institutions followed when the world war showed how important the Soviet Union would be in the world order. Analysis of the Soviet system led to a comparative investigation of other highly governed huge states, the so-called universal empires of the past. Examination of the imperial order in turn entailed consideration of the opposite condition; systems of interacting sovereignties, such as the city-states of classical Greece or the nation-states of Europe after the fifteenth century, the kind of societies which alone have been capable of free political institutions. Turning to Latin American politics added another dimension; the differences between the advanced industrial states and the Third World, in which Latin America is the best contemporary political laboratory for the study of democracy or partial democracy versus authoritarianism.

This book endeavors to bring these various subjects into a single vision, to make a work of theory in the broadest sense. Its basic premise is that human psychology and the bases of social and political relations are much the same everywhere and always, however different the political results of different structures bringing different motivations to the fore.

Overwhelming problems arise from our incredible success as an intelligent species; but most, if not all, of them should be solvable if the peoples of the earth can learn to guide themselves without allowing themselves to be enslaved. This work represents an effort to improve, however slightly, our understanding of relations of superiority and inferiority, domination and responsibility, or self-seeking and cooperation on the highest level—that of human societies. It represents an effort to improve our understanding of how humans are governed or misgoverned or might be better governed.

R.W.

# Introduction

The paradigm of the modern miracle, the computer, is made up of very many switches, which can be either on or off. With a single switch or junction, or even a few dozen, one can do very little. But millions or billions can be linked together to perform extremely complex operations, such as designing an airplane or playing a masterly game of chess. Perhaps the designers will one day produce a genuine electro-mechanical intelligence.

Humans are like computer elements in that a lone individual has very limited innate capacities and can react to the environment only in animal-like fashion; even a community of hundreds or a few thousand in isolation could carry on only a primitive existence. But the cooperation of many millions of minds, building on the immense data bank called culture and utilizing a huge volume of software called institutions, has made possible technological civilization, including the ability to construct computers.

The efficacy of the computer lies in the way switches and chips containing thousands of switches are linked. This is equally true of human society: the degree to which persons or groups can be creative and productive depends on the complex network of interrelations holding together the society and forming the framework of the lives, thoughts, and deeds of the members. A person watching swarms of Egyptians hauling huge stones up ramps to build the pyramids several thousand years ago would surely have been impressed with the marvelous coordination making possible such works. The flight of a huge airliner or the reading of the code of a gene are testimony to the good functioning of the vastly more intricate interrelationships of modern society.

A fundamental difference between the computer and human society is that the former has only such purpose as is built into it by the engineers, whereas the latter is self-motivated. This is closely related to another major difference; whereas engineers design computers, no one has had much success in planning a human society. Seldom, and then only partially, have architects of the state been able to introduce new, rationally devised instititions; even the philosophers' utopias look backwards. Such lawgivers as Solon among the ancient Greeks and the drafters of the United States Constitution in Philadelphia in 1787 invented little that was really new but built on existing institutions. Politicologues like to see the state as far more systematic and purposeful than it is; even the founders of new states have almost always tried to meet the exigencies of the day, rarely giving thought to the distant future. The structures of human society have grown up in virtually incomprehensible, often unpredictable ways.

There has been as much irrationality in affairs of state as there has been intelligence in the higher reaches of physical science. Careful and objective thought, sophisticated experimentation, and laboriously constructed edifices of fact-based theory have enabled humans to delve into the interior of the proton, to measure surfaces with an error less than the diameter of an atomic nucleus, and to send probes billions of miles to the outer reaches of the solar system. Yet the leadership of great nations is seldom coherently systematic, and there is little pressure for truthfulness in political practice. To the contrary, although the appearance of candor is an asset, to practice much of it is not helpful to a political career.

Politics takes in all of human nature, including domination, submissiveness, ambition, laziness, love, hatred, cooperation, and jealousy, and is as unknowable as it is complex. In its realm there is no complex and methodical thinking like that of mathematics. Overabundant and fuzzy data confuse the mind, and there is no scientific theory to guide leaders in novel situations. They are not, of course, usually trained in political science, but we cannot be confident that professors from the best universities would necessarily show better judgment.

There is no system for placing in power the persons best equipped to decide on behalf of the community; indeed, there are no clear criteria for deciding who such persons may be. And power corrupts judgment; even the middling great are beset by sycophants. Moreover, people have a wonderful ability to disregard evidence that does not fit their preconceptions and to believe what suits them for material or psychological reasons; and they hunger for simple answers in the confusion of facts. Tobacco salesmen can apparently convince themselves that they are doing good in the world, and high intelligence does not seem to make people less likely to be misled by appealing theories. Crude, egotistical dictators may well believe themselves the savior of the state and persuade the multitudes to agree.

The highest officials of great nations, who are subject to all manner of accidents of personality and often bring limited abilities to the most demanding positions, frequently make ill-founded decisions based more on prejudice and emotion (if not self-interest) than on careful consideration of the needs of their country. The results of the chemist are usually reliable; the wisest statesman is, however, as capable of gross errors as the humblest citizen. German generals thought America's entry into World War I could have little military effect; Hitler insisted on attacking the Soviet Union without waiting to end the war with Britain, despite Stalin's desperate desire for peace; and Franklin Roosevelt—an expert in American, but not Soviet, politics—believed he could win Stalin's cooperation by joviality.

It is the more difficult to analyze political problems because the structure of human society remains largely beyond our understanding. No one really knows how different or how much alike New Yorkers, Bolivian peasants, or Pygmy hunters in Zaire may be, as they cope with their respective worlds; and no one can describe a society in such a way as to make it theoretically possible to reconstruct it. All manner of relations would have to enter into such a description: within families and between unrelated persons, between the sexes, between leaders and led, between stronger and weaker, and so forth, all mixed with acquired and inborn drives. No one can give a clear-cut answer even to such an apparently simple question as why one nation is more apt than another to develop democratic institutions. No society can ever really understand itself, and the more sophisticated, the more difficult a society is to understand.

The present book cannot, of course, treat all aspects of society. The bases of our social existence—the way we regard and treat one another—are the subject of many specialists, from priests to psychologists, most of whom would reform our behavior. The subject here can be only a single crucial area of the enormously intricate web of human relations and institutions—namely the state, the broadest and highest-level structure of society.

Political organization rests on institutions, motivations, customs, and other social phenomena; and it influences them and at the same time is affected by and merges with them. It is a suitable subject for separate inquiry, however, because it is rather definite, tangible, and, to a degree, knowable. Psychological, social, or economic factors favoring dictatorial government are vague and indefinite; but that one person commands the apparatus of government in an arbitrary fashion is a clear fact. And the state, which calls itself sovereign and claims a monopoly of legal coercion, obviously may be a major cause of many other things, a primary independent variable. For example, the two Germanies, like the two Koreas, despite shared background, inhabit decidedly different worlds, are immersed in different cultures, and seem to have developed different value systems, all for a single apparent cause; the fact that one fraction has a Soviet-influenced government, and the other, a looser, more pluralistic Western-affiliated government.

It is seldom possible, however, to point confidently to such a clear and unambiguous cause. There are few broad yet definite and scientifically defensible conclusions in political matters. Politics is inscrutable because we have limited and unreliable information about exceedingly complex interactions of people acting more or less irrationally. Generalizations must be qualified by "other things being equal," and other things are never quite equal. All too many statements in this book are weakened by a *probably* or a *perhaps*. One may speak of "tendencies" in certain directions, which may be modified by "special circumstances." Statements in political matters are relative, and what one makes of relative statements depends on one's attitude. There are far too many facts and supposed facts to work with, yet very many or most facts are missing.

For example, we know little of the inner workings of most Third World governments simply because they prefer to close the shutters. We make largely intuitive judgments on the basis of selected data, and the most effective political assertions are gross overstatements of emotion-laden ideas.

Much depends on unpredictable personalities. For example, the greatest factors leading Cuba to Marxism-Leninism and Spain to democracy seem to have been the characters of Fidel Castro and King Juan Carlos respectively. Hitlerism and Leninism were partly the result of preexistent conditions, but they were shaped by idiosyncratic personalities. It is unsatisfactory to say that a course was followed because that was what the president decided, but this may be the most realistic answer.

Yet we should not surrender in the face of the impossibility of finding exact and provable truth in political questions. If deductions are unprovable, this does not mean that they cannot be based on many well-attested facts, clear thinking, and careful analysis. Very many things that we know about democratic states, for example, hang together and give some confidence in our general understanding. The wielders of great power continually have to draw conclusions and reach decisions; it is our task to understand the workings of the state as best we can while confessing that we never understand absolutely.

It is consequently the purpose of this volume to consider something of the problems of government, the use and misuse of political authority, and, by implication, how it may be better managed. An essential for the betterment of the human condition is improvement of the social fabric, just as better design is the essence of building more powerful computers. It may be necessary first to bring about a better society in order to have a better state atop it, and this is a theme of the present work. But the chief hope of reformers is to improve society through its most powerful and purposeful institution, the state.

# The Principles of Government

## 1

## THE HUMAN DUALITY

The realm of politics is a jungle landscape, across which there are no highways and few trails to understanding. But by standing back one can perceive a certain order in the tangle. A few fundamentals run through politics and government across the whole panorama from savagery to the most cultivated civilization: relations of leadership and subordination and of command and consultation or responsibility, the vesting of authority in one or a few, and the rights and duties of many. However different the proportions and the mode of expression in despotisms or democracies, old or new, one can interpret all political systems in these terms.

Basic relations in the ordering of society, as in the ordering of the family, obviously derive from the social nature of humans. Human society is caught up in countless difficulties and uncertainties because *Homo sapiens* is only ambivalently a social being. Other highly developed societies, such as the colonies or hives of ants, bees, and termites, rest on the instinctual, genetically fixed subordination of the individual to the collectivity. A bee has no destiny but that of the hive; anthropomorphically stated, its values are only those of the collective. But humans have individual destinies, and each is biologically or genetically keyed to his or her own lineage; and favor for one's kin, especially one's children, is a large factor in the complication of politics. A human society is a conglomerate of many individuals, each with particular needs, drives, and purposes, yet all tied by common interests, specializations, and mutual dependence. In contrast to the social insects, humans have scanty, ill-defined, and often contradictory social instincts, which might better be called tendencies. They probably developed through the survival value of cooperative behavior to small bands,[1] and are mostly derivative of familial relations and the in- and out-group antithesis. The efforts of sociobiologists to find definite genetic bases for human behavior have had little success.[2]

Yet humans are quite as dependent on society as social insects, and the human community is as much a superorganism as is an anthill. Humans are not merely willful, self-sufficient individuals but are parts of a large aggregate apart from which they, like the cells of a metazoan body, cannot function. We are formed by society as much as we form ourselves. There is hence ceaseless tension between self-regarding needs and impulses and the needs and demands of the group, and human nature is a complex compound of egoistic and altruistic drives.[3] This unresolvable ambivalence causes endless conflict and complications and is at the heart of most of our dramas.

Because a large majority of higher animals are more or less social, contrary selfish and altruistic traits are common in nature, both evidently favored by evolution: wolves cooperate in the hunt and fight for leadership; in some species of monkeys, mothers feed the young of others; in other species, females kill their rivals' offspring. The conflict of selfishness and altruism is the essence of the human condition, and only through the interaction of these dual aspects has it been possible for evolution to give rise to high multiform intelligence, indefinitely cumulative culture, and the fantastic powers of technology. Social insects, bound by instinct to serve the hive or colony, whose organization is more reasonably called slavery than cooperation, are fixed into rigid patterns.

Humans, flexible and capable of change, have potentialities—genetically based but not genetically determined—for advancing self-interests either alone, in harmony with a smaller or larger community, or at the expense of others, and also for promoting broader interests, with or without sacrificing personal ones. Motivation is mixed beyond disentanglement. One may join the army because it is required, or because it offers good pay with opportunities for training, or to become part of a close group, or from the desire to serve the national community. Normally self-centered people gladly accept sacrifices when called upon by inspiring leaders. People act as much from shared values as from personal self-interest, if not more so; and persons in similar economic situations often have very different political ideals.[4]

It is in a sense irrational to sacrifice oneself in any way for the group. On the other hand, it is essential for the group that individuals subordinate their needs to a considerable degree to the group's needs. This dilemma is only partially resolved by the fact that they receive satisfactions through their relations with their fellows and like to feel themselves part of a larger whole, because these satisfactions may be sought in ways congruent or incongruent with its needs. The group with which an individual identifies may be a small fraction of the community, or the community, or even humanity as a whole. While the group prospers by the altruism of its members, individuals may prosper both materially and psychologically at the expense of the group. The organization of the community responds partly to the individual drives of power holders and partly to the collective needs of the community, mingled in undeterminable proportions. These contrary aspects are sometimes harmoniously joined, sometimes sharply contradictory, the degree of harmony or discord being a measure of the quality of the society.

## THE STATE

Because of the duality of human nature, a close social existence is possible, yet a synthetic regulatory authority is necessary for any group too large to be guided by well-understood personal relations. The lack or weakness and irregularity of social instincts requires the formation of a coordinating organization, the state.

Inevitably, the state, like its component individuals, has a dual nature, corresponding both to unselfish and to selfish drives, individual and shared. One can imagine that a primitive state may take shape because a clan subdues its neighbors and exacts obedience and tribute from them, or a gang asserts its mastery over the more passive members of the community. Contrariwise, a number of villages may recognize that to carry on common affairs—to build a bridge, or to fend off hostile raids—they need to have recognized leaders; perhaps tax gatherers are required to make sure people contribute for the general needs, or a chief priest to represent the community in dealing with higher powers, or judges to reconcile differences. The state, that is, may represent largely aggressive and selfish motives, as some stand over and take advantage of others; or it may represent the social aspect of human nature, as an organization to do for the community whatever people cannot do for themselves. Of course, it cannot be entirely given to either of these directions. The most oppressive state necessarily does something useful; and in the most communitarian state only occasional saints will entirely refrain from using position for their own benefit.

If the incredible successes of humanity are made possible by the effective structuring of society, the greatest human failure is bad government. In the most important human affairs, one may rise by skilled maneuvering among personalities, by sharp domination, by the ability to appeal to passion, or by the capacity for persuasive simplification. Self-deception grows with power over others, and rewards are seldom geared to encourage leaders to seek the welfare of the community over their own or that of a narrow group. In all professions there is some incongruence between contribution to the overt goals of the profession and status acquired by manipulation of symbols and personal relations; this is probably greatest in politics.

In ordinary definitions of the state, emphasis is laid on its coercive aspect. It is commonly called the agency that has a monopoly of legitimate force (except for parents physically chastising their young ones *in loco rei publicae*) over the people of a defined territory. This is realistic, considering the demonstrated capacity of states, ancient and modern, for maltreating their subjects. This definition is inadequate, however, since even harsh dictatorial states rarely spend a large part of their energies in coercion. Resort to force represents a failure, a breakdown of the normal means of securing obedience. The state acts through persuasion and prestige as well as threat, and its most-used power is the ability to take or control property, taking from some and giving to others. Even harsh dictatorships make much more use of rewards than physical punishments, especially to motivate their servants. The signal fact is that the state is the all-embracing authority from which there is no appeal by the prevalent rules.

It is equally relevant that the state is an expression of the group—the territorial nature of society—separating the world into "us" and "them." Much of the solidarity of the state rests on the antithesis between those who belong and those who do not and commonly on hostility to the outsiders. The state, or the government that incorporates it, is the institution whereby the community regularly makes effective and ordinarily enforceable decisions. It may be simple and primitive; if a tribal people has the custom of convoking the elders or the bearers of arms to decide on war or peace under recognized leaders, this may be considered a prototypical state, with basic features found in all government: allocation of authority, a fixed leadership, and mechanisms for consultation and for execution of decisions.

The smaller the self-ruling group, the more personal the state is and the more like a family; in small primitive bands the leadership roughly corresponding to the state is not far from the headship of an extended family. In fundamentals, the state is the family unit writ large; and the well-ordered family has traditionally been the model for the good state. Even modern states regard themselves to some extent as a sort of superfamily, as the Japanese, for example, considered themselves children of the emperor. Attitudes toward state authority may derive in large part from attitudes toward parents, and such feelings are reflected in language; we speak of *paternalistic* government and of the *brotherhood* of the citizens of the *fatherland*.

### Purposes of the State

The first and most essential purpose of the state is self-preservation, in which it resembles any organization that is rewarding to those who compose it. The original purpose of organization above the family was probably the defense of the tribe, and the primary purpose of the state is to stand for its people in relation to other peoples and states. Defending itself against internal as well as external foes, the state protects the community over which it presides and the basic social order, the class system or structure of society. Only in a rare revolutionary situation does a freshly constituted state seek deeply to change the social order. Ordinarily the chief business of the state is to keep society functioning much as it has been.

Governments can logically be considered good or bad only in terms of what one expects of them. Many have served little purpose beyond the transfer of income from producers—mostly peasants—to an upper class,[5] causing insecurity and injustice and depriving many of liberty and welfare while taxing, conscripting, and repressing them. But under modern conditions all governments do much more, or claim to. Among the commonly desired political goods that the state is called upon to furnish are security, justice, liberty, and the general welfare.[6] Good rulers and bad ones have generally asserted, in ancient times as well as in modern, their love for their people. Hammurabi (1750 B.C.) was proclaimed to be the good father of his subjects, as were Pharaohs long before him. The beneficent purpose of the state was taken for granted in the Greek city-states of classical times and was often expressed by the Roman Caesars. Confucius was preoccupied with the welfare of the people as the true goal of imperial Chinese statecraft. "But the end of the state," according to Aristotle, "is not mere life; it is, rather, a good quality of life." [7]

Expectations of the state are as innumerable and diverse as people's values and needs. People generally want services such as the protection of life, property, and "the pursuit of happiness," schools, roads, security for the nation, help in emergencies, and an almost endless list that always grows longer. Somewhat less obviously, they want the state to be restrained; to refrain from not overtaxing them, to not penalize or repress them improperly, to permit them to act and express their feelings—in short, to not abuse its command of force. For some states, the fostering of freedom and responsibility to the people has high priority; for others, indoctrination and conformity take precedence, for the benefit of the holders of state power and perhaps at some sacrifice of the material welfare as well as freedom of the majority.

Demands on the state proliferate with the complications of modern life, and its citizens are inclined to blame it or the leaders' policies for whatever goes wrong, except obviously uncontrollable natural calamities. It is up to the government to keep cities livable, enable people to earn an adequate living, and support the needy, not only in countries with state-managed economies but also in those that rely on private enterprise. The authority above us should assist us in all ways toward what we imagine to be the good life.

More than any other single agency, the state makes an environment favorable or unfavorable for modern civilization. It encourages or discourages learning, the flow of information, scientific and artistic creativity, productive or unproductive activity, honesty or thievery. In many ways, the state makes life more open or closed, more rewarding or more frustrating. It reassures or intimidates, stimulates or depresses, promotes equality or inequality, preserves or wastes. It is not easy for people of the Western world to realize how fortunate they are to have a reasonably well-functioning political apparatus.

The political authority has and must have strong powers, including the ability to deprive people of property and freedom; yet it should use those powers for the general good, not to benefit a minority of power holders. It is less remarkable that the state is sometimes brutal and exploitative than that it is often fairly enlightened and decent, making possible this infinitely complex and delicately balanced technological civilization. It incorporates the self-guidance of the community, requiring a higher level of understanding or rationality than problem solving on the part of beings who are not only self-seeking but often irrational—if it is possible to discern rationality in the contradictions of civilization.

In ordinary affairs the state represents a settled order—whether voluntary, traditional, or imposed—and it must do so to keep human affairs running. Any government needs the active support of many people and the acquiescence of many more; the regime must enjoy some legitimacy—that is, be seen as justified—and correspond to some notion of right or equity. A functioning society requires that people behave in predictable fashion; and most behavior conforms closely to the norms and expectations of the group and remains within the accepted rules (which may differ from the formal regulations). Traffic has to follow some sort of code for people to get from one place to another.

Yet there must be space for deviance to permit improvement in the governance of affairs, just as the tiny fraction of positive genetic mutations are the building blocks of evolutionary progress. Most conduct departing from social norms is doubtless for individual gain at the expense of the group; and deviant acts, like violations of the vehicular code, are commonly negative if they are significant. But without dissidents to seek new ways, the state decays.

## THE URGE TO POWER

If humans were instinctually communitarian, there would be no need for a coercive state except to deal with other states. But people desire benefits for themselves at the expense of others; the state consequently becomes everywhere an arena of conflict.

Nonetheless, the political contest would be fairly manageable if self-seeking were merely for material benefits; parties could probably come to an agreement on cutting the cake. The tensions and bitterness of politics arise because much more is involved—namely, who is to be the boss, who is to lay down the rules, who is to be respected as the chief personage, whose ideals and principles shall prevail. It is not enough to find a way to divide the cake; the political struggle is about who decides how goods are to be allocated now and in the future, which is a far more serious and threatening matter. Politics, in other words, is about power, the ability to raise oneself over one's fellows and to shape their actions.

So far as power is formalized, it is political; and the essence of politics is the contest for power to win and hold economic, social, and political superiority, the three aspects ordinarily coinciding rather closely. The autonomy of many is restricted to give greater capacity to the few. Some occupy positions of authority over others, whether because interests inevitably come into conflict and must be adjudicated, or because a leader must act for the community, or because some impose themselves on the rest. Power is as necessary as it is dangerous.

It is not easy to define power, but in practice it is recognizable. To have it is to be able to act—as in the French term *pouvoir*—in ways as complex as human emotions. It is a relation of inequality, whereby one's will is superior to that of others. It is exercised by persuasion mixed with coercion. The urge to achieve it is fed by ambition, vanity, altruism, and responsibility in varying amounts. Through power, good and evil achieve fulfillment. It is held desirable as almost nothing else. Even in the most primitive human groups a few achieve power and prestige, some fail, and some never try.[8] To preside over the kill, to lead a victory, to command the attention of the multitude, or to win an election are equally realizations of power. Often power is a vindication of masculinity and manhood.

### The Will to Power

The will to power arises from the conjunction of individual and social natures, and it is so total because it satisfies both individual and social drives: as individuals we seek standing and control in the group. This is the essence of the political struggle.

Some have a much stronger will to power than others, and some wish to be admired or loved, whereas others wish to be feared; but the taste of power is almost always sweet. Even those who gain power without really wanting it get satisfaction from it: they speak and others listen, applaud, and obey; they make their fellows instruments of their will. It is the acme of social success, as one works with, uses, and rises over others, whether helping or hurting them. People do worse deeds and better ones for power than for material gain.

Power expands life and lends it significance; it is a projection of the personality. Those who go into positions of leadership for the benefit of the community often stay on because of enjoyment of power. Power is an aphrodisiac, as has often been observed, and subordinates do their best to make the powerful feel grand. Much of the desire for luxury is really for power; it is more important that elegant cars show the status of the owner than that they ride smoothly, and a numerous servant staff is needed less for service than as an assertion of superiority.[9] The urge to power, unlike biological needs, knows no limits.

Although too complete power distorts the personality, power is generally good for you. The powerless suffer more depression and are psychologically less well integrated. According to psychological researchers, the powerful are above average in health and freer of mental problems, although they have tendencies toward grandiosity and uncontrolled behavior. The pursuit of power to the neglect of family and lesser personal pleasures becomes an addiction. To be stripped of power shakes the personality.[10]

Fortunately, power has many shapes. Political power is closely tied to economic power, or ownership, which is an institution dependent on the state. Beyond the satisfaction of material wants, economic power is desirable mostly for the same reasons as political power: to give superiority over others and to extend one's capacities for action, and to give social status and perhaps political power. The corporate executive, like the political leader, stands over many subordinates. The desire to accumulate wealth, like political power, is unbounded. A person goes on to pile up a second billion at the cost of the ability to enjoy the first.[11]

On the other hand, political standing is commonly convertible into material gain. In most countries, high position in the state gives access to large wealth. Even in the most orderly and democratic countries, one can step from high political status to corporate directorships or a lucrative legal or consultative practice. The emperor or dictator wants palaces as manifestations of power and power in order to enjoy palaces.

### Collective Power

Not only individuals but also organizations and groups, small and large, strive for power and status or to defend or enlarge their turf or territory. They especially fight to uphold positions of superiority, which the group, much more than the individual, consecrates as a right. Thus bureaus within a department and departments within an administration jostle for superiority, parties seek power in or over the government, and nations assert themselves as "powers" on the world scene.

The assertion of collective power over vulnerable groups regarded as different is a general practice, as in the cases of Afrikaners over Blacks, Israelis over Arabs, Malays over Chinese, Africans over Asians, and Whites over Blacks in the American South before the 1960s. It may be that the aliens are indistinguishable by either appearance or culture, as are Koreans and Burakumin in Japan. Nonetheless the Japanese, who are egalitarian among themselves, contrary to official policy refuse to dilute their superiority by socially accepting their inferiors.

Strong collective claims to power and position are commonly accompanied by an ideology, either clearly expressed (as in the case of Communist parties) or largely implicit (as in the case of most premodern imperialisms). Most strongly of all, contests between sovereign states have been waged for power or for advantages equivalent to power, but often in the name of an ideology or religion, that is, unnegotiable principles. What is really unnegotiable is the question of which side is to prevail, of who will be the victors and who the vanquished.

## MONISTIC AND PLURALISTIC SOCIETIES

There is no evidence that the will to power or the ability to cooperate for the general good is different in Chinese, Indians, or Americans. Yet the nature and results of political power are obviously very different from Japan to Uganda, from Ecuador to the Soviet Union or the United States. The most obvious difference is in the dispersal or concentration of power within the society. Those states in which authority is split among a number of entities are called *pluralist*; those in which authority is highly concentrated and uncontestable are called *monistic* or, more commonly, *authoritarian*. The crucial effect is that power divided is somewhat neutralized and leaves more room for individual and nonpolitical drives, whereas unchallenged power is more coercive and exploitative. Likewise, where power over society is less centralized, it has to be more responsible to those without power, that is, more democratic; and where it is more centralized, it increases inequality between elite leaders and led.

### Classifying States

There is no wholly satisfactory way of classifying states, since classification depends on whatever aspects one may emphasize: modern against traditional, secular against religious, decentralized against centralized, leftist (more egalitarian and reformist) against rightist (more aristocratic and traditional), legalistic against arbitrary, consensual against repressive, libertarian against intrusive, and so forth. But probably the most useful classification is based on the responsibility or irresponsibility of the state or the degree of centralization of its power, varying from the virtually unlimited despotism (in theory) to the decidedly restricted democracy, from the hegemonic to the polyarchic,[12] or from the monistic to the pluralistic.

For the most part, qualities of government are related: the repressive state rests more on tradition, religion, or ideology (which it can impose); it is centralized (decentralization weakens power), arbitrary (law is the basis of freedom), less legitimate (legitimacy derives from the consent of the ruled), and inegalitarian (political power creates privilege). Hence the most significant spectrum is a single band, expressive of the antithesis of imposed, arbitrary rule and cooperative, responsible rule, or of the imperial-coercive aspect of the state versus the pluralistic-consultative.

This classification is synonymous with the common description of states as authoritarian or dictatorial, in contrast to the democratic. Here *authoritarian* is not used as the designation of strong government that is less than totalitarian but as a general term, *totalitarian* being only the extreme of authoritarianism. This dimension might also be stated in terms of the degree to which the state apparatus is checked by internal division of power or by independent groups. This in turn is linked to the degree to which power is concentrated in the hands of those directly profiting from the state, or to which the governing apparatus operates more for its own benefit than for that of the community as a whole. It says nothing about what kind of rationale or ideology the rulership may proclaim, but whether the state is guided by the idea of consultation for the sake of cooperation and justice or the idea of submission to leadership for the sake of order and decisiveness. Both principles are inherent in the human condition, however much one or the other may come to the fore in different conditions.

### The Basic Antithesis

The state rules over society to serve society and also to serve itself; this admixture ranges from beneficence to sadism. The state may in general try to give people what they ask for, or it may manage and use people, giving them what the leadership wants for them and itself.[13] Those in power may be self-selected or chosen by and answerable to people outside the state. But neither democratic (pluralistic, or polyarchic) nor authoritarian (monistic, hegemonic, or dictatorial) represents a total condition. On the one hand, humans are not selfless; or if they approximate selflessness, they are not likely to climb high on the pyramid of power. On the other hand, in the modern situation where the outside world cannot be completely walled out, every state must do much, at least to reward its supporters.

This basic antithesis is close to that of legitimacy and illegitimacy, but it is not the same. Popular consent is the chief source of political virtue in the modern world; but legitimacy—that is, acceptance as right—is a broader concept. Success has much to do with it; a democracy that fails to satisfy its people loses legitimacy, whereas an authoritarian government gains legitimacy if it brings prosperity or victory. Constraint mingles with consensus, and power gives the means of claiming or earning legitimacy.

The antithesis of democratic-polyarchic-pluralistic and authoritarian-hegemonic-monocratic states also corresponds roughly to that of "open" and "closed" societies, freedom of information being closely cor-

related with responsibility and legality of government, just as civil liberties are nearly equivalent to political rights.[14] Other antitheses run more
or less closely parallel: individualism versus collectivism, rationalism
versus dogmatism, freedom versus order, social mobility versus fixed
status, responsible government versus insulated government, relativist
versus absolutist, market economy versus controlled economy, open versus secretive, legalistic versus arbitrary.[15] The fundamental difference
may also be viewed as the rights of the many (freedoms) against the
rights of the few (prerogatives). Political theory has shown the same dichotomy since the days of Plato, who advocated a monistic community
dedicated to virtue, and Aristotle, who wanted power checked within a
moderate political order; the divide is between those who are concerned
to use power for ideal ends and those who wish freedom for people to
pursue their own ends.[16]

In the closed society, where politics is reserved for insiders, the
rulership is self-perpetuating and based on intrigue and manipulation;
where politics is open and competitive, candidates for leadership come
forward through the interaction of groups more or less independent of
the state. In the former case, economic power, or its equivalent, is gained
mostly by official relations, and prestige derives mostly from political
position or relations. In the latter case, money made nonpolitically gives
prestige and perhaps assists to political position; and there are independent classes, as of teachers, lawyers, entrepreneurs, journalists, and so
forth. The means by which leadership is achieved in turn shape the
values of the elite and of the state.

The contrast of democratic and authoritarian regimes corresponds
roughly to that of societies wherein people get ahead primarily by producing goods or services and those wherein status is achieved mostly by
some kind of manipulation or favor. In the former, success is basically
economic; in the latter, it is political. In all societies, of course, the two
aspects are interwoven in most activities; but the difference is rather
strong between, for example, the United States, where most successful
persons are in business, and the Soviet Union, where one can rise high
only within the political framework or secondarily by one's usefulness
to it, as in the case of sports stars and scientists.

Institutions are culturally conditioned, yet they have to do with
human relations deeper than cultural or historical differences of expression. For example, some egregious twentieth-century tyrannies, such as
Hitler's court, have strikingly resembled despotisms of the distant past,
such as that of Genghis Khan or even that of the nonliterate empire of
the Incas. The basic features of democracy in classical Greece or even
earlier cultures are fully understandable in terms of modern democracy,
whatever the differences in customs. Most of Pericles' Funeral Oration [17]
could be put in the mouth of a political orator of our day with only

minor changes. And it is reasonable to assume that relative freedom had much to do with the creativity of ancient Greece as well as of the modern West.

## PLURALIST STATES AND UNIVERSAL EMPIRES

The basic dichotomy may also be seen in the opposition of the imperial and the competitive principles of government.[18] At one extreme in the historic panorama stand the great empires, formerly called Oriental despotisms, which Europeans saw as the prevalent form of government in the past. The millennial Chinese empire, covering a huge realm that was virtually a world unto itself, is perhaps the best example. At the other extreme are sets of small or smallish independent states with more or less republican, popular, or at least relatively limited government. The congeries of city-states of ancient Greece and the nation-states of Europe are the best examples.

### The Universal Empires

The great continental empires, which have felt themselves a world apart, have had unlimited government under an autocrat whose will was law. They have also necessarily been bureaucratic, governed by an overgrown administrative apparatus. Under such a system, this bureaucracy becomes a ruling class, enriching itself with little interference from the personal sovereign. The universal empire has the ordinary concomitants of tyranny: agencies to repress potential rebellion, censorship, and a more or less compulsory belief system rationalizing the political order. This creed or ideology probably contains the vision of a noncompetitive world based on the virtues of faith, submission, and service, as in Neo-Confucianism.[19] Its ideal is universal citizenship and perfect order.

Beneath varying symbolism, the grand empires have had much in common because they shared the overriding purpose of securing obedience and sustaining unity. States of a pluralistic system have more varied outlooks and differ more in their institutions. Any political organization has the purpose of self-preservation, but in competitive states this is partly or largely turned outward against foreign states; in the universal empire, the danger is mostly internal and power is directed inward.

The universal empire is despotic for lack of the conditions favoring responsible government in pluralistic systems. The competitive state has to encourage a productive economy—that is, a more or less free economy—to avoid weakness in relation to other states, whereas the imperial court may be fairly well satisfied by an unproductive economy as long as its luxuries are supplied. Trade between independent states gives some autonomy to the merchant interests; the ruler who wishes his state to be strong and prosperous must make it congenial to business. Hence the commercial sector is influential; and commerce is rationalistic (based on realistic calculation), antiauthoritarian (commerce does not prosper under political controls), and republican (merchants want a predictable government in which they can share).

The emperor can deify himself as the leader of one of many states cannot. Cut off from independent influences, the people of a great continental domain are more controllable than the peoples of small states interacting through trade, travel, and communications with foreigners. For the former, it is as though all the world is under the same exalted rulership; but citizens of small states know that the writ of their rulers is bounded and more or less escapable. Learning about the ways of other governments raises expectations of one's own, and those who travel abroad are poor subjects for despotism. For the emperor, power consists in part in the ability to ignore popular wishes; for the leader of a competitive state, power requires the support of the people, who are his strength against foreign rivals.

### The Competitive States

The contest of sovereignties is equalizing. It makes people valuable as workers and fighters, and those who fight in the wars are admitted as equal citizens. For example, military needs gave status to ordinary men in both classical Greece and Rome before it became an encompassing empire. An essential element of the democracy of medieval towns was the role of the citizen armies; when mercenaries were later engaged for defense, democracy was dead or dying. The need for soldiers brought liberation of the serfs in eighteenth-century Prussia.[20] Defeat in the Crimean War led the Russian tsar Alexander II to emancipate the serfs (who formed the largest fraction of the population) and to inaugurate other reforms to broaden support for his government. Likewise, the great wars of this century have been equalizing and destructive of inherited status,[21] and countries with high military participation have better income distribution under elites more willing to share privileges.[22]

For parallel reasons, the competitive states of the pluralistic international system are far more creative than the big empires. The open system better stimulates intelligence. It promotes a present-future orientation, a sense of responsibility, trust in people, and personal ambition. Free classes support diverse activities, there is no single commanding center, the valuation of production favors technological innovation, and higher productivity supports more art and science. Pluralism and individualism bring more social mobility, more rewards for talent and creativity, and more esteem for factual learning, with openness to new ideas. Competition necessitates the confronting of reality and elevates truth. The association of political freedom with science, the industrial revolution, and modernization is no accident.

### Pluralism versus Monism

Science looks for new truth, but the empire is pleased with its old truth. The elites of the empire have the best of all possible worlds, and they desire to maintain things as they are, not to improve them. Art probes meanings and seeks to give new significance to life, but for the empire, inquiry is inherently subversive. The isolated empire, concentrated on power and its symbols, is uncreative and often incredibly suffocating. The Roman empire in its early days was less compressive than most because it was the heir of the exceptionally free and vibrant Greek civilization and was relatively decentralized by geography; but in a few generations it choked the once so flourishing art, literature, philosophy, and science of the classical world; even practical techniques deteriorated into the Dark Ages. The Inca empire similarly wiped out the culture of conquered peoples and had little interest in developing its own; it even banned the art of writing that had already come into being.

To compensate for their sterility the empires glorify themselves with imposing monuments and exalt their rulers. If the freer states have the stronger society, the empires have the stronger, or at least the greater, government; and they make themselves respected: their power is deemed holy, and it is deemed a sin to transgress their laws. People are deeply impressed by their glories; historians of later ages treat them kindly.

The government of the great empire is artificial in the sense that it does not grow out of the needs and feelings of those beneath it. People obey or worship faraway personages whom they know only by repute, and they give much, perhaps most, of their produce to an elite that has set itself over them. But it is the transcendent virtue of the empire that it has seemed inevitable, a necessary replacement of the quarrelsome (and sometimes mutually murderous) independencies. It vaunts its stewardship of peace and unity.

Interstate interaction and competition favor more egalitarian or democratic, or at least nondespotic, political systems. The measuring of an in-group against outsiders develops common values and purposes, within which there can be freedom without tearing the society apart. Collective egoism takes the place of individual egoism. Patriotism, generated by nonviolent or violent rivalry, integrates a society and makes it possible and desirable to bring many or all into the political sphere. It is also helpful to the democratic society for the people to see themselves as a higher breed than neighbors against whom they measure themselves. Equality and community come naturally to the close in-group, with the psychology of a fraternity.

The imperial or autocratic state, however elaborate in its organization and rituals, is essentially primitive, like the chieftaincy of a tribe or the boss-ship of a gang; it results directly from the drive to power. Its institutions require little preparation, and conquerors have only to adapt to peacetime the methods they used to crush their rivals; the craft of despotism is not subtle. The institutions of the free states, on the other hand, are the fruit of a labored and difficult evolution. They are fragile, cohering in a delicate balance between independence, cooperation, and antagonism, like the competing sovereignties of a state system.

Although universal empire and the pluralistic state system are opposites, both incorporate the duality of human nature, the antithesis of individual striving and group coherence. In the empire loyalties shift away from the central power, which no longer excites self-sacrifice, and smaller groups, such as clan or family, become the focus of life. In contending states, on the other hand, there is more incentive to fulfill personal ambitions in common endeavors. The difference lies in the way groups are structured, and the competitive states provide a more appropriate framework for productive activity.

Because empires are more easily constructed than loose international systems of competitive and balancing states, they have prevailed in history. Once the independent states are undone, as in the conquest of the Hellenistic world by Rome, they cannot be restored short of the secular gestation of a new society and new modes of sovereignty, as happened in Europe during and after the Middle Ages. But when an empire crumbles, there are always leaders eager to replace it, and the rotted remnants of old empires make fertile soil for new ones, as has many times occurred in China, India, and the Near East.

The career of France from revolutionary democracy to empire is illustrative of the facility of instituting imperial ways. The first French republic, established in 1789, was inspired by vague ideals of "Liberty, Equality, and Fraternity." But when an outsider, Napoleon Bonaparte, by his victories made himself master not only of France but of much of Europe, he much more than restored the theoretically absolutist but actually rather feeble rule of the overthrown Bourbons and made himself an autocrat like the Son of Heaven in imperial China. Napoleon indulged a fulsome cult of his personality, censored writing, had the arts devoted to his glory, persecuted those who doubted, rewrote history, and had the catechism equate duty toward himself with duty to God. In typical imperial fashion, flamboyance was the mode. Also as usual in great empires, patriotism died out despite much propaganda; the people were indifferent to the entry of foreign troops into Paris in 1814.[23]

The empire is also stable because it gives full power to a class whose overwhelming purpose is the enjoyment and preservation of its power. To some extent this occurs in all political systems: those who are on top and can exercise the most influence on the direction of society have ipso facto an interest in keeping things more or less as they are; but in the looser society elites are fluid and fluctuating, many persons desirous of reform have voice and vote and a place in the unsteady power structure, and ideas and organizations outside the ambit of the state can press change on it. In the empire those who might gain by change are kept powerless.

The very fact that the great empires are intellectually and technologically stagnant contributes to their stability. The pluralistic states, on the other hand, outmode themselves by improvements in the arts of war and communications, with many subtle or obvious changes in the nature of international relations and society, until the independence of states becomes increasingly precarious. Some are engulfed by others, the international contest becomes more bitter, and the way is open for the world-uniting conquerors.

The contending states would be more secure if attainments in the arts of war and administration could be kept at home. But authoritarian states on the fringes of the primary cultural area, although uncreative, can learn to make war as efficiently as the freer states and to use their greater resources to throw them down. Thus Macedon and Rome learned from the Greeks the means of conquering Greece and much more. There was a similar sequence in both India and China in the fourth and third centuries B.C., and partially in the subjection of the Italian republics by France and Spain in the late fifteenth to early sixteenth centuries. The scientific-technological prowess of the nation-states of the West and its spread, especially in military applications, to politically non-Western areas, may conceivably result in a similar loss of autonomy to a more ruthless state, if not the nuclear destruction of the state system.

Despite many differences in form, these basic themes of the political spectrum, from the democratic-polyarchic-pluralistic-open to the authoritarian-hegemonic-monistic-closed formation, have persisted for thousands of years: the antitheses of the Greeks and the Persians in the fifth century B.C. and of the Dutch and the Spanish in the sixteenth century were basically like those of the modern West and Soviet bloc. There can be no more universal empires, however (unless one power should conquer the globe), and it is no longer possible for a state to slumber in semi-isolation and technological stagnation without resigning itself to powerlessness. Ideas spread everywhere, and political forms are borrowed, at least in pretense; for example, there are Soviet "elections" for a pseudoparliament. Much of the language of politics is universal, although there is a range from mean and narrow tyrannies to deeply democratic communities. But the contrariety of the two fundamental political directions persists as an antithesis inherent in human destiny. It must continue, in one or another form, as long as human nature retains its ambiguity.

## THE WORLD PANORAMA

Diversity is the most striking fact of the contemporary constellation of sovereignties. Although information goes instantly anywhere and one can travel between any two major cities on earth more quickly than one could go from London to Paris a hundred and fifty years ago, disparities are enormous. About a fifth of the world's population, in the so-called advanced industrial states, enjoy at least twenty times as much material goods—as well as enjoying many other advantages—as the poorest quarter, the less fortunate of the so-called developing or, less euphemistically, less-developed countries. Whereas the privileged minority have an abundance not only of necessities but of entertainments and luxuries, hundreds of millions exist on the margin of subsistence, are malnourished and chronically diseased, know little beyond the native village, and have received few or no benefits of the scientific-industrial revolution. Many states, especially in Africa, are sovereign principally by virtue of international recognition, and some subsist thanks mostly to foreign aid.[24] Technical information—the knowledge basis for modern riches—is (except for the latest innovations) easily available, capital flows freely (except where stopped by political barriers), world markets are accessible, and nations have both economic and political compulsions to learn the ways of wealth and power. Yet the gap in development widens.

The political unevenness of the world is equally great and equally difficult to understand in view of the general similarity of human nature everywhere, so far as is known. Some governments are highly orderly and solicitous of the well-being of all (even to an excessive degree in some opinions) and promote about as much freedom for their people as seems consonant with the rights of their fellows. On the same planet other regimes have shown themselves ruthless, killing large numbers of their people on slight suspicion that they might be hostile to the authorities. Many more states, although not grossly murderous, have acted virtually as sovereign robbers, or kleptocracies, dedicated to taking from producers for the benefit of nonproducers. Numerous governments are so distrustful of their people that they severely limit information, communication, and movement. Only about a quarter of the world's roughly 160 sovereign states can well be classified as democratic; the remainder, not being responsible to their people, must be considered more or less irresponsible and consequently abusive.

**Pluralism and Prosperity**

The economic and political landscapes largely coincide, and economic prosperity almost always goes with political pluralism. The category of democratic or pluralist fairly well defines the group of wealthier nations, whereas the poorer ones generally have nondemocratic or dictatorial governments. There are exceptions on both sides. For example, a few oil-rich authoritarian countries enjoy wealth produced by nature and technologies from democratic societies. In the case of Eastern European countries under communist rule, productivity is high by world standards. Nonetheless, it is low by Western European standards, and it seems clear that the development of these countries has been held back by the repressive political structures imposed on them as a result of World War II. Historically, no tightly controlled economy has ever prospered long, and there is no reason to suppose that the Marxist-Leninist states have found a recipe denied their autocratic predecessors.

More challenging exceptions to the correlation between democratic institutions and economic growth are Singapore, Taiwan, and South Korea, which have achieved rapid growth of output under nondemocratic regimes. They have, however, not been very oppressive, and they have given considerable freedom and security to economic enterprises. The most obvious reason for adherence to sound economic policies in the cases of Taiwan and South Korea has been their sharp antagonism to communist neighbors, the People's Republic of China and North Korea, respectively. The anticommunist governments of Taiwan and South Korea have encouraged production and provide benefits for their people for the sake of national security. Their opposition to communism is translated into devotion to the principles of the market economy. For Singapore, it is important that the Chinese forming the majority of the population stand up against the much larger numbers of Malays in surrounding territories, and their traditional means of self-defense has been money making. Whether the government is organized to give political power to the masses is obviously not crucial for economic growth. But it is difficult to suppose that political powers will be permanently restrained from maltreating the productive economy unless there is a framework of constitutional responsibility, and all three of these countries are under strong and apparently mounting pressure to permit more freedom and democracy.

On the other side, some poor Third World countries have found democratic institutions no quick cure for poverty. These include India and Sri Lanka in Asia (the democratic condition of the latter having become questionable), Jamaica in the Caribbean, and several Latin American countries. However, in all of these it is uncertain that democratization runs deep. These poor countries, with markedly divided societies, acquired democratic institutions through British colonial tutelage or, in

Latin America, borrowed substantially from the United States and else-where. Their democracy may result as much from inertia and from efforts to impose ideas of what a modern government should look like as from social forces. It is also the fortune of the democratic ex-British colonies that no brand of authoritarianism has had the opportunity to establish itself, since they were given constitutional regimes along with independence a few decades ago.

Various Latin American countries have swung repeatedly between military and constitutional regimes, and they have shown no clear correlation between economic growth and democratic institutions.[25] This has probably been because neither dictatorship nor democracy has run deep enough to change radically the structure of society and the conditions of production. In Third World countries, despite regular elections which may be honestly conducted, political power is held by a small elite. So far as economic and social equality are necessary for democracy, there is not much of it.

In sum, the correlation between pluralistic political structures and modern productive economies is clear although by no means complete. If one considered not current productivity but innovativeness and inventiveness, which lie behind productivity, the correlation would be stronger. Innovation is weak in the communist countries, rich or poor, and in authoritarian countries generally. The flourishing of South Korea and others like it requires no native invention, merely favorable conditions for productive enterprises to apply imported technology. Japan, which expanded its economy by imitation quite rapidly in the decades prior to World War II, continues as a democratic country to raise its capacities not only by adaptation of foreign ideas but by increasingly successful research and development.

The causal relation of democracy to economic success goes partly from the economy to politics, as it is obviously easier for a relatively wealthy country to have a constitutional government responsible to its citizens. Wealth supports broad education and health care, which qualify people for political participation, and also extensive communications, which make participation fuller and more meaningful. A productive modern economy tends to escape controls by virtue of its very complexity. Prosperity, or a sense of prosperity, gives the masses a stake in the political system and reduces social conflict. On the other hand, poverty increases inequality in an unequal world, and the gap between the modernizing sector and the backward sector makes democracy difficult or unreal.

In the other direction, political freedom makes possible higher productivity and prosperity. The Netherlands, Switzerland, Britain, the Scandinavian countries, and the United States were all relatively democratic, or at least unburdened by harsh government, long before they were notably rich. A legal democratic political system almost by definition creates a favorable environment for production. Representative-pluralistic states are characterized by: the rule of law enforced by independent courts, permitting rational economic calculations; the freedom to criticize abuses of power and to promote different ideas, facilitating improvements in management of the economy; the freedom for people to organize themselves in many different ways to promote their interests and ideas; and the security of persons and property and the freedom (within limits) to produce desired goods. Authoritarian states lack these characteristics or at least do not have them reliably and permanently. But lack of any of them implies the abuse of power, hence waste and unproductive values, insecurity for producers, and rewards for manipulators. The growth of industry and commerce since the seventeenth century would hardly have been possible without the breakdown of feudal shackles and the lightening of the burden of official controls. Economic growth, in turn, made possible the evolution of modern political systems.

There are many obvious causes of underdevelopment, including a heritage of backwardness, a shortage of natural resources or good land, ignorance, a lack of capital and economic infrastructure, high population growth rates and perhaps an enervating climate and chronic disease. But it seems that the problems could be overcome if government—or more broadly speaking, institutions and values—were different. The necessary technology is available, and the capital is ready to flow to any country where it has relative freedom and security.

On the other hand, when Third World countries have come into the possession of great natural wealth, especially oil, this has seldom brought much improvement for the mass of citizens. The late shah of Iran seems to have made a real effort to buy his country's modernization, but the inertia was too great, or the vision of the palace was too cramped; and Iran has undergone an extraordinary reversion to political primitivism. Elsewhere, petroleum riches have produced as much trouble as benefit.[26] Mexico came into an oil bonanza after 1974, but many billions of dollars have done much more for corruption and elite enrichment than for general welfare. Nigeria's oil likewise brought riches to a few but nearly ruined the nation's basic livelihood, agriculture.

The Third World comes from far behind; it cannot catch up quickly. Even the Japanese have taken well over a century, since 1853 when Commodore Perry sailed into Tokyo Bay and demanded that the kingdom end its isolation, to reach the forefront of modernity. But the problem of the Third World is not merely a late start. The University of San Marcos in Lima, Peru, is a century older than Harvard, but it has been vitiated by politics as well as poverty. Argentina and Uruguay, with extremely rich agricultural endowments, became prosperous by world standards in the first part of this century, only to lag and become middle-tier Third World nations. In the roughly twenty years since gaining independence, nearly all African states have declined relatively; most have become poorer in absolute terms. If a very few states, headed by the East Asian economic minigiants, have narrowed the gap, the majority of the non-Western world have seen the gap widen in the past generation.

It may be surmised that defective institutions, perhaps especially bad government, are the chief hindrance to many countries in their striving to join the modern industrialized world. Development requires an atmosphere in which people can trust authorities and expect fair treatment, an environment encouraging innovation, incentives for merit and effort, and reliability of conditions making planning possible.[27] Extortion, corruption, insecurity of persons and property, malfunctioning of basic services, the preference for personal over general interests, policy making by persons whose only qualification is political connection, official unreliability, irrational regulations, and monopolistic exploitation all stand in the way of the implantation of modern technology.

Relatively legal, democratic governments have many faults, but incompetent, if not rapacious, regimes deserve the largest share of the blame for the failure of most contemporary societies to better satisfy their citizens. The only reliable way to reduce such defects is to open government to criticism and make it more responsible to its citizens.

### Notes

1. Edward O. Wilson, *On Human Nature* (Cambridge: Harvard University Press, 1978), pp. 153–54.
2. Edward O. Wilson, *Sociobiology*, abridged ed. (Cambridge, Mass.: Belknap Press, 1980), chap. 26.
3. Howard P. Kainz, *Democracy East & West: A Philosophical Overview* (London, Macmillan, 1984), p. 49.
4. Sidney Verba and Gary R. Orren, "The Meaning of Equality in America," *Political Science Quarterly*, 100 (Fall 1985), 371–73.
5. John N. Kautsky, *The Politics of Aristocratic Empires* (Chapel Hill: University of North Carolina Press, 1982).
6. Roland Pennock, "Political Development, Political Systems, and Political Goods," *World Politics*, 18 (April 1966), 420.
7. Aristotle, *Politics*, trans. Benjamin Jowett (Oxford: Clarendon Press, 1923), chap. 9, sec. 6.
8. Wilson, *Sociobiology*, p. 272.
9. E. L. Jones, *The European Miracle* (Cambridge: Cambridge University Press, 1981), p. 109.
10. Daniel Goleman, "Seat of Power and Woe," *New York Times*, March 8, 1985, p. 22.
11. Cf. John Kenneth Galbraith, *The Anatomy of Power* (Boston: Houghton Mifflin, 1984).
12. In the terminology of Robert A. Dahl, *Modern Political Analysis* (Englewood Cliffs, N.J.: Prentice-Hall, 1976), chap. 7.
13. Peter Calvert, *Politics, Power, and Revolution: An Introduction to Comparative Politics* (Brighton; Sussex Wheatsheaf Books, 1983), p. 75.
14. Ratings of Raymond D. Gastil, *Freedom in the World: Political Rights and Civil Liberties, 1984–1985, 1985–1986* (Westport, Conn.: Greenwood Press, 1986), p.

35–47; political rights and civil liberties are usually the same for 167 sovereignties, never much different.

15. Robert Wesson, *Modern Government: Democracy and Authoritarianism*, 2d ed. (Englewood Cliffs, N.J.: Prentice-Hall, 1985), p. 23.

16. Robert Nisbet, *The Social Philosophers* (New York: Crowell and Co., 1973), p. 396.

17. Thucydides, *The Peloponnesian War*, trans. B. Jowett (Oxford: Clarendon Press, 1881), pp. 37–40.

18. They are treated in some detail in Robert Wesson's *The Imperial Order and State Systems: International Pluralism, Politics and Culture* (Berkeley: University of California Press, 1967).

19. David S. Nivision and Arthur F. Wright, eds., *Confucianism in Action* (Stanford: Stanford University Press, 1959), p. 18.

20. Otto Hintze, "The State in Historical Perspective," in *Society and Politics*, ed. Werner Braungart, (Englewood Cliffs, N.J.: Prentice-Hall, 1976), pp. 63–78.

21. William H. McNeill, *The Rise of the West: A History of the Human Community* (Chicago: University of Chicago Press, 1963), p. 336.

22. Erich Weide and Horst Tiefenback, "Some Recent Explanations of Income Equality," in *The Gap Between Rich and Poor: Contending Perspectives in the Political Economy of Development*, ed. Mitchell A. Seligson, (Boulder: Westview, 1984), p. 250.

23. Jean Robiquet, *Daily Life in France Under Napolean* (New York: Macmillan, 1963), pp. 68, 273–75.

24. Robert H. Jackson, "Sovereignty and Underdevelopment: Juridical Statehood in the African Crisis" (paper for International Political Science Association, World Congress, July 1985, Paris), p. 2.

25. Robert Wesson, "Conclusion," in *Politics, Policies and Economic Development in Latin America*, ed. Robert Wesson (Stanford: Hoover Institution Press, 1984), p. 235–37.

26. Jahangir Amuzegar, "Oil Wealth," *Foreign Affairs*, 60 (Spring 1982), 814–35; and David Morawetz, "The Gap Between Rich and Poor Countries," in *The Gap Between Rich and Poor: Contending Perspectives on the Political Economy of Development*, ed. Mitchell A. Seligson, (Boulder: Westview, 1984), p. 11.

27. Lawrence E. Harrison, *Underdevelopment is a State of Mind* (Lanham, Md.: University Press of America, 1985), p. 3.

# The Historical
# Background

## 2

As Laski stated, "The character of the modern state is a consequence of the history through which it has passed, and it would be unin-
telligible save in the light of history." [1] The present convoluted and para-
doxical international constellation, with its phenomenal political and
economic differences, has evolved through an endlessly complicated history. Innumerable accidents of geography, culture, events, and personalities have given rise to seemingly predestined directions, as the irregular
accumulation of culture and technical capacities has propelled political
change.

## THE BEGINNINGS OF THE STATE

Although the history of the state begins some six thousand years ago in
the Near East, political institutions or patterns of authority have no beginning. There are hierarchy and structure in mammal and bird societies,
with domination and cooperation in reproduction, hunting, territories,
and so forth. Monkey troops have leaders enjoying perquisites (general
respect and priority for their wants) and performing duties (watching
over and protecting the "citizens"). A large majority of encounters within
chimpanzee bands are friendly, and the discoverer of a fruiting tree calls
out to share the find. There is also "simian war": a stronger group may
destroy a weaker one, killing the males and taking the females. Troops
of around fifty have their understood territories, which they will fight
to defend. [2]

   But ape bands, although they may have leadership, have no modes
of decision making; a statelike organization is as much a part of being
human as is language. The emergence of some kind of coordinating authority may have resulted from the transition of our ancestors from the
jungle to the savanna, where the individual was all too vulnerable to
predators—humans can run less than half as fast as large four-legged
animals—and hunting called for cooperation. Large game, from the mam-
moth down, could be utilized efficiently only by a sizable group; on the
other hand, taking big animals offered a more abundant life than scroung-
ing small prey. Collaboration in the chase implied coordination not only
by means of language but also by social organization, with leaders and
cooperative followers; and leadership in the hunt probably became institutionalized as enlargement of bands beyond a few dozen required better
organization. [3]

   The importance of the hearth probably helped to cement early
Paleolithic societies. Social development advanced with the more or less
permanent bonding of the sexes, instead of the irregular mating of the
apes, and the assumption by the male of some responsibility for the
sustenance of his mate and children. The growth of familial bonds permit-

ted the long immaturity and socialization essential for the accumulation of culture and laid the basis for the cohesion of larger groups.

The beginnings of culture deeply altered social relations. Something as simple as a spear made it possible for a weaker individual to kill a stronger one. Dominance could no longer rest simply on individual strength, as in the ape band. Leadership came to require, as it has to this day, support and protection by at least a few and acceptance by many or most of one's fellows. Neanderthal man seems to have had a complex social life, in which handicapped persons were supported by the group.[4]

Social instincts doubtless were genetically favored by the contest that must have arisen between groups. The earliest humans had to cope not only with the great beasts but with the most dangerous of creatures, other humans. They came into rivalry and competition, we may assume, as a result of many causes: the need for prestige or for vengeance for real or supposed offenses, the demands of witchcraft, or disputes over hunting grounds.[5] Survival and prosperity was the reward for the best coordinated and directed fighters.

Probably most relations were friendly; neolithic trade over distances of hundreds of miles more likely indicates peaceful tolerance than primitive empire. Agriculture, with rights to land and problems of storage of crops, greater density of population, fixed abodes, specialization, and free time part of the year, facilitated the growth of culture and a much more complex society. This implied the need for controls, as did irrigation. The earliest civilizations all arose in dry valleys of great rivers.[6]

### The Emergence of the State

The state begins when authority grows beyond the kinship group to become an artificial entity, and people have to deal with and obey persons to whom they are not related or whom they may not know.[7] Amalgamation would feed on itself, as conquest gave resources for further conquest. Thus there may have been something like a state long before the historical record. From the beginnings of agriculture, if not before, intergroup conflict must have often meant conquest, the subjection of the conquered, the imposition of tribute, or enslavement. At the least there was inequality, as shown by high-class, middle-class, and low-class neolithic interments. The opulence of some children's graves shows that these differences were not entirely the result of individual achievement.[8]

The primitive state presumably secured consent both coerced by force and by management of trade and religion and filling defensive needs. The control of land and water was both a means of giving benefits and a lever of compulsion.[9] As soon as thousands were under a single headship, there had to be something like police, judges, taxes, and social classes. The emergent state reinforced itself by giving power and material privileges to those who served it. It fostered proto-cities, in which people were more dependent and more controllable; and it probably lent itself grandeur and purpose by monumental constructions, such as Stonehenge.[10]

It may be guessed that the incipient state was closely associated with religion or a belief system, leaders being ritualists or working with them. The expansion of the state would spread its cult, somewhat as imperialism in modern times has supported and been supported by ideology. Perhaps with the backing of religious practice, the idea of the state seems to have spread from the Near East to East Asia, possibly to the Americas, and from Mesoamerica to the Andes. In prehistoric times there may have been large empires. In both the Andean region and Mexico, elaborately organized governments extended over hundreds, even thousands, of miles, without the use of writing, wheeled vehicles, or even riding animals.

Improvements in transportation and communication made it easier to build up and administer large political units, and throughout history most of civilized humanity has lived under middling to very extensive empires—Egyptian, Babylonian, Persian, Roman, Indian, Chinese, and many others—some transient, others as though eternal in the sight of their people. Empires have commonly proclaimed their greatness by mobilizing thousands or hundreds of thousands to build awe-inspiring palaces and grandiose works, from the pyramids and spectacular temples of Egypt to the Great Wall of China; and by their power and law they have made a deep imprint on their peoples.

### Early State Systems

There have also been groups of smaller states, less imposing for their monuments but far more creative of ideas, such as the city-states of classical Greece and the nation-states of Europe.[11] In a few places, for reasons mostly unclear, there have grown up loose collections of independent sovereignties interacting closely and for the most part peacefully through trade and shared culture and religion, but sometimes hostilely in rivalry and war, although not fighting so desperately as to destroy the international system. They have been a little like members of a loosely organized community, sharing common values but driven by independent ambitions, a sociopolitical universe opposite to the centralized empires.

Such state systems have laid the bases of the major civilizations of the Near East, India, China, classical antiquity, and the West, in undefinable but momentous ways laying the foundations for enormous and enduring achievements. They may have been the cultural builders in all cases, although the historical record of the background of the earliest civilizations, including the native American civilizations, is very sketchy. Great empires have regularly been inheritors, rather than originators, of ideas. They have spread civilization and, in a sense, consolidated it; but they have been more content with preservation, which comes to mean stagnation, than zestful for progress and have stifled the creative impulse. Even in the case of China after the unification of 221 B.C., invention and innovation seem to have come mostly in times of what is called political decay, that is, of dynastic breakup; almost half the time from 221 B.C. to the end of the Qing Dynasty in 1912 China has been irregularly split into regional states,[12] not forming a state system, properly speaking, but allowing some release from imperial strictures.

We have knowledge of less than a dozen clear-cut state systems with corresponding episodes of creativity and discovery. The earliest known and one of the most fertile was that of the Sumerian city-states of Mesopotamia, in the late fourth and early third millennia. They were responsible for a host of inventions, from writing to sailing vessels and the wheel. They left behind the oldest known literature, and they had schools and school books of a sort. They had in some places and at some times consultative institutions in the spirit of modern democratic government. A primitive Magna Carta of about 2400 B.C. limited taxes and promised certain rights for everyone. The small states traded, quarreled, and warred among themselves until their international system became unstable. They were swallowed up by the first empire of history, the Akkadian, about 2350 B.C., and Sumerian creativity was thereby ended.

Through the following millennia, large or medium empires succeeded one another, coming to fullness and breaking up. During many centuries civilization was in some ways refined and more widely extended, but not much advanced except in the techniques of imperial rule.[13] The Assyrian empire of the seventh century B.C. represented little improvement of the arts and sciences (except for some inventions, such as the smelting of iron) over its predecessors nearly two millennia before.

## ANCIENT DEMOCRACY

Around this time there arose for reasons not well understood a new wave of intellectual progress leading toward classical civilizations in India, China, and Greece—offshoots of the weary civilization of the Near East. Buddha and Confucius (sixth to fifth centuries B.C.) were contemporaries and were immediate predecessors of Socrates. In each case, a group of many small, interacting independent sovereignties displayed historically phenomenal creativity for a few centuries, in widely separated cultural flowerings roughly at the same level, well above the parent civilization of the Near East.

In Greece democracy became widespread, although not universal, after the kings of Homeric times lost power to aristocratic councils or citizens' assemblies. It was promoted mostly by commercial interests, against the opposition of landholders; and usually the more commercial a city, the more democratic.[14] Institutions were sophisticatedly developed. The only ancient constitution known in detail was that of Athens, described by Aristotle. Its democracy was far-reaching and effective, the common interests of the citizens being strengthened by exclusion of slaves and the large foreign population. To share in the state was the duty and privilege of the ordinary male Athenian, both as a voter in the assembly and as an officeholder in the administration.

The Greeks were responsible for much of the modern political vocabulary, including "politics" (from *polis*, city-state), "democracy" (people power), "monarchy" (single rule), "oligarchy" (few rule), and many other terms. They apparently invented the abstract idea of liberty, which they enthusiastically exalted. "Better starve free than be a fat slave," said Aesop. The bases of Greek democracy were the same as those of modern democracy, including rule of law, freedom of expression, responsibility of the government, frequent elections, and courts independent of the executive. The state prided itself on its openness—most of the city-states were ports, with a highway to the world—and trade was minimally controlled. The chief power lay in the assembly, where all citizens had voice and vote. Government was by committees—the most important being elected, the others chosen by lot—so that most male citizens shared at some time in the business of the state.[15] The courts, with juries of hundreds, were a key institution; law was enforced mostly by public opinion.[16]

Greek democracy could be more far-reaching than conventional modern democracy because the state was limited to an area whose people could assemble conveniently. The citizens were like members of a fraternity, enjoying less freedom than those of a democracy today but more equality, community, and participation. There were rich men and noble families, but display of wealth was frowned upon, and the wealthy were required to contribute to the festivals and defense of the community. The poor had a vital role as soldiers and as oarsmen in the navy.[17] Competition for civic honor was intense not only among the city-states but within them, and the atmosphere was so stimulating that Greece set the West on its course for the next two thousand years.

Republics flourished in India about the same time. Not much is known of them, but they were reputed to be patriotic, just, and well administered. Many questions seem to have been decided by the assembly, which elected leaders and decided on war or peace. In monarchical states kings were restricted and sometimes subject to election. Commerce was promoted and respected in what appears to have been a rather bourgeois society.[18] If there is no record of republicanism in China, this may be because the chronicles have been transmitted by a series of determinedly despotic and history-minded dynasties. The empires that took over the heritage of Indian and Hellenic civilization were authoritarian enough; but they never did anything comparable to the burning of books when China's unifiers sought to affirm their rule by destroying the literature of the previous freer times.

Some reasons why a system of independent sovereign units is conducive to more open and consultative and less arbitrary and autocratic politics have already been noted. They are mostly obvious and much the same today as thousands of years ago and include the ability to compare different governments, the greater difficulty of censorship, the freedom of emigration, the lesser elevation of rulers, and the importance of trade and the mercantile class. The states of an international system are continually engaged in rivalry and contention and sometimes war. Confrontation with the outside world imposes realism and develops an achievement ethic.[19] A shared cause nourishes community spirit and brings aristocrats and commoners closer together;[20] among the Greeks there was no shame in manual labor, and all mingled easily. Community spirit and better government, along with superior weaponry, enabled the small and quarrelsome Greek city-states to stand against the mighty Persian Empire.

But the balancing of powers in a system of independent sovereign units is inherently unstable. Each state system has broken down after a few centuries, perhaps mostly because technological changes made it easier to govern larger areas and improved arts of war gave advantages to larger and more aggressive states. The Chinese Contending States (before 221 B.C.) and the Indian republics and small kingdoms were thus swallowed up by empires covering their whole cultural world. Despite many often chaotic interruptions, empire remained the ideal in China and India.

Greek civilization outgrew the tiny city-states, but after the Macedonian conquest and Alexander's spectacular empire building, his dominion fell apart. Greek culture then had a sort of afterlife in the Hellenistic period, which was dominated by middle-sized kingdoms around the eastern Mediterranean, some of them comparable in size to modern European nation-states.

Hellenistic culture, although less original than that of classical Greece, was more varied and more voluminous; and it carried Greek science to a higher level. But after little more than a century and a half the independent states were engulfed by Rome, a power farther from the Greek cultural center than Macedon and correspondingly less Hellenized and more warlike. The Roman empire was at first less centralized and repressive than comparable universal powers, but it also subsided into classic despotism, with a deified Caesar standing over a rapacious bureaucracy. After centuries of cultural and political decay, the Roman Empire collapsed in the fifth century under the assaults of less organized Germanic peoples whom it would have easily repelled in its days of vigor. A long period of disorder, the so-called Dark Ages, ensued.

## THE RISE OF THE WEST

Renewal began in the ninth century within the framework of carry-overs of the old empire, the Roman Catholic Church and the Holy Roman Empire. Towns slowly grew up as trade revived, and groups of small autonomous units slightly suggestive of free Greek city-states of an earlier age arose in Italy, Spain, France, the Low Countries, Germany, and elsewhere, even as far away as western Russia. They became the new centers of economic and cultural growth. Thanks to the protection of the papacy, they were especially strong in Italy, where they remained independent longest (until the end of the fifteenth century). During the Renaissance the art, wealth, and intellectual activity of Europe were concentrated in the Italian statelets. Italian was the modish language of Europe in Shakespeare's day; Milton wrote much verse in it.

The free towns of Europe raised Western civilization to near-modern levels of sophistication and to an elegance hardly surpassed since, at least in the visual arts: one recalls Da Vinci, Michelangelo, Raphael, Cellini, and a host of near equals. The sovereign or semisovereign cities, usually called communes, were in their inception quite republican or democratic, with citizens' assemblies and much government by committee; but they gradually lost freedom and became oligarchies, tyrannies, or dependencies of larger powers. They were always politically handicapped by having to function under the shadow of the Holy Roman Empire, sundry feudal powers, and especially the monarchies that were making Europe into a collection of nation-states. Thanks to the development of technology, especially gunpowder and artillery, territorial consolidation was continuous, although gradual, from the early Middle Ages. From the fifteenth century, the free cities were engulfed or dominated by the rising kingdoms, headed by Spain and France; and the political map began taking on modern contours.

### The European Nation State System

In Europe, unlike Mesopotamia, India, China, and the Greco-Mediterranean world, the process of consolidation halted short of universal empire. The most obvious reason was the dissected geography of the continent, a peninsula with many natural barriers, such as the Alps, the

Pyrenees, many lesser ranges, the marshes of Holland, the English Channel, and the Baltic Sea. Because of such obstacles, territorial expansion in Western Europe was checked, although communication was relatively easy. The accident that the Holy Roman Empire and the papacy, with their conflicting claims to universal sway, spent their energies battling each other for centuries also facilitated the formation and solidification of independent sovereignties. Ambitious states were restrained, too, by the balance of power, that is, the tendency of weaker states to combine against any that seemed threatening to the freedom of all, which became a basic principle of European statecraft.

It was further essential for the stability of the state system of Western and Central Europe that it formed, despite countless wars, something of a community. One faith united the West against the heathens; in the Middle Ages and afterward, Poland and Austria saw themselves as defenders of Christian Europe against the Mongols and Turks. The educated always had a lingua franca. Latin was central in education and was widely used until the sixteenth century and in some parts into the nineteenth. In the Renaissance, Italian was preferred; and in the seventeenth century, French became fashionable as the language of Versailles, the Sun King (Louis XIV), and diplomats and aristocrats as far as Russia. Scholars traveled and corresponded very widely, and fashions of dress, furniture, art, and music were copied across the continent.[21] Within this community, political pluralism gave a degree of freedom: there could be no absolute repression, as dissidents in one country could migrate elsewhere; there was no general censorship, although kings commonly tried to limit their subjects' reading. Improvements of communications and travel, without corresponding enlargement of political jurisdictions, tended to lighten the political atmosphere.

Europe thus became a patchwork of medium-sized units, intermediate between city-states and great empires. But the maintenance of national independence from the fifteenth to the twentieth century, through profound changes in warfare, communications, production, and trade, was almost miraculous. The freedom of Europe was often placed in jeopardy by men ambitious of reunifying the continent, from Charlemagne through Charles V, Louis XIV, Napoleon, and Hitler. They were all defeated by the balance of power (assisted by geography, especially the English Channel) or in this century by the inability of European conquerors to cope with extra-European powers, namely Russia and America.

### Europe's Ascendancy

The power and productivity of Europe waxed through the Middle Ages. Especially from the thirteenth century there was a swelling flow of inventions, and Western culture leaped forward in the fifteenth century with the invention of printing and the beginning of overseas voyages of discovery. Up to the fifteenth century, China was technologically roughly equal to Europe, but Europe progressed as a nation-state system while China stagnated as an empire. Chinese vessels reached the Indian Ocean at roughly the same time as the Portuguese, who were soon challenged and outdone by the Spanish, Dutch, and English; but the Chinese navigators were reined in and kept home. Printing in Europe spread into all corners and a thousand uses and revolutionized intellectual life; in China it was controlled, used mostly for ornamental and ceremonial purposes, and had little effect. Production in China remained regulated; in Europe the growth of trade broke up the guild system.[22]

European government was generally monarchic but much less severe than the autocracies of the East. Rulership in the Middle Ages was divided by a multitude of often conflicting jurisdictions, and medieval monarchy was much qualified by feudal rights. Kings swore to respect the privileges of nobles, towns, the Church, and other groups with a stake in the society, and it was assumed that they were subject to the law of the land.[23] There were more or less representative assemblies—estates of the realm—the consent of which was deemed necessary for new laws or new taxes. There was a balance between crown and nobility, which was vital for the emergence of a middle class and the growth of liberties.[24] By comparison with Asia, Western Europe was quite egalitarian, and persons of lowly origin could rise in trade, the army, or the church.[25]

The initial effect of consolidation of European nation-states and the loss of freedom of the towns was a hardening of government and a separation of classes. Absolutist monarchy became the mode, rationalized by the theory of the divine right of kings, but it was more complete in theory than in practice. Guilds, towns, nobles, and other groups retained traditional rights, and no one contemplated arbitrary management of society. Representative feudal institutions were not forgotten, and the republican ideal was uninterrupted in some places, as in Switzerland since the Middle Ages. The Reformation in the fifteenth century, which was made possible by both printing and the growth of nation-states, brought a division of spiritual authority, that is, its relaxation. As the level of culture rose without much further territorial enlargement of the European kingdoms, the tide began flowing toward liberalism, constitutionalism, and representative government.

A monumental move to freedom was the revolt of the Netherlands against Spanish imperial rule in the late sixteenth and early seventeenth centuries. The Netherlands became a virtual model of the free, pluralistic, and progressive state. Despite, or more likely because of, its "jerry-built and seemingly ineffectual state machinery,"[26] with a small population and no natural resources, and without even much good agricultural land, the Netherlands became a world economic hegemon for the greater part of a century. The Dutch excelled in agriculture, industry, commerce, and finance; their shipping tonnage surpassed that of all their rivals together; and their experts were hired to assist factories, waterworks, construction, and military engineering across Europe. The state was cumbersome and divided, but it favored entrepreneurs and did more for social welfare than any other.[27] Its upsurge was brought to a halt by contrary causes: the nation was too small to compete militarily with other dynamic powers, especially the British; and the Netherlands sacrificed something of its character by acquiring an overseas empire.

The libertarian trend continued in the English civil war (midseventeenth century) and in the firm establishment of parliamentary authority by the "Glorious Revolution" of 1688. Monarchies justified themselves less by ascriptive right and more by their supposed benevolence. It seemed necessary to find a rationale for the authority of the state; contract theories of government, to the effect that the people had somehow compacted with their rulers, led toward ideas of individual rights and liberties.

The old order was creaking well before the American Revolution (1776) announced a new era of freedom and the French Revolution (1789) proclaimed "Liberty, Equality, Fraternity," the Rights of Man, and the equality of citizens. Revolutionary France went to war against most of Europe and was for a time victorious, even as it fell under the tyranny of Napoleon. France and Napoleon were defeated in 1815 by the conservative powers, including Russia, Austria, and Prussia; but their conservatism was qualified by the presence of liberal England in their coalition. The strength of the long-term liberalizing tide was shown when in 1830 the French dethroned their last Bourbon, and by 1848 revolution was again marching over Europe, restoring the ideals of the French Revolution.

The technological, scientific, and cultural progress of the West accelerated from the fifteenth century. The seventeenth century was a time of basic advances by such geniuses as Newton and Descartes; it was followed by the upsurge of chemistry and physics in the eighteenth century, accompanied by the beginnings of the industrial revolution. Education, technology, and science reinforced each other: free craftsmen improved technology, which gave science better instruments to develop theories that further advanced technology. The beginnings of mechanical civilization, burgeoning in the Netherlands even in the long war against Spain, flowered in England in the eighteenth century and spread to neighboring lands. The nineteenth century saw the ripening of coal-and-iron industrialization; science grew from the hobby of a few to the preoccupation or vocation of many, and brought a new self-perception of humanity.

With the overseas voyages starting from Portugal in the latter part of the fifteenth century, Europe began achieving worldwide hegemony, based not on unity and martial organization but on technological superiority. Portugal and Spain acquired huge empires in Asia and the Americas with minimal military effort; after them, the Netherlands, Britain, and France staked out overseas possessions dwarfing the European homeland. Oceanic exploration was basically complete by 1700, and exploration of habitable lands by 1850.

The nineteenth century saw the zenith of the European state system, with a near monopoly of world industry, commerce, and military power, shared only with overseas offshoots, headed by the United States. As though to celebrate, or perhaps to compensate for incipient decline, in the latter decades of that century the leading European powers carved up most of the non-European world that remained unclaimed (mostly because of its low productivity of tradable goods) in Africa and Asia. This period also saw the maturing of representative and increasingly democratic, as well as constitutional, government, which was regarded as the inevitable way of enlightenment. As early as the 1870s and 1880s there were moves toward constitutionalism and representative government in the Turkish Empire, Thailand, and other unlikely havens for democracy. European-based civilization, spreading to vast new lands and successful beyond the dreams of earlier civilizations, seemed destined to convert and civilize all peoples and prevail universally.

## FROM EUROPEAN TO WORLD SYSTEM

The nation-state system of the West endured half a millennium, but it, like earlier state systems, eventually made itself obsolete by technological progress and became unstable. New weaponry made war no longer suitable as a form of international relations, and territorial conquest in Europe lost sense. Yet growing mass armies made national power ever more expensive, and the emerging politics of democracy and nationalism raised tensions between powers representing the old order and the new.

The balance of power was undermined in the second half of the nineteenth century by the unification and industrialization of Germany, potentially the strongest of European powers (except still backward Russia). The division of Germany into many small states and principalities, consecrated by the Peace of Westphalia (1648), had been a major factor in the maintenance of the balance of power, because it immobilized the center of Europe. The unification of Germany after 1870 under the leadership of militaristic-authoritarian Prussia made difficult the containment of what was rapidly becoming the leading industrial power of Europe, a Germany that felt its ambitions had been cheated. European politics was rigidified as republican France stood in opposition to semiautocratic Germany and both sought allies.

Optimism in the steady growth of science, education, material well-being, and the arts and graces of civilization was shattered by the First World War. This was triggered by a problem of trivial concern for most Europeans, the alleged complicity of Serbia in the assassination of an Austrian prince. The underlying causes were the nervousness of the anachronistic Austro-Hungarian Empire in the face of advancing liberal nationalism, and the fear of the German elite for its outdated authoritarian order and its determination to use its military might when it seemed advantageous to do so.

There could be no compromise in the long, grinding, and grossly murderous war because each side feared that victory of the opponent would be fatal for its way of life or national existence. Victory came to the more libertarian side because the Germans blindly brought the United States into the fray. But the senseless struggle largely destroyed the morale and influence of Europe.

In this disorder and demoralization, the Russian Empire fell to a radical ideology and an extremist party under Lenin. The revolution he led amounted to an energetic reassertion of the imperial vocation of Russia with modern organization and dogmatic garb, adapting Western notions of equality and social change to Russian political purposes.[28] Claiming to represent not a state but a movement of universal salvation, Leninism launched a broadside on everything the state system stood for, including nationalism, individualism, legality, freedom, representative government, and "bourgeois" virtues in general. Such a rejection of the Westernization that had long been gaining ground in Russia was possible only because the war largely cut Russia off from the West, which was morally discredited by the bloody and futile war. Because of widespread disillusionment, the Leninist rebellion against the Western system gained many adherents in the West despite the material weakness of the new Soviet state; and it injected a powerful alien and violent element into the political contentions of Europe.

The nation-state system, having failed politically, failed economically. The war was followed by maladjustments, impoverishment, unemployment, and crises of trade and confidence. Then, little more than a decade after its end, came the Great Depression of the 1930s. The virtue of the pluralistic system had been its ability to invent, improve, and produce, bringing relative material prosperity to its peoples. In the depression, the promise of welfare, like the promise of peace, seemed fraudulent; and the way was open to a bitter political reaction. Fascism in Italy, Nazism in Germany, and parallel movements in several countries of Eastern Europe mixed hypernationalism evoked by anger at the outcome of the war with an effort to use state powers to cut through the economic problems that seemed beyond the capacity of the old liberal order. They were also a reassertion of native authoritarian ideas and institutions, repudiating democracy as poisonous of true national values, while adapting democratic modes such as the mass political party to dictatorship and applying modern techniques of propaganda and repression to premodern politics.

The Western reactionaries borrowed much from the successful Leninist proponents of reshaped Russian authoritarianism. Setting themselves up as the most determined enemies of Bolshevism, they used Bolshevik methods of organization, leadership, and control; Communists and fascists alike rejected liberalism, capitalism, and democracy. German fascism was distinguished by virulent anti-Semitism, which Hitler brought from the broken Austrian empire; but its distinctiveness was decreased as Stalin quietly reverted to traditional Russian anti-Semitism.

The dynamism of the Nazi reaction and its lust for triumph led to something like a renewal of the 1914–1918 struggle. After Hitler took office in 1933, he rearmed the Reich; and by 1938 the Nazis were embarked on a career of aggrandizement. Austria, Czechoslovakia, and Poland were the first items on the menu. By 1939 all of Eastern Europe was under dictatorship, and totalitarianism seemed the way, or the wave, of the future.

Britain and France resolved to halt the onrush of Nazi power, less from democratic convictions than from fear of loss of national independence. They drew a line against further German expansion, in the old spirit of the balance of power, and went to war when the Hitlerites invaded Poland on September 1, 1939. The Germans won spectacular victories and overran the bulk of the continent west of Russia. They were joined by the Italian fascists and by the Japanese militarists, who sought to take over the Asian holdings of Western powers as well as China. However, the Germans made the mistake of attacking the Soviet Union, and they repeated their error of 1917, adding the United States to their enemies.

## THE CONTEMPORARY INTERNATIONAL SCENE

After World War I, Europe still viewed itself as the cockpit of history; after World War II, it had obviously receded. The leadership of world affairs fell to the new category of superpowers, the holders of strategic strength and the only states capable of projecting power around the globe. The nation-state system that had brought the scientific-industrial revolution was at an end, even as its achievements were becoming universalized.

Again, as in Renaissance times, it was the fortune of the West that the supersession of smaller units did not lead to the blanketing of a single universal empire. On the contrary, the victory over fascism seemed to open new horizons not only for the United States but for

Europe, which suffered terrible material destruction but found a new albeit more modest spirit. Within the Western world, political primitivism was purged by the defeat of the totalitarian-militaristic powers, and since 1945 there has been no serious political conflict between Western powers. Europe surrendered its overseas empires, partly because the vocation was lost, and partly because it was too difficult to maintain domination of alien peoples who had absorbed ideas of nationalism and freedom, as appeared most clearly in the wars in Vietnam and Algeria. But Europe was healthier to be relieved of colonies.

The entire globe has become a single international system, in which the distance between continents in terms of travel time and ease of communication has become far less than between states of Western Europe a century ago. The world buys and sells in a single market, and in many cases production is farmed out in countries thousands of miles apart. International commerce has grown many times over and is more important than ever for most nations. People listen to broadcasts from half a world away, and internationalized television seems on the way to homogenizing culture.

The new international system, however, is ambiguous, caught up in rapid technological change of unknowable potentials and subject to fears that its first big war would be its last. It is deeply divided by extreme differences of power and economic level. The fundamental division of the world remains between the sphere made rich and powerful by the capacities of the unique Western state system (with the significant addition of Japan) and the mostly poorer remainder, from Russia and China to South Asia, Africa, and (partially) Latin America. This division corresponds fairly closely to that between countries taking elections and constitutions seriously and those subject to more or less arbitrary government.

Of these groups of societies, the former is (since World War II) remarkably united. All its members are effectively democratic, and their per capita income levels hardly vary by a factor of more than two or three. Their economic and political systems are sufficiently similar that it would represent no great shock for the people of any Western nation to find themselves under the government of any other; and there is no grave political quarrel between any two of them. On the other hand, in the non-Western sphere there are differing types of government, many strong antagonisms, and not a few low-grade wars. Per capita income levels vary by a factor of ten or twenty or more. Political forms include the democratic or quasidemocratic (such as Venezuela or India), military-bureaucratic (such as Burma or Nigeria), oligarchic authoritarian (such as Thailand), personal authoritarian (such as Paraguay), traditional monarchic (such as Saudi Arabia), theocratic (such as Iran), one-party semi-dictatorial regimes (such as Mexico), Marxist-Leninist dictatorships (such as Angola), and Marxist-Leninist party-states (headed by the Soviet Union). Many must be simply called mixed.

Most non-Western states, especially the weaker ones, are friendly to the West, or the "capitalist world system," and dependent on it and are more or less subject to its influence. Yet there is a basic political alienation. Few African or Asian countries have voted with the United States on more than 20 percent of the issues in the UN General Assembly recently; in the Americas, even such friendly countries as Venezuela, Argentina, and Brazil have been on the side opposite the United States on more than 80 percent of the roll calls. Africa agrees with the United States only a little more often than does the Soviet bloc.[29] Much of the Third World is nearly as alien to the West as the overtly hostile Marxist-Leninist states.

In a sense, however, the victory of Western patterns, like Western fashions, is universal. People everywhere want products of Western civilization, such as automobiles and television, follow Western styles (China has accepted the ordinary business suit), and adopt Western culture (Moscow has surrendered to Western music). The democratic philosophy is accepted as the chief claim to political legitimacy, in modified form even in the Soviet Union. Military governments—militocracies—also represent a partial Westernization, taking over organizational patterns as well as means of force and using them for non-Western, but not usually anti-Western forms of rulership, while usually claiming to have ultimately democratic aims. Even the Ayatollah's Iran, devoted to Islamic fundamentalism, has elections and a parliament.

Yet the standoff between the more pluralistic or democratic Western states and the more authoritarian non-Western or anti-Western states seems deep and lasting. Perhaps it is built into the international system, with its enduring mixture of cooperation and confrontation, which might be overcome only by the victory of one power and the imposition of its universal mandate.

The political division is linked to the permanent economic division of the world. Poverty or relative backwardness, like strong government, tends to perpetuate or reinforce itself. If underdevelopment is the relation between material achievements and technical possibilities, the world is becoming more unequal rather than less so. If a less affluent country a few decades ago could contemplate importing a steel industry or even machine-building at a technological level near that of the leading producers, only the most favored (such as Brazil, Mexico, or Taiwan) can reasonably dream of inaugurating a computer or gene-splicing industry.

Present trends offer less-developed countries no chance of closing the gap within a thousand years. Brains go to where brains are successfully working, and no less-developed country can come near to matching the scientific facilities and attractions of the leading powers. There is no research or institutional basis for beginning to catch up. Advanced enterprises farm out labor-intensive operations to low-wage countries, but the control centers and most of the profits remain where skills, information, and communications are most abundant.

At the same time, the poorer countries find it difficult to move away from oligarchic regimes of low legitimacy and responsibility. Political shortcomings in turn handicap economic innovation, rationalization, and the kind of social and economic progress that would promise political renewal. The contemporary international system is riven by deep differences impeding understanding and cooperation between political and economic opposites.

## Notes

1. Harold Laski, *Politics* (London: J. B. Lippincott, 1931), p. 147.
2. Michael P. Ghigheri, "The Social Ecology of Chimpanzees," *Scientific American*, 252 (June 1985), 110–112; Edward O. Wilson, *On Human Nature* (Cambridge: Harvard University Press, 1978), pp. 27–28; and Jane Goodall, *The Chimpanzees of Gombe: Patterns of Behavior* (Cambridge: Harvard University Press, 1986), chap. 17.
3. John E. Pfeiffer, *The Emergence of Society* (New York: McGraw-Hill, 1977), p. 33.
4. Robert J. Wenke, *Patterns in Prehistory: Mankind's First Three Million Years* (New York: Oxford University Press, 1980), pp. 114, 138.
5. Robert L. Carneiro, "Political Expansion," In *Origins of the State: The Anthropology of Political Evolution*, ed. Ronald Cohen and Elman R. Service (Philadelphia: Institute for the Study of Human Issues, 1978), p. 211.
6. William H. McNeill, *The Rise of the West: A History of the Human Community* (Chicago: University of Chicago Press, 1963), p. 65.
7. Eli Sagan, *At the Dawn of Tyranny* (New York: Alfred A. Knopf, 1985), p. 239.
8. Marek Zvelebil, "Postglacial Foraging in the Forests of Europe," *Scientific American*, 254 (May 1986), 110.
9. Jonathan Haas, *The Evolution of the Prehistoric State* (New York: Columbia University Press, 1982), pp. 82, 209.
10. Haas, *The Prehistoric State*, pp. 82, 209, 211, 214.
11. This chapter is based on Robert G. Wesson's *State Systems* (New York: The Free Press, 1978).
12. Alan P. L. Liu, "The Dragon's Teeth of Mao tse-tung," *Issues and Studies*, 21 (August 1985), 9.
13. William H. McNeill, *The Rise of the West: A History of the Human Community* (Chicago: University of Chicago Press, 1963), p. 126.
14. George H. Sabine, *A History of Political Theory*, rev. ed. (New York: Holt, Rinehart and Winston, 1955) p. 23.
15. Donald Kagan, *The Great Dialogue: History of Greek Political Thought from Homer to Polybius* (New York: Free Press, 1965), chap. 5.
16. Sabine, *History*, pp. 9–10.
17. McNeill, *Rise*, p. 256.
18. Wesson, *State Systems*, pp. 47–48.
19. As seen by McClelland. For the Greek condition, see pp. 108–129. David C. McClelland, *The Achieving Society* (New York: Irvington Publishers, 1976), pp. 108–129.
20. Wesson, *State Systems*, pp. 80–90.

21. E. L. Jones, *The European Miracle* (Cambridge: Cambridge University Press, 1981), pp. 112–14.
22. Jones, *European Miracle*, pp. 61, 67, 99.
23. Sabine, *History*, p. 207.
24. Barrington Moore, Jr., *Social Origins of Dictatorship and Democracy: Lord and Peasant in the Making of the Modern World* (Boston: Beacon Press, 1966), pp. 417–18.
25. McNeill, *Rise*, p. 558.
26. Immanuel Wallerstein, *The Modern World System*, vol. 2, *Mercantilism and the Consolidation of the European World Economy, 1600–1750* (New York: Academic Press, 1980), p. 38.
27. Wallerstein, *Modern World System*, pp. 46, 61–63.
28. As outlined in Robert Wessons, *The Russian Dilemma*, rev. ed. (New York: Praeger Publishers, 1986), chap. 3.
29. *Report to Congress on Voting Practices in the United Nations*, Department of State, (Washington, D.C.: 1985); Jeane J. Kirkpatrick, "The U.S. Leads; Who Follows?" *Washington Post*, June 9, 1986, p. 21.

# The Divided World

---

## 3

## THE REACTION TO THE WEST

The overwhelming historical fact of the past thousand years has been the material and cultural triumph of the Western state system. It has, for better or worse, swamped the peoples of the world, and its effects are the subject of modern history. Infinitely varied, they have impinged in many different ways, positive and negative, on the diverse non-Western peoples.

Modern civilization has brought preventive medicine, many amenities of life, and a vast broadening of horizons and experience, down to the television set that now lightens evenings for hamlets from the Amazon to India and China. But the onrush of modernization has also disrupted patterns of society and smashed values. The strange machines, ways, and ideas have been profoundly injurious to once proud peoples made aware of their weakness. Local gods are denigrated, implicitly if not overtly; and old institutions and peoples are made to seem poor and backward, like the dugout against the airplane. Frictions are inevitable, if only because there is no way to define fairness in dealings between the technological society and the wooden plow society. The big problems of international relations, both the North-South and East-West conflicts, stem from the impact of the West on the rest of the world.

The assaulted peoples, having acquired some knowledge of Western ways and the dangers to their society, have been moved by two basic drives. One was to seek to catch up with the West by learning its secrets, which meant first adopting tools, then modernizing administration and the institutions behind modernization, including political modes such as a constitution and elected government, and along the way changing national mores and character to suit a modern economy. The alternative was to try to defend culture, character, and independence by putting up barriers to the invasion and cultivating native virtues.

The first approach implies greater psychological sacrifice—the surrender of pride and way of life—but it has been supported by fear and respect for the achievements and power of the West. The second is for many peoples the more attractive, especially for those who have felt maltreated or at least humiliated by the intrusion of mechanically better equipped and more effectively organized nations. This option had and has strong political appeal, because it implies defending customary ways and mentality, the national personality.

Both drives or approaches have been mingled not only in countries but in individuals who at the same time love and hate the alien culture and prize and despise the traditional ways. The result has been a varying set of usually unconscious compromises between Westernization and nativism in the effort to gain materially while saving spiritual independence. The accommodation achieved has usually worked badly, neither securing very effective borrowing nor saving self-respect, and it has led to confusion of values and uncertainty, with bitterness and ambivalence. The West is much admired and accused of many sins of injustice and immorality.[1]

## RUSSIAN REACTION

The problem first came to the fore in Russia, a Eurasian power in close cultural, economic, and military contact with Western Europe. From the days of Ivan IV (1530 to 1584) Russia was compelled to learn from the West to extend its autocratic empire eastward and defend itself against the West. After being defeated by the Swedes, Peter I (1672 to 1725) undertook massive Westernization to reinforce his power and his rule. He not only imported shipbuilders but required his nobles to change their style of dress, shave their beards, and smoke tobacco.

Post-Petrine Russia, split into the Westernized upper layer and the dark masses, was always uncertain how much to borrow, how fully to shut itself off from corrosive Western ideas. It had to borrow to try to acquire the economic and military strength of the West, yet it had to protect the autocracy that stood for Russian greatness. As the industrial revolution ripened in the nineteenth century and as Western-style education perforce expanded, the dilemma became a serious intellectual problem. As Western influence became more pervasive, the need to reconcile the contrary requirements turned more acute. Russian intellectuals tended to divide into two currents: the Westernizers would generally replace Russian ways by those of the more progressive West, whereas the Slavophiles (the majority) would protect Russian values, idealize the virtues of the simple peasants, and repel the West through a renovated autocracy.[2] Eventually the Bolsheviks, taking advantage of the breakdown of the old order in 1917, imposed a synthesis of the two inclinations. Promoting a restored authoritarianism, they claimed Russian virtues of equality and fraternity plus unity and order, and boasted of taking over the ways, not of the corrupt bourgeois West of the present, but of the more advanced socialist West predicted by Marxist theory.

The Russian Empire, long accustomed to the borrowing of Western technology within an autocratic-imperial framework, thus reframed the imperial vocation in utopian terms. In many ways, however, the extremist Russian response was typical of Third World reactions to the Western impact: it bowed to modernism and science (in Marxism and "scientific socialism") but reinterpreted imported ideas to suit native political purposes. While borrowing technology, the Leninists asserted the moral superiority of Russia (renamed the Soviet Union) leading the world to the socialist order. Neglecting agriculture in favor of industry, they looked to the solution of all problems by a combination of technology with political controls. Lenin equated electrification plus Soviet power with the utopia of communism, and Stalin promised to build socialism by the grandiose industrialization of the Five-Year Plan. His "revolution from above" imposed outward westernization (as Peter the Great once did) by non-Western political means.

The revolution, however, was short-lived. The Soviet system, forged by Stalin's despotism atop Lenin's dictatorship, necessarily lost its impetus for change and came to base itself more on force than on ideology or the pretended will of the people. The utopianism of renewal having worn out, the Soviet Union has gradually become, politically and economically, more like a Third World society while ever claiming a messianic role in the Russian tradition and continuing in determined hostility to the ideals, if not the very independence, of the West.

The Russian reaction to the pressure of Western pluralist civilization forms the basis of the great political contest of our time, the East-West standoff. Marxism-Leninism is itself a hybrid, an adaptation of Western doctrine to anti-Western authoritarianism. Although Lenin originally intended his revolution as a summons to revolution in the West (as called for by Marx's thories), the communist movement has gained support there only as an answer to the barbarism of fascism or as a refuge from disillusionment with war, disorder, and depression. In recent years of considerable world prosperity, while the Soviet Union and its satellites were falling behind rather than catching up with the advanced industrial countries, European parties have been riven by factionalism and uncertainty as to the relevance of their message for modern economies, and communism has largely and probably finally faded from the Western European scene.

## THE SOVIET MODEL

Russia has instead made itself a supportive model and organizational rationale for non-Western regimes desirous of escaping the political threat of the West and asserting a new and more effective absolutism. The Leninists of the 1920s and their successors transferred their hopes to those who shared their grievances against the prevalent world economic and political order, the peoples of colonial areas then and of the Third World today. Although there have been many efforts at radical Westernization, from Egypt to China, nowhere except in Russia did conditions and circumstances combine to produce a strong, lasting movement of anti-Western mobilization. Consequently Leninist communism has become a model, the only widely propagated model, for those who want the benefit of modern technology but feel deeply threatened by modern social and political institutions. It offers an appeal to nativist values, traditional collectivism, the prestige of a sophisticated and purportedly scientific teaching, a means of building a new statehood from disparate ethnic groups, a claim to legitimacy in the world order, and a promise of future glory.

The Russian answer to the Western intrusion helped to unite and rejuvenate another great nation of imperial tradition, China, which seemed helpless before foreign forces for generations until the victory of a party patterned after that of the Soviets (with Soviet assistance) in 1949. China attempted to develop first in an anti-Western posture in close alliance with the Soviet Union and then in limited cooperation with the West, under its own authoritarian system of management. The communist form was also imposed on a number of smaller nations from Cuba to Vietnam, with similar institutions despite diverse backgrounds and economic levels, using the same basic political means for the same end, the total power of a small minority.

As the idealism and vocation of social change faded, the Leninist formula appealed less to the deprived masses than to the holders of power. It has met the needs of many dictators, such as the rulers of Cuba, Guyana, Benin, and half a dozen other states in the Americas, Africa, and the Near East. In this use, Marxism-Leninism has undergone a metamorphosis. The class struggle is not the means of gaining power but the result of seizing power; the army becomes a "revolutionary" group, more or less equivalent to the Leninist party; [3] and the essence of their communism is not the organization of the economy and society but the apparatus of control and solidarity with the Soviet Union and its allies.

Despite the political attractiveness of this strategy, only a small minority of Third World dictatorships use it. This is partly because of religion and traditional ways and partly because weak and impoverished countries are compelled to adopt more or less capitalist economic methods, their material needs being better met not by the inefficient Soviets but by the Western powers.

In 1955 Soviet Premier Bulganin offered Soviet help for the development of Third World countries,[4] but for many years Soviet aid has been largely limited to military assistance in promising situations. The governments most inclined to follow the Leninist way have been those militarily dependent on the Soviets, such as Ethiopia, Mozambique, and Angola. A majority of Third World countries have subscribed to Western political ideals superficially, while accepting military, personal, or single-party governments and welcoming assistance from wherever it might be forthcoming. Others, such as the People's Republic of the Congo and various other African states, subscribe officially to the Marxist-Leninist persuasion but look for economic assistance from the West. China seeks Western and Japanese technology and investment and partly opens its own economy to entrepreneurial money making but still flaunts banners with the portraits of two Germans, Marx and Engels and two leaders of the disliked Russian nation, Lenin and Stalin. The saints of totalitarianism are exalted to ward off the dangers of modernization and Westernization.

### Democracy versus Authoritarianism

In Latin America centuries of exploitative colonial rule generated little pride in native institutions, and there has hardly been any imperial vocation on the part of these mostly weak countries. Independence was achieved early in the nineteenth century with the inspiration of the French Revolution (of which the Latin Americans received an idealized image) and the example of the newly freed and formed United States. Hence, although social structures were and have largely remained uncongenial to democracy, this has almost always and everywhere been an aspiration. Latin American countries generally would like to regard themselves as parts of the Western world, only needing a little adaptation and improvement to find full membership; and they have aspired, with varying success, to democratic politics, while making progress toward economic modernization. Some have had formally democratic institutions for a long period, but in Latin America as nowhere else there have been pendular swings between looser democratic and harsher military rule, neither usually bringing deep social change.[5] There has been a strong anti-Western revulsion only in the areas most dominated by the United States, the Caribbean and Central America.

Only in Japan has Western democracy been successfully transplanted—a democracy rather different from that of Western Europe but strong nonetheless. Exceptional circumstances made this possible. For one, Japan had a tradition of selective borrowing from Chinese culture for centuries. Consequently, when the Japanese realized in the mid-nineteenth century that they had to learn much very rapidly from the West to safeguard their independence, it came easy for them to set about systematically to adapt both technology and institutions. Moreover, Japan, dissected by mountains and ocean, had a somewhat decentralized feudal government, with much autonomy for local powers and a relatively open society.[6] Innovation was easier than in centralized China, tied up in imperial bureaucracy. The Japanese had in Confucianism an antidemocratic philosophic heritage, and they had no tradition of rights or representation, but a sacred emperor; yet they had customs of group leadership and collective decision making that adapted easily to democratic politics.[7]

Whatever its capacity for importation of Western institutions, as well as machinery and techniques of production, Japan in the 1930s turned to military authoritarianism, in part because of a feeling of being disdained by the dominant West and excluded from Western-dominated markets. But Japanese militarism in the long run could hardly have proved more productive or better suited to modernization than military rule elsewhere. It collapsed in the failure of its grand adventure, the huge Japanese "Co-prosperity Sphere" in Eastern and Southeastern Asia.

Not only were the materialistic authoritarians discredited and swept away; the Japanese were socially leveled, as possessions were destroyed or lost. The humbled people then docilely adopted the democratic institutions prescribed for them and undertook to make their way by production. Both ideas fitted Japanese traditions. Democracy fitted Japanese modes of solidarity and consultation, and the people had long excelled in crafts and had done very well in mechanical production. The example of Japan, the sole non-Western nation to become effectively democratic, is in one sense negative, however: it suggests that military defeat and occupation by a democratic power may be the only sure means, or at least the only rapid means, of transition to thorough democracy.

The United States had another opportunity to impose democracy—in the Philippines—but American rulership implanted democratic forms without reshaping Philippine society. From 1946 on, the islands had rather turbulent electoral government, and in 1972 Ferdinand Marcos used conditions of violence and unrest as an excuse to establish martial law. He was unable, however, really to institutionalize dictatorship; and in February 1986 the Filipino people gave a remarkable demonstration of the power of democratic ideals among a relatively poor people. There have also seemed to be possibilities of democratization in Taiwan and South Korea because of close relations with and dependence on the United States, together with pressures of intense antagonism to communist powers; but old power structures have persisted.

Spain and Portugal moved from dictatorship to democracy in the latter 1970s, in effect reentering the Western community of which they were integral parts in the sixteenth century but from which they had become partly separated by their empires and the superior economic growth of Northern Europe. A losing war for African colonies released Portugal from dictatorship. For Spain, accidents of personality, particularly the convictions of Franco's Bourbon successor, seem to have been very important; but democratization would have been impossible without great economic progress and close relations with the European Economic Community.[8]

The remainder of Eurasia, from East Germany to Korea, with Southern and Southeastern Asia, is fairly solidly authoritarian. The chief exception is India, which has managed to maintain functioning democratic institutions brought by the British. The Near East and Africa, both north and south of the Sahara, are inhospitable to representative government. In the Arab world, peoples with memories of conquest and brilliance have found the material superiority of the West particularly galling and have turned, in the failure of modernization, to antirationalism, fundamentalism, and the revival of traditional law.[9]

Africa, having seen European colonial empires carved into over forty countries with little basis for democratic government, has mostly gone to regimes of force. African countries have been much more bent than Latin American countries on asserting nativist values—such as "Familyism" in Tanzania and "Africanism" in Zaire, and "Conscienc- ism," the pseudoscientific rationale for anticolonialism put together by Nkrumah of Ghana—although there has not been much correlation be- tween ideology and policy.[10] Such doctrines seem less necessary as West- ern-trained leaders pass from the scene and national liberation becomes history. But from Africa to China there is a strong undercurrent of hostility to Western political values, even on the part of those who have gained most from world trade, such as the leaders of Singapore.[11]

## THE OBSTACLES TO DEMOCRACY

The failure of democratic forms to spread effectively much beyond their Western center of development, their collapse in some places where they seemed well established (as in Chile) or at least promising (as in Nigeria), and the difficulty of translating economic growth into political develop- ment (as in the shah's Iran) should cause no surprise. The Third World has lacked the historical-political formation of the West; prima facie, it should not be expected to generate, or be receptive to, the same institu- tions. Democratic government is part of a complex of interrelated institu- tions and customs in pluralistic-individualistic societies formed by the experience of the European nation-state system. Its main ideas, that people should be consulted about matters that concern them, that leaders should be bound by law and answer for their stewardship, and that everyone has rights of political participation, are comprehensible enough to Chi- nese, Indians, and Africans. This does not mean, however, that the sophis- ticated ways of democratic government can easily be made to function or that traditional value systems will support pluralistic politics. Democ- racy requires not only democratic ideas but democratic institutions and manners.

It is not to be concluded, however, that countries cannot sustain democratic governments unless they share centuries of the competitive history of the West or have the fortune to be defeated and forcibly re- shaped by a democratic power. Unless democracy or its lack are mystically conceived, they should be explicable in concrete terms, and it should be possible to find specific factors and conditions that have thwarted earnest democratic intentions in many lands. So far as they can be dis- cerned, such factors may conceivably be attenuated if not eliminated.

### External Pressures

The less developed nations are not entirely free to decide how they will govern themselves. They are psychologically, politically, and economically overshadowed. Dependence, economic or political, is injurious to national pride, consensus, and solidarity. The social structure is slanted toward foreign sources of wealth and power, and there is probably a sense of exploitation and futility. Foreign investment and close relations with international corporations and commercial and financial powers are wanted for growth and progress and hated for their superiority and their presence in, if not interference with, national affairs. To the extent that the economy is foreign-dominated and subject to forces beyond the control of the state, the state loses its validity as maker of the national destiny.

Understandably, Latin Americans and other peoples of the Third World blame many or most of their woes on dependency, "peripheral capitalism," or neocolonialism. However vague this concept, it represents a reality; a colony does not become confidently self-reliant simply by raising a new flag. Latin American social structures were molded by three centuries of Spanish oppression. In a weaker sense, the region has continued to lack autonomy economically and to some extent politically during its century and a half of formal independence.

Dependence and helplessness reduce the people's and the government's sense of responsibility. It is divisive and demoralizing for a state to shape policies to please a wealthier or stronger state even if relations are quite friendly. Some leaders are happy to cooperate; some seem grateful for aid but inwardly resent it; some view liberation from the domination of the outside power as the highest goal. Castro, for example, seems to have wished above all to get out of the economic and political embrace of the United States, although it had been in many ways advantageous for Cuba. He hailed it as liberation when the United States ceased paying several times the world market price for Cuban sugar. Economic policies are distorted by political relations; even persons friendly to the United States and the Western economic system resort to state enterprise to save the nation's assets from alienation, thereby weakening the domestic private sector and making it more difficult to manage the state democratically.

The logically relevant question is not why some are poor—most people have always been poor—but by what miracle some have become rich. But for the poor in a world dominated by the rich, the appalling question is why all cannot share in the miracle, and the bitter implication is inferiority. Peoples of the Third World, status conscious and sensitive, are embittered and humiliated by weakness. The Arabs have been hurt more by the success and power of Israel in the region the Arabs thought theirs than by the loss of territories; it is all the worse because the Israelis are fellow Semites. Part of the ungovernability of Argentina doubtless arises from the vexation of its relative decline from one of the richest Third World nations to middle-tier status (although in absolute terms the Argentines are better off than fifty years ago). All Third World countries, we may assume, have in different ways (as exemplified by Cuba and Iran as well as by the Philippines and Mexico) deeply ambivalent attitudes toward the United States, the stronger as contact is more intense. The powerful rich world compresses the nationhood and culture of the weaker and poorer, although it regards itself as just and generous. The result is political incapacity and cultural malaise.

***The East-West Conflict and the Third World***   International tensions also poison the politics of weaker countries as global conflict washes over national boundaries to complicate already difficult conditions. The image or specter of revolution generates hopes of radical improvement in some and fear of moderate reform in others. To outsiders it seems hypocritical for Third World tyrants or elites to see communism behind almost any program of serious change; but those making such charges, usually not very sophisticated analysts, are sincerely afraid of losing their way of life and deeply held values in the face of incomprehensible and disturbing forces. On the other hand, those who are discontented with present conditions naturally seek support from the proponents of revolutionary change, at home and abroad.

The Russian revolution, which spread a politics of violence and intolerance, won great and broad prestige by the successes of Soviet armies in World War II. In the times of Lenin and Stalin, the Soviet Union was preoccupied with its own reconstruction and lacked the power to reach out to distant lands. However, from the ascendance of Khrushchev in 1955, the Soviet Union began courting Third World countries. The results were uneven and in retrospect not very significant, but they alarmed Western, especially American, leaders. Soviet ambitions were the more disturbing because they coincided with the creation out of the old colonial empires of many new nations, the political directions of which were unpredictable. The Soviets did not insist on conversion to Marxism-Leninism but welcomed into the fold almost any anti-Western movement. But the ideological issue raised the temperature of political struggle in unstable societies.

Communism seemed a real threat to many in the Americas after Cuba turned to the Soviets in 1960 to 1961 for support against the United States. Castro proclaimed Cuba "socialist" in the Soviet sense and moved to destroy U.S. influence—"American imperialism"—in Latin America by popular revolutions or guerrilla warfare like that which led to Castro's seizure of power. Revolutionary doctrines took on a new meaning for the possessing classes and for many of the non possessors, especially déclassé intellectuals. But the upper classes and military officers, observing what had happened to the Cuban well-to-do and to the officers of the old Cuban army, resolved to quash any movement that might give power to radical elements. This meant putting a lid on democracy.

While Khrushchev looked to the radicalization of the Third World to swing the global balance to the Soviet side, the United States, fearful of unknown new forces in alien societies, envisioned that he might succeed and that the movement might be cumulative and avalanchelike. A Marxist atmosphere (intellectual Marxism is much more prevalent than political Marxism in the Third World) putting politics in terms of class struggle helped to make any ripple of political change look like a gathering tide.

Hence the United States became apprehensive that any popular or radical movement might possibly turn toward communism. It seemed safer and more convenient to support conservative, albeit more or less dictatorial, governments that took a firm anticommunist stance. Although the United States probably would have at all times preferred orderly, moderate democratic governments, which would assuredly be respectful of private property and friendly to this country, it has often feared that popular movements in the Third World would oppose foreign, especially U.S., corporations and U.S. interests in general, would turn into demagogic radicalism, and would open the door to extremism. In its anxiety over potential communism, the United States has sometimes tended to forget its commitment to democratization, as in the Dominican Republic in the 1960s.[12]

On the other hand, populist leaders often looked for inspiration and assistance to the Soviet Union or, in this hemisphere, to Castro's Cuba. They took for granted that the United States would oppose any attack on property interests, which for the radicals were the enemy, the native owners being tied up with the foreign. Adherence to the concept of private property in the Third World became an ideology of fixity and privilege and hence seemed to many to be antidemocratic. Democracy to the leftists became a matter not of free and responsible government but of combating the ruling social class, leading to the acceptance of a more or less Leninist formulation of democracy.

Third World politics thus became entangled, despite the desire of most Third World leaders, in extraneous Cold War issues. Foreign interference became a major issue on both the Left and the Right, with Castroism and its "progressive" allies against the CIA, the Pentagon, and multinational corporations. Such complications made it more difficult for Third World countries to find a democratic consensus. The political order is discredited by the belief that a foreign-affiliated group or socioeconomic class is using it, or would like to use it, for selfish purposes. Liberties that can be misused by foreign powers lose validity; for example, there is no value in freedom of a press subject to external manipulation. If important political parties are, or are believed to be, in the service of foreign powers, the contest of parties loses its meaning. Elected governments in Brazil, Chile, and Uruguay might have been overturned in 1964, 1973, and 1974, respectively, because of purely internal conflicts; but external encouragement of radicalism on the one hand and of anticommunism on the other helped provoke military coups. Under ideological strains, and subject to the meddling of greater external powers, democracy is problematic.

### Divided Societies

Much of the vulnerability of non-Western societies to pressures from abroad is due to divisions within them—antagonisms, mutual incomprehension, and feebleness of shared purpose—which invite foreign powers to play on differences. But even if the outside world takes no notice of them, most non-Western societies are too fissured to develop the consensus on fundamentals essential for a well-ordered constitutional representative system. Democracy can function only if people are tolerably in agreement; it has no means of bringing opposites together. Between communities that feel themselves incompatible, issues are not subject to mutually satisfactory adjustment. On the contrary, democratic politics may focus and inflame differences of class or ethnicity, and perhaps the strongest argument against free competition of political parties is that it splits the nation.

Divisions may be religious, ethnic, or social; few Third World states, except the smallest, are reasonably homogeneous. Some small Western democracies, such as Belgium and Switzerland, manage to surmount divisive differences, but Third World "nations" are far more divided and lack a unifying historical experience. They are more like Northern Ireland, where conflicting religious and ethnic traditions make democracy unworkable despite long experience with British representative constitutions and legal tradition.

The majority of Asian and African countries have dozens of languages and in many cases a multiplicity of mutually intolerant religions. Such large countries as India and Pakistan, like the majority of sub-Saharan African states, use the language of a former colonial power—English, French, or Portuguese—as a lingua franca of the educated and a medium of the business of government. Not over 5 percent of the population of Haiti can communicate freely in the official language, French.[13] In many Latin American countries there is more or less division going back to the Spanish conquest between an upper class of largely European origin and lower classes of more Indian background and, in some cases, Indian culture. Ethnic conflict destroyed Nigeria's first republic and contributed to the downfall of the second. The belief of Tamils and Sinhalese in the injustice of the other side reduced Sri Lanka from a functioning democracy to a semidictatorship.

The divisiveness of ethnic-racial differences is much intensified as they parallel economic and social differences. Usually a politically and economically dominant group, superior in education, prestige, and influence as well as wealth, is more or less separated from inferiors by race, ethnicity, or customs. This is the case in most Third World countries, although the separation is seldom legally fixed as in South Africa. Sometimes the situation is more complex, as in African countries where trade may be dominated by Asians although Africans control the State. In Malaysia the Malays have superior political rights, but the Chinese dominate the economy.

If they are free to organize, people come together along the lines of the identities most important to them; and democratic parties can hardly fail to be lobbies for ethnic, religious, or other such groupings. That much-divided India has functioned fairly well as a democracy is explainable in part by the common religious background of the large majority, Hinduism, and by the multitude of caste and other divisions too numerous for political representation. The castes also tend to moderate demands by sanctioning the social status quo. In a deeply divided society, democracy is manageable only because of the resignation or impotence of the masses; the organization of one small but self-assertive minority, the Sikhs, has been very disruptive for India. The fact that Japan is the most homogeneous of major nations has been a major factor facilitating its democratization.

***The Rich and the Poor***    The fundamental inequality, however, is between rich and poor. Income statistics are unreliable, but they indicate clearly that an inordinate share of wealth and income goes to a small elite in almost all Third World countries. Even in democratic Uruguay there was a ruling oligarchy of about six hundred families when the military took power in 1973.[14] By corollary, the middle-income sectors are relatively weak, and the equation is valid, No bourgeoisie equals no democracy. The inherited grievances of such profound inequality make for bitterness on the part of the deprived and insecurity and arrogance on the part of the upper layers; there is little tendency to reduction of inequality.[15] Disunity and lack of civic feeling contribute to inequality; love for the patria is respect for its people and a desire for equality.

The income gulf, usually having an ethnic-racial correlation, is reinforced by differences of social standing, education, and outward marks of manners and garb, all of which make the classes more reluctant to accept the right of the masses to decide the government and laws by electoral process. Inequality is not only economic and social but physical. The poor are usually malnourished, getting insufficient protein and deficient food, if not actually undernourished in terms of calories. They are more or less underdeveloped physically and, to some extent, mentally, are of less stature than the upper classes, and have smaller craniums. In addition, very many of the poor are rendered less capable of both work and self-assertion by chronic disease. It was reported that 95 percent of Brazilian school children suffered parasitic infestation.[16]

Hungry people do not make good citizens of a democracy. Their concern is for their immediate wants, not for the management of the state, much less abstract rights. In relatively developed Brazil, a 1985 poll showed that two-thirds of the people had heard of a major proposal, for a constituent assembly to lay a basis for the newly democratic government, but only 9 percent had any idea what it was about.[17]

For such reasons inequality tends to be self-reinforcing. The born and bred aristocrats have great confidence in the rightness of their position; the upper classes do not accept the uneducated and unwashed as political equals. For its beneficiaries the unequal society is successful; they know that their advantages are deserved or are part of the natural order, and they regard any idea of substantial social change as unjust. Traditional hierarchical structures, sustained by a rigid political and social structure, have historically been as though written in stone, virtually changeless for generations.

***Inequality of Nations and Classes***   In the modern world, moreover, there is a secondary cause of inequality: the technological and economic superiority of the industrialized countries. In the felt inferiority of their nation, the upper classes would assert themselves, as far as possible, as equals of the world's elite, while looking down on the lower classes at home. The more integrated the world becomes, culturally and economically, the more this inequality is felt. A small sector of the Third World nations are in close contact with the international world, very likely know English, may have been educated abroad, and live in an international cultural environment. In Malawi, where only a quarter of the children get to school, the students at Kamuzu Academy study Latin, Greek, and classical history, wear boaters, and play rugby and golf.[18]

Industrialists, traders, and top professionals perform the same kind of work as their counterparts in the wealthy countries and expect to be rewarded more or less like the world's well-to-do. Corporate executives in Latin America, for example, may have earnings comparable to their counterparts in the United States or West Germany, whereas their factory workers earn ten to twenty times less than factory workers in the United States or Germany. This is not merely a matter of exploitative conditions. Engineers in Africa expect earnings commensurate to their training, like engineers in the United States; and if they do not get what they see as their due, they may emigrate. The workers, who are in oversupply in any case, are lucky to be paid much more than they could earn in the fields. Similarly, pilots for a Peruvian or Argentine international airline feel entitled to salary levels not far below world levels, whereas bus or taxi drivers live in a different world. The tastes and consumption goals of the cosmopolitan elite filter down, but not the corresponding buying power.

The importation of technology into a relatively less advanced society puts wealth and power into the hands of those best able to exploit the improved technology. A new elite of foreign-related capitalists, technocrats, and high civil servants form something like a caste separated from the masses.[19] Modern technology coexists with primitive, and the policy makers, favoring capital-intensive technology, mostly help those who need it least and further concentrate wealth.[20]

Modernization widens the gap between urban and rural life. Education improves in towns much more than in the countryside, crafts are destroyed, and the city masses are politically mobilized to press for advantages—especially low food prices—at the expense of the farmers. The Green Revolution helped the Third World farmers who were best able to buy new seeds, use fertilizer and insecticide, and market their crops, that is, those who had more education and capital to begin with. Those less well equipped often suffered an actual decline of earnings as they lost markets.

Political tensions, however, do not come from the poor. They see the rich as unjustly fortunate, but they will probably passively accept their condition, which has long been changeless. Their chief idea of improvement is to climb to higher status or to set their children on the way to education and prosperity. The drive for change comes from the middle classes, particularly indignant intellectuals, who identify their own disappointments with the misfortunes of the many. Many articulate middle-class people in the unevenly modernizing society feel cheated and hope to prosper by changing the social order, which they regard as backward and inhumane.

But it leads to excessive strains if a party strives seriously to put democracy into effect in a highly unequal society. It is unrealistic to expect the upper classes to renounce their means of power because of the votes of the ignorant, ragged, and perhaps diseased. Voting strength is too much at variance with real power, and conflicting interests are stronger than attachment to constitutional democracy.

It is a little as in the United Nations: it is impossible for a body representing poor, weak states equally with the rich and strong—or for a body hypothetically representing the people of the world on a basis of equality—to impose decisions on the small minority who control the bulk of wealth and force. The ideals of international order and equal sovereignty are strong enough to make a United Nations representing all states seem desirable but do not give it real strength. It may have some small influence for peace keeping; as a redistributive agency, however, it is a nullity. The same is true of many superficially democratic governments: they may keep order, but they cannot change society.

### Political Culture

There are many other factors in the frailty of democracy, such as the incapacity of trade unions; the weakness or subordination to the state of professional and economic organizations; narrow, impractical, and politicized higher education; and the preference for social status (as shown especially by fondness for landholding) over production. Self-government must be based on information, but the press suffers from poverty and venality and is subject to a multitude of influences, above all from the government, which can reward richly for conformity and punish severely for disrespect. The broadcast media are even more subject to regulation or, in most countries, government operation. The police are little restrained. Murder is sometimes a major activity of government; rulers of Uganda, Equatorial Guinea, Burundi and other countries have killed a considerable fraction of their people without consequential disapproval of the international community.[21] The state is regarded less as the representative of the people than as a club of politicians, and bad government elicits resignation to bad government. Excessive centralization overburdens the national administration, hamstrings local responsibility, and separates the people from politics.[22] There is a nearly universal penchant for economic controls and state enterprise. This is supported by the prevalence of a Marxist orientation among elites, or at least intellectuals, a mentality inherently uncongenial to democracy.

When basic consensus is weak, toleration of an opposition seems to be an invitation to instability or disorder.[23] A multiplicity of parties is felt to undermine national unity, to waste labor and time, and to endanger independence.[24] At the same time, there are no other groups competent to mobilize opinion.[25] The primary role of the single party is communication from leader to masses, not vice versa. Many people admire a strong leader, a macho caudillo, who cracks heads and gets things done; to be respectful of law and procedures is to appear weak.

*Corruption*  A crucial weakness is an ambiance of corruption, as is to be expected of irresponsible governments with feeble national vocations.[26] The state is a treasure chest to be grabbed; parties strive to get hold of as much as they can for their clientele. This undermines both the capacity of government and faith in its betterment without revolution. Presidents and ministers suck princely fortunes out of poor countries; an egregious example was Joseph Mobutu of Zaire, who was believed to have taken some four billion dollars from a country in which three-fourths of the population lacked electricity.[27] Officials of the Shagari government in Nigeria seem to have taken some five to seven billion dollars out of the country in a few years,[28] and Ferdinand Marcos squeezed a similar amount from the Filipinos.

In Kenya, politics is said to be "the only way to make a lot of money." If a politician fails to take advantage of the prerogatives of power, he is regarded as a failure.[29] At the lower end of the scale, in much of the world clerks and police have to take bribes to supplement tiny salaries; they are poorly paid because it is taken for granted that they will compensate themselves irregularly. Mail clerks remove stamps from letters to resell them. If bribes are required to expedite legal actions, they can also bring about illegal actions.

Corruption further shackles the economy by giving an incentive for multiplication of formalities. The more requirements and regulations there are, the more need for greasing the way past them. For example, in Peru a fisherman must pay the equivalent of two hundred days of work to obtain a license to operate legally; having obtained it he finds himself subject to many restrictions and heavy taxes. For such reasons over half the business of the country is unauthorized and illegal, tolerated but subject to many penalties and discriminations.[30] Similarly, nationalization is desirable because state enterprises in the Third World are not only a shelter for bureaucrats but also a fountain of wealth for administrators.

Kleptocracy, like all political systems, has much inertia. Talk of reform leads to little action, and actions soon lapse. It is dangerous for journalists to publicize graft. According to an observer in Kenya, "The problem is that there are too many people in positions of power who don't want to see it changed." [31]

Whereas business and politics are fairly well separated in the West, in the Third World politics is the handmaiden of business and itself is profit oriented. In nearly all Third World countries (Singapore being a striking exception) politics is probably the best or easiest way to wealth. Corruption is related to the atmosphere of general insecurity and the tendency to rely on family and friends. It grows with the importance of public-service jobs, police power, the inefficiency of the bureaucracy, large expenditures by the state, the mass of regulations, and state ownership of a large part of the economy, all furnishing resources for political dealers. It is unavoidable where officials are badly paid, have discretionary authority, and are not closely supervised—except perhaps by superiors who claim a share of their subordinates' take. For example, Mexican police have to get their "bite" because the state cannot or does not give them a living salary; they must in part pay for their jobs, as they buy much of their equipment and "rent" profitable locations.[32]

These conditions, plus the long stay in power of one party, have made corruption notorious in Mexico, where payoffs override or bend the law at all levels. Almost any important business requires dozens of permits, which mean equivalent payments. It is simply counted as part of the costs, usually amounting in foreign deals to about 15 percent.[33] It is an old tradition, but amounts grew greatly as money flowed freely after 1975, first from the oil boom and then from the generous lending of the international bankers; former President Lopez Portillo is credited with having siphoned from one to three billion dollars. There are no conflict of interest laws, no public accounting, and no publicity of the earnings of high officials. It is almost obligatory to enrich oneself during a possibly brief term of office, for one's own security and the family's.

It should not be difficult to understand how government can function badly in Asia, Africa, or Latin America if one remembers the difficulty of securing efficiency and rationality of administration in the richer and better organized society of the United States. But the misgoverned society is unproductive and wasteful.[34] It is also inherently undemocratic.

## THE SHORTFALL OF THE STATE

In a modernizing society, the state, as the successor of a more or less autocratic colonial or traditional domination, is more developed than other social forces. The visible means of national progress, it dominates and co-opts other organizations such as unions and producer groups. There is little tradition of limitation of political authority; to the contrary, the state claims to represent modernization and is the obvious instrument to secure it, as well as the assumed means to social justice.

To set up a semimodern state over a premodern society is to place a potent instrument in the hands of a few. There is little to prevent redistributing resources from the producing poor to the consuming rich. For example, many a state procurement agency in Latin America and Africa has had a franchise to buy crops at fixed prices. The state wants to hold down food costs for the cities and also thirsts for revenue; consequently it pays much less than market prices. This has often amounted to a heavy, if not ruinous, tax on the sector that should make the prosperity of the country. It has had something to do with the decline of per capita grain production in Africa by 25 percent in twenty years, and a situation in which "farmers are growing less food, factories are breaking down or closing, roads and railways are falling into disrepair, civil services are disintegrating." [35]

It is a form of corruption also found in the West that the state functions as a provider of employment for the upper classes, often answering the purposes less of the people than of those needing employment. Allocated by influence or connections, jobs become a possession, a virtually guaranteed livelihood with limited relation to work performed. This leads to egregious overstaffing. In the People's Republic of the Congo, for example, salaries of agricultural advisers came to a sum comparable to all peasant cash income.[36] The public servants, with their intense interest in politics, form probably the most effective lobby; the armed forces can intervene decisively but find it difficult to exercise the steady pressure that comes naturally to the bureaucracy. The need to give employment is a major reason for the prevalence of state enterprises, such as the Argentine state corporations, which include monopolies or near monopolies in oil, minerals, telephones, shipyards, banking, and many other branches, all operating at losses which are sometimes greater than gross revenues.

The addiction to controlled exchange rates would be inexplicable if they were not in effect a tax on exports—and a subsidization of favored imports. Access to foreign currency at official rates is a gold mine and an excellent way of profiting from the state without exactly stealing. This and the relative ease with which a substantial fraction of money borrowed by the state can be diverted to private welfare make understandable the avidity with which Third World countries seek foreign loans.

The problem of underproductivity is hardly one of underequipment or lack of capital. The Third World, especially Africa and Southern Asia, is strewn with underutilized or abandoned manufacturing plants and other projects. Some African countries receive more foreign aid than they collect in taxes.[37] Tanzania has remained impoverished despite, or because of, the largest flow of foreign aid per capita in sub-Saharan Africa; it suffers food shortages despite abundant fertile land.[38]

Many Third World countries have produced statistics of fairly rapid growth, but progress is overstated as people shift from rural self-sufficiency to urban dependence on commercial goods, and the quality of life may decrease while income is rising. For example, about a third of the children of Brazil are virtually abandoned, despite striking industrial development.[39] It is possible to go backward; real wages in Zaire are said to have fallen by 90 percent from 1960, when the country became independent, to 1980.[40] The Central African Republic has virtually no telephones, and Chad (population about 5.5 million) has only about a half dozen physicians.[41] For more than a decade Uganda built not a single school, hospital, or surfaced road for its rapidly growing population.[42]

Modernization and industrialization are necessary to support an increasing and ever more urbanized population and to provide a surplus for patronage to fuel the political system. But education is commonly more of a social sieve than a builder of human capital,[43] and the importation of technology is costly. The less-developed countries do only 2 to 3 percent of the world's research and development and get poor returns from their small expenditures. Their scientists work in isolation and do little for their own countries.[44] Modernization is not so much a question of capital or capital accumulation or even the transfer of technological data as it is a political or semipolitical problem of management, basic know-how, values, incentives, and innovative capacity. The obvious way to acquire such capacities is from those countries that possess more of them. But the state is often more an obstacle to, than a force for, change. It may even decide to opt out of the modern world. Burma, having shut itself off in 1962, became one of the world's poorest nations, almost completely without machinery or new construction.[45]

## THE PROBLEM OF REFORM

It is truistic to say that there is not much good government in the less-developed countries because any state with good government would rapidly graduate to the more favored category. The very poor countries, especially of Africa, have mostly gone backward in the past decade, because of the inability to carry out any economic policy, or the rapacity of rulerships which squander whatever they can squeeze out of the economy, or brutality, as in the case of Idi Amin, who killed or removed two-thirds of the Ugandans with any technical qualifications. Of many countries it may be realistically said that the ship of state is not trying to go anywhere, only to stay afloat.[46] The nations of higher productivity and more wealth—such as the "newly industrializing countries" of Latin America and Eastern Asia—have better chances of orderly government, but they too face severe problems of relating people to production.

Deep change is needed. Some contend that violence and social trauma are necessary, but the revolutionaries have no real political program beyond the revolution beside the assumption of their own virtue. They have to be antidemocratic in practice, whatever their theory, because the masses are usually apathetic and conservative. The deepest noncommunist revolutions of Latin America, the Mexican (1910) and Bolivian (1952), only partially or temporarily changed the underlying hierarchic structure. Inequality today is much greater in Mexico than in Argentina, although the former was the beneficiary of a social revolution and has been governed since 1917 by leaders supposedly dedicated to the well-being of the masses, whereas the latter has been ruled mostly by the military since 1943; but Argentina is much more homogeneous than Mexico.

The military may take charge. The trained soldiers, free from political limitations and presumably patriotic, should be able to guide their country in the most rational course. But the military organization is anticommercial in spirit and ill-equipped to make economic policy, and military rule is not promising for the modern age.

No form of government has been notably successful in solving the basic problems of disunity, inequality, corruption, and abuse of the power of the state. In most non-Western societies, the state is overwhelmingly the source of status, and probably of wealth; beside it everything else is marginal. There is little self-criticism or serious thought of reshaping society because basic change would be hurtful to the governing sectors. Those to whom the state gives wealth and status use their wealth and status to protect their positions and the system that has favored them, as do the politically privileged everywhere, so far as they can.

The Third World, like the Marxist-Leninist states, cannot easily get out of this trap. If new forces gradually ripen with economic progress and if expectations of human rights take hold and it becomes accepted that the state is for the people, the less-developed countries can hope. But recent history is not promising.

### Notes

1. Marjorie Kelly, "Muslim Nation-States," in *Islam: The Religious and Political Life of a World Community*, ed. Marjorie Kelly (New York: Praeger Publishers, 1984), pp. 174, 193.
2. Robert Wesson, *The Russian Dilemma*, rev. ed. (New York: Praeger Publishers, 1986), chap. 2.
3. Walter Laqueur, *Germany Today* (Boston: Little, Brown & Co., 1985), p. 18.
4. F. Parkinson, *Latin America, the Cold War, and the World Powers, 1945–1973* (Beverly Hills: Sage Publications, 1974), p. 55.
5. Robert Wesson, *Democracy in Latin America* (New York: Praeger Publishers, 1982).
6. Edwin O. Reischauer, *The Japanese* (Cambridge, Mass.: Belknap Press, 1977), p. 8; and G. B. Sansom, *Japan: A Short Cultural History* (London: Cresset Press, 1956), p. 460.
7. Reischauer, *The Japanese*, pp. 237–40.
8. Donald Share, *Making of Spanish Democracy* (New York: Praeger Publishers, 1986).
9. John L. Esposito, *Islam and Politics* (Syracuse: Syracuse University Press, 1984), p. 213.
10. Crawford Young, *Ideology and Development in Africa* (New Haven: Yale University Press, 1982), pp. 304–5.
11. *New York Times*, April 11, 1985, p. 4.
12. Cf. Edward S. Herman and Frank Brodhead, *Demonstration Elections* (Boston: South End Press, 1984), p. 25.
13. Charles R. Valdman, "The Linguistic Situation of Haiti," in *Haiti—Today and Tomorrow*, ed. Charles R. Foster and Albert Valdman, (Lanham, Md.: University Press of America, 1984), p. 79.
14. Edy Kaufman, *Uruguay in Transition: From Civilian to Military Rule* (New York: Transaction Books, 1979), p. 43.
15. Mitchell A. Seligson, ed., *The Gap between Rich and Poor: Contending Perspectives in the Political Economy of Development* (Boulder: Westview, 1984).

16. James J. Horn, "Brazil: The Health Care Model of the Military Modernizers and Technocrats," *International Journal of Health Services*, 15, no. 1 (1985), 54.
17. *Visão*, Brazil: June 5, 1985, p. 14.
18. *Christian Science Monitor*, April 28, 1986, p. 40.
19. Jean-Yves Calvez, *Politics and Soviet in the Third World* (Maryknoll, N.Y.: Orbis Books, 1973), p. 263.
20. John W. Sloan, *Public Policy in Latin America: A Comparative Survey* (Pittsburgh: University of Pittsburgh Press, 1984), p. 41–43.
21. Irma Adelson and Cynthia T. Morris, "Economic Development and Distribution of Income," in *The Gap between Rich and Poor*, ed. Seligson, p. 153.
22. Henry Maddick, *Democracy, Decentralization, and Development* (Bombay: Asia Publishing House, 1966), p. 37.
23. Robert H. Jackson and Carl G. Rosberg, *Personal Rule in Black Africa: Prince, Autocrat, Prophet, Tyrant* (Berkeley: University of California Press, 1982), p. 189.
24. Fred R. van der Mehden, *Politics of the Developing Nations* (Englewood Cliffs, N.J.: Prentice-Hall, 1969), p. 61.
25. Carl Stone, *Democracy and Clientelism in Jamaica* (New Brunswick, N.J.: Transaction Books, 1983), p. 108.
26. Jackson and Rosberg, *Personal Rule*, p. 184.
27. *Los Angeles Times*, October 19, 1983, p. 23.
28. Robert H. Jackson, "Sovereignty and Underdevelopment: Juridical Statehood in the African Crisis" (paper for International Political Science Association, World Congress, July 1985, Paris).
29. *Christian Science Monitor*, March 24, 1986, p. 13.
30. *Caretas* (Lima), May 26, 1986, p. 43.
31. *Christian Science Monitor*, March 24, 1986, p. 13.
32. Alan Riding, *Distant Neighbors: A Portrait of the Mexicans* (New York: Alfred A. Knopf, 1985), p. 117.
33. Riding, *Distant Neighbors*, pp. 118–21.
34. Lloyd G. Reynolds, "The Spread of Economic Growth to the Third World," *Journal of Economic Literature*, 21 (September 1983), 941–76.
35. Clifford D. May, "The Famine Workers," *New York Times*, December 1, 1985, p. 73.
36. Young, *Ideology*, p. 40; and William McCord and Arline McCord, *Paths to Progress: Bread and Freedom in Developing Societies* (New York: W. W. Norton & Co., 1986), pp. 36–37.
37. Sanford Ungar, *Africa* (New York: Simon & Schuster, 1985), p. 353.
38. *Christian Science Monitor*, January 23, 1986, p. 11.
39. James J. Horn, "Brazil: The Health Care Model of the Military Modernizers and Technocrats," *International Journal of Health Services*, 15, no. 1 (1985), 53.
40. Ungar, *Africa*, p. 361.
41. Ungar, *Africa*, pp. 412, 417.
42. Young, *Ideology*, p. 5.
43. As in Haiti; see Mats Lundahl's "The Roots of Haitian Underdevelopment," in *Haiti—Today and Tomorrow*, ed. Charles R. Foster and Albert Valdman, (Lanham, Md.: University Press of America, 1984), p. 195.
44. Nicholas Wade, "The Third World: Science and Technology Contribute Feebly to Development," *Science*, 189 (September 5, 1975), 770–71.
45. *Time*, January 20, 1986, pp. 32–33.
46. Jackson and Rosberg, *Personal*, p. 18.

# Authoritarianism

---

## 4

There are many criticisms of democratic government: it is not really representative of the nation, it fails to maintain order, it is incapable of decisive action, it results in a dissolute society, and so forth. But the foundations of authoritarian rule and the sources of its legitimacy are unrelated to comparisons with the democratic way. Strong government comes naturally because it corresponds to some basic elements of human nature: the desire for order, stability, simplicity, and certainty; the dislike of having to decide for oneself; the feeling that someone has to be in charge; the receptivity to indoctrination; and the willingness to be led. It claims to give security, and it may appear at times as conducive to the happiness of the masses as the less structured, and more anarchic and uncertain order that places more responsibility on individual shoulders.

## THE PSYCHOLOGICAL BASIS FOR AUTHORITARIANISM

Acceptance of authority lies in the social nature of many animals as a means of securing harmony. Societies of higher animals have strong rank order, which is seldom contested once established. The alpha, or leader, commonly assumes responsibility for defense and the keeping of order.[1] Those defeated in a contest submit humbly to the victor, often exposing vulnerable parts, such as the throat. Willingness to subordinate oneself to the group seems inborn and is indispensable for social existence.

It is postulated that humans may have an instinct for obedience, like the innate capacity for language. There is certainly much training for it. One grows up under the discipline of the family and school, which rewards compliance and penalizes defiance even in the most democratic society. To get along people continually yield their autonomy to others somehow placed over them. One follows the leader without being aware of being led.[2] It is comforting to trust the superior wisdom of those in charge, just as it is troublesome to doubt; the mere fact that a Stalin or a Brezhnev is glorified seems proof enough of his genius.

An American psychologist, Stanley Milgram, showed that educated citizens of the world's most individualistic society were prepared to perform cruel actions, contrary to their inclinations, if commanded by a proper authority (the experimenter) despite the lack of any real compulsion. It seems that people feel responsible to the authority, not to their consciences, for their actions. Becoming agents, they suppress their own judgment; and once a person has accepted, for whatever reasons, the role of being an instrument of the authority, it is very hard to break free. Ideals and morality are forgotten as one responds mechanically.[3] In the structured situation, very ordinary people behave quite monstrously, like those who carried out Nazi orders for the "final solution." [4]

The authoritarian regime encourages dependence, and by reducing the capacity for self-government, it makes anarchy a greater threat. The traits associated by psychologists with the authoritarian personality prosper: conventionality, acceptance of stereotypes, emotional immaturity, preoccupation with status, cynicism regarding humane values, and negativism toward nonconformists.[5] Such a personality dislikes the uncertainty and disorder of democracy.

### The Imposition of Rulership

If sufficient organized force is available, an authoritarian regime can be imposed anywhere, at any cultural level. Authoritarian regimes perhaps began when neolithic conquerors discovered the advantages of enslaving, rather than killing, the vanquished.[6] Modern technology, giving new means both of exerting and of escaping control, has changed the modes and appearances of rulership but not its essence. It facilitates police action, propaganda, and effective political organization. At the same time, people learn to evade regulations, and modern communications help to obtain and spread information undesired by the state. Controls are complicated as the state is driven to admit external influences in order to reduce backwardness. The level of modernization has little to do with the aptitude for authoritarianism. A repressive East Germany can be more effectively regimented than a primitive Benin.

The authoritarian state can hardly refrain from using its authority over the economy, as the ideals of equality and social justice are translated into political possession of the sources of wealth. This implies the political use of economic power, and also its use for economic benefit, that is, the privileges and luxuries of the elite. Some degree of free enterprise may be allowed for practical reasons, but it has no security in the arbitrary state. Some states seek to regiment almost everything; whatever is not commanded is prohibited, it may be said with literal exaggeration but basic realism.

Unlimited governments may be fairly intelligent, managing more suavely without giving away powers, or they may indulge the rulers' paranoia and sadism. It is usually recognized that killing large numbers of people is counterproductive. Stalin's purges endangered his regime and might have brought defeat in war if the Hitlerite leadership had not been equally or more stupid. The barbarities of Pol Pot, Idi Amin, and others like them caused their downfall.

The authoritarian regime, except when riding on a wave of national feeling, has to use at least a little violence and brutality, the more as it feels insecure. Various communist states have engaged in widespread murder, especially when solidifying power. Kampuchea, where the Khmer Rouge killed perhaps a fifth of the population, is only an extreme.

Ruthlessness, however, has little relation to political directions. Soviet Stalinists, Genghis Khan, and the followers of African autocrats, however diverse in their ideologies, all committed unspeakable savageries. The Nazis, in one of the most sophisticated nations of Europe, were as brutal in their way as the illiterate Kampuchean Communists.

Murderousness is not closely correlated with degree of totality of the state. Unsystematic regimes, such as that of Idi Amin in Uganda, have left little to be desired in the way of insane killing. Rather stable oligarchic states with military-dominated governments and privately owned economies, such as El Salvador and Guatemala, have also used murder as a regular means of control while making formal concessions to democracy. Thus Salvadoran death squads kept peasants from organizing, checked trade unions, censored the press, and made it difficult for opposition parties to function, all in the absence of repressive laws for these purposes. It is a simple, decentralized, and inexpensive means of political action. It also has the advantage of committing people irretrievably to the party for whom they commit terroristic acts: they cannot permit the opposition to gain power without endangering their own lives. On the other hand, sophisticated authoritarianism, such as that in the post-Stalinist Soviet Union, appeals to the practical advantages of conformism. It resorts to force only when the deviants are really principled and determined, and actually kills few. But if people begin to feel secure enough to press for more freedom, they must be reminded of reality.

Grotesquely harsh or not, the authoritarian system amounts to institutionalized discrimination with elements of parasitism. It rests basically on personal, not legal, relations, with corresponding advantages for a minority. Strong, more or less revolutionary rulerships, such as the Marxist-Leninist states and to some extent the Nazis, have attacked the inequities of the previous social order, but they have done so to make way for a new and stronger inequality; inequality is the essence of authoritarianism. The principal bond of the elite in all authoritarian regimes is shared privilege, superior power, prestige or social standing, and material benefits. The less favored are seen as sinful and needing guidance or are treated like the children of the rulers (at best) or their chattels (at worst), lacking self-determination or the rights of full-fledged persons. This is as true of the workers in communist factories as of the peasants who raise the export crops of Third World dictatorships.

The deeper the inequality, the more essential it is to maintain it. The Afrikaner government of South Africa, representing a people of basically libertarian (Dutch) background and Christian faith and enmeshed with the Western world, could strongly rationalize forcible, often brutal repression because the possibility of a government dominated by a racially different and culturally distant majority became unthinkable. Any means to avoid it seemed admissible to the superior community. It is similarly inconceivable for ruling communist parties to surrender voluntarily any share of power. The feeling of group need is stiffened by the sense of ideological-historical necessity, duty to the revolution, and the effects of long self-indoctrination. There would seem to be no limit to what the elite might do if they believed it necessary to preserve their control.

## VARIETIES OF AUTHORITARIANISM

The societies near the pluralistic-libertarian-legalistic end of the spectrum are much alike: there are no really different kinds of democracies except in the directness of relations between powers and people and the degree to which power is checked by fractioning. Some, of which Switzerland is the best example, place more emphasis on freedom and particularistic rights; others, such as Sweden, stress the welfare of the majority. All have some kind of electoral process in which organized groups freely contend, limited terms of office, a constitutional framework of government, independent courts, freedom of expression and organization, personal freedoms, and, to a greater or lesser degree, economic freedom.

The states toward the authoritarian-monocratic end of the spectrum are more diverse, because they form the residual category of those lacking a formal scheme of responsibility of the government. In place of the single legitimation of the democratic order, there can be various rationales for political power: tradition, religion, ideology, revolution, the vocation of the armed forces, or sheer force. There is a radical to conservative spectrum of politics, as well as the pluralistic-democratic to monistic-authoritarian spectrum, and the authoritarian state may be either radical or conservative. However, whereas democracies tend to moderation, never excluding reform or proposing revolution, the authoritarian state probably has a much stronger commitment in one direction or the other, to maintenance of a traditional status quo or at times—in the aftermath of a revolution—to drastic change. Dictatorships may be violently leftist (that is, outwardly egalitarian) or rightist (that is, assertive of the value of hierarchic order). For this reason it is less obvious that authoritarian states are similar beneath the surface. Primitive democracy is obviously democratic, whereas the idea that a Marxist-Leninist dictatorship is of the same genus as a primitive despotism is not widely accepted. Confusion is increased because many or most undemocratic governments, especially the most antidemocratic, pretend to be democratic.

Yet authoritarian states are similar in that all the regular characteristics of the pluralistic society are absent, or nearly so. For example, the press is kept in line by various pressures, mostly economic in the softer authoritarian countries and coercive in the harsher. The courts may be fair in ordinary cases, but they do not protect rights against the state. There may be nominal freedom to organize politically, but it is impossible for the opposition to win elections. All nondemocratic regimes, however varied in particulars, stand on the same basic tripod: the control of information, with some sort of official teaching; the monopoly of politically effective organization; and the readiness to use force. However opposed in rhetoric, extreme authoritarians of the Right and the Left are much alike in practice, not only in methods of control but in styles, from fondness for processions to promotion of heroic art and dedication to sports. They also often coincide in policies, from militarism to opposition to population control and general dislike of frivolity.

The principal species of authoritarianism are (1) traditional rulership, which rests on the assumption that whatever has lasted a long time, particularly whatever has seemed successful in the past, is not to be challenged; (2) personal dictatorship, which is based on personal positions of strength or force of personality and respect for the leader plus the shared self-interests of a ruling clique and which earns acceptance both through fear and because it fills social or psychological needs; (3) militocracy, which is the commonest of all in the Third World and which differs from simple dictatorship in that an organization geared to wield instruments of coercion for generally accepted purposes displaces other rulership without reliance on any particular personality (although an individual is usually dominant); and (4) ideological totalitarian party government, which requires a doctrinaire rationalization and an organization to incarnate the dogmatic authority and mobilize the people. In contemporary affairs, this is mostly communist but may be of fascistic or other inspiration, as demonstrated by the Islamic-fundamentalist Khomeini dictatorship in Iran.

### Traditional Rulership

The commonest form of authoritarian government until recent generations was hereditary monarchy, supported by a more or less hereditary elite, an aristocracy, or the powers that be, allegedly ordained by God.[7] It usually rests on a traditional ideology, that is, a state religion, such as the sacred law legitimizing Moslem rulers.[8] Monarchs represent the national glory and its heritage, continuity, and order; above parties and interest groups, they stand for the state as a whole. They enjoy the respect and love of the people and let evil counselors be blamed for failure and abuses.[9] Monarchs are not only, or not chiefly, decision makers or commanders but symbols of unity and values; they are the axis and focal point of society. They need not have exceptional personal qualities; it is sufficient that they dwell in the palace, wear a crown, and are the center of public ritual binding them and their people.[10] One proudly serves king and country.

Even though the emperor may be formally absolute, traditional rulership has a framework of law and custom, because the ruler is sovereign not by virtue of special abilities but by the right of inheritance. So far as it feels secure, the traditional rulership may allow a considerable degree of personal freedom, leaving people and local powers substantially to their own devices as long as they pay their respects and taxes.

The symbolism of royalty is popular. The British maintain a family in great luxury at considerable cost for purely symbolic purposes, and millions avidly follow its doings; for democratically minded Americans, the visit of the Prince of Wales is the social event of the year. The depth of the monarchic appeal is apparent in the faithfulness of many to even a discredited royal lineage. A Bourbon pretender was visible in France well over a century after the chance of a Bourbon being crowned king had become nil. Seventy years after the abdication of Nicholas II, Grand Duke Vladimir had a well-organized following to support his claim to be the legitimate ruler of Russia.

It is the strength of the traditional order that most people are conservative, accepting the given and fearing the unknown. Change is threatening; people are comfortable with accustomed leaders, and to remove them implies a crisis. This is also true in nonmonarchic societies without a firm constitutional order. Heads of communist and other strong states have ordinarily retired, or been retired, only by physical incapacity or death. Franco could remain for thirty-six years at the top of the Spanish government he inaugurated because no one had much idea what would happen without him. Konrad Adenauer, first leader of the Federal Republic of Germany, likewise was kept in place from 1949 to 1963 (when he was eighty-seven) because he seemed to stabilize the untested constitutional system.

Continuity is served by succession of an eldest child. The offspring is a continuation or virtual reincarnation of the old ruler, and across the generations the dynasty comes to seem part of the way of existence. In a nondynamic, static authoritarian society, hereditary rulership seems almost inevitable. Even leaders of ostensibly revolutionary societies are prone to place relatives in high places, as is evident in Kim Il-Song's making his son his heir and Ceausescu's surrounding himself with family; and at least for the time being the respective communist parties have accepted this flouting of ideological principles. In democratically organized India, the Nehru dynasty has governed with only brief interruptions since independence in 1947.

Hereditary monarchy assumes that the prince inherits kingly virtues. The founder of a royal house is prima facie an imposing character, and royal offspring should resemble their forebears. Princes also have the benefit of the supposedly finest schooling for the governance of their people. But genetics do not guarantee the inheritance of statesmanship in humans as reliably as speed in horses, and no one has ever learned how to prepare children for kingship. The fetid atmosphere of the palace does not improve character. Monarchy is consequently vulnerable if it really exercises power, and it is most secure where it is largely symbolic, for which no talent is required. The Japanese imperial house, for example, has maintained itself for over a millennium because it has exercised little or no power.

It is not advantageous for an aging monarch to foster a really regal heir. The crown prince who is competent and vigorous is virtually certain to come into conflict with the father, whose corresponding qualities decline with age. The prince becomes the focus of a separate party, and the smoothness of transition that is a major advantage of royalty may be lost.

The principle of inheritance not only applies to the supreme office but is the normal criterion of elitehood in monarchic systems. In the aristocracy the hereditary principle functions better than in the royal house because occasional bad individuals are no disaster for the class. There is usually some competition among aristocrats, bringing the better to the fore; and the milieu of the young noble is not so abnormal and stultifying as for the heir to the throne.

The inheritance of status is better suited to poor or premodern societies than to modern societies. To the extent that schooling is for the few, the aristocrats have a claim to rule on the basis of education. Although the noble youths have probably given more attention to sports than to factual learning, they are fairly sure to be brought up with polish, self-confidence, and the arts, or at least the attitudes, of leadership or domination of inferiors.

In many traditional societies the aristocracy can regard itself as a natural ruling class not only by education but also by physique. The nourishment of the majority is probably inadequate for their full development. The aristocrats, or upper classes in general in most of the world, regard themselves as obviously superior to the lower classes—stronger, taller, and apparently more intelligent. Status seems simply a fact of life and natural condition.

The hereditary principle is omnipresent and prevails to some degree even in theoretically egalitarian states. It must continue to have some effect as long as the human species is composed of self-perpetuating individuals and families. It rests on the universal biological as well as social commitment of humans to their offspring. The successful want to pass on whatever they can of their success to their children, and they can do so in many ways, from wealth to titles, schooling, character training, personal example, and a boost on the ladder of office. So far as the political system permits—and it always permits to some extent—status is transmitted across the generations. The more authoritarian a stable system, the more it lends itself to the inheritance of authority.

### Personal Dictatorship

Traditional or hereditary authority begins as a personal achievement: a conqueror founds a dynasty. The initiator of a ruling lineage has usually been a victorious captain, such as Julius Caesar, Genghis Khan, or William the Conqueror, who replaced the Saxon rulers of England with a Norman kingship and a Norman nobility. The founder of each Chinese dynasty waded through corpse-strewn fields to the throne. Personal rule is normal in new states lacking fixed institutions.

In modern times, however, the rulership seldom outlives a forceful personality. Only in a few relatively backward countries have dictators been able to pass power even to the next generation. Nicaragua and Haiti, among the poorest countries of the hemisphere, are the only ones in which a dictator has been able to bequeath his power; in neither could the son hold on nearly as long as the father. African dictatorship thus far has not been transmissible; and it remains to be seen whether communist rulers, such as those of Romania and North Korea, can keep power in the family after their demise.

Cruelty and treachery have been in many primitive and not so primitive countries a prime qualification for clawing one's way to the top, and personal dictatorship is probably more arbitrary and ruthless than hereditary monarchy. Benevolent or even moderate characters are not likely to best all rivals in the political jungle, and it is probably necessary to be more or less tyrannical and deceitful to remain in power. Moreover, self-made rulers are usually less secure than the traditional monarch, less bound by conventions, and less restricted by persons whose title is not by their gift or favor. They raise people to please themselves. Personal rulership, however, is usually subject to a veto by persons below the chief, especially the military.

Why millions of people accept the elevation of a particular individual to be their unrestricted master often appears mysterious. But some personalities glow with charisma, or the ability to inspire loyalty, and intelligent persons can give body and soul to one who somehow satisfies deep needs, as though hypnotized into eager subjection of their will. Some people, deeming their ruler to be more than humanly inspired, want him or her to be absolute, perhaps more than he or she desires.[11] This may be in part a search for intellectual and emotional security, such as is furnished by many modern cults. Commitment on purely personal grounds may be very deep: James Jones led over six hundred devoted followers to mass suicide in their retreat in the Guyana jungle in 1978.[12]

Messiahs whom few would listen to in normal times prosper in times of turmoil and uncertainty. If Russia had not been militarily defeated, Lenin would have earned only brief mention in the history of Marxism. He became great because he seemed to know clearly where he wanted to take his country when most Russians were depressed and confused by defeat and disorder. Although Lenin, too, had only a nebulous program, a compass rather than a blueprint, he vehemently offered land, bread, and peace—none of which he gave—to be followed by utopia.

Hitler was a more charismatic leader who dominated the fledgling Nazi party by his rhetorical abilities. He had only to threaten to resign for the party to subordinate itself utterly to his will. In the economic depression, Germans, previously shocked by defeat and the humiliation of the Treaty of Versailles, disoriented by inflation, and depressed by unemployment heard him passionately promise a glorious future under new inspiration of national will and flocked to his banner. On the other hand, Stalin's great talent lay in making himself useful to the organization and in raising up a new class beholden to him. Whatever charisma he had was synthetic, a product of power and propaganda rather than the source of power.

There is usually much conflict beneath the surface of a dictatorship. However, in time, dictators, like traditional rulers, come to stand for order and regularity. Their government becomes customary and accepted, a part of the order of things, the loss of which would be threatening. The fact that despots remain in power is seeming evidence that they are chosen, or at least favored, by God or history, and it is deemed irrational to oppose them. As long as the regime is reasonably competent, there is something to be gained by going along, a risk in defying it, and uncertainty in its failure.

The obvious beneficiary of any dictatorship is the dictator, but there always must be sufficient payoff for strategically placed persons to make a workable system of control; the narrowest dictatorship must please a certain faction of the community. But the number of real zealots does not have to be more than a tiny minority as long as the opposition is immobilized.

The principles of dictatorship were blatant in the "government by franchise" of the Duvaliers in Haiti.[13] Governmental functions and powers were assigned to trusted persons and families, who were free to exploit them with the help of armed bullies, subject only to the financial and security needs of the center. In return, holders of privileges or franchises supported the "president for life" and the system that put an estimated 44 percent of the national income in the hands of 1 percent of the population.[14]

Like traditional rulership, personal power is ordinarily—at least if it is sophisticated and lasting—bolstered by idealism of some kind, such as association with religious values (Franco's rule in Spain was allied with the church), nationalism and identification with a national cause (it is difficult to attack a tyrant while the country is contending with foreign powers), or an ideology. Stalin, for example, rationalized his atrocities in terms of the imperatives of Marxist-Leninist doctrine: to oppose the purges was to oppose the sacred revolution.

### Militocracy

The founder of a dictatorship usually comes to the top as a commander of armed force. The politician, such as Hitler, Mussolini, or Khomeini, who forges total dictatorship by nonmilitary means is exceptional. Even in such cases, paramilitary formations were essential in the thrust for absolutism. Many a Latin American dictator of the nineteenth century gathered a band of armed followers, called himself general, and pushed a less effective ruler aside. Others rose on the military ladder and converted command of the army into command of the state.

Militarized societies are as old as history; Sparta is a famous example. The makers of the Turkish Empire in the eleventh to thirteenth centuries were practically an army organized as a state. The Tatars similarly formed an army, under Genghis Khan, that was equivalent to a nomadic people. It is a modern phenomenon that the professional officers exercise power more or less as a corporate body. This has become possible only as the soldiers, especially the officers, have become organization-bound and separated from civilian society by virtue of specialization, lengthy training, and much indoctrination. The modern professional military establishment is somewhat like a religious order; its members adopt its values and identify with it. The armed force, with its rules of order, procedure, and hierarchy, becomes a self-regarding and self-managing organization with purposes of its own, something of a state within or over the state.

Usually the militocracy is as responsible as any other authoritarianism, but it may be abusive, especially when professionalism is feeble. In much of Africa and to some extent elsewhere, there has evolved a sort of ruling warrior caste, a privileged elite responsible to no one, free to treat the country as they wish, taking for themselves the best it can offer. Soldiering is a steady job in lands of high unemployment, with a secure living for relatively light work and opportunities for betterment.[15] Its "ideology" is order, obedience, and the soldiers' welfare, to be secured by the right of the gun. It is not easy to see how the bearers of arms are to be stripped of power.

The soldiers have great advantages in the political contest. The imported technology of killing is disproportionately powerful in relatively backward societies with weak institutions and values. Having little defensive purpose in most Third World countries, they are free to turn their force against their own state. They claim to be, and sometimes are, more above class and ethnic divisions than any civilian group in their much divided societies. They probably have relatively modern, or at least technological, attitudes in largely premodern countries. They also probably control an unrestrained national intelligence agency and secret security forces.

Officers may be better educated than civilian politicians or at least have had more formal schooling. They believe themselves capable of managing the state, partly because of their supposed disinterestedness and partly because their training is the more impressive by comparison with the disorder and impracticality of many Third World universities. They do not have much else to do than to prepare themselves in one way or another for potential responsibilities, and at higher levels they probably study national problems more than battle tactics. No other professionals spend such a large part of their career in school—perhaps one-fourth to one-half.[16] They are also probably indoctrinated to preparedness, willpower, and self-denial, and trained to work in a coordinated, systematic fashion as civilians seldom are.

The ability to subordinate self to superior orders is very positive for a political organization, and the officers are probably the most coherent force in the poorly structured societies of most Third World countries. Forming something of a fraternity and sharing not only education but housing, clubs, recreation, commissaries, medical facilities, and pensions, they are bound by tighter friendships than are usual among civilian politicians. They not only hold the guns, but they are the most purposeful sector of the society. When the Sudanese ruler, Gaafar-al-Nimeiry, was asked why he placed so many soldiers in high places, he replied that they were the most disciplined leaders and that Africa needed more military in government to overcome backwardness and tribalism.[17] Many across the Third World have agreed with him in practice.

It is consequently natural that a majority of the governments of the world are subject to military influence, and in very many the armed forces exercise a militocracy. But the soldiers take power primarily because of the debility or absence of other forces. They do not make coups against orderly, legitimate, and respected civilian governments. Soldiers overthrow corrupt regimes unable to keep order, ordinarily with the indifference, if not the positive support, of the civilian population. There is no obvious example of a thorough-going democracy falling, even in hard times, to a military coup.

***Military Government*** Despite some reluctance to take on the responsibilities of administration, the officers are certainly disposed to watch over the government and check it if it should seem to go too much contrary to their ideas. It is not difficult for the officers to agree on a low opinion of civilian politicians and to blame them for corruption, disorder, and economic mismanagement. Depending on the degree to which they reject the civilian authority, the role of the military may range from the frank and complete assumption of state power through participation in a generally civilian cabinet to behind-the-scenes oversight. They are at least the residual power in almost all Third World countries.

No clear line can be drawn between personal government by a military man and government by the military corporation. For example, although the overthrow of Chile's Salvador Allende in 1973 was the work of the armed services—the army, the navy, and the air force acting jointly—General Augusto Pinochet gradually made himself supreme ruler. In Guatemala, Efrain Rios Montt was placed in power by a coup in March 1982 as one member of a three-man junta. By a minicoup of his own he got rid of his fellow junta members, only to be ousted in turn a year later by his top officers. Argentine presidents after 1976 remained in office on sufferance of the junta of commanders, which could always overrule or eject them, as Generals Viola and Galtieri were ejected. The military presidents of Brazil had more latitude than those of Argentina, but they were not in a position either to extend their own terms of office or to adopt policies unacceptable to large numbers of their subordinates, who knew that the chief's position rested on their acceptance.

***The Military Mission*** So far as the military forms an effective corporate unity, it represents itself, not a social class. It is probable that the high officers, being powerful and prestigious, feel a community of values with those who prize social stability, that is, law and order. However, the well-organized corps with a career ladder open only at the bottom does not attract the scions of the aristocracy. They lack the patience for the long road they would have to traverse along with social inferiors, probably with modest pay and perhaps in unpleasant posts. But the military offers social mobility in otherwise mostly immobile societies and is a good means of advancement for middle-class boys who can acquire enough education to qualify as cadets. Hence the majority of a well-organized officer corps are generally of rather modest social origins.

This does not mean that the officers represent the middle layers of society. They feel equal to the upper classes with whom higher officers socialize, and they share upper-class attitudes. On the other hand, they are aware of the middle classes from which they come and often sympathize with middle-class resentment of aristocratic privilege. They may also be concerned for the lower classes, whom they see close at hand as recruits. The ignorance and poor physique of the men whom the officers expect to carry out their orders may make them social reformers. National strength and security obviously require that the conditions of life of the masses be improved: more social justice or economic improvement is essential to produce better soldiers and sailors.

An example of a militocracy energetically undertaking a social mission is the Peruvian regime of 1968 to 1975, which endeavored to place much of the economy nominally in the hands of workers and peasants—although there was no more notion of giving real power to the common people than of depriving officers of command over their troops. In many other countries of Latin America and Africa, military regimes have advocated agrarian reform, workers' participation in management, and nationalization of parts of the economy. They have seldom carried out such programs with much vigor, however; and promises have mostly remained on paper.[18] Soldiers are trained for organization and hierarchy, not for ideas or utopias; they are likely to wish to change the social order only for specific concrete purposes. They are not much interested in control of the economy for reasons of principle. State enterprises are desired to provide soft landing places for retiring officers, not to promote socialism.

The force represented by the army does not much need justification beyond the basic ideas of order, nation, and the interests of the services themselves. Discipline harshly enforced by physical punishment seems inherent in the nature of armed forces, and they have been inclined to extend their discipline to populations under their domination. The physical elimination of the enemy—that is, the subversives—also comes easily to the military mind. Regimes dominated by professionalized armed forces have often been severe by ordinary standards of dictatorship, such as those of Chile, Argentina, and Uruguay, the socially most advanced countries of Latin America. In Uruguay, for example, in the first two years of the military government (1973 to 1975), one out of fifty citizens had been imprisoned or interrogated, and a law provided four to six years imprisonment for merely being dangerous even in the absence of any criminal act.[19] The Argentine officers seem to have felt that the "disappearances" without trial of thousands of suspects in the latter 1970s were entirely justified.

***The Military Way***   Militocracy has the combined aspects of domination by possession of instruments of force and domination by virtue of coherent, tight, and purposeful organization. It thus shares something with personal dictatorship on the one hand and with one-party government on the other. Military rule may also be technocratic. The officers of a modern army are trained to achieve their objectives by systematic material means, with emphasis on skills and equipment rather than on values and procedures. Hence soldiers in power are likely to look to technical means to achieve results (so far as the army has a modern outlook), preferring to ignore political considerations, irrational sensitivities, and selfish interests, or what they see as divisive and short-sighted concerns. Militocracy may thus bring technocrats to positions of de facto influence, although not of great authority. Government may be by a loosely structured military-bureaucratic-technocratic elite, as in Brazil under the military presidencies of 1964 to 1984, a form commonly dubbed "bureaucratic authoritarianism."

The military are better prepared to take power than to manage it. Officers are usually uncomfortable in political positions. They value clarity and unity, but deciding national policy, especially economic policy, is divisive. Their organization is not structured for political bargaining or representation of the various sectors or interests of the nation, the concurrence of which is necessary for effective national leadership—all of which goes contrary to the military's hierarchic ways. They must engage civilians to administer the nation, effectively sharing power with outsiders, such as business leaders and bureaucrats, who may have no stake in military government.

But militocracy has the virtue that the generals can withdraw from administration without surrendering their means of intervention. Consequently, if the military government becomes excessively unpopular, the officers can easily yield to the call for more legitimate government, permit elections, and go back to the barracks. They have done so in many Latin American and African countries, under no more compulsion than public opinion and weariness with a task for which they were not prepared. They can continue to receive the material support of the civilian government and enjoy a comfortable and uncomplicated life.

Paradoxically, government by professional political managers may be more militarized than government by professional soldiers, who do not care to try to run everything, to mobilize the masses, or greatly to enlarge their forces. For communists, as for fascists and Nazis, uniforms, military ceremony, and subordination to military-style hierarchy have been the stuff of politics to a much greater extent than for those for whom military discipline is the way of life. Marxist regimes keep more than twice as large a percentage of the population in the armed forces as non-Marxist regimes, and the force-to-population ratio bears no relation to internal or external threats. For example, military-dominated Guatemala, facing a chronic guerrilla movement, had 2 to 3 persons per 1000 in the armed forces; Mongolia, with no visible military needs, had 21.2. In Cuba the replacement of the semimilitary dictatorship of a soldier, Fulgencio Batista, by the Marxist-Leninist dictatorship of a former law student, Fidel Castro, brought a twelvefold increase in the armed forces. There was a similar increase in Sandinista Nicaragua even before guerrilla conflict began.[20] The Sandinistas teach their children to read "rifle" before they can read "cat," and they learn to add and subtract not oranges but hand grenades.[21] The military ethos is the core of modern absolutism.

Party political mobilization uses military methods much more than military government uses party political-mobilization methods. The vertical, rigidly authoritarian political system organizes society along military lines, not only training and drilling but exalting heroes of battle, cultivating the memory of war in all possible ways, and giving military meaning to civilian life. Communist states call good workers brigadiers and fight the "battle" of the harvest or of railroad construction. The totalitarian party is designed to gain and hold power by essentially military means, while soldiers are trained for professional efficiency.

### Party Rule

There have been parties of sorts from ancient times—groups pressing for certain policies or supporting certain leaders, as in Greece and republican Rome—but the political party designed to contest elections is largely a nineteenth-century innovation. The very large, penetrating, and monopolistic party, designed to govern alone and permanently and guiding the state apparatus even in details, is a twentieth-century transfiguration, practically invented by Lenin and perfected by Stalin.

A "party," by etymology, is a part or a fraction, typically uniting those supporting a certain outlook or policies against parties upholding other views. In the party-state, to the contrary, there is a single party, *the* party. If, as in the case of several Eastern European countries, minor "parties" are permitted a shadowy existence without any real influence, this is a concession to appearances, intended to make more effective the rule of the governing party by organizing sectors (such as farmers or church-oriented folk) that are not to be affiliated directly with *the* party. Or opposition parties may be allowed conditionally to operate for the sake of democratic appearances, as in Mexico.

***The Party and the State***   The party, instead of seeking benefits from the state, absorbs the state or stands as a superstate over the administrative apparatus. Party and state overlap in fascist or communist systems and to some extent in Third World one-party systems, as in Mexico and several African countries. Since the state obeys the party or belongs to it, the locus of significant decision making may be shifted to party organizations. In Marxist-Leninist states, the supreme body is conventionally the policy bureau of the party's central committee, or the politburo, as it is called in Russian. It is difficult to decide how far the party is to become involved in details of administration, with emphasis shifting between close supervision and general oversight. For practical purposes, the party is the political sovereign, and the state is its administrative arm, as the trade unions are its labor arm, the political police its repressive arm, the writers' union its literary organ, and so forth.

The relation of the leader to the party is variable. There is no government, strictly speaking, by a party, because a collective cannot make decisions, and there is always an element of personal dictatorship. Most parties of one-party states, as in Africa, are essentially personal followings. The Nazi party was Hitler's instrument. Well-organized communist parties come nearer to acting as ruling organs, but a very strong chief (with his coterie) may quite dominate the party apparatus, as Stalin did, balancing the political police and administrative hierarchy against it. Mao in his Cultural Revolution intimidated the party and came near to dissolving it. It seems clear that the North Korean party is an instrument of Kim Il-Sung. But instruments acquire power, and as the revolutionary party turns into a stable rulership it is unlikely to promote leaders capable of injuring it.

If party rule is less total, as in noncommunist one-party states generally, political decision making is more likely to take place in the state apparatus. The Mexican president, for example, finds it suitable to meet with his ministers; the president of the party is his subordinate with little authority. For African one-party states the party is likewise the instrument of the state rather than vice versa.

***Controlling the Population***   It is desirable to organize as many persons as possible in party-dominated organizations, from school children to pensioners, in order to preempt organizations of possibly undesirable character, to monitor the population, and to indoctrinate and involve people with official purposes. Organization goes down to the local neighborhood, as in Cuba's Committees for the Defense of the Revolution, apartment committees in the Soviet Union, and house committees in China. In communist countries, there are associations under political guidance for almost any approved activity; becoming engaged in high jumping or theater means becoming involved in the political system. Milder party rule is less compelled to organize.

There are many specific means of control even in a relatively loose one-party state such as Mexico. They include the ability to exert pressure on peasants through land allotments and the granting or withholding of credit and other facilities, on workers through unions and access to jobs, on professionals through their societies and licensing, and on private businesses through government contracts and dealings with state enterprises and banks. Schools are all or nearly all state run, with prescribed curricula. Newspapers are kept in line by providing or denying newsprint, access to news, and government advertising; and reporters may be rewarded or penalized for their reporting even if there is no official censorship. Broadcast stations are subject to license. State employment is for the deserving. Voters are subject to pressure as well as propaganda, and electoral results can be altered if necessary. Opposition leaders can be co-opted, intimidated, or if necessary repressed.

More thorough party-states use violence more freely. An important aspect of repression is the involvement of large numbers of people as informers, making them participants in the misdeeds of the secret police. It seems that millions are recruited by the Soviet KGB, for example; and it is the practice to coerce even persons unfriendly to the regime into cooperating, thereby sacrificing their personal integrity. The strongest rationale for coercion is that party rule is the alternative to anarchy, and it may seem the only way to hold together a society that defies unification by the conventional state.[22]

Rule by a single party might be expected to make the state responsible to a politically active minority of the population—typically 5 to 10 percent of adults in Marxist-Leninist countries. But if the party were open to all who desired to participate and were itself democratically organized with freely contending sectors and views, it would be a long step toward democracy. Many countries have claimed to have one-party democracy. In practice, however, the party controls its own membership, and it is managed from the top. The chief basis for advancement has to be devotion to party purposes, that is, to the will of the party center or to the boss.

## IDEOLOGY

Everywhere and always, there is some sort of ideal justification for the power of the state over individuals, and rulers are guided by an explicit or implicit understanding of their right. In a loosely structured pluralistic society such concepts are rather vague, correspond to the ideas floating in the society, and are brought to the government rather than imposed by it. If authority is arbitrary and imposed, it is accompanied by a special rationalization or ideology, consciously developed and refined, if not invented, for political purposes. This may vary greatly, ranging from a religious drive (as in the Iran of Ayatollah Khomeini) or a revolutionary myth (as in the Mexico of the Institutional Revolutionary Party) to ad hoc formulations (as in Italian fascism or Argentine Peronism), personality cults, or the "scientific socialism" of Marxism-Leninism.

The doctrine may be mystic or pseudorationalistic, naive or scholastically elaborated; but its precise content is generally not important. Its purpose is always to dominate. Its primary message is that those in power are fulfilling a lofty purpose that people must support. It is like the signs and rituals of a secret society or lodge, the importance of which resides not in any rational meaning conveyed but in the symbolism of the fraternity. The fullest understanding of the doctrine is reserved to the inner core, but ordinary people are expected to know enough of it to respect the adepts.

More arbitrary or authoritarian states give more attention to ideology. The greater coercive power of the strong state invites the use of its power to give people the "right" ideas and exclude harmful ones. Many democratic leaders would no doubt like very much to be able to impose their views, educate the people properly, and protect them from wrong ideas; but they lack police powers, the ability to censor, or control of the media. To accept arbitrary rule is to accept an arbitrary creed.

The arbitrary state has more need for rationalization. On the one hand, it lacks basic legitimacy and needs synthetic justification. Otherwise expressed, ideology serves to clothe "the beastliness of power" [23] and makes force into justice. The exercise of authority must correspond reasonably well to the modes of thought of the people, at least of those possessing the means of influence, especially the more or less educated who are needed to carry on a modern government. People want to believe there is a logic in the duties imposed on them; the powerless need to see power as right.[24] Ideology may be clear and fairly coherent or diffuse and contradictory, but the essence is that the powers are somehow sanctioned by a universal higher law. It need not really be understood or understandable. Its truth is proved by endless repetition, which ultimately becomes hypnotic.

Strong states, imposing heavier burdens on their people, have to convince them of the need to sacrifice. Faith is essential to enable a leader to persuade people to willingly subordinate themselves at all levels, from those near the summit to humble workers. Compressive closed regimes could not be stable, at least not in the modern world where many persons come into contact with the outside, if the command structure did not have an acceptable rationalization. Persuasion is always preferable so far as it can succeed; and despots claim to rule, and probably believe that they rule, by the will of the people or as the representative of the community. Hitler was the incarnation of the German people, and Stalin represented the workers of the Soviet Union and the world. Roman emperors had the faculty of lawmaking because the people by the *lex regia* (supposedly adopted on an unknown occasion) vested their power in them.[25] Latin American militocracies have adopted a "National Security Doctrine," making them the guardians of the nation.

### The Functions of Ideology

Ideology serves many functions. It helps set off the elect from the masses, and it gives the former a more or less esoteric means of communication. It helps the leaders to work effectively together and checks cynicism and the decay of political power into pure self-seeking. It preempts minds; even if it does not really convince people, the drum-beat of indoctrination makes it difficult to think in undesirable ways. It erases morality: few humans would choke or stab another for personal reasons, but in the name of an ideal, leaders will freely authorize, and people will accept, the killing of countless persons who have done no wrong by ordinary standards. It gives an interpretation of history in which the rulership is justified. It gives a purpose to the sociopolitical structure, in relation to which dedication is in order, personal pleasures are down-graded, and selfish individualism is evil. If everyone around the leader were devoted merely to self-interest, the system would break down as all pulled in different directions or tried to enlarge their share. The aware-ness of shared self-interest is a powerful cement, but it works best when buttressed by loyalty to a cause.

The beneficiaries of the system like to think that they are doing good. To what extent they believe the doctrines that they espouse can hardly be guessed, but they know that their version of the world is useful. For the people, too, ideology carries satisfactions, even if it is not totally credible. Symbols carry much weight; people like to have answers to the big questions, whether the answers help them materially or not.

It is comforting to fit into a scheme, even as a small cog. It may seem that giving up liberty means losing the better part of being human, and that it is degrading to accept servitude to a power based primarily on force and so pretentious as to try to dictate one's thoughts. But the modern affirmation of individual personality and rights is far from univer-sal; many have feared self-rule as anarchy, and almost everyone some-times prefers security. Coercion makes conviction; the burden of fear is eased by accepting the message and will of those against whom it is senseless to rebel, and one may actually resent those so contumacious as to defy authority. Ideology or a broadly accepted premise justifies bowing to the superior will. To be contrary is disruptive and socially irrational. There is even a certain reassurance in being commanded; Soviet writers have said they would rather be harassed by the KGB than ignored, as émigrés often are in the United States.

People may be quite consumed by a belief that is not contradicted by their experience. Thus victims of the Zulu king Shaka sang his praise as they were being carried away to be butchered.[26] It is reported that "the two million members linked together in the organization [of the

Korean Workers' Party] find their identity, and indeed their purpose in life, only in striving to fulfill the leader's directives." [27]

Whatever the psychological power of ideology, its specific content and ideas are much less significant than they are frequently made to seem. Power and personality are far more decisive, but ideology is a better subject for disquisitions. Stalin's opinions on sundry subjects were once analyzed in detail; now we realize that his paranoia was far more important. In the final analysis, faith is only the frosting on the cake of power. Except in unusual and transitional situations, the biggest factor in personal rulership is the use of force. An ideological movement soon finds that persuasion alone does not suffice, and it must offer firmer reasons for obedience.

As long as Hitler relied chiefly on his oratory, people were swayed but not bound to him; the number of votes for his party shrank substantially in the last free election. He became potent when he was made chancellor and took over the levers of the state, especially the police. He became absolute when he got the army to swear personal allegiance to him and could replace independent-minded generals. He liquidated opposition parties, unions, and other independent organizations, not through eloquence or the appeal of his program, but through the Gestapo and brute force. Marxism-Leninism blessed Stalin's whip; the political police destroyed the old guard, cowed the entire population, and put a substantial fraction of it into concentration camps. Seldom has any government based itself more unreservedly on religion than the theocracy of Khomeini in Iran; yet it has killed tens of thousands of people who were not adequately persuaded. Ideals or ideological propaganda and force are maximized together, as is evident in the adulation surrounding various egregious butchers. Propaganda softens, but force crushes.

## ABSOLUTIST AND LIMITED AUTHORITARIAN STATES

The one-party system provides a mechanism for more complete regimentation of society than is achieved under traditional monarchy, ordinary dictatorship, or militocracy. That is, the monopolistic governing party, separating the political brotherhood from the rest of the community, is a seemingly necessary condition of modern absolutism. [28] Primitive empires, such as that of the Incas, have exercised very penetrating state control over the lives and activities of their citizens; but to rule a large modern or semimodern society thoroughly and securely, it seems indispensable to have a special agency for political direction apart from and above the administrative organization.

Because of their focus on the maximization of political power, totalitarian systems—those claiming control of the totality of society or all aspects of life—are fairly similar in basic outlines. The less total states are much more diverse, and there is no designation covering such different forms as the semipluralist communism of Yugoslavia, personal dictatorships, one-party African states, and corporate military regimes. It is hardly adequate simply to call them authoritarian or *merely* authoritarian, because the totalitarians stand at the extreme of the authoritarian-democratic gamut. For lack of a better term they may be called *limited* authoritarian. They might also be called oligarchic, in line with Aristotle's basic classification of states into the monarchic, the oligarchic, and the democratic. An absolutist-totalitarian system may be oligarchic in that the top personage cannot go much counter to the wishes of a small summit group. Such is apparently the relation of the Soviet general secretary to the Politburo since the passing of Stalin. However, in the totalitarian regime, one has standing only by relation to the central authority, and anyone is subject to removal. Limited authoritarian systems, on the contrary, have a looser structure with more or less autonomous secondary power centers; [29] and some persons are influential in their own right, beside or around the chief leadership. There is some pluralism in high politics.

The basic distinction between absolutist-totalitarian and limited authoritarian states is manifest in the contrast between states in which the rulership asserts a monopoly of organization (using this to dominate all sectors of society, including the armed forces) and those that rely on political management of critical institutions without trying to envelop all of society in the party–organizational web. Systems asserting a monopoly of organization are naturally much more tense and shrill, as well as more ideological, not merely because of the political utility of doctrine but because it is an integral part of the system and its mentality. Less fully authoritarian regimes can be more relaxed.

For the totalitarian, the mere fact of autonomy is an affront if not a danger. All should stay in their proper places, and there should be a place for everyone. Differences of status should derive from political standing. Limited authoritarians are less intrusive. They do not try to control the movement of people but allow emigration; they would rather be rid of the discontented than have the problem of managing them. They permit independent organizations, cultural, professional, or even political, as long as these are not overtly oppositionist and perhaps even if they are, as long as they represent no political threat. They allow—probably encourage—private money making. They use only occasional, irregular violence and have prisons but not forced labor camps.

The absolutist regime must claim to stand for a new kind of life both to justify sacrifices and to set the state off from the external enemy. It exaggerates its own virtues and other systems' faults, seeing itself beset by evil forces in order to justify its claims on its citizens by permanent emergency. Limited authoritarianism has little of a state religion or arbitrary creed to place life in the service of a vision. It represses criticism but otherwise lets people publish more or less as they please and does not try to dictate much of the content of the media.

Limited authoritarian governments are usually more friendly to the Western world and its general ways. This is not merely a matter of foreign policy but is inherent in their nature. The absolutist essence is rejection of Western pluralism and individualism; the oligarchic rejects certain aspects of Western society but broadly wishes not to combat it but to be respected by it and to profit economically from it.

### Leadership

The two types also differ in their leadership. It seems that the more demanding the government, the greater the necessity for a preeminent individual to serve both as symbol and as unquestionable authority and arbiter of differences. The history of communist states has been marked by many exalted figures—Lenin, Stalin, Tito, Mao, Castro, Kim, Hoxha,—all presented as larger than life. The power of the state suffices to inflate any mediocrity, and the lack of obvious great talents did not keep Brezhnev from receiving adulation like that given to Stalin; or hinder Kim Il-sung from being made, or making himself, a demigod, honored by a statue nearly as tall as the Washington Monument; or prevent Ceausescu from being treated as a superman at the same time that he was mismanaging the Romanian economy and imposing the most grievous hardships on his people. Even the short-term Soviet rulers Andropov and Chernenko were rapidly built up to heroic stature in their few months' reign.

The single leader was even more essential for fascism or nazism, which had only a potpourri of an ideology. The charismatic head was the foundation of the state, and there was tremendous emphasis on unconditional obedience. The exaltation of the chief was not only de facto but also theoretical (unlike Marxist-rationalized communism, which theoretically downplays the individual). Hitler was personally omnipotent; he could make the biggest decisions, such as to invade Poland, without consultation.[30] It may be significant that fascistic movements came to power in monarchies or formerly monarchic countries (Italy, Germany, Spain, and Romania).[31]

Nonabsolutist states lack the power to institute really Stalinesque cults. The image of a Perón in Argentina or of a Trujillo in the Dominican Republic may be blown up by much advertising, but it lacks conviction: where there are shades of independence, there is skepticism. The limited authoritarian regime can function well with only a moderately exalted headship or no strong head at all, as in the case of military-civilian oligarchies (as in El Salvador, 1932 to 1979), or with a leader limited to a fixed term (as in Mexico).

***Fixity*** It has been said that limited authoritarian regimes can move to democratic institutions, whereas the absolutist-totalitarian cannot. This is logical, because the latter have farther to go. The former leave space for movement and permit independent property and organizations, which may serve as nuclei for an opposition to take hold, grow, and nurture ideas of freer government. Many dictatorships and governments of Latin America have given way, mostly nonviolently or voluntarily, to elected governments; the Southern European democracies in Spain, Portugal, and Greece replaced the respective dictatorial governments. On the other hand, the example of a communist state turning noncommunist is yet to be recorded, although Yugoslavia and China have modified the institutions of more ideological times.

But the distinction is not clear-cut. Many less than total authoritarian regimes have been seemingly everlasting to the people under them. For example, the Mexican regime has remained in place about as long as that of the Soviets. The Somozas ruled Nicaragua for forty-five years, and El Salvador had about half a century of military-oligarchic government. Haiti and Guatemala likewise had several decades of uninterrupted dictatorial rule prior to regime changes in 1986. On the other side, Poland, Hungary, and Czechoslovakia have at different times seemed capable of ending communist power, being held to Marxist-Leninist patterns only by the Soviet military presence. This may indicate that external influences are as important as internal structures in determining the potential for evolution of a regime. The chief reason for attempted democratization in Eastern Europe is probably the same as in Spain, Portugal, and Greece—namely, the influence of the prosperous pluralistic Western world nearby.

***Establishing Total Power*** If a totalitarian regime is more difficult to undo, it is likewise more difficult to establish. It is anomalous that a ragtag, rather threadbare bunch of agitators previously without solid backing in the community, such as Lenin's party or Hitler's brown shirts and strong-arm squads, should not only thrust themselves into the seats of power but assert virtual ownership of society. The large majority of the population, perhaps over 95 percent, permitted a few persons without previous standing to take to themselves the whole of the country and mastery over the lives of all.

The outsiders who form the nucleus of a radical movement can seldom do this. For example, the Allende forces in Chile in 1970 to 1973 talked of the need to make their regime irreversible by nationalizing the economy, that is, placing in charge persons owing their positions not to ownership or managerial ability but to political position, whose first priority would be to preserve a revolutionary socialist order. The Allende radicals could expropriate most businesses, but they could not operate them effectively. At the same time, they could not replace the old constitutional system; most crucially, they could not reduce the armed forces. Their government was consequently easily removed by a coup despite the passionate support of many persons and the radicals' planning for civil war.

The Nazi dictatorship could be made more total because it promised everything to a society badly shaken by unemployment and depression and fearful of communism. It was less impeded by institutional structures, having been voted full powers by the Reichstag; it was totally unscrupulous in the use of coercion; and it chalked up national successes that paralyzed opposition and enabled Hitler to subjugate the armed forces. Thus the Nazis could follow the natural inclinations of an outsider group suddenly placed in the driver's seat and make themselves absolute bosses. They continually broadened their area of control and extended political organization over the economy. Although they had no program of socialization, they practically annulled the private ownership they ideologically supported.

Perón in Argentina tried to do much the same as the Nazis, whom he admired. He built a mass party, manipulated the trade unions, and attempted to direct the economy. But conditions were less propitious for such change. Argentina was fairly prosperous and had not been traumatized by war and defeat. Perón failed to destroy the upper classes, he fell into an unwinnable conflict with the church, and the dominant sector of the armed forces turned against him.

Castro was probably no more authoritarian by temperament or conviction than Perón and no more skilled politically, but he could make his power total because the armed forces of Batista had disintegrated and Castro could count on a guerrilla band whose ideology was loyalty to him. Cuba had more frictions than Argentina with the United States, the foreign policy of which facilitated Castro's slide to the Soviet orbit and adoption of Soviet-style institutions. Small-scale hostilities energized Castro's synthetic social revolution; and in the patriotic emergency of the Bay of Pigs incursion, Castro was able to uproot the opposition, organize the people to stand guard for a new invasion, and declare Cuba socialist.

It is not easy to liquidate forces that have a strong social basis. Even the Leninists needed about ten years to make their rule total and several more to subjugate the peasantry. It is not sure, in fact, how far Lenin's revolution would have gone toward totality if his party had not fought a desperate civil war against adherents of the old regime assisted by the Western Allies. War has hardened, if not shaped, successful communist movements, from the Soviet Union to China, North Korea, Vietnam, former Portuguese colonies in Africa (Mozambique and Angola), Ethiopia, and Cuba (in rhetoric as well as in CIA-sponsored paramilitary activities). It has yet to be demonstrated that a communist order can be instituted by a native party without large-scale violence and nationalistic mobilization.

Although absolutist does not necessarily mean communist, the Soviet state as brought to completion by Stalin has been the sole important model since fascism was crushed in World War II. It draws on the socialist tradition and the ideal of social justice to rationalize collectivism and tyranny; and strongly antipluralist or anticapitalist states naturally look to the Soviet Union for support as well as inspiration (Albania being a conspicuous exception) and hence are anti-Western in foreign as well as domestic policy. The maker of a revolution may seek to find an alternative form of total rule; Castro did so, but after 1968 he took the easier course of following the tried-and-true Soviet way.

## ABSOLUTISM: THE SOCIAL BASIS

Authoritarianism becomes most effective through the elevation—in both theory and practice—of depressed persons in an unequal society. Without proletarianism, communism could not carry out its radical transformation of society. The doctrine of uplift of the deprived was necessary to reverse the general trend toward liberalization in the generations preceding the Russian revolution. Although the Leninist leadership were of the middle-class intelligentsia, the party recruited persons of humble origins to provide the dedicated and uncritical troops who imposed its absolute dominion—persons promoted to positions of importance, not because of their general qualifications, but at least partly because of their lack of qualifications as ordinarily conceived. Rootless city workers were preferable to peasants. The best recruits were those who felt cheated by the previous social order, such as the aggrieved Jews, Balts, Caucasians, and Poles who were Lenin's most loyal followers.

Much of the appeal of the party lay in its ostensible concern for the lower classes, which gave the Communist leadership a rationale for despotic power. More important, those who owed everything to the party could be counted on to use their new power ruthlessly and to grip it firmly. Stalin got rid of the more independent Leninists by advancing less educated proletarians to strategic positions, a move that the formerly émigré middle-class leaders had to accept in accordance with Marxist principles.

The principle of relying on those who owe everything to the party has been followed in all communist countries. The Chinese Communist party recruited poor peasants of suitable character—egalitarian, anti-intellectual, disposed to action, and ready to follow the leader.[32] In 1969 seventy-eight percent of Cuban party members had less than a sixth-grade education, and higher education severely reduced a member's chances of reaching a position of leadership. Forty percent of state farm administrators in 1964 lacked even a third-grade education.[33] Castro has not improved the lot of the average Cuban, but he has helped many of the poor and given them a new dignity; they are consequently devoted. The same drive caused the Khmer Rouge to kill most literate people in Kampuchea as unsuitable for communism.

Persons from the prerevolutionary educated classes have been mostly barred from politically important positions and their children have been more or less excluded from the higher education that is the gateway to elitehood. Especially insecure or illegitimate communist regimes, such as those of East Germany or Czechoslovakia, have been most systematic in advancing young people of working-class or peasant origin and excluding those of bourgeois background. They do not seek to win over the formerly better-situated classes but visit on the children the class sins of their fathers. Communist parties distrust intellectuals because these have a life outside the party and a will of their own. Poor workers or peasants who rise to become cadres are readier to agree with whatever the party proposes. The regime can count on the new status groups it creates, not only political bosses but professionals. Idealism soon wears thin, but dependence on the new order for good living, privilege, and power is solid.

### The Strategy Applied Elsewhere

Not only the Leninists but numerous autocracies without the benefit of Marxist ideas have used the same strategy. It is a key contrast between the more ruthless authoritarianisms and more moderate or traditional dictatorships, which rely on the support of prestige classes. It is particularly characteristic of antitraditional tyrannies and has been a major factor in their solidity.

Hitler, for example, followed Lenin in gathering a group of full-time revolutionaries; his intimates and most loyal supporters were nobodies outside their Nazi party roles, mostly uneducated drifters without regular occupation. When the depression and President Hindenburg's folly gave power to Hitler, his gang determined to keep it instead of going back to nowhere. Hitler removed the rightist aristocrats who formed a majority of his first cabinet; not one of the top Nazis appeared among fifteen thousand names of the pre-Nazi German *Who's Who.*[34] Hitler, who had the manners of a man of the people, made young nobles drill with plebeians, reduced the difference between officers and troops, and had owners socialize with their workers.[35]

The result was exceptional political strength, despite the incoherence of the Nazis' ideology of racism plus hypernationalism—it was clear only that they were against Jews, communism, and liberalism and for German power. Their determination, ruthlessness, and unity in the depressed and divided country enabled them to eliminate other parties that had a sounder basis in German life. They went on to victories on the world stage first by threat and then by force of arms and made their position so firm that they remained almost unchallenged even after it became clear that continuation of the war only compounded the disaster.

Strong despots have regularly surrounded themselves with persons who owe everything to themselves. For example, freedmen were raised to high posts in imperial Rome.[36] Peter the Great publicly burned the record books of the aristocracy and raised thousands of commoners, even serfs, to nobility.[37] Ivan the Terrible before him elevated his servants and murdered the boyars of ancient lineage. Turkish sultans pampered slaves and placed them in the highest positions next to the throne.[38] The favored slaves could not conceivably be rivals for the crown and could be decapitated without fuss or returned to ordinary slavery; and they served faithfully, at least until the whole regime became rotten.

The harshest Latin American dictators, such as Juan Manuel de Rosas in mid-nineteenth-century Argentina and Juan Vincente Gómez of Venezuela (1908 to 1935), relied on crude, ignorant, wholly devoted bullies to keep polite society in awe of them. More recently, Somoza recruited illiterate peasant boys into the National Guard, trained them in soldiery, brutality, and loyalty, isolated them, and gave them good pay, guns, power, and privileges over civilians.[39] The Guard became a loyal instrument, faithful to its master to the end. Stupid cruelties alienated the bulk of the population, especially in the towns; but the Guard fought bitterly for Somoza and for itself. Despite the fact that a large majority of the people were opposed to the dictatorship, the civil war, unlike the usual Latin American revolution, was a bitter, bloody, and prolonged struggle that the Sandinista-led rebels could not have won without foreign support. The Guardsmen did not give up in the usual Latin American manner when they saw the contest going against them because they had too much to lose and nowhere to go. In defeat they were embittered, unreconciled, and ready to return to the fight as "Contras."

The foregoing implies that totalitarianism is revolutionary absolutism, most total when it is fresh. As soon as the new class becomes fixed in place and wants its children to have a head start in life, it will no longer be possible to secure complete loyalty by raising people from deprivation and separating them from their old background. This has occurred to a considerable degree in the Soviet Union, and the expected result is to be observed: the fiats of the government are no longer so absolute and people shop during working hours, exchange favors, take bribes, and so forth; and the second economy has become enormous. But the effect is slow. People still say, "My parents were poor peasants, and my son is an engineer," and today's top leaders are still mostly of humble origins. The aristocratic principle has been slow to advance, partly because Stalin kept Soviet society in turmoil through the 1930s and opened up careers by purging most well-placed persons. The ordeal of the war had some of the same effect. But the loss of social mobility is unavoidable, and as it disappears the totalitarian state becomes more like the oligarchic or limited authoritarian state.

## COMMUNISM

### The Building of Communism

In communism the rulership strengthens the state to a degree seldom seen in history—a result inherent in Lenin's idea of the totally obedient party dedicated to a supremely important goal (the revolution and transformation of society) and therefore morally superior to ordinary people and entitled to absolute power. Power is to be exercised not for the party but for the cause; but the party defines the cause and the manner of serving it and inevitably serves itself, or the leadership that sets the party's goals. The party thus takes to itself the rights of the people—or of the proletariat, theoretically the leading part of the people—and its business is to maintain its position. Thus a small minority makes the entire nation theirs.

There is no psychological contradiction between attacking an enfeebled old tyranny and putting a new and stronger one in its place. In its Russian beginning, communism was a reassertion in distressed times of deeply laid imperial values: Lenin did not so much make a new system as modernize and reintensify the Russian empire.[40] Before the revolution, Lenin feared that the workers, left to themselves, would develop a trade union mentality; this would mean that they would become Westernized and take on the outlook of the pluralistic society. They had to be guided— or commanded—by an elite. The workers were the readier to accept guidance because they were accustomed to looking to upper-class elements for direction. Russian society being socially as well as economically hierarchic, Lenin was able to extend old relations of inequality while claiming to stand for the ultimate equality. In deference to the democratic principles that were penetrating Russia early in this century, he paid verbal tribute to modern political ideas and used them to give all power to the few in the name of all power for the working masses.

***Circumstances of the Bolshevik Revolution***    The Soviet party-state could arise only in the unique conditions of Russia in 1917: the defeat and breakdown of the decadent empire, the long custom of combining borrowing from the West with autocratic politics, the weakness of democratically inclined parties, and the need for an integrating force for the multinational realm. It required a theory of historical inevitability, anticapitalism, egalitarianism, and internationalism to justify casting away old values and uniting the peoples of the empire; and it would have been impossible if Marxism, which fitted like a key into the Russian political lock, had not been popular with the intelligentsia. It could not have come without Lenin's personality and his obsession with the idea of a party of professionals solely dedicated to the party and its power.

The de-Westernization of Russia and the demonstration of how potent the state can be were made possible by a series of contingent events. The world war, defeats, and the loss of western territories staggered the Russian economy, destroyed the prestige of the ruling house and privileged classes, caused widespread desperation, and made the people responsive to demagoguery. The discontent of maltreated minorities of the tsarist empire was also crucial. The victims of discrimination, who sought not to destroy the empire but to obtain justice from it, were the most faithful of Lenin's party.

***The German Connection***    An important, probably essential circumstance was the interest of the German Reich, after the abdication of Nicholas II in 1917, in disrupting the Western-inclined provisional government and undermining the Russian army—an interest that it shared with Lenin. The equivalent of several tens of millions of dollars—a pittance by today's standards but a very large amount in the impoverished Russia of 1917—was for the Germans a small price to pay for the sabotaging of the Russian war effort by Lenin's antiwar party.[41] For Lenin it was the means not only of supporting a large noncommercial party press but also of employing many more professional party workers than rival parties could afford and an apparatus that would have been impossible if he had had to rely on workers' donations.

But Lenin, having accepted money from the enemy, had either to achieve power or be punished for treason; hence his frantic insistence in the summer of 1917 on an immediate Bolshevik coup. Moreover, having gained power, he had to hold it or quite likely be hanged. This meant a commitment to power unlike that of other parties, not only for ideological reasons (as often stated not only by the Leninists but by their critics) but also for criminal reasons (in terms of "bourgeois" codes, not Lenin's morality). Power was not only sweet but necessary for survival.

This may have been why Lenin was determined, contrary to most of his henchmen, not to share power in a coalition after the coup; outsiders near the center of power might learn too much. Lenin's guilt was an additional reason to restore censorship and the political police, contrary to the libertarian ethos of the antitsarist revolution. It also makes more understandable Lenin's insistence in March 1918 on acceptance of the German-dictated Treaty of Brest-Litovsk, against the judgment of a large majority of the party, and the August 1918 treaty whereby the Soviet government gave a large part of its scanty gold reserves to the Germans, who were already facing defeat in the west.

The same compulsion applied not only to Bolshevik leaders who were more or less aware of Lenin's guilt or were participants in it but also to the rank and file. Although they assuredly believed their leader's passionate declarations of persecuted innocence, they knew that their party was accused of acting on behalf of Germany. When the civil war inevitably followed the takeover, they had to win not only because of the fierceness of the class struggle but also because their opponents damned them as German agents and would have liked to string them up as such. The merciless conflict thus toughened the new Soviet state.

**The Effects of the Revolution**   The Bolshevik victory plus disorder and famine effectively did away with what there had been of independent urban middle classes. The chief survivors of the formerly affluent or educated sectors were some professionals with useful nonpolitical skills and bureaucrats who were prepared to work for the new masters as they had for the old. Lenin's party, having won the civil war, instead of relaxing its monopoly and permitting a more conventional political order, stiffened central control and tightened party discipline. The Leninists outlawed the non-Bolshevik socialist organizations that had earned a right to exist by fighting for the revolution and proscribed the independent parties previously permitted a somewhat marginal existence, not because the ruling party enjoyed but because it lacked support. The people were weary of hardships and dictatorship; the Bolsheviks would certainly have been expelled from power in 1921 to 1922 if there had been institutions whereby popular feeling could have political effect. The efforts of peasants and the Kronshtadt sailors to throw off controls were repressed as mercilessly as the civil war had been fought. Only by dictatorial means could the party assure its power; ergo, it became fully dictatorial.

**Stalin and the Climax of Totalitarianism**   The climax of the party's totality of power under Stalin owed something to the fact that he was a non-Russian, an outsider in the basically Russian realm, and at the same time a man of less ideological sophistication than many others in Lenin's entourage when proficiency in Marxism was still an important qualification for leadership. The only man whom Lenin in his "Testament" specifically asked to be removed from his position, Stalin seems to have felt highly insecure—there is ample testimony to his para-noia—and, in a sense, illegitimate beyond the illegitimacy of the Bolsheviks in general. Consequently, he applied within the party the basic principle of the party's control over society and raised up persons of crude and humble ("proletarian") background, as sanctioned by Marxism. With their help, he destroyed private farming, brought the peasant majority back under landholders—that is, the party-nominated administrators of state or collectivized plantations—and displaced and destroyed the more edu-cated Leninists. The terror was propelled not only by Stalin but by thou-sands of otherwise insignificant people given power and convinced by Stalin that party rule—that is, their well-being and perhaps their life—was in peril unless they were unconditionally loyal.

Stalin destroyed not only potential oppositionists but the spirit of opposition as completely as brutality would allow. He thereby realized the potentialities of modernized despotism that were only dimly percepti-ble when the Soviet state was being born in 1917 and which hardened almost continually during the next twenty years. Stalin fixed the Marxist-Leninist system in the Soviet Union as it has endured without marked change—except for loss of dynamism in repression and slackening of its grip.

### Strengths of Communism

From the Soviet Union, communist rule has spread, or been spread, to about fifteen countries ranging in size from China to Albania and in longitude from Laos to Cuba. The extension of the Marxist-Leninist realm has been almost entirely by military means: in some cases by the victory of Communist parties in civil wars (as in China and Vietnam); in others, by Soviet arms (as in most of Eastern Europe and Afghanistan); and in still others (as in Cuba and Ethiopia), by the decision of native rulers reliant on Soviet military assistance.

Communist ideologues are heartened that territorial expansion has seemed to confirm their thesis of the irreversible march of history. No communist regime has thus far been replaced by a noncommunist government. Democracies, dictatorships, and sundry tyrannies come and go in many lands; but communism, in our historical experience, never goes.

The communist states have not only maintained themselves but have also shown a great capacity to keep order. Riots and mass protests in communist countries have been newsworthy partly because of their fewness. Disorders suppressed by troops in Novocherkassk in 1962, in Lithuania in 1972, and in Kazakhstan in 1986 have been the chief blem-ishes on outward Soviet placidity for the past seventy years. The excesses of collectivization and Stalin's mad terror were borne with resignation,

as was the even more atrocious butchery of the Khmer Rouge in Kampuchea in the latter 1970s. The recession of terror after Stalin was greeted
with relief, and a few citizens took advantage of the relaxation to publish
surreptitiously in *Samizdat*, or even to unfurl a banner in Red Square
for a few seconds before the police pounced on them. But without fuss
or difficulty, the authorities in the 1980s brought back a climate of some
fear and demoralized, scattered, or punished the dissidents. The relatively
youthful and sophisticated Gorbachev called for "openness" and released
some prisoners, but one may doubt that many would object aloud if
executions of nonconformists were resumed.

The Poles, with an only partially communist society (having
mostly private farming and a powerful independent church), have shown
more ability to raise their voices than the people of any other communist
country. They took to the streets in 1956, 1970, and 1976 to get more
meat and sausage; and in 1980 to 1981 they enjoyed the florescence of
the free unionism of Solidarity, which briefly seemed stronger than the
faltering state. But coercive authority was restored without direct Soviet
intervention. Under Mao, the Chinese masses had ample cause for unhap-
piness, but the country was thrown into the turmoil of the Cultural Revolution (1964 to 1969) not by popular discontent but by the anger of the
Great Helmsman, who saw himself losing control. After the rioting calmed
down, rule by the military and the party was as total as before. The
Hungarians rose against communist rule in 1956 when it was relatively
new and was discredited by de-Stalinization, but Soviet forces taught
them a bloody lesson, and they have been quiet since. The Czechs seemed
capable in 1968 of changing the regime, but the Soviet army vetoed the
experiment; and they, like the Hungarians, seem to have learned the
nature of the power over them.

The grip of communist regimes, moreover, seems little affected
by massive social and economic change, in defiance of theories that relate
political institutions to such things as industrialization, mass communications, and literacy. Leninism came to a Russia that was overwhelmingly
agricultural, 80 percent rural, and largely illiterate; the country has since
been industrialized, urbanized, and schooled, yet the party is more firmly
in charge now than sixty years ago. Such formerly rather backward lands
as Romania and North Korea have likewise built much more modern
economies, but the rule of the party seems only to have been strengthened
thereby.

Just as the communist establishment maintains itself tenaciously
despite changes through time, it prevails over a wide range of conditions
in countries of very different background, from Vietnam to Russia and
from East Germany to Cuba. Systems of control, ideology, and management, with leadership by general secretary, politburo, central committee,
and so forth, are similar in such diverse nations, which call one another

"brother socialist." The purposefully structured party-state is a coherent whole. The exclusive party with controls from top down, the separation of the political class, ostensible egalitarianism, censorship, obligatory dogma, political police, monopoly of organization, and control of the economy all fit together, reinforce one another, and form a viable political structure applicable anywhere.

In a number of Marxist-Leninist states—including the most highly industrialized, East Germany and Czechoslovakia—the Communist regime was imposed by Soviet armed forces and could hardly be sustained without them. But the governments of these states, however unpopular or antinational, have been able to keep order and secure fair to good economic growth, especially in the case of East Germany. Eastern Europe has not seethed nearly as much as one would expect of proud nations subject to foreign domination and an alien political system.

***Communism versus Modernism***   The viability of communist systems cries out for explanation because they directly counter the principal long-term tendencies of modern civilization since the Renaissance. These include trends toward empirical rationality, representative and responsible government, and personal autonomy—trends the importance of which is attested by the Leninists' claims to fulfill most of them by representing the height of reason and science applied to society, providing the fullest democracy, and guaranteeing true freedom.

Communist methods are opposite to those that have promoted modernization in the past; they might be called the political negation of modernization. The rise of science and industry required release from political controls to permit inquiry, innovation, and initiative. A progressive modern state presupposes a free flow of information from varied sources. Yet the communist state frankly rejects "bourgeois objectivity" and strongly controls communications. The Maoists preferred "Redness" over expertise, and the Khmer Rouge deurbanized Kampuchea. In the same spirit is the Soviet insistence on "party spirit" over intellectual inquiry and the communist dislike for modernism in painting, literature, and music and general distrust of intellectuals. Almost synonymous with the growth of scientific-industrial civilization has been the development of well-defined legal, instead of more arbitrary traditional or political, relations. But communism unabashedly, even proudly, places the will of the governing power over "bourgeois" concepts of law or constitutionalism.

The progress of history in the West since the invention of the printing press has been toward the emancipation of the individual from obligatory beliefs (freedom of religion), from foreign domination (the independence of the nation-state and national self-determination), and from economic rigidities (freedom of contract and occupation). Communist states have gone determinedly in the opposite direction, imposing an obligatory faith, maintaining foreign domination over many peoples (when old colonial empires have been dissolved), replacing the market by the planning authority, and compelling people to work for approved enterprises, sometimes fixing them to the workplace or the land like medieval serfs. The primary axiom of communism, in defiance of the modern mode of democracy and egalitarianism, is the right of a self-selected organization called the party to command the entire society.

*Politicization of Society* This reversal of historical trends is a political tour de force, a phenomenal application of the powers of the state directed by a purposeful, well-organized minority. It is possible only through maximum and uninhibited use of the sovereign capacity to coerce and direct, while minimizing the self-expression of persons and sectors of society more concerned with rationality, freedom of information, legality, and individual or corporate autonomy. The strength of communism may thus be summarized as the concentration of power in the hands of those primarily dedicated to the control system—those whose profession is the promotion of the interests of the party [42]—and the exclusion from influence of those with other values. Its durability rests on the ability of those advantaged by the system to keep powerless those who might gain by political change.

In a less directed society, many persons outside the hierarchic power structure, such as lawyers, businessmen, union leaders, journalists, writers, and teachers, are aware of the need for change and have some means of pressing for it. Historically, modernization has entailed the growth and strengthening of unofficial classes and has given them importance in the community. Influence thus has flowed to sectors concerned with legality, individual and group autonomy, the protection of personal and property rights from the arbitrary power of the state, and the participation of outsiders in the political process. In the settled communist state, to the contrary, channels of information, influence, and organization are closed to independent forces so far as possible (and very far is possible). Not only officials at all levels but industrial executives, newspaper editors, farm managers, cultural administrators, and so forth, hold primarily political positions and enjoy primarily political standing.

Productive scientists and sports champions may be well rewarded, but they are politically impotent. People hold positions of power because of their standing in the power structure, only secondarily or marginally because of their nonpolitical ability or their contribution to satisfying social needs; and their primary concern is maintenance of the political ensemble. Politics is itself the prime profession; members of the nomenklatura, the political elite, are generalists who may be detailed to industry, agriculture, or governmental administration.

Almost everything is politicized—that is, managed—so far as feasible, by, and for the benefit of, the system. Circus clowns have a political message, chess is of political concern, and sports are treated as a political contest with other nations. Abstract humanism, being independent of the party, is considered a serious vice. A recent Soviet youth festival was wholly given over to politics and propaganda; to minimize unplanned contacts, Moscow was closed to traffic and nonofficial young people were sent away.[43] Nothing is to be unplanned or spontaneous; the mourners for the leader's funeral are permitted (or required) to come only in organized groups. The communist state thus contradicts what seemed to be the modern movement toward the diffusion and fluidity of influence in society.

The society ostensibly oriented toward social change is actually oriented toward fixity. The elite have an overriding interest in the regnant order—their order—made by and for them. This applies not only to those near the top of the pyramid but also to the masses beneath them, especially to those who have acted harshly against the citizenry, such as the political police, who might well lose more than their career if their state were overthrown. Millions of informers, whom the KGB recruits to involve them morally, would face reprisals. Countless bureaucrats and controllers would lose their jobs and way of life; many would face prosecution for abuses and corruption. Even substantial reforms would be directly threatening to many. Managers of the planned economy would be replaced by others with more economic, as opposed to political, skills. Without censorship, not only the censors would be unemployed; administrators of art and literature would cease to be bosses over more talented artists and writers, and many a thriving hack would be jobless. In all societies, of course, extensive political change is costly to some people, but the breakup of a communist state would injure, perhaps mortally, nearly everyone in a position of influence.

In pluralistic societies, people are not such faithful servants of the state or party because those who lose out politically can go into private activities. Persons of superior education or professional or economic standing in the community are not so much impressed by political position. To take office may well represent a financial sacrifice; they consequently tend to be independent. Similarly, military rulers can step aside comfortably without great personal loss. In the communist state, those who do not conform can take nothing with them and have to accept whatever pittance the party allows. Malenkov went from heading the Soviet government to managing a power station and Dubcek reminisced as a forest ranger about his leadership of Czechoslovakia.

*Unity* Not only are the party-advanced elite and the enormous bureaucratic apparatus wholly committed to the status quo; they are also united and organized, whereas their opponents or potential challengers are divided and denied means of organization. As Lev Kopelev said, "Believe what you want. Say what you want. Be a monarchist if you wish. They don't care. But start to organize, no matter on how small a scale, and—wham—they'll get you." [44] That a group in the Soviet Union is independent suffices to condemn it even though its purposes may be identical with those of the party.[45] People are not allowed to organize independently to support an antialcohol campaign, because they could use the organization to petition the state and cause unrest.

The obverse of the atomization of society is the coherence of the party. A key element of the Leninist doctrine is the absolute priority of the party's collectivity (*partiinost*, or "party spirit," as the Russians call it), an idealization of collective self-interest. The monolithism of the rulership stands omnipotent over the dividedness of the subjects. A major step in the consolidation of the Soviet system was the outlawing of factionalism in 1921. If this prohibition were repealed or even softened, it would represent a major loosening of the system; but of this there is no sign in any ruling party. The universal doctrine is "Democratic Centralism," that is, the undemocratic supremacy of the center.

Not only are the many weak and the few tightly organized; there is also no visible alternative to party leadership but anarchy. From the viewpoint of the individual's material interest, opposition is irrational; and the authorities have a stronger and more direct interest in maintaining the power structure than their opponents have in overturning it. To take up a cudgel against the almighty state entails sure penalties for uncertain spiritual rewards. It is logical to consign dissidents to psychiatric wards.

Solidarity being so vital, Communist parties make willingness to identify completely with the party the supreme virtue.[46] It is difficult to enter, and the militant is wedded to the party as adherents are not wedded to less single-minded political movements. It is much worse, in communist countries, to be an ex-member than never to have joined. Freedom of divorce would suggest a conditional commitment where commitment must be unconditional.

Near the start of his career as an agitator, Lenin insisted on a party of full-time revolutionaries in the Russian conspiratorial tradition to pull the Marxist movement out of the morass of futility into which it seemed to be sinking around the turn of the century. This theme, which he set forth in *What Is to Be Done* (1902), was Lenin's great contribution to the making of the communist state. His explanation of why he preferred "fewer but better" members in his party—that selectivity was necessary to guard against police action—was not convincing. He knew the party was readily infiltrated, in any case, and he kept up the same insistence after he acquired the police power.

The stronger reason was that the full-time revolutionary would have to accept completely the ideas and orders of the leadership; to rebel would mean losing a way of life. The leader has the satisfaction, like an army commander, of having followers upon whom he can rely completely despite difficulties or changes of policy. The followers enjoy the psychological security of the close group with a strongly shared purpose; they have only to follow orders. Welded together, they form an excellent instrument for seizing power in a time of crisis, confusion, and division of other forces. But if they attain power, the full-time devotees cannot slacken their grip lest they lose it totally and forever.

### Marxism-Leninism

The chief dogma of communism, the need for solidarity in order to survive, is translated into a conviction of the naturalness and rightness of maintaining it, a conviction justifying any action. To maintain this conviction a chronic emergency is necessary, a sense of danger from innately hostile foreign powers. The party sustains this antithesis partly to fortify its position, partly because of fear and distrust of whatever it cannot control, and partly because of a sense of insecurity and illegitimacy; and Marxism furnishes its rationale.

In the formation and organization of the Communist Party, Marxism plays a complex and equivocal role. If Lenin had taken it literally, he would never have attempted a socialist revolution in a backward country—a venture that more consistent Russian Marxists warned would lead to tyranny. He would have enlisted workers not only in the ranks but also in the leadership; hardly any of those near Lenin were members of the class the party was supposed to represent. And a truly Marxist party in power would feel the need to listen to the workers and secure their approval.

But the Marxist-Leninists, uninhibited by inconsistencies, have used Marxism, or derivatives of it, as a political and psychological tool. Claiming to represent the acme of social science and the fulfillment of history moving toward predestined higher justice, they presented themselves as saviors. They turned ideas borrowed from the liberal Western world into means of control, contrary to their original meaning and intention: from "democracy," which is made into a synonym for management of opinion and repression of individualism, to "proletarian internationalism," a euphemism for Soviet domination of the proletariat and everyone else. The world, impressed by their insistence and fervor, has been very loth to bracket the proclaimed leaders of the proletariat with ordinary despotism. They are the more convincing because they speak, or shout, with total self-righteousness in whatever circumstances: the East Germans celebrate the nobility of the Berlin Wall with music and parades.

Ideology takes the place of the theocratic religion that has been an integral element of older imperial societies, such as imperial Russia, which for centuries had a state church. A shared ideal gives coherence and community of purpose, first to would-be revolutionaries and then to the masters of the state. Radicals, as rejectors of authority, are almost by definition a fractious lot: the Far Left is usually splintered. Successful organization needs a joint purpose that can be seen as eminently noble even while it serves self-interest. The conviction of rightness fortifies the comrades not only in the struggle for power but in the resolve to keep and enlarge it, especially so far as it lays duties, even symbolically, on the rulers.

Marxism blends democratic or populist feeling into the authoritarian impulse and gives the people some reason to accept the claim of the party to command them, or it at least confuses the opposition. Marxism, or Marxism-Leninism, thus lends a bit of sense to a situation that is otherwise hardly comprehensible to the nonbeneficiaries. The ideology enables the party, claiming moral virtue, to overlook material conditions.[47] But the real function of Marxism-Leninism, to fortify power, becomes more evident in the waning of egalitarianism. The communist leaders seem to be aware, however disinclined they are to admit it, that theirs is the right of the strong. The state uses propaganda and education but rests on force and really respects only force. Stalin asked how many divisions the Pope had, and the Soviets have seemed to regard Japan, with the world's second largest economy, as inconsequential because its armed forces are inconsequential.[48]

Marxism-Leninism makes the individual feel trivial beside the collective and the state of which he is a small component.[49] It facilitates the rewriting of history. It denies political reality: all normal citizens of a communist state are held to be eager supporters (as demonstrated by "elections"), and they are deemed free, whereas it is the citizens of democratic states who are considered enslaved. For the Soviets, as for the imperial Romans, freedom equals obedience to necessity, which is made by the party. The operative elements of Marxism-Leninism consecrate the party's right as representative of the progressive class; the preference for "workers" whose devotion to the party will be undiluted, the need for socialization (that is, control) of the economy, the priority of heavy (especially defense) industry, the monopoly of foreign trade, the inadmissibility of alien or independent ("bourgeois") influences, and the priority of class (that is, party) over nation. In 1968, the Soviet Union required of the Czech party not that it care better for the workers or increase their political role, but that it restore censorship and protect its monopoly. The Soviets give their blessing to Third World dictatorships, not on the basis of their social ideals or policies, but according to the Leninist character of the governing party and its support for Soviet foreign policy.

### The Ways of Communism

If the communist state felt itself legitimate, it would be less troubled by a little criticism, most of it constructively intended, and would permit people freely to choose a different way of life and leave its jurisdiction. It would encourage contacts between its citizens and foreigners on the assumption that it would not suffer by comparison. The comfortably legitimate communist state would let people freely do things that cause no harm to others, such as raising lemons in Georgia to sell in Moscow or mending shoes for pay. It would not worry about the practice of religion, the formation of clubs, or the teaching of Hebrew. Khrushchev in his memoirs expressed the fear, upon the death of Stalin, that popular feeling might rise like a tide to sweep the party out of power,[50] a fear that would have hardly occurred to him if he had not felt that the masses hated party rule. He also hoped that Soviet socialism would mature sufficiently to permit free movement and freedom of expression in the manner of modern states.[51]

Popularity is secondary, if not irrelevant, for the communist state. We may assume that communist rulers wish to be loved. However, except for a few at the very top who are symbols of the political order, they live secluded from the masses and have no need to be popular. They seem to have been popular only where communism was fused with nationalism, as in the Soviet Union battling the Nazi invasion, in Yugoslavia fighting German occupiers and then facing a threat from Stalin, or in the struggle of North Vietnam against first French and then American forces. After victory in World War II, Stalin could have had immense popularity and probably greater personal security by allowing his people some of the freedom vaguely promised to them when the struggle was most difficult; but he chose to reimpose ideological strictures, political repression, and economic sacrifices.

After the revolutionary phase, communism is based not on the union but on the separation of rulers and people, a separation marked by the many privileges of the elite well beyond the practice of pluralist societies. The elite form a sort of club, socializing and sharing entertainments and ideas,[52] and a host of perquisites bind them: the ability to travel abroad, access to special entertainment, quality of medical care, restricted stores, and special vacation accommodations, among others. Privileges are not only material; censorship, for example, not only suppresses information and ideas but also divides the informed from the uninformed and reduces the capacity of the latter to judge the actions of the leaders.

The bosses can hardly know whether they are liked or disliked. Underlings have no interest either in learning the true sentiments of the masses or in telling their superiors anything disagreeable. The only critical journalism the leaders can read—if they desire—is that of the ideological enemy. The people bow; if a few dissidents raise complaints, they can be dismissed—if the leaders are even aware of them—as eccentrics or foreign hirelings. It is necessary that the subjects be obedient, not that they be eager. The purpose of the great expenditures on propaganda and indoctrination is probably less to inculcate positive beliefs than to exclude bad thinking. The ethos of communist rulership is not to appeal to people or satisfy their wants but to manage them. Real elections are not desirable, even if winnable, because they would acknowledge the authority of the people.

The essence is not to seek consent but to do away with the need for consent, thus throwing back the challenge of modernity to absolutism. If status depends on pandering to the people, they may demand different things; if the people are to be satisfied, they may become dissatisfied and press for change. It is a capital sin for a communist to look for support from the masses or any nonparty source; this would threaten the basis of the regime. It is undesirable or dangerous for a communist leader (other than the chief) to enjoy personal popularity. Soviet leaders (except the leader) have never sought broad support since Stalin crushed his rivals in the 1920s.

The management of people goes much beyond the strictly political. Communist states tend to be puritanical watchdogs, probably less from political calculation than from the feeling of the rulers that they know how people should behave. The Soviets prohibit things sexually suggestive and compulsorily (but ineffectively) register those with a drinking problem. Cuba fights homosexuality. The Khmer Rouge of Kampuchea banned family names and folk songs. The Bulgarians require Turks to take Bulgarian names. The Soviets try to homogenize the people; for example, Balts are pressured to leave the Baltic region as Russians move into it, and interethnic marriage is encouraged. Everybody should learn Russian and be a model of *Homo sovieticus*, who is much like *Homo cubanus* and other related species.

We have no idea what percentage of citizens of communist countries are pleased or displeased with the government. Very likely the rulers do not either. The number of the discontented probably varies a great deal. It is certainly high in Poland and East Germany, in the former because of nationalistic urges and the economic failure of the regime, in the latter because of contacts and comparisons with West Germany as well as negative attitudes toward Russians. Communist countries generally betray a lack of confidence by allowing very few to choose to live elsewhere.

Foreign observers have the impression that Soviet Russians usually support their regime; at least, they do so in talking with outsiders. Even many persons discontented with the Soviet system are inclined to identify with it and to fear the anarchy of its possible overthrow. There are satisfactions of security; life is simple and straightforward, and choices are few. Americans are alarmed to the edge of hysteria by statistically trivial dangers of terrorism; Soviet citizens are reassured by their government that a nuclear meltdown is unthreatening. The Russians also enjoy superiority over many lesser peoples. Some of the few who manage to emigrate return to the Soviet Union or try to (they may be refused), complaining of the anarchy of life in the West and burdened by independence but perhaps suffering even more from loss of their importance as Russians.

Emigrés or escapees from totalitarian countries almost always meet difficulties in adjusting to the more permissive societies, where they see pornography, prostitution, and commercialization of all aspects of life.[53] Worse, they are burdened with too much choice. For example, new arrivals from across the Elbe, going into a department store or supermarket in West Germany, are made delirious by the need to reject so many attractive things.[54] The idea of looking for a job is appalling.

It may be, however, that even people who accept the government would welcome a change. In Spain and Portugal, where the grievances of the people were much less weighty and domestic tranquillity reigned, nearly everyone seems to have rejoiced at the departure of the respective dictators.[55] The fall of Latin American tyrants has regularly been celebrated by dancing in the streets. The people of Czechoslovakia and Poland gave every sign of enjoying the breath of freedom in 1968 and in 1981.

Even a high degree of illegitimacy need not prevent a communist state from governing effectively. In fact, it may be just as well if cadres are aware that they have to justify their status by results. Their situation is like that of the Spartans, who ruled parasitically over an overwhelming majority of Helots. In order to stay on top, the Spartans had to be brave, skilled warriors, united and dedicated to the Spartan ideal. In a sense they earned their status and held it for three centuries.

The rulers of East Germany, who have inherited something of the Spartan-Prussian tradition, are a tiny, self-chosen minority, acting on behalf of Russian occupiers, who control the entire state, its resources, and its people. Moreover, they have to deal with a population that is well informed by West German television. To make the state function tolerably, the East German Communists have had to administer it well; and under pressure of necessity, they have managed the economy fairly effectively and have implanted intelligent social policies. It may be inferred that illegitimacy, of which they must be better aware than most communist elites, and the inescapable comparisons with West Germany have made them more effective communists.

The Stalinist economic model brought rapid growth of output in the Soviet Union over many years and in Eastern Europe, China, Cuba, and North Korea for a shorter time; and the system gained much strength thereby. Rapid growth ceased, and in Cuba, Vietnam, and various African countries of "scientific socialism" there has never been an impressive economic upsurge; but the strength of the respective regimes has not visibly been affected. No economic failure can convince the cadres that they should surrender their privileges and well-being, nor can it generate an alternative authority.

As long as the few are united in preserving their status and the others are leaderless and unorganized, if not resigned, the minority is secure. In some ways, too, the structure is self-restorative. If the regime feels threatened, it can allow limited freedom and make small concessions, correcting abuses and satisfying grievances without giving away real power. If the state displays a modicum of flexibility and the intelligence to attend to, or seem to attend to, the most urgent demands of the populace while binding its supporters by special status, it is unshakable.

The catastrophe of collectivization brought no move to oust Stalin, much less the party. To defuse the desperation of the peasants, who were a large majority of the population, it sufficed to allow them to retain small garden plots for their own use under severe restrictions. The Romanians, having heard their leaders boast for years of unexampled economic progress, shivered through winters in almost unheated buildings and stood in long lines for meager food supplies; but they remained silent. Maoism was an economic failure for twenty years, but the adoration of Mao remained hyperbolic, more exaggeratedly so in the later years of poorer performance. Failure may lead the cadres to work more devotedly for the party, as they become concerned for the loss of their livelihood, just as corruption makes it more necessary to uphold the system to escape retribution.

These priorities help the party to maintain its precious unity. Infighting is inevitable where there is an irregular contest for supremacy, but the beneficiaries of the system have been remarkably successful in presenting a common front to outsiders. Covert factionalism has had little effect in softening the system. Ordinary dictators cannot usually liquidate their allies because as landholders, generals, or whatever they have a base of their own in society. However, Stalin or Kim Il-sung could annihilate any group within the party because it had no ground outside the party. Thus the followings of Kamenev and Zinoviev, Trotsky, and Bukharin in the 1920s and of Malenkov and Molotov in the 1950s could be quite destroyed or at least driven underground by Stalin or Khrushchev because they had no standing against the party apparatus. The Workers' Opposition in the Soviet Union in the early 1920s could not even call on the support of the workers for whom it spoke. The Workers' Oppositionists, like their enemies, owed their position in the trade unions to force and fraud; and it was out of the question to appeal to genuine workers who were in any event leaderless and powerless.

***Military Advantages***   The compulsion for unity and the reliance on force provide a basis for military excellence. In the systematic and purposeful use of violence, loyalty and dedication are of special importance; the communist system gives strength in combat, just as the marriage of nationalism with totalitarianism made superb fighters of the Nazis. The organizational advantage shows itself most clearly where technology, in which the communists are weaker, is less important. Thus the communists do best at guerrilla warfare and underground resistance. In occupied Europe during World War II, for example, they came to lead the field nearly everywhere. However, they have also performed magnificently in regular battles, as in the Soviet Union, Korea, and Vietnam.

The communists also have the military advantage that they can require indefinite sacrifices in the name of the highest ideal, communism. The Sandinistas of Nicaragua, despite the newness of their regime, are not much hurt by economic pressures as long as people can be told they are suffering for the revolutionary cause. If there is less to buy, the people are more dependent on the state and less distracted from their duties. Communism is at its finest struggling under privations and pressures. If the United States government had understood this, it would not have assumed that a rain of bombs would make the North Vietnamese turn reasonable and sue for peace. The effect was the opposite.

War, calling upon the strengths of communism, at the same time reinforces them. Years of bitter civil and antiforeign war tempered the Soviet, Chinese, Korean, Vietnamese, and Yugoslav parties. Prior to World War II, as the numbing purges ran out, the Stalinist state had become a corrupt despotism; and it performed miserably in the 1939 to 1940 conflict with Finland and the first weeks of Hitler's onslaught. But it responded to the invasion and the challenge to do what it was best prepared to do, renewed itself, and went on to excel on the battlefield. Communist states pay enormous attention to the memory of wars not only for reasons of morale building but also because those were the good days when the system functioned best.

Communism thrives on struggle and the in- versus out-group antithesis, the virtuous state against the evil outside. This becomes a sort of nationalism; the theoretically internationalist Leninist revolution behaved nationalistically almost from its inception. Many communist states have exaggerated their national character in quite un-Marxist fashion, from Albania, sole depository of revolutionary virtue, to the Soviet Union, bringer of the new dawn to humanity, and North Korea, carrier of the banner of "Juche." As Kim said, "We Communists love our fatherland and nation more than anyone else." [56]

Through military strength communism saved the Russian empire after 1917 and in World War II gave it the greatest victory of its long history. It kept North Korea in existence and made the North Vietnamese rulers of all Indochina. A would-be conqueror would do well to adopt it or imitate it.

The strength of communism lies in organization, people's need for security and social direction, and their willingness to accept superior power. Its great weakness is the failure to take into account and utilize the other side of human nature, individual self-will.

## Notes

1. Robert Ardrey, *The Social Contract* (New York: Atheneum Publishers, 1970), pp. 132, 135.
2. Irving Janis, *Victims of Groupthink: A Psychological Study of Foreign Policy Decisions and Fiascos* (Boston: Houghton Mifflin, 1972).
3. Stanley Milgram, *Obedience to Authority: An Experimental View* (New York: Harper & Row, Publishers, 1974), pp. 146, 148, 164.
4. Max Rosenberg, "Compliance," in *Compliant Behavior: Beyond Obedience to Authority*, ed. Max Rosenberg (New York: Human Sciences Press, 1983), p. 34.
5. John P. Kirscht and Ronald C. Dillehay, *Dimensions of Authoritarianism* (Lexington: University of Kentucky Press, 1967), pp. vi, 5–6.
6. Orlando Patterson, *Slavery and Social Death* (Cambridge: Harvard University Press, 1982), pp. 40–41.
7. Romans 13:2.
8. John L. Esposito, *Islam and Politics* (Syracuse: Syracuse University Press, 1984), p. 221.
9. See Reinhard Bendix, *Force, Fate, and Freedom* (Berkeley: University of California Press, 1984), p. 82, for the Russian case.
10. M. Fortes and E. E. Evans-Pritchard, "Introduction," in *African Political System*, ed. Fortes and Evans-Pritchard (New York: Oxford University Press, 1940), pp. 16, 19.
11. Dennis H. Wrong, *Power: Its Forms, Bases & Uses* (New York: Harper & Row, Publishers, 1979), p. 96.
12. Hugo J. Zee, "The Guyana Incident," in *Compliant Behavior: Beyond Obedience to Authority*, ed. Max Rosenberg (New York: Human Sciences Press, 1983) pp. 229–40.
13. Brian Weinstein and Aaron Segal, *Haiti: Political Failures, Cultural Successes* (New York: Praeger Publishers, 1984), p. 30.
14. Weinstein and Segal, *Haiti*, p. 84.
15. Clifford D. May, "Africa's Men in Khaki," *New York Times*, October 1, 1985, p. E3.
16. For Latin America, see Robert Wessons, ed. *The Latin American Military Institution* (New York: Praeger Publishers, 1986), pp. 20–45.
17. Alan Cowell, "Egypt's Friend in Need," *New York Times Magazine*, December 20, 1981, p. 40.
18. As in the case of Uruguay. Edy Kaufman, *Uruguay in Transition: From Civilian to Military Rule* (New York: Transition Books, 1979), pp. 64–65.
19. Kaufman, *Uruguay in Transition*, pp. 77–79.
20. James L. Payne, "Marx's Heirs Retire the Pacifist Promise," *Wall Street Journal*, April 5, 1985, p. 16.

21. David N. Dorn and Xavier Z. Cuadra, "Understanding the Sandinistas Is as Easy as Uno-Dos-Tres," *Washington Post Weekly Edition*, September 2, 1985, p. 23.
22. Samuel P. Huntington, "Social and Institutional Dynamics of One-Party Systems," in *Authoritarian Politics in Modern Society: The Dynamics of Established One-Party Systems*, ed. Samuel P. Huntington and Clement H. Moore (New York: Basic Books, 1970), p. 10.
23. Patterson, *Slavery*, p. 18.
24. Wrong, *Power*, p. 111.
25. George H. Sabine, *A History of Political Theory*, rev. ed. (New York: Holt, Rinehart and Winston, 1955), p. 171.
26. Wrong, *Power*, p. 96.
27. Chong-sik Lee, *The Korean Workers' Party: A Short History* (Stanford: Hoover Institution Press, 1978), p. 134.
28. Huntington, "Social and Institutional Dynamics," p. 13.
29. As pointed out by Zbigniew Brzezinski in *Ideology and Power in Soviet Politics* (New York: Praeger Publishers, 1962), pp. 14–20.
30. Carl J. Friedrich, "The Failure of a One-Party System: Hitler Germany," in *Authoritarian Politics*, ed. Huntington and Moore, p. 242.
31. Amos Perlmutter, *Modern Authoritarianism: A Comparative Institutional Analysis* (New Haven: Yale University Press, 1981), p. 27.
32. Alan P. L. Liu, "The Dragon's Teeth of Mao Tse-tung," *Issues and Studies*, 21 (August 1985), 16.
33. Jorge Dominguez, *Cuba: Order and Revolution* (Cambridge, Mass.: Belknap Press, 1978), pp. 316–17, 320.
34. Juan J. Linz, "Comparative Study of Fascism," in *Fascism, A Reader's Guide*, ed. Walter Laqueur (Berkeley: University of California Press, 1976), p. 43.
35. Staninlav Andreski, "Italian Military Efficiency," *Journal of Strategic Studies*, 5 (June 1982), 251–52.
36. Patterson, *Slavery*, pp. 306–7.
37. B. H. Sumner, *Peter the Great and the Emergence of Russia* (New York: Macmillan, 1951), p. 8.
38. Hamilton Gibb and Harold Bowen, *Islamic Society and the West* (London: Oxford University Press, 1950), vol. 1, pt. 1, p. 43.
39. Bernard Dietrich, *Somoza and the Legacy of U.S. Involvement in Central America* (New York: E. P. Dutton & Co., 1981), pp. 34, 62.
40. Cf. Robert Wesson, *The Russian Dilemma*, rev. ed. (New York: Praeger Publishers, 1985), chap. 3.
41. Zbynek A. Zeman and W. B. Scharlau, *The Merchant of Revolution: The Life of Alexande Israel Helphand (Parvus), 1867–1924* (London: Oxford University Press, 1965); and Zbynek A. Zeman, *Germany and the Revolution in Russia, 1915–1918* (London: Oxford University Press, 1958), p. 176.
42. Konstantin Simis, "The Gorbachev Generation," *Foreign Policy*, 59 (Summer 1985), 9.
43. *New York Times*, July 27, 1985, p. 2.
44. Lev Kopelev, *New York Times*, October 11, 1980, p. 2.
45. Geller, *Mashina i Vintiki* (London: Overseas Publishing Interchange, 1985), p. 182.
46. Simis, "The Gorbachev Generation," p. 7.
47. Susan L. Shirk, *Competitive Comrades: Career Incentives and Student Strategies in China* (Berkeley: University of California Press, 1982), p. 196.
48. The Nazi ideoogical mishmash also showed the primacy of power: although Nazism was inherently limited to Germans or Aryans and treated non-Germans, especially swarthy peoples, as inferiors, it was widely admired and imitated prior to World War II by eastern Europeans, such as Hungarians and Romanians, by some South Americans, and even to a degree by the Japanese.
49. Geller, *Mashina*, p. 10.
50. Nikita Khrushchev, *Khrushchev Remembers* (Boston: Little, Brown, 1970), p. 323.
51. Nikita Khrushchev, *Khrushchev Remembers: The Last Testament* (Boston: Little, Brown, 1974), p. 84.

52. Andrew Nagorski, *Reluctant Farewell* (New York: Holt, Rinehart and Winston, 1985), p. 145.
53. John F. Burn, "China on the Move: Will the Changes Last?" *New York Times Magazine*, December 8, 1985, p. 41.
54. Ernest Gill, "Foreigners in Their Own Land," *New York Times Magazine*, February 16, 1986, p. 55.
55. A. T. Shtromas, "Dissent and Political Change in the Soviet Union," *Studies in Comparative Communism*, 12 (Summer/Autumn 1978), 174, 220–21.
56. Peter Zwick, *National Communism* (Boulder: Westview, 1983), p. 182.

# The Decadence
# of Authoritarianism

## 5

Many an empire formed by vigorous conquerors has established a vigorous and effective government. For example, the legions spread Roman law over a huge territory, ended local wars, built roads, and let commerce flourish. The empire taxed moderately and erected countless monumental edifices; Augustus boasted of leaving Rome a city of marble. Chinese dynasties have likewise repeatedly set up an honest administration, built public works from the Great Wall onward, and imposed a more or less beneficent rule. Modern absolutisms also have established order and admirably raised industries and monuments. Moreover, ancient and recent states alike have deeply impressed themselves on their people, convincing them in a few decades that the rulership is, so to speak, decreed by heaven, and that any alternative would be disaster. Conformity becomes the rule: Soviet writers accept self-censorship as the price of being able to write at all,[1] just as writers of imperial China would not think of putting heretical ideas on paper.

But very strong states begin to decay long before they get old. Art and literature decline to imitation, and science shrinks. The rulers discourage enterprise by extortion or taxation that is near extortion. They waste the fruits of the multitudes' toil on the luxuries of parasitic power holders of low and high rank. They demean and humiliate the masses. Society becomes demoralized; people seek chiefly to protect themselves from the government, retreating to private concerns and the shelter of family or clan.

The ebbing Roman Empire hired Germans to protect it against other Germans, and became their booty. The Roman, Chinese, Persian, Indian, and many other less celebrated empires sank to amazing weakness as monopolistic power lost the capacity to defend what it most treasured. In the most self-sufficient of imperial universes, the Chinese, the sequence from strength, grandeur, and order to feebleness, breakdown, and revolution has been played out many times. Leaders were not so stupid as to be unaware of what was happening and where it was leading, but they could not halt the corrosion. The history-minded Chinese particularly studied the causes of the fall of the preceding dynasty and tried in vain to avoid them.

The ills of unchecked rule have been most obvious and most dramatic in the imperial autocracies, whose conceit is as ample as their territory; but they appear wherever states lack responsibility and balance. The failure has many aspects, all interrelated and perhaps manifestations of a single sickness, for which there is no good term. The syndrome includes lowered quality of leadership at the top; separation of rulers from ruled, with loss of community; rigidity of institutions and decreased ability of the state to command its servants; loss of morale and the sense of mission that may have given direction to the elite; permeating corruption; choking of information, with failure of inventiveness and lowering of the general intellectual level; and depression of production with impoverishment of the majority.

## QUALITY OF LEADERSHIP

Among wolves or apes, rank is determined primarily by violence, by physical contest or threats; and the idea of jousting for kingship is not unknown to humans: in many primitive kingdoms the new monarch had to be strong or crafty enough to kill his brothers. Similarly, in a situation where force prevails, as in a revolution or coup of some kind, the question of authority is solved by the ability to command force: Julius Caesar forged an army to defeat rival generals; Lenin was placed at the top in 1917 by his Red Guards; and Mussolini was elevated as chief of his "fasci" marching on Rome and threatening civil war. This implies that the dictator, emperor, or however he may be designated (rarely if ever has a woman come to the top in this manner) is gifted, certainly active, dynamic, and capable of organizing a following. His lieutenants also have probably been selected for proven ability.

A new group is likely to govern effectively, at least for a few years. But the seizure of power by a new rulership is not a state of being or an institution; it is commotion. Revolution gives no good way to remove a leader who may become outworn or incapable or to establish a competent succession, and the quality of leadership usually declines, just as the son of the founder of the dynasty is seldom the equal of his father.

A ruler cannot prepare for his demise without some sacrifice of power, and modern absolutist rulers have rarely been able to bequeath their power to a desired successor. In the uncertainty after a leader who has long been in power, however, a relatively capable person may succeed in pushing to the top, as Khrushchev after Stalin, Deng after Mao, and Gorbachev (with the interludes of two sick men) after Brezhnev. A domineering personality leaves his colleagues with a desire for more relaxation; a more relaxed but less effective regime bequeaths willingness for an activist. But as the state matures and ages, the quality of leadership is fairly sure on the average to decline, partly because those on top do not advance persons who make them uncomfortable, partly because rising in the hierarchy has more to do with intrigue than with the improvement of the state.

"As omnipotence becomes routinized, more and more people feel they are entitled to partake of kingly power," among modern Russians as well as nineteenth-century Bantus.[2] In the solidification of structures, effective power probably falls to a small clique. To renew this group, the survivors co-opt new members to replace those who fall out, but their quality is unlikely to be raised. Those in charge want colleagues who will help in the business of the state but be no threat to those on top. Most of all, no doubt, they want aides who will help to maintain the political status quo, that is, persons wedded to fixity.

A corollary is the tendency to aging of the upper echelon. The Leninists, like the Hitlerites, were a party of youth when they came to power; but in the absence of any regular procedure for removal, leaders cling to high positions well past their prime, if not into their dotage, and only a new revolution or near-revolutionary violence (as in Stalin's purges) can rejuvenate the state. The age levels of politburos, central committees, and ministries have been generally rising in the communist sphere, from Vietnam to Eastern Europe, with little access to power for persons under age fifty.[3] In the Soviet Union enfeebled gerontocrats, Andropov and Chernenko, succeeded to the top position after Brezhnev had lasted well beyond his capacities; well before his death in November 1982, he could neither check Andropov's gathering power nor quash a scandal involving his own daughter.[4]

Eventually, the overaging of the top level forces change, and there may be a renewal, as under Deng Xiaoping or Gorbachev; but there is nowhere in the absolutist state for persons short of retirement age to retire with dignity, and the youngsters brought forward are in their fifties and sixties. Gorbachev in his first year largely replaced the top echelon, but he promoted very few younger than himself (then fifty-four).[5]

There is a swing back and forth. Each new succession represents something of an opening or opportunity for change. There is a relaxation of structures, but as the new authority is built up, the new chief wishes to distance himself from this initial freedom to make a new start. After the partial renewal, the aging process begins again. It may even be disadvantageous if a young man takes over, because it probably means that there will be little change for very many years.

Quality of leadership is also subject to erosion. It is hard to purge any but the most egregious incompetents, because the organization protects its own. Advancement in the supremely political hierarchy comes mostly through pleasing superiors; there is every temptation to sycophancy, deceit, and intrigue. Patrons protect followers, dismissal of one is a threat to the security of all, and careerists coming to the top favor their own kind.

The top bosses are informed or misinformed by persons wholly dependent on them, and only by a mighty effort could they break out of the cocoon. Kim Il-sung could hardly fail to have been persuaded by chorused repetition that he was godlike, and something similar must occur with all adulated rulers. Romania's Ceausescu presumably believes that the bear he shot was the largest ever bagged in Europe, and the trees are especially verdant where he travels, thanks to spray paint applied before his visit.[6]

Less outlandishly, the whole elite is self-deceived. The ideologists whose business is to persuade must first persuade themselves, and the self-informed party lacks feedback. Unpleasant facts have to be forced on people, who can find endless reasons to deny obvious realities by selective perception; and cognitive dissonance excludes ideas and information that do not harmonize with accepted views. Rationality is perpetually at risk even in the openest society, where conflicting opinions circulate freely and no views are completely protected from criticism; but there is nothing in the communist education to encourage ferreting out disagreeable truths.

The condition of the tightly organized party is the worse because the more cohesive a group is, the less able are its members to deviate from preconceptions. What has been called "group-think"[7]—which amounts to mutually reinforced irrationality with illusions of certainty—thrives on faith in the morality of the group, esteem for unanimity, the ability to ignore outsiders, and a stereotyped view of opponents—all characteristic of the absolutist system. For the party, the ability to believe and to reject doubts is not only acceptable but necessary for organizational solidarity.

## RULERS AND RULED

Marx thought that ownership of the means of production was sufficient to define a governing class, but the elect of the absolutist state not only in effect own all major property but also control the means of coercion and of communication and are tightly organized for their own benefit. They hence form a closed ruling stratum, or a new class which becomes a new nobility,[8] in a society characterized by much snobbery and emphasis on status.[9] Even the lowliest of those who have political standing are superior to ordinary citizens. New cadres are no longer drawn from the poor but from the educated and privileged. The offspring of the new class, who feel entitled by both family and education to everything they get, have a weaker commitment to the system they did not build and feel less driven to justify status by performance. But the elite favor their children, not only because of parental instincts but also because those born to the class are seen as reliable. Special schools lead onto the ladder of success; for example, academies train officers' sons to be officers.[10]

Government without responsibility becomes the enjoyment of the privileged, who acquire the ability to protect themselves both from the arbitrariness of the leader and from demands from below.[11] No devices succeed against the dynamics of position. Chinese rulers tried to choose able servants by permitting all to compete through the examination system, but this theoretically excellent system was corrupted. The Turkish sultanate sought to guarantee the total loyalty of its guardians by drawing them (the Janissaries) from poor, non-Muslim families and rewarding them generously. They were also prohibited from marrying to prevent their passing their position or fortune to their children. But this system, too, became hereditary and totally corrupt.

Once-revolutionary states as diverse as Mexico, the Soviet Union, and China have become increasingly class divided. The separation of elite from masses is most striking in the case of the ostensibly utopian Leninist revolution.[12] Soviet aristocrats live more separated from the masses, both physically and in terms of the goods and services to which they are entitled, than any Western upper class.[13] They enjoy perquisites rather than property, and their privileges are usually screened from view; but the inequality is no less for these reasons. They enjoy entertainments considered sinful for the commoners. Big official cars are exempt from traffic regulations that bear heavily on ordinary folk.[14] The elite are largely immune to the law.[15] There are layers; lower ranking officials compensate for their inferiority to the upper class by asserting their own superiority over ordinary mortals.[16] The aristocratic mentality is also shown by carelessness about industrial safety, the prevention of peasants moving to the cities, the exclusion of almost everyone from residence in the capital, inequalities of ethnic groups, and categories of privilege among workers.

Cuba has seen increased inequality since the maturation of Castroism in the beginning of the 1970s.[17] In China, the turn from Maoism after the Helmsman's demise brought more separation of classes and greater urban-rural differences as a bureaucratic-administrative elite solidified.[18] New recruits for the party are drawn preferentially from the most elite universities. In Eastern Europe, openings for workers or opportunities for their children to move into the managerial-professional class decrease, while barriers rise between commoners and bureaucrats.[19] As in the Third World in general, in mature communist states an upper class strives to live like the world's wealthy while the masses remain poor. There is also an emotional divorce of elite and masses. The former needed people to share their purposes when they were setting up a new state; when the state is fixed, it is not important what people think as long as they can be commanded.[20]

In the first years, or even decades, of the Soviet state, there was much feeling of common endeavor, of building for a better future under the leadership of the party, however grim the present. As late as the death of Stalin, many felt attached enough to the tyrant to weep for his passing, and the crowding of mourners was such as to crush many to death. But rulers and ruled come to have different purposes, ways, and values; and neither side cares much about the other. When Brezhnev died, it seemed that no one but his immediate family wept. Apparently most Russians hardly noticed the passing of the leader whose portraits were as huge as those of Stalin had been.

The authoritarian society claims to be firmly united, and it has ample formal means of binding the people through its multiple controls. But by relieving the rulership of responsibility to the people, it sets those with political position against those without; this basic conflict of interests—to dominate and to be relieved of domination—makes the few into antagonists of the many. This has been clear in Spain, Portugal, and Latin American and Asian dictatorships, and it seems obvious from what little is known of public opinion in Eastern Europe. It has seemingly been true of the Soviet Union, to judge from the warm welcome Nazi invaders initially received from people who had voted unanimously for Stalin's party. However much the people may accept the power over them, compulsion does not make a genuine political community.

## RIGIDITY

The new authoritarian state is fluid and can be reshaped to suit its makers. They are the builders of the new, from the outwardly unprecedented Soviet state of 1917 and 1918 to Hitler's New Order in Nazi-occupied Europe. The Brazilian military enacted a new constitution and thought they would remake their nation, as did General Pinochet in Chile. But innovations turn into accepted ways, and institutions become more rigid than those of more legalistic, pluralistic, or democratic states because authoritarianism means relations of fixed superiority and inferiority.

The rulers lose both the authority and the drive to change, and they probably cannot conceive any serious political change that would suit them. The leader does not come to the top of the huge apparatus by making waves or disturbing superiors. The general secretary, whose powers are superficially unlimited, probably enjoys less political space than a British prime minister or an American president.[21] Any large organization is inherently conservative in its internal order, and in the highly authoritarian state everything pertains to the internal order. The better organized a system is and the more satisfactory it is for its beneficiaries, the more implacable its decay. There is no motivation for reform. Whatever changes the party once proposed have been made or abandoned. It is more important to avoid mistakes than to achieve positive merit. In the cases of dozens of military dictatorships, the coup has proposed a purification of politics and the imposition of a rational order through national discipline; when these things have been attempted and have mostly failed, there remains little to do, and any proposal for radical action would be a reproach to the regime if not a call for a new coup.

The existing state represents the victory of the cause, and failures are to be ascribed to a falling away from earlier virtues—a failure, for example, to follow the teachings of Lenin—and are not to be deemed evidence that Lenin could have erred. Functionaries who have qualified by their mastery of the ideology and unconditional loyalty to party ideals want their underlings and successors to qualify in the same way. Since communist officials respond not to inferiors or equals but to superiors, there is little input from below to those on top.[22]

The state rests on the conviction of its power-holding beneficiaries that it represents the best possible world for them. To injure them brings the raison d'être of the system into question not only for the victims but also for all who count on the rewards of unconditional loyalty. Even in relatively minor matters, it is easier and safer to stick with the tried and trusted. For example, official Soviet culture has remained virtually frozen since 1965, while the Western world has been swept by many fads or fashions. Ballet is fettered for no obvious reason but a generalized dislike for spontaneity and experimentation.

Officials stake out their spheres and build up defensive structures in their fiefdoms. They learn to cooperate for mutual protection and to deal with any policy they dislike, perhaps bowing while ignoring or sabotaging it. Position is an important form of property, so organizations, such as factories, collective farms, and technical institutes, become something like possessions of their directors or directorates. Even a retail clerkship is valuable for the ability to divert scarce goods. It becomes very difficult to carry through any changes seriously threatening any important group of functionaries. Khrushchev failed; his successors avoided trouble by not trying.

"Soviet society is not only stratified but also arranged in a series of enclaves, each insular and impenetrable as a walled city. Every individual's profession places him in a circle of privilege and deprivation, providing him special access to what is within his borders and often denying him what is without." [23] And as long as such little centers are not grossly misused, the central authorities may cease trying to control the lower bureaucracy.[24] Territorial jurisdictions also tend to acquire a little, or perhaps considerable, de facto autonomy. It is less the role of the apparatus to move new policies than to coordinate and mediate among the parts of the state, responding to social forces rather than changing society. Despotism historically has declined by erosion and fractioning of authority, not by increasing the rights of individuals.

## THE LOSS OF PURPOSE

The excuse for imposing total controls on a country in the era of mass communications is a claim to a new truth and better justice for the making of a blissful life. The Soviets were remarkably successful in keeping up an atmosphere of enthusiasm and dedication for many years, thanks to Stalin's "Second Revolution" of collectivization and planned industrialization and to victory in World War II. The belief that the revolution represented a supreme value and the promise of a glorious future was pounded into the people to make it unquestionable as long as Stalin lived. Even in Khrushchev's day there was some vibrancy: the Soviet Union was on its way to the building of a better, happier, utopian way of life. According to the 1961 Party Program, "The Party solemnly promises that this generation of Soviet people shall live under communism" [i.e., nonmonetary society].

But hopes peaked around 1957 and thereafter subsided.[25] Very little utopianism remains in the Soviet Union or any communist country. The failures and broken promises have been too many for the sacrifices, and economic stagnation and social division falsify the fundamental claims of Marxism-Leninism. The party, instead of promising abundance, attacks consumerism and emphasizes collective ideals and military virtues. The "shining future of communism" is no more, in Eastern Europe as in the Soviet Union. The central doctrine of inevitable victory has collapsed under Gorbachev's far-reaching criticism, and the party preaches not ideology but good citizenship.[26] Some Soviet writers proposed that religion should be brought back to restore moral values. The interesting question becomes not what Lenin promised, but where meat or shoes are to be found. A recent survey of Soviet émigrés showed the young to be more critical than their elders of the Soviet system, although the opposite was the case into the late 1940s.[27]

The ideology continues in use as a substitute for reason, a code for communication, a symbolic bond of the elite, and a ready way of avoiding thinking about problems. But it is permeated by cynicism; in the Soviet Union any sign of real belief in Marxism-Leninism may be seen as a sign of naiveté or bad taste.[28] Most of those who attend ideological sessions do so under compulsion.[29] In the 1960s, Poles or Hungarians who disliked the rule of the party still usually expressed adherence to a vague "socialism"; they no longer do so. Thirty years of Mao's moral crusading left people only more alienated from the state and one another; a questionnaire of college students after the Cultural Revolution showed 85 percent believing in fatalism and none in socialism.[30] Even isolated North Korea has become less spartan and has lost confidence in its peculiar virtue.[31]

The Soviet Party Program of 1919 promised a new world; Khrushchev's 1961 version offered a pallid vision of utopia; Gorbachev's in 1985 gave up the goals of communism and promises of victory, proposing hardly anything more radical than the platform of an American political party.[32] The verbal ideology is rehearsed insistently,[33] but it is shallow despite intense indoctrination. The adoration of Stalin in 1953 gave way to de-Stalinization in 1956. The Chinese came rapidly and apparently gleefully from outwardly absolute Maoist dedication to the free-wheeling, get-rich-quick sentiments of the 1980s.

It is entirely to be expected that the urge to social change should give way, as the new possessors settle down, to collective self-interest, stability and security for the apparatus, and nationalism for the country. Yet phrases of worn-out revolutionism are part of the system and cannot be dispensed with. They are consecrated self-righteousness, and their loss would threaten unity. In China too, despite the more pragmatic post-Mao approach, the party needs to keep up at least a pretext of social transformation; otherwise, its right to govern would come into question [34]—arbitrary rule requires arbitrary values. It is fitting, in view of frequent shortages, for the Soviet press to denounce "consumerism," although both the elite and the masses display a passion for consumer goods beyond the worst of the "materialistic West."

Less total authoritarianisms are less tied to doctrine, and they are even less able to sustain enthusiasm. Perón's synthetic creed, *Justicialismo*, which was supposed to outmode communism and capitalism, was exhausted before Perón had been a half-dozen years in office. Franco's unheroic efforts to develop and implant an official philosophy were likewise nugatory long before he died.

A firm and vibrant political idea requires a strong sense of shared endeavor, without which no organizational devices can keep people firmly united. A long-past conflict and the myths built around it cannot sustain forever the spirit needed by the highly inegalitarian mobilizing state.

## CORRUPTION

Any autonomous bureaucracy serves itself, and in the best of governments individual officials use their authority to some extent for their own benefit. But the more authoritarian the system, the greater the possibilities of the misuse of authority, as though by simple geometry: the more the government covers, the more extensive the opportunities for making position profitable.[35] Control of people can always be turned to advantage.

Not only does political coverage of society give opportunities for abuse; so far as the government is imposed, it is illegitimate, and official interests and injunctions lack a moral basis. If the powerful have little respect for their own laws,[36] people are morally free to please themselves. If the state is more or less shameless—as it blatantly is, for example, when the East Germans sell prisoners to West Germany for hundreds of millions of dollars yearly [37]—there is little to restrain its servants' cheating.

Privileges that are morally close to corruption are a regular and authorized part of the authoritarian state, loyalty being rewarded by license. If leaders fight corruption, as they occasionally do—ordinarily halfheartedly except in the aftermath of a change of power at the top— they do so mostly because they do not wish so much of the benefits to go to the underlings. The anticorruption campaign is usually directed against minor villains, although punishing their equally guilty superiors would have more deterrent effect. The party is far more concerned with disloyalty than with the use of power for private benefit. The whole system, after all, is designed for the party's use of power.

In the weakness and insecurity of private enterprise, the official apparatus is almost the only means of personal advancement. To climb the career ladder is easy in the fluidity of a revolution or a disturbance like the Stalinist purges. But when the state settles down and people become fixed in their positions, promotions are slow and officials have less both to hope for and to fear. Then the greedy or ambitious, or perhaps those who merely try to keep up their standard of living, use their position to better themselves materially.[38] The important fact about a job is not the salary but how much is to be made on the side.[39] The Soviet state may thus allow persons to accumulate substantial wealth, although it gives no security against confiscation.

Bribery or influence can open the doors to higher education and the start of a career,[40] and progress thereafter depends to a large extent on relations. Since political power is arbitrary, it can hardly be allocated in any regular fashion. The absolutist state cannot institute a merit civil service, as loyalty and personal affiliation have priority. If positions were won in accord with objective criteria and officials had security of tenure, they would owe their standing to their own qualifications and efforts. They would not owe everything to the party, and their abilities would presumably continue to be valuable in a changed political system. Communist systems may, of course, promote capable persons, but they are always vulnerable to disfavor. Cliques inevitably dominate careers; and clique politics means exchange of favors, discourages honesty, and requires pretense, if not falsification. Honesty is disadvantaged, because those above lack the means, if not the will, to find out the truth.

Misuse of political position occurs in relatively well ordered democratic societies, although it is inconspicuous in some of the well-ordered small countries of Europe, such as Switzerland and Scandinavia. In nondemocratic societies irregular profiteering from political position is almost inescapable; monetary grease may be essential for almost any governmental action or restraint, or at least smooths the transaction. In a circular effect, jobs are valuable, hence they are for sale; and jobholders, having paid for their position, have to use it to remunerate themselves. Petitioners may even be eager to pay without officials having to express demands.[41]

Rewards can be large; various Latin American and African presidents have taken hundreds of millions or billions of dollars. Corruption is less visible in the more tightly controlled totalitarian state, but it is an overwhelming fact.[42] It is worse because the interaction of party and state apparatuses makes legal irregularity the rule; and it ranges from the nurse needing a ruble or two to provide a clean sheet or the freedom of a few to travel abroad and sell the treasures they bring back, to virtually conventional fees for dropping criminal charges. Other communist states are not much different from the Soviet Union, although some, such as Hungary and East Germany, seem to be less affected. China is not exempt; one study showed nearly all families to have been bribe payers in 1981 to an extent averaging one-fifth of their ordinary wages.[43]

In the politically dominated, essentially anomic society, relations of protection are necessary for survival. Corruption is only part of a general amorality, which ranges from occasional sadistic maltreatment and officially protected robbery to expected gifts and deference and friendly exchanges of favors. To some extent illegal practices are useful; the planned economy would come to a halt if managers could not secure materials, transportation, and equipment outside prescribed channels. But corruption represents misuse of resources. In its various aspects, it may be the greatest cause of low productivity in the Third World,[44] and it must be a major reason for economic sluggishness in the Marxist-Leninist states.

Corruption represents an erosion of the political edifice. The reward system becomes partly privatized, and a sort of free-enterprise economy grows up within or alongside the authoritarian state. The mobilizing state that assumed total power is partially immobilized. Illegal activities become more remunerative than legal ones, and outsiders acquire some of the power the ruling group would keep to itself.

The diffusion of power through corruption weakens the state, but it does not create an opposition. Those who profit by misuse of authority have no desire to see it removed. This is also true of those outside the apparatus who gain by lawbreaking—smugglers, black marketeers, and the like—and whose activities are made profitable by the restrictions and failures of the official economy.

## IGNORANCE

The arbitrary authority both hides and deceives. Falsification is inherent in the need to persuade people that the state is something that it is not, and ideology must be defended by coercion. Hence censorship is inevitable. Having set out to stop political attacks, censorship extends to anything distasteful to the authorities. In the Soviet case, for example, natural catastrophes such as drought or floods are unreported, unless too extensive to escape notice or, of course, occurring in the capitalist world. The Soviets (at least prior to Gorbachev's "glasnost") would admit to no problem of political or near-political nature, indeed, to no important disagreement.[45]

The leader is the father, the state is the mother, and the children should trust and obey. A Soviet official, explaining the paucity of information about the Chernobyl nuclear disaster, said, "If we are treating a patient for cancer, we will never tell them. . . . We treat the population like children." [46] Questioning is not useful; it is well not to think beyond practical necessity or idle dreams; and spontaneity is evil. But without spontaneity there is no creativity; and the more complex the society, the greater the need for ventilation and criticism.

The modern "information society" is not at home in the absolutist state. For example, in the Soviet Union and other communist countries copying machines are strictly policed and kept under lock except for authorized personnel. There are few telephones, and their utility is decreased by the near absence of telephone books—the Moscow directory published in 1978 included only state offices and stores. There is no direct dialing between cities, and since 1979 calls abroad have to be placed through an operator. The passion for secrecy also seems to be a major impediment to the large-scale introduction of computers—a proliferation of printouts is a little like freedom of the press. Large libraries are accessible by permission only, different sections requiring different clearances and "need to know." There is a shortage of data; statistics are limited and unreliable. After Stalin the Soviet Union, with some confidence in its future, began divulging more about the economy and society. Under Brezhnev, however, there was much less accurate information than ten to twenty years before.[47] Planning became practically a system of concealment.[48]

Education is weighed down by indoctrination. The communist state is proud of promoting literacy, but schools discourage inquisitive thinking. Higher education is professionally very specialized: one becomes not a civil engineer but a ceramics engineer. It is more serious that higher education becomes the prey of politics. A higher degree is deemed a political qualification, and directorship of an academic institution is prestigious; when the politically worthy receive higher degrees and retiring magnates take over rectorships, the result is politicization, favoritism, and replacement of intellectual by political criteria. Education prospers only in the propaganda of the regime. Even high leaders have little real knowledge of the outside world.[49] People lose interest in affairs concerning which they are not informed, and to be brilliant is suspect.

With the lack of innovative capacity, creativity is stultified. Despite great expenditures, Soviet science declines. In a few years, 1975 to 1981, the number of scientific items in Soviet journals decreased by 20 percent, while their number in the world was rising by 67 percent, and citation abroad of Soviet scientific findings shrank even more.[50]

Credulity flourishes. The Soviet press reports all manner of paranormal phenomena, as well as fossilized salamanders that come to life, men over 150 years old, abominable snowmen, touch healers, and so forth, in contradiction to the official materialistic philosophy. The polygraph is useless on Soviet citizens because lying is taken for granted and arouses no guilt feelings. Truth is operational, one says what seems appropriate, and the government does not expect people to tell the truth.[51]

In a large society with a strong intellectual tradition, such as that of Russia, some individuals uphold intellectual integrity and independence, perhaps actively assert themselves against the prevalent order, and find freedom in moral rebellion and rejection of the official falsification.[52] But they are few, lack information, and in this context may be seen as irrational—mentally ill in the view of Soviet psychiatry. Intelligence suffers under political suffocation and disincentives to thinking.

## IMPOVERISHMENT

Shortage of information hinders not only the modernization of the economy and the furtherance of immensely complex industrialization but also the basics of production. The government, trying to control too much, cannot adequately define needs and priorities. Planned production is feasible only if it is clear what should be produced (as fairly well occurs in wartime or with military production), but planners lack knowledge of the requirements for millions of products. The controlled economy, as in the Soviet Union, suffers less from lack of goods than from lack of the right kinds of goods. Moreover, controllers have no way of calculating rational prices; only a market can do this reasonably well.

It is difficult to motivate innovation on the part of managers; entrepreneurship is for the illegal sector. The idea of performance criteria is contrary to party dominance. Responsibility gets lost in the bureaucratic apparatus, and state monopoly has the vices of private monopoly.[53] Soviet writers admit that workers lose the urge to produce; they perform poorly because there is little incentive to do better and take their reward partly in leisure.[54] In the words of a Czech philosopher turned factory worker, "In this 'socialist' society the energy of the people is used in scheming against society more than on behalf of society." [55]

The revolution promised not merely to lift Russia out of its secular backwardness but also to propel it far ahead of the decadent West. Something of this dream continued in the euphoria of victory in World War

II and reconstruction. But the performance of communist states has been poor to mediocre by world standards after the ideological drive is exhausted and the effects of radical mobilization are spent. Their real performance is poorer than indicated by statistics furnished by themselves because figures are subject to inflation at all stages, and quantitative data also fail to take into account quality, choice, and availability of goods. Central planners cannot have a very accurate notion of what is produced.

While output growth is modest, modernization lags and the technological gap increases. The number of robots in Soviet factories is comparable to those in factories in Finland. In the 1960s many persons thought the computer would come to the rescue of central planning, but the electronic and computer revolution has been a disaster for the communist economic system.

Investments in housing, medicine, and education have been steadily reduced and are below the level of a generation ago. There are worsening shortages of many basic materials.[56] Soviet industry uses 2.5 times as much energy as that of the Japanese for the same amount of production.[57] Agricultural shortcomings are notorious; although agriculture is relatively simple technologically, it defies the planners because of variability and unpredictability of conditions. Hence 60 percent of Soviet potatoes come from the inherently very uneconomical private garden plots. It is difficult to take into account long-range agricultural needs, such as checking soil erosion.

There is a huge black or gray market in goods the official economy fails to provide, not only for many necessities but also for variety, novelty, and thrill.[58] Private enterprise is especially strong in the moonshine industry. According to a Soviet report, in one district nearly every household had its still.[59] Nonstate construction workers, generally using government machinery and materials, earn three or four times as much as ordinary industrial workers; but they are occasionally punished.[60]

Inflation is denied and held down for some goods—especially for foodstuffs—by costly subsidies; but it goes on steadily, making Soviet figures of output growth unrealistic. It is partly concealed by product change—a higher price for new packaging or the same price for an adulterated product—but was apparently quite comparable to that in the Western world in the early 1980s. Irresponsible authority makes counterproductive decisions; for example, the use of amalgam for dental fillings was abolished in 1984 in favor of plastic, which lasts only about a year and requires six times as much dentistry.[61]

Health care, supposedly gratis, becomes either poor or costly because of the need for gratuities; medicine is kept functional only by the "second economy."[62] Mortality rises, especially for working-age males; between 1964 and 1980 life expectancy for men declined by six years, to about sixty (against seventy to seventy-five in the West), and the overall death rate rose from 6.9 to 10.8.[63] Through the 1950s and early 1960s, life expectancy rose in Eastern Europe; since then it has halted or declined, apparently because of increased tobacco and liquor consumption as well as inferior health care.[64] According to Soviet reports, workers in some regions averaged a bottle of vodka per day.[65] In sum, an American employed in the Soviet Union characterized it as "an exhausted society trying to catch up with the West while hiding its backwardness from foreign eyes," and "the most developed of the world's undeveloped nations." [66]

Third World communist countries, such as Vietnam and Mozambique, have fallen into extreme depression. Cuba (hurt, to be sure, by very low sugar prices) has lagged badly despite Soviet aid approximating one-third of its GNP. In 1959 it was third in Latin America in per capita product; two decades of Castroism with Soviet assistance lowered it to fifteenth place. Poland has suffered a virtual collapse, with Romania not far behind. Alienation may be so intense, as in Poland, that people refrain from doing for themselves because it would help the party.[67] China is the principal exception, as it has since the death of Mao become one of the rapidly growing nations. Relaxation of controls and inviting people to profit by their work have enabled the country to recoup losses of years of stagnation.

The malfunctioning of the economy is no doubt the chief cause of discontent in absolutist-totalitarian countries. Many persons would like to be freer to travel, to obtain forbidden books, to read informative newspapers, and to have some say about who governs them. But such matters hardly seem to trouble most people very long; if life is regulated, it is comforting. Shortages and the poor quality of goods and services are more annoying, especially when material standards decline. More important, the leaders are concerned with poor performance of the economy because it is the basis of national strength and standing in the world and the foundation of military power. Hence economic failure is the propellant of reform.

## REFORM

Leaders must perceive, albeit probably confusedly, the need for change; they have trained specialists who advocate reform measures, and their legal powers are unlimited. Why do they not take obvious steps to rationalize the management of the state?

One might ask this question not only of communist leaders but also of various Third World dictators whose regimes begin to totter and who obviously can save themselves only by timely housecleaning and reforms. Despite urgings from their foreign friends, the shah of Iran, Anastasio Somoza of Nicaragua, Ferdinand Marcos of the Philippines, and many others stubbornly stood pat and in due course lost everything. The reason is partly self-deception; they could not believe that they had done so badly. But regimes that know what has to be done cannot remake themselves, because significant reforms would undercut the pillars on which the rulership rests. Marcos of the Philippines, for example, could not take abusive monopolies away from his cronies because they were his source of power; and if he tried to discipline a few, others would take fright and withdraw support, leaving him to the mercy of unforgiving enemies.

Problems are even more deeply rooted in the absolutist system crafted over a long period to maximize party power. For example, it is obvious that Soviet consumers would be better served by allowing much small-scale private enterprise, especially in services; and some is permitted in the more relaxed countries of the bloc, Poland and Hungary. But any serious relaxation would be injurious to the power of the party, the chief and most profitable business of which is the management of production.[68] The managers are trained to political, not economic needs. They and the controllers and planners would become superfluous in a liberalized economy, which needs entrepreneurs, not bureaucratic managers. The consumers who would benefit from a slackening of planning have little voice.

Those who have a voice see many reasons for maximum control. The strongest is that the chief claim of the system, economic justice unattainable in the capitalist world, would be shadowed by burgeoning inequality. Market economy spells "spiritual pollution" for Russians as for Chinese. Workers are said to defend socialistic practices such as pay not tied to productivity, fixed prices, and paternalistic benefits.[69] Some of the elite may not be altogether unhappy if the masses stand in line or do without goods readily available to those who hold the necessary tickets.

Economists in the Soviet Union have been permitted in recent years to publish strong criticisms of the economic system, and they are aware of the good results of loosening controls in Hungary and China. But they see, especially in the latter, inflation (there is no good way either to fix prices or to let them float freely in the semimarket economy), unemployment (which results when enterprises are allowed to prune their labor force), increased tensions of inequality (which gives independence from the party), and corruption nourished by the wealth of the new entrepreneurs. There are, indeed, severe problems of mixing controls over the bulk of the economy with freedom of enrichment and opportunities for misuse of authority. Blending socialism and capitalism is problematic where the idea of legal boundaries is weak.[70] Officials turned entrepreneurs misuse their powers, and capitalism is problematic.

It is always easy to defend the ideologically sanctioned ways, and socialism is vastly more important than catering to consumers. The party ideologues—who are not philosophers of Marxism-Leninism but watchdogs of party domination—hate private enterprise because it conflicts with their ingrained values; it must annoy cadres to see Muscovites swarming around black market dealers in Western records or mobs in Beijing rioting to buy televisions and jewelry. Not less important, private enterprise competes with their state enterprises, shows up their inefficiency, and outbids them for labor and materials. To expect the bureaucracy to foster market-oriented reform is like having the goats raise the cabbages.

Loosening of controls suggests possibilities of good living outside the party framework and hence makes loyalty less essential, weakens the party grip, and decreases political privileges, such as access to special stores. Even if the higher authorities would tolerate modest private enterprises for the sake of the economy, local controllers would tax and squeeze them. The party bosses are probably correct in believing that privatization will lead to abuses, profiteering, and tax evasion, because people have grown accustomed to avoiding the law and cheating the state. Private wealth is dangerous, moreover, because it would permit private persons to buy political influence.

Similarly, it is not for ideological reasons that the inefficient collective farms cannot be broken up. Soviet peasants have often shown that they can double harvests or better when less submerged in the collective, and a variety of arrangements could easily be squared with ideology, such as the small collectives favored shortly after the revolution or individual cultivation with cooperative ownership of heavy machinery. But the collective farms are, in effect, property of the party bosses and not to be surrendered. Their dissolution would deprive supervisory functionaries of their functions; worse, it would permit people to prosper independently of the party and so reduce both the party role and the compulsions to conform.

The nationality problem enters too: if non-Russian peasants, especially of Central Asia, were released from the collectives, it would be harder to prevent nationalistic stirrings. Any important degree of economic freedom would nourish political dissidence, especially in areas of minority nationalities that are already inclined to believe they are exploited by Moscow. Moreover, the Soviet Union, as leader and guardian of the bloc or empire and maker and model of socialist justice, must stand uncompromisingly for the pure "socialist" faith and reject anything that may appear to be a compromise with the enemy system.[71]

### Prospects for Reform

It was commonly assumed that Gorbachev, as a younger, more vigorous, and intelligent leader, would make major changes in economic management, as seems essential to bring the Soviet Union really into the modern age. His speeches indicated a keen awareness of the gravity of the problems. But he produced no real economic program, and he has sought not to relax but to improve political controls. He has talked of going back to Lenin; and instead of structural change, he would improve the Soviet Union by getting people to behave better, tightening labor discipline, emphasizing collectivism and dedication, and trying to banish vodka. Being unable to abolish the parallel economy, he has tried to register, regulate, and tax it.

But Brezhnev for many years talked of discipline, while discipline was crumbling around him.[72] More political education is not a promising remedy for the failure of political education, and the results of exhortation are not likely to be deep unless Gorbachev can offer people a greater share in the management and benefits of the state. But this would require transferring power away from the apparatus on which he rests. Hence Gorbachev has attacked symptoms, not causes, of failure, as in cracking down on the parallel economy.[73] Castro similarly decreed the abolition of farmers' markets as seedbeds of capitalism.[74]

The Soviet Union has attempted to improve the economic system many times since it began to slow down markedly in the early 1960s; but the measures taken have never been far-reaching, and they have never brought any important improvement.[75] The decades-long effort to increase management initiative and central control at the same time is futile.[76] Nor is there much hope for a technocratic solution—improvement by rationalization and technology—because the values of the system are not technical but political. Genuine concessions to economic autonomy—entrepreneurship for profit—are contrary to the first axiom of communism, the subordination of the individual to the regime.

Major economic reform seems to require political change, as the absolutist-polity and the absolutist-economy system support each other. But political reform is at least equally difficult. For example, an electoral contest would clearly be beneficial for public morale and the legitimacy of party rule. Even if all candidates are party approved and represented similar philosophies, an open competition of personalities would enliven the now ceremonial "elections." But in such a contest, winners would owe their places partly to their own merits and to the voters, not merely to the favor of the party. Hence this is difficult in the Soviet Union, although Poland and Hungary can permit a few more candidates than positions to be filled in nearly powerless bodies because the political order is guaranteed by the Soviet presence. In 1970 and after, the Cuban party sought to gain legitimacy from elections, but in a few years the idea was abandoned.

A possible step in the direction of political change is the openness or *glasnost* proclaimed and practiced by Gorbachev. Many books, plays, and motion pictures long held under censorship have been released, and the press has received new freedom to report shortcomings and many unpleasant things. This relaxation, however, is relative; criticism of party privilege was quickly halted. There has been no latitude for pluralistic organizations; much of the new freedom is mostly for the elite, not the mass audience; and all concessions could be withdrawn at any time.

Nonetheless, the idea that people may be able to speak out once allowed cannot be easily stamped out; and no regime is immune to change. Some hints of the Soviet future may be seen in Yugoslavia, Hungary, and China. In the first, the impetus to reform was the 1948 quarrel with Stalin and the desire to differentiate Yugoslavia by legitimating its brand of communism and to secure popular backing; relaxation was not threatening to Tito's position after the break because nationalistic support was strong and the system was so new that vested interests had not been built up.

Since Tito's death, the federal structure and the difficulty of domination by any one ethnic group (Serbs being slightly over one-third of the population) have been the principal factors in considerably easing the system. Yet the effort to reform economic management while keeping the political monopoly of the party has not been entirely successful. Although Yugoslavia has far more material glitter than most of the Soviet bloc, the average workday was 3.5 hours in 1985, and the standard of living decreased 30 percent from 1980 to 1985. Exports, productivity, and industrial output declined, more than a million were unemployed, and the income level of Slovenia is eight times that of Kosovo. Party dogmatists grumbled about betrayal of the revolution by creeping capitalism, and dissent is irregularly repressed. It is not a very encouraging example for communist reform. In the face of growing pluralism, a high official stated, "We will not allow any tendencies to pluralism. We have to defend the interests of the establishment." [77]

Hungary has undertaken important reforms since 1968, legalizing private services and permitting considerable private farming and small-scale production. The nonstate sector, thanks to large-scale corruption, may comprise a third of the economy.[78] No less important, state farms and factories have much latitude to buy and sell freely, produce partly on their own initiative and discretion, fix wages, and go bankrupt if unprofitable. Private employment is much more profitable than state employment, to the neglect of the latter. In consequence, Hungary has suffered inflation, growing inequality, and a decline in real wages after 1980, although it enjoys abundance by Soviet bloc standards. At the same time, there has been political softening, with some freedom of speech and travel [79] and slightly meaningful elections. But everyone knows that the Soviet Union sets limits.

The reforms of Deng Xiaoping have been even more successful than those in Hungary in rapidly raising average standards of living, especially for the peasantry. China has the usual problem, however, of irregular enrichment and corruption, as politics conflicts with economic rationality and there is little comprehension of the rule of law. Because of numerous strictures, foreign investment has been far less successful than anticipated.[80] Economic liberalization has been stubbornly resisted by a sector of the party and has not been accompanied by political relaxation except for increased freedom of criticism and some local electoral contests. Deng has felt it necessary to reaffirm the value of "Mao Zedong–Thought." Prolonged student demonstrations calling for more democracy in December 1986 brought out the dilemma of communist reformers: for modernization and economic strength, it is necessary to educate the new elite and expose them to foreign (that is, Western) political ideas. Apparently alarmed, Deng's government reverted to denunciation of the Western evil and reined in the reformers.

The new policies are less secure because they are very largely the work of one aged man whose character was formed in precommunist times, assisted by victims of the Cultural Revolution. A new generation educated under communism and not scarred by repression may be less prepared to carry on pragmatic policies. However, there can be economic and even some political relaxation without endangering basic authoritarian rule. The government of Taiwan, under far more pressure to democratize itself, has allowed a remarkably freewheeling economy and permitted fairly meaningful elections yet kept central rulership unimpaired.

## VIABILITY

It might be logically supposed that the society governed by and for a small elite without responsibility or clear limits on arbitrary action must rapidly degenerate to a condition of bare subsistence for the masses, superstitious ignorance, dull routine, total corruption, capricious oppression, and parasitic luxury for a few at the center. These have been the circumstances of decadent empires, such as the Roman in its later generations or the Chinese in the decline of dynasties. Some African countries, such as Idi Amin's Uganda, have seemed totally misgoverned. Such is by no means the case, however, of the Soviet Union or its satellites, of China, or of numerous other more or less dictatorial, if not totalitarian, countries.

Authoritarian or imperial systems bespeak collective selfishness and idealized deceit, but they also have values of faith, order, and security. Soviet citizens, guaranteed a job of sorts and almost immune to discharge, are spared many of the uncertainties and conflicts of the Western world. The economy works, more or less—in the case of the Soviet Union and its European satellites rather well by world standards. People are tolerably fed, clothed, and provided with some amenities; and standards of living have tended to improve over the years. Modernization gradually advances, even in Stalinist Albania.

In noneconomic matters, the totalist system may be decidedly successful. The performance of communists and Nazis in war was superb. The totalitarian order is in principle like an army, and armies sometimes function very well. In a related area, the Soviet Union, with inferior technology, has developed a broader and better planned space program than the United States.[81] The communists generally do well in strictly political competition; for example, the Soviets with fewer resources seem to wield more influence than the United States in the United Nations. Communist states, moreover, know how to make the most of their achievements; for example Castro's Cuba has convinced the world of great merits in education and health, although the record is no better than that of other Latin American states that receive little credit.[82]

Refugees from the Soviet Union often complain that they had a "better cultural life" at home, while they bemoan the anarchy of the West.[83] Soviet citizens who manage with great difficulty to get out sometimes return—although, having tasted life in the West, they may change their minds and want out again. Like the Caesars, the Soviet authorities provide many and sometimes excellent circuses. A very extensive and well-supported sports program engages youthful spirits.[84] Although the system of justice spares party people and treats harshly not only political dissidents but also those accused of common crimes, in ordinary matters, such as family affairs, housing (a major subject of litigation), and property disputes, it is fair, accessible, and far more expeditious than American courts.[85] The Soviets make concessions to democratic principles at the lower level, not only holding pseudoelections but also inviting discussion of promotions of officials and organizing popular participation in local affairs and law enforcement.

The most gangsterish government does something for many and much for at least a few. Strong governments seldom squeeze their people as much as they might, or as much as many officials would probably like; and they usually allow people to petition for redress. Even the abysmally misgoverned Turkish Empire provided some justice and security and protected traders in order to obtain money to pay its soldiers.[86] Murderous Pol Pot regimes, even those on the level of Nguema Macias, scourge of Equatorial Guinea until 1980, are exceptional; most dictatorships, from Hungary to Chile, allow the large majority to exist fairly normally. Governments without constitutional limitations may even, as in the already noted cases of Taiwan, Singapore, and South Korea, restrain the state, provide a good environment for productive enterprise, educate, and promote social mobility. Nationalistic, meritocratic, and egalitarian, they mix market incentives with state guidance for the world's best economic growth.[87] Holding wages down, repressing unions, and facilitating production, the military government of Brazil fostered something of an economic miracle in 1968 to 1974 and earned great popularity.[88]

Authoritarian leaders may behave decently because they perceive the wisdom of providing incentives and making concessions. Political leaders, like other humans, envision themselves doing good, for which they will be praised and thanked after they have ceased to exercise sway. It is sobering for newly installed autocrats to observe the rapid dismantling of the cult of their predecessor. There is some noblesse oblige in imperial rule, a claim to lofty purpose and service to the people, the counterpart of the popular ideal of kingly benevolence giving order and stability, or the Confucianist Mandate of Heaven conditioned on service to the people.

Having attained their material goals, leaders probably seek to fulfill a faith or philosophy. Those educated in Christianity or Buddhism or other religions have surely felt at least a little responsibility toward those over whom they have shepherdship. It is claimed in communist countries that the elect necessarily serve the people because they are the best trained in Marxism-Leninism, and this is not totally false. At least for a few, especially those who are dedicated to the system and have risen rapidly in it, there is a sense of fulfillment in carrying out the endlessly repeated purposes. Just as Soviet officials appear to be sincerely convinced that anything anti-Soviet is sinful, there seems to be a feeling that what contributes to the well-being of the people and so to Soviet power and prestige is virtuous.

Although it is comforting for leaders to believe that they are acting nobly, the ideological factor is nonetheless marginal. It is too easy for persons in high places, whom no one is going to remind of the conflict between policies and moral principles, to find a justification for anything. "Reasons of state" or "military needs" can excuse any crime. If leaders have doubts, loyal subordinates will provide a thousand reasons; and it is easy to forget a duty to those with whom one feels nothing in common. Nazis in charge of death camps doubtless thought they were acting according to some kind of morality.

## FOREIGN INFLUENCE

More important than idealism is the fact that there is no isolated empire in the modern world. Radio goes everywhere; jamming is not completely effective, and it adds to the attractiveness of the exotic message. A survey of Soviet émigrés found that 77 percent of blue-collar workers and 96 percent of professionals listened to foreign broadcasts.[89] Foreign coverage has been a prime factor for the morale of dissidents in the Soviet Union and Eastern Europe. The Polish Solidarity movement would have been impossible without it.

Western television reaches a broad band of Soviet Eastern Europe and Estonia in the Soviet Union. It is increasingly accessible throughout the Soviet sphere, as it becomes easier to rig rooftop antennas for satellite broadcasts and the slackening of the state permits getting the necessary materials and technical assistance to install them. It is possible that a large fraction of the people, especially the better placed, will come to rely on foreign broadcasts. East Germany has long since surrendered, probably with good effects.

Competition has obviously made the Soviet press and radio more informative; Western reporting, for example gave the impetus for fuller reporting of the Chernobyl nuclear accident.[90] East German television has been driven to make itself a virtual copy of West German television, except for the content of news reporting. With a rather wide window open to the world, the Soviet system cannot be the same.

Freer access to foreign entertainment undermines ideology, but it lessens a major grievance and may even make official propaganda more credible. People learn not only about material abundance in the West (of which they may have an exaggerated idea already) but also about strikes, disorders, and sundry problems, reports of which in the local press might be discounted.

Perhaps more significant are the foreign contacts promoted by the state itself. Commercial and other contacts across the borders are essential for a modern state, and many influential people in would-be exclusive states are exposed to foreign influences and values. They transmit ideas and attitudes if they do not carry or smuggle literature. At the same time, large numbers—in the Soviet case, hundreds of thousands—of émigrés and their families keep up some contact by letter or telephone with people in the homeland.

People, especially the upper classes, are everywhere at least slightly aware of world opinion and standards. Leaders have some notion of what the world thinks of them, and they wish to enjoy the respect, perhaps the esteem, of the international community. Latin American or African dictator-presidents, flattered at home, want the good opinion of their peers abroad as vindication of their worth, and they would have their governments regarded as legitimate if not democratic. Marxist-Leninist leaders desire to stand well with the "socialist community" and even more so with the prestigious West; it has obviously been important for Soviet general secretaries to feel that their state is accepted as the peer of the United States.

The outside world also gives feedback and provides information the monistic state cannot furnish itself. Just as the world market helps socialist planners fix prices, the world news tells the leaders much about themselves that they would otherwise not know. They can ignore the foreign press or dismiss it as biased, but they find it interesting—far more readable and lively than their own—and they enjoy access to it.

The authoritarian state can neither compete with nor fully exclude attractive foreign goods and modes. Marxist-Leninist states have spent much energy combating Western music, art, and various styles; to some extent they have surrendered and allow imports or imitations. A large fraction of Soviet youth, especially of the privileged classes, are fans of Western pop culture, which they acquire in any possible way—clothes, books, records, and a thousand things bespeaking a more sophisticated culture. Smuggled videotapes can easily be copied, and there are technicians to make electronic adaptations.[91] Such material treasures do not translate into longings for democracy, but they may make the pretensions of "scientific socialism" a trifle ridiculous.

The government virtually concedes intellectual inferiority as it looks abroad for technological improvement. This is necessary to keep the economy from falling disastrously behind; it is even more essential for military strength. To shut down contacts, as Stalin did, is to invite backwardness. Equally, the politicization of education is checked by the necessity of objective science to manage a modern economy, if not to construct strategic weapons.

## No State Is Alone

Even the largest and strongest states live in a competitive, if not dangerous, universe, the effects and influence of which cannot be entirely excluded. However imperial any government would like to be, it cannot without endangering its own existence remove itself from an international system in some ways more interlocked than state systems of the past. All countries are subject to the stimulation and restraints that historic universal empires sought to banish.

A modern government is unlikely to be allowed to become so very bad as the most rotten empires of the past. The regimes of Pol Pot and Idi Amin, for example, were ended by invasions from Vietnam and Tanzania, invasions that were made possible by the extreme brutality of the tyrants. The Soviet Union is not likely to be invaded, barring an incredible degree of rotting; but it might fear a dissident movement in Central Asia or the Ukraine, encouraged and assisted from across the border.

Even if the Soviet Union could count itself physically secure, it has deep pride to sustain; and not only the leaders but the masses find strength exhilarating and weakness humiliating. Actively competitive authoritarianisms, like those of Sparta, Prussia, or Japan after the Meiji Restoration, can be strong indeed under an oligarchy aware of overwhelming national need. Somewhat in the same way, the oligarchic imperial Japanese government after the Meiji Restoration undertook systematically to borrow Western learning and techniques; and it industrialized and modernized Japan sufficiently well to become a formidable antagonist for the United States in 1941. Nonliberal but orderly Bismarckian Germany likewise showed outstanding economic growth during the two generations preceding 1914. The Nazis so pounded into the people the sense of all Germans together—"Ein Volk, ein Reich, ein Fuehrer"—dedicated to the common destiny, as to make them excellent fighters in a bad cause, prepared to endure unspeakable hardships for a degraded leadership.

The Soviet Union does best in the areas most subject to international competition: sports and the military. The Soviet leader, Gorbachev, campaigning to raise production, tells the people they must work harder for the national defense. Renovation of the Soviet economy might come out of the dismal recognition that China, with a more open economy, is outpacing the Soviet Union and is on the way to relegating it to fourth place in the world. Pride in national strength is a major Soviet asset, when Marxist revolutionary inspiration is long since dead. It is the excuse for shortages: "We must do without because we are threatened by the evil powers outside. If we work well, we can get the better of the proud Americans; but sloth, carelessness, disorder, and self-indulgence play into the hands of imperialism." The arms race not only drives military production to high quality but also generates concern for the general health of the economy.[92]

The image of the endangered motherland translates into the international struggle of clashing social systems; and rivalry with the United States seems to be a chief cause of keeping the cumbersome system functional. If there were no external enemy, the Soviets would have to fabricate one. The we-group feeling of confrontation gives legitimacy to the government: to oppose it is to put oneself at the service of the evil "bourgeois" abroad. Stalin said that the enemies of socialism were becoming more desperately aggressive as they were losing out. The reverse may be true if the absolutist state becomes more truculent as its inappropriateness for a modern technological civilization becomes more marked.

Conflict was the heart of the Nazi or fascist way; and military dictatorships, especially when insecure, have often had recourse to external quarrels. For example, in 1978 the Argentine military regime made much of the dispute with Chile over some valueless islets by the Strait of Magellan and in 1982 undertook to fortify itself by seizing the national irredenta, the Falkland (Malvinas) Islands. This was momentarily successful, as Argentines of all persuasions rallied to the national cause. In a different way, Taiwan has been under great pressure ever since the defeat on the mainland in 1949. The outstanding educational, social, and economic performance of the government coming out of the ineffective autocratic regime that lost the mainland is to be explained largely in terms of felt needs for unity and dedication in the face of the power of the communist mainland. The one-party regime of Singapore has been helped to honest and capable government by the psychology of a small state formed with a siege mentality and surrounded by alien peoples to whom the Chinese majority in Singapore feel superior.[93]

Why external pressure and dangers sometimes evoke the strengths of the integrated authoritarian order and sometimes fail to do so is difficult to explain. Thus, in the Vietnamese war, the North Vietnamese were very effective, but the South Vietnamese regime failed to mobilize, wasted energies, and was destroyed. The Chinese Nationalists in 1945 had a far better position than the Communists under Mao, with international recognition and much larger and better equipped forces. But they broke down in corruption and inefficiency; only when remnants retreated to Taiwan did they pull themselves into shape to defend their way of life.

If the leadership is reasonably enlightened, however, the political shortcomings of the internally noncompetitive state can be offset by external competition and the challenges that continually grow in the modern world. For this reason, closed-elite societies are inherently more inclined to hostility toward other societies. Conflict does not have to be with philosophically different powers; to the contrary, one closed society (such as China or Albania) may see the principal danger in another with the same basic ideology and a similar party-led regime (that is, the Soviet Union). But contest with an external force takes the place of open internal political contest.

## BREAKDOWN

Although the outside world drives the monocratic society to modernize and refurbish itself, we do not know how effectively it can do so over a long period. Modernization, although it provides improved means of coercion and organization, is basically contrary to the extreme authoritarian society and government. It is not clear whether the absolutist state can prevent indefinitely the creeping petrifaction of the apparatus, the politicization of education, the stultification of intelligence, and the demoralization of society.

The prospects are not encouraging. Khrushchev tried to open a little and in some ways to modernize Soviet society, but the trend of the past decade has been mixed. Contacts between Russians and foreigners have been curtailed; by comparison with the exuberant youth festival of 1957, that of 1985 was sadly dead and dry. It is difficult really to check the self-seeking of the officialdom or convert the call of patriotism into reality in a society riddled with sham. The state cannot fully claim legitimacy as long as it pretends to base itself on an unmodern and largely irrelevant mythology.

Scores of empires facing external attack in their time of decadence have failed to respond adequately. Their weaknesses, like those of ailing Third World dictatorships, have been apparent, yet the political system has been unable to make the obviously necessary adjustments and has eventually succumbed. The Soviet Union in this regard is especially handicapped. China, like Yugoslavia, may have possibilities of adaptation without grievous loss; for the Soviet-dominated realm, the way to serious change requires a sacrifice still too painful to contemplate, the sacrifice of Russian supremacy.

Elites are not overthrown unless they are thoroughly demoralized, as in Russia in 1917, Mexico in 1910, and Cuba in 1959. Of this there is no sign in the Soviet Union or Eastern Europe. The communist elite has sometimes become violently divided, as in China during the Cultural Revolution, in Grenada in 1983 before the American occupation, and in the civil war in South Yemen in 1985. But a state lasting generations, such as that of the Soviets, seems to build more stability into itself.

While it holds together, the decaying imperial system develops its compensations. The slackening of central control permits a little autonomy and independent spirit in the provinces. Consumers' needs in the Soviet Union are increasingly met by the black or gray markets and unauthorized but tolerated enterprise, just as the planning system functions thanks to dealers and fixers. When a few discontented intellectuals are allowed to emigrate, the opposition loses much of its leadership. A little freedom of criticism reduces tensions and improves morale. Institutions acquire a bit of autonomy and function better. When the center can no longer command, a partially pluralist society grows up with enough flexibility to satisfy many needs. It would be safest to predict a fairly long life for the Soviet system.

But a long life is not forever. The best organized imperial dynasties have hardly lasted much more than two hundred years without a major breakdown, usually much less. Change rushes much more rapidly in modern times; and the Soviet Union, as the oldest communist state, has been overtaken by visible decadence in a single generation. Judging from comparisons with past empires, one may doubt that the Leninist state will survive to its centennial.

Rupture of the legal continuity of any authoritarian government is inevitable at intervals, probably of decades at most. Where there is no way for the system to renew itself legally, as the democracy can through regular elections, groups and families make positions in the state their property; and they become less efficient and probably more corrupt with passing years. Discontents and the desire for change grow, above all because of the failure of the economy to fulfill expectations; and the morale of the elite wears down. The Poles in 1980 to 1981 showed how a rather young communist party could disintegrate in the face of popular disappointment.

The rupture of the authoritarian continuity may be slight or severe, bringing moderate or deeper renewal. In the former case one speaks of a coup; in the latter, of revolution. After the collapse of Chinese dynasties, years, even decades, of turbulence and anarchy made possible a wholly new start and the establishment of a new dynasty to last a century or so.[94] In a different way, Mexico, installing a new president with near dictatorial powers every six years accompanied by a massive overturn of personnel at high levels, has largely avoided the decay usual in prolonged dictatorship. But there has been much continuity of the elite for half a century, and it has gradually become less responsible and more self-seeking.

Commonest are palace coups that get rid of only the outworn dictator-leader and a few henchmen, doing little to refresh the system. There has already been such a break in the Soviet Union: on the death of Stalin, a group of seven insiders, including Khrushchev, Malenkov, and several whom Stalin was about to purge, set aside the existing party Presidium and asserted their power by no authority except their command of the police. There followed a decade of mildly renewed Soviet idealism and the reforms of Khrushchev, which his successors characterized as "hare-brained." But discontent was not strong enough or the system was not sufficiently discredited for change to go very deep, and Khrushchev was ousted by the conservative bureaucratic forces. If a clique should seize the reins in some future time of disillusionment and uncertainty, they might conceivably proclaim a new government.

The longer the period of decay and the worse the condition of the country, the more likely that pressures for change will come from outside the center. The Poles (1980 to 1981) and the Czechs (1968) showed that communist controls can collapse in a troubled atmosphere. The Russians have also shown themselves capable of rebellion in the past. But whereas communism is antinational for most Eastern Europeans, for Russians it will continue to jibe with nationalism unless the conviction should grow that communism is a cause of weakness, backwardness, and discredit in the world.

It is not easy, however, to imagine popular pressures bringing a turnover of the entrenched Soviet elite. On the contrary, the deeper the discontent the stronger the fear of "forces of darkness." More probable than any sort of mass movement is that the ruling party may lose the ability to control the armed forces. The Soviet army seemed to be gaining a greater voice at the top until Gorbachev—whose Politburo has no representative of the military but three of the KGB—and the army would differ markedly from other armies if it did not resent the political role of the police organization.

As the economy deteriorates, it may become difficult for the party to satisfy the wants of the military and its needs for the posture of a superpower rivaling America. In this case, party management of the army would become difficult; and the soldiers might well, like those of many Third World countries, deem it their duty to cleanse the rot from the Kremlin. This would mean liquidation of the leftovers of the revolutionary order.

Militocracy in the Soviet Union and other communist states would, however, not mean full renewal. In all probability, the apparatus, with its infinity of vested interests, would remain essentially in place, subject to some purging and reimposition of discipline; in the Soviet society there is no one to take the place of the exhausted elites and cadres of the official apparatus. Really to rejuvenate the society would require a deeper change and more pervasive violence, perhaps like Stalin's hammering of the 1930s, perhaps another revolution like that of 1917 to 1920. But this would become possible only after defeat in war. The likely, perhaps inevitable, outcome of the Soviet experiment in evolution toward more normal politics will be like that of the Third World today: The grip of the party becomes more parasitic and weakens. Minority nationality discontent rises, and the government has no means either of repressing it or of accommodating it. The Central Asians, deeply alien to the Slavic majority, represent the largest problem, as was shown by two weeks of rioting in Alma-Ata in December 1986 against the replacement of a Kazakh by a Russian first secretary.

The "convergence theory" popular in the 1960s postulated that because of industrialization and modernization the Soviet Union would converge politically with the Western world. This was illusory because in the communist way politics has priority over economic development. Convergence comes not because of industrialization but because of the wearing out of the revolutionary way, and not with the West but with the Third World.

The old style of politics of jockeying factions and sectors returns, with strains and divisions and the incapacity of the state to change things. The class system gradually grows more like that of Third World countries. The influence of the military inevitably looms larger. Repression softens or becomes more irregular as the elite feel freer to please themselves.

Censorship loses force. Soviet anti-Westernism moves from its Marxist basis and turns more like the simple resentment and envy of Third World states toward the richer nations. The Soviets no longer cultivate a general or ideal cause but their national interests. At the same time, for practical reasons, the Soviet Union and other communist countries become more involved in the world economy; like most Third World nations, the Soviet Union becomes heavily indebted to foreign banks.

East Germany, contrary to the general trend of the communist world, has gone backward toward greater centralization and rigid monopolistic controls, probably because of the insecurity of the leadership. The result has been the choking of previous economic advances and the virtual rejection of the computer age.[95] Similarly, unless the Soviet leadership is prepared to do the unthinkable and partly sacrifice its political system, it must decline.

## Notes

1. Mikhail Geller, *Mashina i Vintiki* (London: Overseas Publishing Interchange, 1985), p. 256–57.
2. Eli Sagan, *At the Dawn of Tyranny* (New York: Alfred A. Knopf, 1985), p. 336.
3. Daniel Nelson, "Leninists and Political Inequality," *Comparative Politics*, 15 (April 1982), p. 311.
4. Andrew Nagorski, *Reluctant Farewell* (New York: Holt, Rinehart and Winston, 1985), p. 183.
5. Thane Gustafson and Dawn Mann, "Gorbachev's First Year: Building Power and Authority," *Problems of Communism*, 35 (May–June 1986), p. 3.
6. *Wall Street Journal*, January 27, 1986, p. 14.
7. Irving Janis, *Victims of Groupthink: A Psychological Study of Foreign Policy Decisions and Fiascos* (Boston: Houghton Mifflin, 1972), pp. 187–98.
8. As elaborated early by Milovan Djilas in *The New Class*. Cf. David Lane, *The End of Social Inequality: Class, Status, and Power under State Socialism* (London: George Allen & Unwin, 1982).
9. Nagorski, *Reluctant Farewell*, pp. 25–26.
10. Timothy J. Colton, *Commissars, Commanders, and Civilian Authority: The Structure of Soviet Military Politics* (Cambridge: Harvard University Press, 1979), p. 269.
11. Seweryn Bialer, *Stalin's Successors: Leadership, Stability and Change in the Soviet Union* (Cambridge: Cambridge University Press, 1980), p. 56.
12. David K. Willis, *Klass: How Russians Really Live* (New York: St. Martins Press, 1985).
13. Adam Westoby, *Communism Since World War II* (New York: St. Martins Press, 1981), p. 308.
14. *New York Times*, August 2, 1981, p. 3.
15. Robert Sharlet, "Politics of Soviet Law," *Problems of Communism*, 35 (January–February 1986), 55–56.
16. Zvi Gitelman, "Working the Soviet System: Citizens and Urban Bureaucracies," in *The Contemporary Soviet City*, ed. Henry W. Morton and Robert C. Stuart, (Armonk, N.Y.: M. C. Sharpe, 1984), p. 223.
17. Jorge Dominguez, *Cuba: Order and Revolution* (Cambridge, Mass.: Belknap Press, 1978), p. 139.
18. Robert F. Dernberger, "Prospects for the Chinese Economy," *Problems of Communism*, 28 (September–December 1979), 15.

19. *New York Times*, November 1, 1979, p. 2.
20. John Plamenatz, *Democracy and Illusion* (London: Longman, 1973), p. 91.
21. David Lane, *State & Politics in the USSR* (New York: New York University Press, 1985), p. 309.
22. Daniel Nelson, "Leninists and Political Inequalities," p. 311.
23. David Shipler, *Russia: Broken Idols, Solemn Dreams* (New York: Times Books, 1983), pp. 208–9.
24. James C. Scott, *Comparative Political Corruption* (Englewood Cliffs, N.J.: Prentice-Hall, 1972), p. 86.
25. Kevin Klose, *Russia and the Russians: Inside the Closed Society* (New York: W. W. Norton, 1984), p. 295.
26. Alfred Evans, Jr., "The Decline of Developed Socialism: Some Trends in Recent Soviet Ideology," *Soviet Studies*, 38 (January 1986), 1–15; and Robert S. Kaiser, "The Soviet Pretense," *Foreign Affairs*, 65 (Winter 1986–1987), 236–41.
27. *Washington Post Weekly National Edition*, February 17, 1986, p. 16.
28. Adam Westoby, *Communism Since World War II* (New York: St. Martins Press, 1981), p. 338.
29. Stephen White, "Propagating Communist Values in the USSR," *Problems of Communism*, 34 (November–December 1985), 3–4.
30. Susan L. Shirk, *Competitive Comrades: Career Incentives and Student Strategies in China* (Berkeley: University of California Press, 1982), p. 2.
31. Dae-Sook Suh, "North Korea in 1985," *Asian Survey*, 20 (January 1986), 83.
32. *New York Times*, October 26, 1985, p. 1.; and *Current Digest of the Soviet Press* (*CD*), 37 (November 27, 1985), 1.
33. Clement H. Moore, "The Single Party as Source of Legitimacy" in *Authoritarian Politics in Modern Society: The Dynamics of Established One-Party Systems*, ed. Samuel P. Huntington and Clement H. Moore, (New York: Basic Books, 1970), p. 64.
34. Shirk, *Competitive Comrades*, p. 194.
35. Scott, *Comparative Political Corruption*, p. 89.
36. Sharlet, "Politics of Soviet Law," p. 55.
37. Ernest Gill, "Foreigners in Their Own Land," *New York Times Magazine*, February 16, 1986, p. 46.
38. Geller, *Mashima*, p. 163.
39. Gitelman, *Working the Soviet System*, p. 240.
40. Ibid., p. 238.
41. Scott, *Comparative Political Corruption*, pp. 15–16.
42. As attested in detail in the Soviet case by Konstantin Simis in *U.S.S.R.: The Corrupt Society* (New York: Simon & Schuster, 1982).
43. Alan P. Liu, "Kleptocracy on Mainland China," *Issues and Studies: A Journal of China Studies and International Affairs*, 20 (August 1984), pp. 13, 22.
44. Scott, *Comparative Political Corruption*, p. 9.
45. Shipler, *Russia*, pp. 126–27.
46. *Science 86*, July–August 1986, p. 11.
47. Robert F. Byrnes, "Moscow Revisited: Summer 1978," *Survey*, 28 (Autumn 1977–78), 9–11.
48. Westoby, *Communism Since World War II*, p. 333.
49. Konstantin Simis, *The Corrupt Society* (New York: Simon & Schuster, 1982), p. 12.
50. Paul J. Flory, "Science in a Divided World," *Freedom at Issue*, March–April 1986, p. 4.
51. Dimitri K. Simes, "Why the Soviets Don't Use the Polygraph," *Christian Science Monitor*, January 9, 1986, p. 12.
52. As reported by Anatoly Shcharansky in the *New York Times*, February 16, 1986, p. 10.
53. Vladimir Kontorovich, "Discipline and Growth in the Soviet Economy," *Problems of Communism*, 34 (November–December 1985), p. 21.
54. Victor Zaslavsky, *The Neo-Stalinist State: Class, Ethnicity, and Consensus in Soviet Society* (Armonk, N.Y.: M. E. Sharp, 1982), p. 160.

55. Henry Kamm, "The Graying of Prague," *New York Times Magazine*, August 20, 1982, p. 52.
56. Boris Rumer, "Revving the Soviet Economic Engine," *Christian Science Monitor*, October 7, 1985, p. 16.
57. *Christian Science Monitor*, January 7, 1986, p. 18.
58. *Newsweek*, September 7, 1981, p. 36.
59. *Izvestia*, October 19, 1985, p. 3; and *Current Digest* 37 (November 27, 1985), 17.
60. Patrick Murphy, "Soviet Shabashniki: Material Incentives at Work," *Problems of Communism*, 34 (November–December 1985), 48–54.
61. *Izvestia*, January 30, 1985, p. 3; and *Current Digest*, 37 (January 30, 1985), p. 3.
62. Nagorski, *Reluctant Farewell*, p. 103.
63. Murray Feshbach, "Symposium," *Public Opinion*, 8 (January 1986), 19.
64. Nicholas Eberstadt, "A Pattern of Soviet Health Reversals," *Wall Street Journal*, April 30, 1986, p. 32.
65. Nagorski, *Reluctant Farewell*, p. 101.
66. Marc Greenfield, "Life Among the Russians," *New York Times Magazine*, October 24, 1982, pp. 94, 108.
67. Nelson, "Leninists and Inequalities," p. 322.
68. Simis, *The Corrupt Society*, p. 12.
69. Specifically in Poland (*New York Times*, November 3, 1985, p. 11), but probably to a similar or greater degree in other countries with planned economies.
70. Jan S. Prybyla, "China's Economic Experiment: From Mao to Market," *Problems of Communism*, 35 (January–February 1986), p. 29.
71. Seweryn Bialer and Joan Afferica, "Gorbachev's World," *Foreign Affairs*, 64, no.3, 612–13.
72. Kontorovich, "Discipline and Growth," p. 20.
73. *Pravda*, May 20, 1986, p. 1; and *Current Digest* 38 (June 25, 1986), p. 7.
74. *New York Times*, May 20, 1986, p. 6.
75. Cf. Henry Norr, "Shchekino: Another Look," *Soviet Studies*, 38 (April 1986), 142.
76. Boris Rumer, "Realities of Gorbachev's Economic Program," *Problems of Communism*, 35 (May–June 1986), 25.
77. *New York Times*, June 26, 1986, p. 6; Fergus M. Burdewich, "Yugoslavia Since Tito," *New York Times Magazine*, April 13, 1986, p. 55; and *Christian Science Monitor*, December 15, 1986, p. 15.
78. Cecilia Rodriguez, "Consommation frénétique et marché noir," *Europ* (Fall 1984), p. 72.
79. William Echikson and Elizabeth Pond, "Shades of Communism: Experiments in Eastern Europe," *Christian Science Monitor*, January 8, 1986, pp. 14–15; and William Echikson, "Trade Embargoes, Inflation Put Squeeze on Hungary's Economy," *Christian Science Monitor*, June 2, 1986, p. 18.
80. *Wall Street Journal*, July 17, 1986, p. 1.
81. *Washington Post National Edition*, July 14, 1986, pp. 18–19.
82. Nicholas Eberstadt, "Did Fidel Fudge the Figures? Literacy and Health: The Cuban Model," *Caribbean Review*, 15, no. 2 (1986), 5–7.
83. *Newsweek*, August 19, 1985, p. 63.
84. James Riordan, *Sport in Soviet Society* (New York: Cambridge University Press, 1980).
85. Louise J. Shelley, "Soviet Justice," *Problems of Communism*, 34 (July–August 1985), pp. 69–73.
86. Frank Tachau, *Turkey: The Politics of Authority, Democracy, and Development* (New York: Praeger Publishers, 1984), pp. 16–17.
87. William H. Overholt, "The Moderation of Politics," *The Pacific Basin: New Challenge for the United States*, Academy of Political Science (New York: 1986), James W. Morley, ed.
88. Youssef Cohen, *Popular Support for Authoritarian Governments: Brazil under Medici* (Ann Arbor: University of Michigan Press, 1979), p. 84.
89. *Washington Post Weekly National Edition*, February 17, 1986, p. 16.
90. *New York Times*, May 14, 1986, p. 8.

91. *New York Times*, December 9, 1985, p. 6.
92. John W. Kiser, "How the Arms Race Helps Moscow," *Foreign Policy*, 60 (Fall 1985), 42, 48.
93. Peter A. Busch, *Legitimacy and Ethnicity: A Case Study of Singapore* (Lexington, Mass.: Lexington Books, 1974), p. 27.
94. Alan P. L. Liu, *How China is Ruled* (Englewood Cliffs, N.J.: Prentice-Hall, 1986), pp. 7–8.
95. *Christian Science Monitor*, January 2, 1987, p. 11.

# The Institutions of
# Democracy

## 6

The Greek meaning of *democracy*, "people rule," is misleading because the people cannot come near ruling in any complex modern state. Yet *democracy* corresponds to a political reality. It may be variously defined or described, and different aspects may be stronger in different countries, but it is easily recognizable. Quarrels among advocates of different kinds of democracy are quarrels within the family, a rather close-knit family whose members usually get along well. Democracies have often copied institutions from one another; and they, unlike authoritarian states, share a common philosophy.

Democracy includes, with varying emphases, many related things: equal rights of citizens, freedom of expression and of political organization and opposition, fair elections to decide who is to rule, limited terms of office, nonviolent politics, nonpolitical police and armed forces, rule of law, and independent courts. A political system has none of these in full measure unless it has all of them; if it has any of them, it probably has them all.

The democratic society has many traits related to these institutions. It is individualistic, pluralistic, permissive of nonconformism, decentralized institutionally and probably territorially, innovative, socially mobile, noncoercive, moderate both in actions and in beliefs, egalitarian in spirit and to some extent in reality, economically oriented, civil in politics, legalistic, achievement bent, open, competitive, humanistic, and more or less rationalistic in temper. As Plato said, "Democracy is a charming form of government, full of variety and disorder."

The nondemocratic society is in all such aspects the opposite. One might define democracy negatively, as the absence of the sociopolitical characteristics of arbitrary government: restrictions on free expression and independent groups, obligatory ideology, arbitrary agents of control, power-holding monopolies, and so forth. To abolish tyranny is to open the way to democracy, and one easily appreciates what tyranny is. It has been often stated that democratic government is not very good but merely less bad than any other known. The commonest reason for longing for democracy is not the yen to cast a ballot but hatred for the repression and corruption of an authoritarian regime.

Democracy cannot mean that all are equal or completely free or that the state is wholly responsible, only that these ends are achieved as well as may be arranged in always difficult conditions.[1] Critics of democracy usually demand a better democracy—more freedom and more equality—or contend that a supposed democracy is not really democratic because it really deceives the people or limits their choice. Hardly anyone proposes that there should be less liberty in principle or less popular participation in government except those with a vested interest in tyranny or inequality.

Democracy is fair government. This means that the state is to serve the people instead of the people serving the state, that the rulers are not self-imposed for their own benefit, and that ordinary people can freely express and forward their preferences and contest for political power.[2] It obviously also means that the political powers have no right to prevent criticism of themselves, that the actions of the state are governed by known rules adopted in some agreed manner and impartially applied, and that there are no unjustifiable discriminations. This implies justice, freedom, and equality, or at least an effort to achieve them.

Democracy rests on legitimacy much more than does authoritarianism. The only broadly accepted and philosophically defensible answer to the question "Why are they in charge?" is that they are approved by the people. To claim legitimacy, nondemocratic governments must pretend to be democratic; they lack a broadly accepted authoritarian principle of order or falsify one that they may claim, as Marxist proletarianism.

Democracy is orderly or systematic government; it is difficult for a nondemocratic system consistently to observe legality. Democracy is characterized by impersonal criteria in decision making, whereas authoritarianisms are more personal. Democracy is also the politics of uncertainty, as leaders may be raised or set aside without violence; the principal uncertainty of authoritarian leadership may be the physical condition of the chief. Democracy admits the possibility of failure and provides the means for change.

In the democracy, ordinary people are treated as mature and autonomous, not infantile in regard to public affairs as in dictatorships. Democracy looks to compromise, in contrast to the rigid antagonisms generated by authoritarianism's arbitrariness. Democracy is the politics of minimal coercion and moderate contestation. If much use of police power is necessary, the democracy is malfunctioning. If one believes all government is repressive, democracy is the system in which repression is lightest, least violent, and most sophisticated.

There is a philosophic presupposition in favor of democracy because there is no rational ground for discrimination.[3] Discriminators have recourse to mystical ideas, such as that Hindus are born high caste or low caste because of merits or demerits in a previous incarnation, that the Jews are engaged in a conspiracy of worldwide domination, that certain races or nations are inherently superior or inferior, and so forth. The philosophic basis of democracy is recognition of all as inherently valuable beings—in religious language, as children of God. It is the assumption of democracy that the members of the polity are to be the judge, so far as feasible, of their own best interest, that the people are reasonably qualified to choose their leaders, and that no special group has a right to decide for all except as they are chosen by the people.

The fundamentals of democracy come easily. Private organizations are commonly democratic if they have a formal structure. The right of members to choose leadership and decide policies is usually assumed, even though one personality may be dominant, or the majority may look to the more trained few, as in some religious groups, or shares are quantified, as in corporations.

Democratic principles are timeless. The conditions of Athens over two thousand years ago were very different from those of today, but the praise of democracy put in the mouth of Pericles by Thucydides rings eloquent today: equality of justice and the rights of citizens, honor for merit regardless of poverty, respect for law, the openness of the city to the world, and the participation of citizens in public affairs.[4] Villagers in India, Africa, or China have some appreciation for not being beaten by the village police, or for being able to express their opinions; and people generally seem to welcome being allowed to participate in choosing who is to lead them. Ignorant peasants in Latin America and Africa are eager to vote when they understand that their vote will decide who is to be in charge.

But modern democracy is the product of the European-Western competitive state system and has not prospered widely outside its sphere. In practice, the principal precondition for democracy seems to be the historical experience of representative government and a corresponding commitment on the part of a political elite to democratic values. But certain other conditions are evidently propitious for democratic institutions: relative economic equality, the absence of excessively unequal landholding in agrarian countries, a substantial middle class, relative homogeneity of the population, autonomous groups limiting state power, nonpolitical armed forces, a vigorous independent press, a relatively high economic and cultural level, and close economic and political relations with democratic powers.

Democracy is relative. Just as no political system can be absolutely fair, none is totally democratic, and the most democratic states sometimes behave in rather undemocratic ways. On the other hand, there is something of democracy in all modern societies, at least a claim to be acting on behalf of the people, and probably some democratic forms, such as elections of some sort.

Democratic performance is to be assessed in terms of civil liberties, open political competition, and responsiveness of authorities.[5] No quantifiable external variable, however, is closely correlated with the democratic character of societies.[6] Democracy is above all a matter of will and character.

### Freedom versus Equality

The two facets of democracy most discussed are freedom and equality. It is sometimes postulated that there is a contradiction between these two, because freedom enables some to raise themselves above others, and equality presumably has to be enforced and thus implies a decrease of freedom. But the inequality arising from freedom (assuming freedom does not extend to violation of the rights of others) is not severe and is not so much resented. The existence of a leading elite is not undemocratic as long as it is fluid and open and the nonelite can turn the elite out. Much worse is the inequality of unfreedom, whereby some assert dominion over others and take advantage of the weaker or those outside the favored group.

Equality cannot really be imposed. If any authority is strong enough to level people, it is also strong enough to create special privileges for itself. That is, in a complex society the great equalizers do not include themselves among those to be equalized. Political inequality in turn is convertible, and is habitually converted, into social and economic inequality.

It is sometimes contended that there are different types of democracy: by the people or for the people. But in human nature government is not likely to be for the people unless it is by the people, and government by the people surely acts more for the people than government by the few. The democratic ends of welfare, justice, and freedom are inseparable from the political means of elections and legal procedures.

Freedom and equality are closely tied and neither is possible without a good measure of the other. There is no liberty without political equality, and severe economic inequality is contrary to democracy and liberty. Liberty means inviting people to seek improvement—equality if they are disadvantaged—by working unburdened by discrimination to improve their condition. Effective liberty is close to equality of opportunity. Liberty and equality clash when the demand is not for equality of opportunity and nondiscrimination but for equality of material results and redistribution of wealth. Modern thinking has tended to go in this direction, toward the provision of benefits for the weaker, which means reducing the advantages of the stronger, partly contradicting the principle of freedom of individuals to improve themselves in any legitimate fashion.

The dichotomy between concern for material equality and for freedom is basic in democratic politics, and where the line is drawn and how the compromise is shaped are the stuff of endless controversy.[7] There is a contradiction between the preservation or enhancement of individual autonomy and the promotion of the well-being of the organized society. For some, the state is inherently bad, a limitation of the freedom of the individual; for others, it is inherently good, the representative of the community and the means of fulfillment of social purposes. Libertarians and collectivists have opposite views of the state (stressing noninterference or shared purposes), of justice (protection of individual rights or sharing of benefits), and of human nature (to be trusted or to be reshaped by persuasion or coercion). For some, the rights of the individual are indefeasible; for others, the people's state is an absolute sovereign.

Many who think more of freedom and prefer government less expensive and less intrusive into economic affairs are well placed and comfortable, political conservatives desirous of stability. Some are consistent libertarians. Many who strongly uphold economic freedom, however, are inclined to favor organized religion, law and order with stern punishments, stricter moral codes (regarding narcotics, sex and abortion especially), patriotism, strong national defense, and an assertive foreign policy. Those more concerned with economic equality are commonly less supportive of organized religion, more politically reformist, more concerned with the equality of the sexes and races, more permissive of individual deviance, and less eager for national self-assertion and strength. The division is by no means clearcut, however: some conservatives find free-wheeling capitalism disturbing or are distrustful of conventional religion,[8] and many capitalists have guilt feelings about wealth. Some who more passionately advocate economic equalization—commonly called social justice—may lose sight of political liberty, claiming that the essence of democracy is economic.

Those who stress freedom favor a more pluralistic idea of democracy based on the autonomy of groups and individuals. They may be inclined to see democracy largely as a means of maintaining a livable degree of harmony among the different interests or sectors making up a modern society, apportioning costs and benefits. As conservatives, they are probably skeptical of popular impulses and rely more on experience or custom and less on reason. Egalitarian-minded democrats emphasize the "general will" of Rousseau, or the power of the central authority to act on behalf of the people,[9] bringing about change according to rational principles. The former tendency is that of the pluralists; the latter, that of the majoritarians; and democracies may incline in one or the other of these directions.[10] But the differences of libertarians and majoritarians, liberals and conservatives, are only nuances compared with the differences of democrats and totalitarians.

## PLURALISM

In theory, the pluralists and majoritarians are quite opposed. However, like the apparently contrasting values of liberty and equality, they are not far apart. Without a fractioning of power it is probably impossible—at least for humans in their present imperfection—to organize the will of the majority without inviting dictatorship. *Pluralistic*, in characterization of a polity, is as nearly equivalent to *democratic* as is *free*. Some democrats, from Rousseau on, have deplored private associations as standing between the people and their state.[11] But they forget that effective action requires organization, and political managers will be omnipotent unless hedged by other powers. The democratic state is like a microcosm of the competitive state system, in which the balancing of powers makes room for freedom, while the monistic state upholds a noncompetitive order like the universal empire. A democracy is a competitive society with numerous autonomous intermediate organizations requiring reciprocity instead of hierarchy.

There are two ways of evolving toward democracy: the recognition of civil and political rights, with growth of the idea of majority rule, and the rise of offsetting balancing powers. Historically, the latter has usually taken the lead. Autonomous sectors of society tend to limit power and hence make democracy possible; on the other hand, democracy is the best way to compromise diversity, as in Switzerland, with its several languages and religions.

The principle of freely operating groups gives rationality and openness to the society. As Laski had it, "Because society is federal in its nature, the more widely power is dispersed in a state, the more effective are its operations likely to be." [12] A pluralist society is not necessarily democratic, but it is moderate and legal even when aristocratic (as in seventeenth century Venice or eighteenth century Netherlands), and it can lead directly to constitutional and representative government. It is as contrary to the monistic society as is the idea of equal rights of individuals.

When democracy has been fully institutionalized, the ideas of group autonomy and majority rule tend to diverge, as do those of freedom and equality. On the one hand, the ideal of the libertarian is to reduce the role of the state to little more than keeping order, assuming generally that people will do good if let alone, or at least better than if under political restraints. On the other hand, the ideal of state welfarism is distrustful of private initiatives as presumably selfish. The latter has been riding a strong modern current, as the governmental share of national income rose inexorably in nearly all the advanced industrial countries up to the 1980s. We have yet to see whether the recent halting of that current is more than a temporary lull.

### Pluralism within the Government

Pluralism within the state apparatus is incorporated in the separation of powers, a fundamental of presidential government. This is best exemplified by the United States, which has the world's most divided political system over one of the world's most pluralistic societies. But the balancing of the legislative, judicial, and executive-administrative powers is historically based, not a priori; and quite different schemes are conceivable. There is overlapping as well as restraint, and there could be fewer than the three traditional powers, or more.

The executive in a presidential system has the advantage of unity, controls most of the government apparatus, and has some authority (veto power) to negate acts of the legislature; the latter has basic control of finances and by a qualified (perhaps two-thirds) majority can overrule the executive, probably even impeach and remove the president. The chief of the government usually proposes policies, and the legislature sanctions them for executive implementation and provides money to support them. The U.S. legislative branch is unique in its ability, through both legal powers and material facilities, not only to check but also to oversee the executive.

Parliamentary regimes usually vest quite full power in the legislative assembly or the prime minister and cabinet sanctioned by it, although there is commonly some restriction as to what the parliament may do— for example, a requirement of special procedures to amend the constitution. In Great Britain there is no such requirement, and the parliament could legally abolish liberties by a simple majority vote. That it does not dream of doing so to keep a government from being voted out of office demonstrates the superiority of social forces and traditions to formal institutions.

Pluralism is also incorporated in local autonomy, whereby provincial or municipal units of elected government manage more or less of their own affairs, sometimes largely de facto, sometimes by legal dispensation from the central government or by constitutional right. Centralization may be of any degree—from the British, in which local councils can do little but act as agents of London, to the European Economic Community, the parliament of which has little more than moral authority.

Federalism is a form of subnational autonomy by which the components of the nation have a share of sovereignty, that is, powers which the center cannot legally take away. There are few successful federal systems, because such arrangements require special preconditions. The greater number came out of the British Empire: the United States (after which all other federal systems, including the Swiss, have been patterned), Canada, Australia, India, and formerly Nigeria. These and Brazil illustrate the appropriateness of federal institutions for very large states. West Germany and Switzerland, however, demonstrate that this rule is not general.[13] Federalism corresponds to practical needs for devolution in divided societies as well as to legal arrangements. In multiethnic India, the constitutional position of the states is very weak, but they are functional and important because they correspond to coherent linguistic or ethnic groups. It is administratively convenient for the central government to act with and through them. Federalism not only checks political power by splitting off parts of it; it also reduces strains on the democratic system by shifting many controversial matters to be decided at the subnational level.

### Managing Divisive Social Forces

Divisions that set people apart automatically and permanently—ethnic, racial, or religious—make problems for the democratic state, especially when they coincide with, and also correspond to, economic groups. All organizations tend toward the assertion of their own purposes—that is, autonomy from any controlling power [14]—and in ordinary practice the government responds as much to private concerns as to the mass of voters. Pluralism means interest-group politics. The United States is the land of pressure groups par excellence, but they are powerful in all democratic and partly democratic polities.

Groups in the democratic society desire to improve their standing; but so long as the system remains open and amenable to compromise, the contention of interests protects freedom. The subsystems of the democracy are themselves mostly democratic, and they help people to know and express their needs and thus to participate politically. They socialize demands and place nonelites in contact with elites and politicians in contact with nonpolitical persons, providing channels between people and state.[15] In freedom, groups form as though spontaneously; in Czechoslovakia in 1968 and in Poland in 1980 all manner of organizations sprang up like flowers after rain in the desert.

Democracy may be defined as the management instead of the repression of social divisions; in 1789 John Adams said, "The essence of a free government consists in an effectual control of rivalries." The mechanisms of power sharing may be adjuncts of democracy, as in Lebanon's elaborate allocations of offices among Christians, Moslems, and Druses—an arrangement that made the country an island of freedom in the Arab world until unbalanced by the differing growth rates of sectors and overwhelmed by the Palestinian conflict. Agreement is sought democratically by conceding to all major groups a veto over policies affecting them, giving all a degree of autonomy, and sharing the benefits of government.[16] In the pluralist concept, nothing is to be done that is passionately opposed by any substantial sector. Minorities should be protected, as they will be if they have a fair chance of becoming or joining a majority.[17] Democracies that emphasize the accommodation of major groups, such as ethnic sectors, sometimes called consociational, require more elaborate mechanisms than more homogeneous states.

## PRIVATE OWNERSHIP

A somewhat different aspect of pluralism is the freedom to own property and to use it for production.[18] "Liberal" democracy in the old sense is closely associated with liberal, or basically free-market, economics. Private property implies pieces of private power—a degree of independence for an indefinite number of persons and organizations holding resources. Wealth gives power; but it produces many different interests—financial, industrial, commercial, landed, and others—not a power elite.[19] It is characteristic of despotisms that all major property pertains to the despot, and individuals hold it only on sufferance. On the other hand, restriction of the power of the rulership is closely correlated with security of private ownership.

An accumulation of personal wealth, like a chestful of gold and jewels, would have little significance. But when property is put to use to produce more, and when it grows beyond the capacity of any individual personally to manage it, it enters the arena of social activity and has political significance. For this reason, nearly all authoritarian states severely restrict rights of private ownership. In the communist viewpoint, private capital is the enemy of community solidarity and is inherently exploitative and divisive. The Soviet authorities permit private ownership of residences and unlimited bank accounts, even paying modest interest; but they are firmly opposed to private use of property to increase it.

In democracies also, the political influence of wealth is commonly seen as unjust, and important parties in nearly all of them have a socialist ideology and favor equalization of wealth, a larger state role in the economy, and public ownership of major property. The United States is unique in lacking a socialist movement of importance. Even in this country, many persons, impressed with the evils of private wealth, would like to have their democracy without it. Impecunious intellectuals especially have believed that democratic government is possible with—perhaps only with—state or "social" control of the means of production, finance, communications, etc. No one, however, seems to have devised how a state is to be kept limited and democratic if it has the whole economy in its hands, disregarding the fact that central control of a modern economy seems to be inefficient. Private property is the backbone of individualism and individual rights. Moreover, economic incentives are generally more salutary than political ones, just as production is generally more beneficial than domination.

### State Enterprise in Democracies

There is no record of a democratic state with a socialized economy. Even in Sweden, a land of socialistic proclivities, where well over half the national product goes through government hands—much of it in the form of transfer payments—industry is almost entirely privately owned. Countries such as Britain, France, and Italy have a large public industrial sector, but the economy remains basically private. There is freedom to establish new enterprises, and those operated by the state are commonly infrastructural and unprofitable; most important, they are divorced from the electoral process.

It would be too much to ask that elections decide not only the political leadership but also the ownership or management of the bulk of the national wealth. Hence a democratic socialized country would seem possible only if the management of nationalized enterprises were independent to a high degree, that is, if the economy were run on a basis not very different from private ownership. The important matter is not ownership but independence and competition. Nationalized industries in Britain, France, Italy, and other democracies are called upon to make a profit (or minimize losses) and are fairly autonomous. So far as they are, it does not seem crucially important that France's Elf-Aquitaine petroleum company, British Petroleum, and Italy's Enti are state owned whereas Exxon is not; all operate in about the same fashion.

The fact that Renault was nationalized as punishment for World War II collaboration does not have much to do with social justice or politics; Renault was not run much differently from its private-enterprise partner, American Motors. Socialized British coal mines face the same problems of costs and productivity as privately owned mines elsewhere, and the miners are not dissuaded from striking by the fact that they are paid or underpaid by the state, which to them is a stingy boss. Some state enterprises, such as Swiss railroads, the French Aerospatiale, and Scandinavian airlines, have proved efficient; the majority have not, either because the state assumed the responsibility of a failing business or because of politicization of management. Private corporations, like state enterprises, may largely separate management from ownership; but the former are under a stronger discipline, the possibility of bankruptcy. So far as state enterprises are run like private corporations, they cheat the principal purpose of state control, to permit political or social considerations to override economic calculations.

It is very difficult to manage economically a politically directed enterprise; this is a reason for the failure of communist states to prosper from the supposedly rational allocation of resources. A progressive economy seems to require something like private enterprise, or enterprise free of central control, no matter how owned, with incentives for innovation and risk taking, rewards for good management, and penalties for bad. Without freedom for innovations and entrepreneurship, any economy is probably destined to a stagnation detrimental not only to the material welfare of the people but also to the political order.

It is also important that small private businesses are often more innovative and more efficient than large ones, and state enterprises are commonly too big. The best size for plants may be two hundred to three hundred workers, not over five hundred, with this number divided into several teams; and successful large corporations set up competitive divisions.[20]

For such reasons, the tendency of recent years has been rather to divest than to nationalize. Not only has the conservative Thatcher government of Great Britain privatized major state enterprises, but France, which went on a rash of takeovers after the socialists came to power under President Francois Mitterrand in 1982, has undertaken to sell stock in government-owned industries. Japan, Canada, West Germany, and many others have moved to trim the state sector.

Capitalism or arrangements preserving the autonomy of productive enterprises seem to be a natural ingredient of the democratic order. If individuals, not the state, are to be the mainspring of the economy, the state will be less omnipotent and more responsible to the nonstate. Business interests, although they seek official aid and protection, do not want a statist, politically dominated society. There is a natural antithesis between the political and the commercial or profit-oriented spheres; and the democratic, pluralistic order is more favorable to productive forces than visible alternatives. Many persons are more attached to free enterprise than to political rights, and capitalism may distort democracy, but it does not favor ideological dictatorship.

Private enterprise serves democracy in another way: it provides comfortable landing places for persons leaving government service and consequently makes easier the turnover of officeholders. If government employment is almost the only career, as in not only communist but also many Third World countries, democracy is impossible. The right to own private property and use it productively is also closely related to other vital rights, such as freedom of speech and the press, which would be difficult to implement unless people were able to use private resources to set up and distribute newspapers, publish magazines and books, operate broadcasting stations with minimal control of the content of programs, and support independent educational and research centers. These freedoms are linked intimately with the right to form organizations and engage in political activity. By joining together, citizens can apply their resources to their political rights.

## FREEDOM

Freedom (or liberty, to use the nearly equivalent Latin-derived term) generates pluralism because people are diverse and will get together to promote diverse interests if free to do so. On the other hand, pluralism, in all its disorder, is the basic guarantor of freedom, especially freedom of expression, the most elemental aspect of democracy from classical Greece [21] to modern America. A traveler to a strange land does not need to ask about its political institutions. If he observes that people express themselves freely about public affairs and that there is an uninhibited confrontation of opinions in the media, he knows that he is in a pluralist democracy.

Such openness is the means of checking the government and holding it to its proper purposes. It is essential for creative thinking; to keep the state healthy it is vital that groups, organizations, and individuals be able to criticize and propose, contributing extensively and intensively to the flow of information. The confrontation of opinions is the only hope for approaching rationality in political affairs. In well-developed democracies basic freedoms are so taken for granted that they are usually forgotten, and controversies turn rather on questions of policy.

It is pointless to ask whether we prefer freedom or democracy because they are inseparable. Freedom is a value in itself. "Liberty," according to Lord Acton, "is not a means to a higher political end. It is itself the highest political end." It enables one to be creative and human at the highest level; in the opinion of its proponents, lean liberty is better than fat slavery—although liberty is surely better nourished than slavery. The way people choose is the essence of character, and democratic freedom gives them the autonomy necessary for moral growth, whereas authoritarianism would hold them in immaturity.

The existence of freedom is an enormous credit for a government; so far as conduct can be guided by good sense and community spirit, the state merits congratulation. Any regime that cannot allow its citizens to think for themselves and to speak out freely and publicize their views has cause for shame. It is often claimed that a higher purpose—such as the building of communism—requires the suppression of criticism, but this implies that the means to the purpose cannot withstand close examination.

### Limits of Freedom

The most important questions of freedom, relating to political opposition, are unambiguous; but the full extent of license to be allowed is not easily defined. It is commonly stated that people should be free so long as their actions are not injurious to the rights of others, but this leaves open how far citizens are free to offend the feelings of others. Controversy centers on moral issues, such as pornography. Some Americans make much of a freedom strange to Europeans and Japanese, that of possessing firearms. Broadly speaking, freedom means not the total absence of restraint but the latitude to develop and fulfill the personality, which includes the ability to exercise political rights.

It has been questioned whether the democratic state should permit freedom of criticism and opposition to be used to destroy democracy and freedom, that is, whether absolutist movements can claim for themselves the rights they would deny to others. This has been a manageable problem, however, in soundly democratic states. Totalitarian parties have little appeal unless many people regard their own society as deeply flawed. But in badly strained democratic polities, totalitarian parties are both a symptom and a cause of grave problems. Nazis and communists combined to destroy the German Weimar Republic in the early 1930s, and the threat or supposed threat of radical movements has been a major excuse, if not motivation, for the overthrow of elected governments in a dozen nations.

It may also be questioned whether the majority has the right to repress basic freedoms, or how far freedom is to be curtailed in order to protect it—a subject of more theoretical interest than practical importance because repression of freedoms by democratic process is trivial compared with the ravages of dictatorship and abuses of democratic power are subject to correction. The argument of the tyranny of the majority has in the past been made mostly by those fearful of the loss of upper-class privileges. But genuinely popular governments—as opposed to those dominated by radical parties probably lacking majority support—have rarely if ever been confiscatory or violently equalitarian. If the majority should indeed misuse its power, whether because of prejudice or emotions, it is at least morally preferable to misuse of power by a minority.

Some have alleged that in the privately owned economy, freedom of the press is for the few or the owners only. It is undeniable that certain ideas or outlooks are more favored than others. But the important fact is that any view that is not widely repugnant—and even some that are— can find a hearing. Publisher-capitalists appear more concerned about their immediate economic interests than the interests of their class; and if there is a market for anticapitalist writing, they will produce and sell it: the shelves of college bookstores are loaded with radical works. The profit motive may be base, but it is nonideological.

The free interplay of ideas and unrestricted organization to advance them are the best means toward the resolution of differences and the adaptation and improvement of society. Although deceit, prejudice, and misinformation confuse issues, one can hope to sort these out not by trying to suppress them but by open discussion and resolution through due political process. This is the value of democracy, the basis for its survival, and the means of preventing the abuse of power.

## COMMUNITY

Pluralism, freedom, limited government, and a legally ordered political system rest on a complex set of institutions; and democratic states, from classical Athens to our day, require careful allocation of powers and regulation of relations between entities. But even with detailed provisions, the existence of many autonomous or partly autonomous units of the polity implies countless potential misunderstandings and conflicts. Hence the democratic apparatus will be paralyzed or will tear itself apart in a crisis unless there is substantial agreement on its principles and a general desire that it should be made to work—unless, that is, its components feel themselves to be a real community.

Community is hardly less important than freedom and equality. Minorities must be willing to accept defeats, or to be voted out of office, with the consolation that they can always try again. There must be agreement or consensus to follow constitutional mandates, to respect the rights of minorities and pacific dissent, and to permit special needs to be overridden by higher values. The citizens should be able to regard one another somewhat as members of a great family, equals in rights and duties and ready to settle differences in an orderly fashion and to abide by the rules while assuming that others do so also. The habit of settlement by democratic process grows with use, and political participation is educational. The democratic citizen should be open-minded, critical, flexible, rational, amenable to compromise, and tolerant; and sharing in the democracy, as far as it is successful, fosters these traits.[22]

Democratic character and sense of community are built primarily by participation; partly in the rites and ceremonies of the state, from voting to celebrations; and partly by sharing in the processes of government and all manner of civic endeavors, from the school board to the town meeting. Teamwork is in the democratic spirit, and community feeling comes best from working together.[23] The United States pioneered in populist democracy because of the frontiersman's spirit of cooperation.

The more homogeneous a society, the more effectively it can function as a democracy. It is difficult for the democratic state, whatever its institutions, to handle deep and strongly felt divisions of any kind; and it is in trouble if any major group or power in the state, from the laboring class to the military, becomes alienated and hostile. Lack of integration is a major, perhaps the chief, reason for the feebleness of democracy in the less-developed countries. It is difficult to prevent or overcome. The community of feeling of Western democracies has grown up through a long history of shared destiny; yet there are problems of minority discontents in the United Kingdom (the Irish and the Scots), France (the Bretons),

Spain (the Basques and the Catalonians), and others, which sometimes lead otherwise decent persons to murder. Heterogeneity and the sense of separation of many minorities detract considerably from the quality of government in the United States. Even in this generally well-ordered country, there seems to be developing a permanent marginal subclass, ghetto bound, with fatherless families, which, if it grows large enough, may severely tax the democratic order.

## ELECTIONS

The mechanism of responsibility to the people is elections, on the almost universally accepted basis of equal votes for adults. The battle for the extension of the franchise was long and hard in the development of democracy, but nowadays universal franchise with secret ballot is taken for granted even in the lands least prepared for its exercise. Voting is the great expression of political equality among otherwise unequal citizens.

The immediate purpose of elections is to choose executive chiefs and members of legislative bodies and possibly (especially in the United States) judges and miscellaneous officials, even some of the most insignificant. Frequent elections—but not so frequent as to bore the voters—strengthen responsibility. Some drafters of the United States constitution believed that representatives should submit yearly to the popular judgment; John Adams said, "Where the annual elections end, there slavery begins." However, the two-year term of members of the House of Representatives is exceptionally short in democratic practice; usually the citizens vote regularly for important officers only once in four or five years.

The fact of being picked by popular choice is the most honest and by far the most widely accepted claim to power. Even if there is no genuine contest, the vote gives some legitimacy, as in Mexico; and the campaign, wherein the candidate travels around the country, shows himself, and shakes hands, and the gesture of placing marked papers in boxes make a bond of sorts between people and leaders. The importance of election is demonstrated by the status it gives the American vice president: hardly anyone casts a vote for him, but the fact that he has appeared on the ballot gives him a standing no appointee can claim.

The vote also contributes to the shaping of policy. In American parlance, this is "sending a message to Washington" or to the statehouse. Policies are changed, of course, if persons representing different views are elected. However, the vote may, without changing leadership, exert pressure to change directions. In Japan, for example, the political contest is mostly of factions within the dominant Liberal-Democratic party, which the electorate has kept in office for a generation; but policies are adjusted to trends manifested in the regular elections. Midterm elections in the United States, by-elections in Britain to fill parliamentary vacancies, state ("Land") elections in Germany, and local elections in many countries, such as France and Italy, are closely watched as indicators of the popular temper.

The degree of dominance of a single party or the frequency of alternation between parties—such as Republican and Democratic in the United States and Conservative and Labour in Britain—is quite varied. In Sweden, Italy, and Japan, a single party has been dominant through almost all the postwar period; in Venezuela and Costa Rica, nearly every election has brought a change. It may be desirable, or at least more democratic, if elections sweep out a possibly stale leadership. It is also healthy to change the governing party from time to time to prove that the electorate really commands.

Yet it is not necessarily undemocratic for one party to remain at the helm. If it adjusts intelligently to the wishes and feelings of the electorate, it may have a good claim to stay in power because another party can hardly do better and represents a possibility of doing worse, and there are practical advantages in continuity. The principal reasons for one-party dominance in both Japan and Italy have been the fact that the chief opposition party proposed a dangerous wrench in national security policy, plus the fact that the stewardship of the governing party has been very successful in raising the economic level. Moreover, fairly frequent changes of top leaders of the ruling party have kept the system from stagnation. The turnover of parties in many countries of highly contested politics, such as Britain and the United States, owes as much to an itch for change as to a judgment of the superiority of the outs.

Political parties are inevitable and necessary intermediaries; it is mostly through them that the voters make their will effective. Everywhere that free elections are held—and in many countries where they are only a hope—there are parties. They come in great variety, from broad coalitions with only the most general orientation (as in the United States) to rather clearly class-oriented groups (such as the British Conservative and Labour parties), ideologically defined parties (such as the Japanese Socialists), or those based on a single issue (such as the Scottish Nationalists). The chief U.S. parties are exceptionally unstructured; ordinarily parties have a dues-paying membership. Party structure is correlated with ideology. Democratic and egalitarian parties go to considerable lengths to keep the leadership at least nominally responsible to the party masses. The supreme party authority, a big convention in which the little wigs have voice and vote along with the big, may actually be influential, whereas authoritarian parties use it as an acclamatory claque. Totalitarian parties, such as the Communist party and the Nazi party when Hitler was seeking power, are hierarchic-authoritarian. It seems better if parties are not closely tied to private organizations; for example, the domination of the British Labour party by the trade unions rigidifies not only the Labour movement but the whole British political system.

In more divided societies and where electoral systems favor party voting people cast ballots more for party organizations than for individuals. All large parties are inevitably to a greater or less extent run by insiders or the professionals who staff the organization, and a larger role for parties means a larger role for these probably nonelected leaders. The United States, with its primary elections, is the chief exception to the rule that candidates are selected by party insiders, subject to the democratic restraint that they want persons capable of winning elections. A vital adjunct of democracy thus at once assists and limits the responsibility of the leadership to the led.

### The Reality of Elections

The best democracy cannot come close to the ideal that political questions be decided entirely in accordance with the will of the people. Elections cannot be very frequent without reducing participation, and the popular vote can be interpreted according to taste. For example, when Ronald Reagan was elected president in 1980, he supposedly received a mandate for balancing the federal budget, reducing regulation of business, increasing defense spending, taking a stronger stance against communism abroad, and prohibiting abortion. On the other hand, voters may have simply been weary of Jimmy Carter and impressed by the well-spoken "great communicator;" a major factor in the election of Reagan was the Iranian hostage crisis, which was resolved before he took office. The reelection of Reagan in 1984 seems to have been most of all a testimony to his general likableness, distrust of his Democratic opponent, and general satisfaction with the state of the economy. It has been contended that in the United States elections are really decided by disposable income, support for the "ins" rising 2.2 percent for each 1 percent of income increase.[24]

People may be allowed to decide specific policies by referendum, for which the voters can preferably take the initiative by petition. This institution is used chiefly in Switzerland and some twenty of the United States. There is much to be said for it: the campaigning surrounding important proposals is educational, and voting laws up or down involves the citizens closely with their government. Measures on the ballot are often beyond the understanding of the ordinary citizen and should be carefully considered by experts, but the voters in practice do not adopt wild propositions.

Polls give frequent readings of opinion on many issues and might well supplement electoral consultations. One assumes that democratic leaders should consider public attitudes, but it is doubtful that they should be obligated to follow the dictates of public opinion, even if this could be reliably determined. It is probably sound that representatives be considered not as instruments of their electors but as persons of good will and intelligence who should share the values of their constituents but exercise independent judgment, according to the Westminster model of democracy. The fact that they are chosen implies that their understanding should be exceptional, and they should be more knowledgeable about public issues than most of those who vote for them. Ease of communications, however, reduces the independence of the representative; and the modern tendency is rather toward plebiscitary democracy.

Very few of the masses—indeed, not many of any sector—have the expertise necessary for informed judgment on educational policy, nuclear power, defense issues, foreign affairs, etc. At best, they can express a sense of priorities. There are strong opinions regarding conservation, inflation, disarmament, support for Israel, offshore drilling, and many other matters that people believe may affect them but concerning which few can inform themselves deeply. Realistically, democracy must require that the people be consulted about major directions, and that they have a broad veto power, not that they make decisions where they are incompetent to decide. A responsible democratic leader will often feel driven to go against prevalent opinion, hoping that history will be more understanding than his or her contemporaries.

Most questions of government, however, are more or less of indifference to the majority. Democracy then loses representativeness as leaders hear the voices of those who lobby them. In practice, the responsibility of the government is less to the people as a whole than to those especially interested in particular issues, that is, "special interests." It also answers to opinion leaders—the journalists and others who are in a position to present information, question actions, and convey judgments to large numbers, including the policy makers and administrators. Although they are outsiders, opinion leaders may be very well informed and are sometimes capable of better judgment than the officials subject to bureaucratic constrictions.

There are also many nontechnical issues in regard to which the people cannot reach definite decisions. These are mostly moral questions, dealing with matters of religion and social control, such as abortion, handgun control (a specialty of U.S. culture), the purposes of education, crime and its control, family matters, and narcotics abuse. These questions are never really decidable, however passionately debated, often under the leadership of persons who specialize in an issue that becomes their avocation or vocation. Many other issues also become emotional—with people differing not because of material or practical interests but because of moral stance—such as the degree to which the nation should act assertively or conciliatorily in the world, and the amount of responsibility society should assume for the poor. Such unresolvable and divisive questions consume a disproportionate fraction of political energies.

The political body cannot be made exactly representative of popular desires. Interest or professional groups overrepresent minorities. The voters cannot possibly give detailed commands to those charged with leadership of the state. At the same time, practical politics and stability require subordinating strictly democratic imperatives to political needs. Thus claims may have to be adjusted in order to gain broader support, to attend to the needs of minorities, to bring different interests together for quiet bargaining, to dodge overly divisive issues, and to give as many as possible a share in the advantages of the state.[25]

In various other ways the electoral process is an imperfect expression of the popular will. One is that not everyone votes; in many local elections only a small minority do. In some countries, such as Australia and Belgium, voting is obligatory, although the logic of forcing people to exercise their prime political right is not clear. Turnout in the United States tends to be relatively low because of some difficulty of registration, the frequency of elections (general and local), the numbers of candidates whom few voters know, and the relative weakness of the party system (American democracy is less party channeled than any other). Low turnout is lamentable, but it surely does not indicate a high level of dissatisfaction.

The electoral system restricts and distorts democratic choice. A district system with a single winner, as is customary in the United States and Britain, leaves the minority in any given district—perhaps a majority, if divided—without representation and distorts the balance of the legislature. It is possible for a smaller number of votes to win a larger number of seats if the votes of one party are more advantageously distributed than those of the other party or parties.

To avoid this and to give minorities their due voice, proportional representation was devised, allocating seats among parties according to the percentage of votes going to each. This, however, ordinarily means voting for party lists, not persons. The choice becomes more ideological and less personal, and hence more divisive. Policies in countries with proportional representation are more likely to be decided by bargaining among parties. In a contradiction typical of political reality, the system for more exact representation of the opinions of the people means giving more power to the political pros. Whether a parliament really becomes more representative thereby is not clear.

There are devices for combining choice of persons and proportional representation of parties. The German scheme, for example, allows voters to pick candidates but adjusts the number elected to party strength. The Japanese compromise deserves attention: several representatives, usually five, are elected from a district, but each elector can vote for only one. By this means, the choice is personalized and there is competition among the candidates of a party, yet small parties can secure representation by concentrating their votes on a single candidate. The American primary system is the most democratic in the world, but doubts have arisen about whether it produces better candidates—especially in the grueling presidential nomination process, which requires not only physical endurance but an enormous urge to become president. The primary system has not been copied elsewhere, either because it is imperfect or because party leaders like to manage nominations.

The impact of elections is also limited by the permanence of the administrative staff. In most European democracies and in Japan, only a few dozen executive positions—the premier and his ministers and their immediate staffs—are at stake in elections. The electorate thus may give broad directions to the government, but the same people carry on the work of government, whatever the electoral outcome, and they do not necessarily make the values of the majority their own. In the United States, a new president makes nominations to approximately a thousand political positions and influences thousands more through the top ranks of the bureaucracy. This amount of turnover is more feasible in a presidential system than in a parliamentary one, in which terms of office are uncertain. But if many more were subject to removal it would strain the democratic system.

The changes to be made by election must be fairly moderate, not only unthreatening to the public service—the largest single segment of the work force, or the educated work force—but not very repugnant to any powerful fraction of the society or the economy. To vote something abhorrent to any major group is seriously to undermine the democratic consensus. It is for this reason preferable, if not essential, that any party likely to win electorally have strength broadly distributed geographically. It is also important that contending parties be multiclass—that there be, for example, conservative workers and peasants along with upper- and middle-class socialists.[26] Crosscutting cleavages and fluctuating majorities hinder the abuse of power. It is often complained in the United States that the two heterogeneous parties give voters little real choice, but it is better for stability and harmony that elections do not decide too much.

With such qualifications, the electoral process remains primordial. It confers legitimate and legal authority on the state. People do not rebel against a government they feel is theirs, and they accept hardships more cheerfully at the hands of those whom they have elected. When parties compete openly for the support of the people and offer themselves as alternative rulers, one can hate a party or a leader yet be wholly loyal to the state and system; where there is no such means of challenge, dislike for the rulership is near disloyalty to the state and opposition means rebellion. The interaction of the people and the government responsible to them generates information and reduces the separation of rulers and ruled. It gives the people a sense of participation and personal worth. The common man becomes significant by voting for or against the most exalted personages, and the use of the ballot is an invitation to more active sharing in political life.

Peoples without the vote exaggerate the benefits to be gained from elections. In the nineteenth century some thought broadening suffrage should lead quickly to a socialist utopia. For those who have long been under arbitrary rule, the establishment or restoration of constitutional processes seems a wonderful dream; and they imagine that as soon as they have an elected government their woes will vanish. Thus in 1984 nearly all Brazilians were caught up by the idea that a directly elected president would quickly restore prosperity, and the peoples of Uganda and many other less-developed countries have hoped that election day was the dawn of a new era. But life flows on in the ruts of poverty and official malfeasance.

Democracy is only part of a social complex. How much real influence lies with the people and how much remains with insiders varies according to modes and structures the workings of which are obscure. The role of the parties gives power to insiders, experts or supposed experts assume decision making, elections usually give only vague mandates, electoral systems cannot exactly reflect the voters' wishes, and narrow economic and ideological interests exert effective power. But the purpose of democracy is more to check the power of the state than to fulfill the will of the people; and a society in which the votes of the people are important is more open, has better social feeling, is more active in thought and discussion, and more creative—perhaps, one might say, more intelligent—than one in which they are denied a share in the making of the state.

## LEADERSHIP

A major part of freedom is choice of whom one must obey. In authoritarian states persons come to the top in a generally unedifying, if not unscrupulous, manner and may stay there indefinitely. The democratic leader should have risen through a legal and rational process and can count on only a restricted span of office.

It seems that a single individual must be given highest powers, although certainly not unlimited powers, in order for decisions to be reached and actions to be taken. If there is an iron law of oligarchy in large organizations, there is an iron law of personal leadership in political bodies. The most democratic committee needs a chairman to give direction, especially to set the agenda. A single personality takes charge in a junta, however attentive to the ideas of junta members, just as in a well-ordered tribe a chief is chosen for wisdom and valor by the elders. Radical movements, communist as well as fascist, are almost always dominated by a leader; rejection of strong leadership incapacitates a party for taking and using power.

### Leadership by Election

It is taken for granted in democratic states that the chief of the government should be elected directly by the people, either as an individual (in presidential systems) or as the head of a party (in parliamentary systems). But democratic presidents may partly select their own successors by placing them in an advantageous position or by undercutting potential competitors, and no means has been devised to prevent party insiders from playing a large role in the selection. In parliamentary systems, the party leader is usually chosen by some sort of conclave of high party figures, frequently the party's membership in the legislature; their selection then is to be ratified by the electorate's choice among parties.

A vigorous public contest for leadership helps to keep the system healthy, and it brings broadest involvement in a fundamental of the democratic order: competition without violence. But there is some truth in the "Dismal Theorem" of political science—that the skills leading to office are not those needed for exercising it [27]—and it is repugnant to choose the nation's highest officer by a sometimes vulgar popularity contest. But free and open election engages popular feelings, confers legitimacy like no other means of choice, is educational for both the people and the leadership, and permits outsiders to enter the inner sanctum. Nothing in politics is so interesting as the choice of the supreme magistrate. Then more than any other time the people debate the issues and personalities of the day. This often fails to lead to the choice of a person of high moral and intellectual qualities, but the citizens of the democracy can take pleasure afterward in berating the follies of those whom they elect.

It is humbling to acknowledge that one's lofty status rests not on dignity of birth or victory in battle but on the will of very ordinary people. The quest for votes brings politicians into the milieu of the masses like nothing else. Those in high position easily lose contact with the commonalty, as they are sheltered by persons subject to their whims and are led to confuse their own with the national needs. Presidents are easily beguiled into surrounding themselves with pomp like that of royalty. But there is no cocoon on the campaign trail.

The electoral process, however, is not a very good way to sieve talent for top leadership. Those who happen to arrive at the political summit of a democracy by nonelectoral means or by chance seem to be no less capable. Those who have reached the American presidency via the vice presidency, that is by choice of the previous president, have hardly been poorer executives than those who fought their way to the office. Rajiv Gandhi, a man of no political vocation, became leader of India simply because he was Indira Gandhi's only remaining son after the death of her favorite Sanjay; yet he has apparently been one of the more capable of India's prime ministers. Corazon Aquino would never have aimed at high office in the Philippines if her husband had not been murdered, but she displayed extraordinary qualities of leadership and political judgment.

Modern leaders cannot possibly fulfill all of their roles—as head of state, as chief of administration, as party leader, as guide of the legislature, as communicator with the people, and as negotiator with foreign powers. Hence they must depend increasingly on subordinates. On the other hand, as the scope of government expands, the power of the office increases, and it becomes increasingly difficult to decide to what the chief's energies should be directed and where the limits should be placed on his or her actions.

How much authority the leader should have and how closely it should be checked are questions usually judged with little reference to political philosophy. Both leftists and rightists press sometimes for strong executive direction and sometimes for restraint of authority, the preference varying according to circumstances. When a leftist, such as Franklin Roosevelt, is in office, conservatives are passionately opposed to the extension of presidential powers, while liberals proclaim the need for a strong executive to provide national directions and carry out reforms; the opposite occurs when a conservative is the villain or hero.

A fundamental check on heads of the government is the fixed term, and their authority softens as people begin to think about the succession. The idea of limited tenure of office is as old as democratic government. The Greek city-states chose officials for one year and (except for some key leaders) prohibited reelection; the president of the Athenian assembly served a single day. This practice was intended, however, not to check power but to share the honors and to give the maximum number of citizens a turn at office. The American founding fathers saw short terms as crucial for democracy; the six-year Senate term was rather an aristocratic provision.

Frequent rotation in office keeps officeholders in touch with the people, makes government more responsible, and increases interest in civic affairs. However, it shifts power to the permanent administrators. In Athens, the citizen-officials who served for a month or a year had to rely on permanent assistants, often slaves. In modern times, short or irregular terms of office imply decision making to a large extent by the permanent staff, especially in unstable parliamentary regimes. A democratic practice has partly undemocratic results.

## THE APPARATUS

When the legislature has made laws and the executive has decided policies, an administrative apparatus or bureaucracy turns them into action. The public servant should be a faithful instrument or tool of the legal political will, but the manner of execution shapes the content of policy, and orders can remain unfulfilled while the chief's attention turns elsewhere. In any government, democratic or authoritarian, the apparatus usurps some part of the political will. It gives the state not only capacity but direction; political superiors have much influence only over the few programs in which they take a special interest.

The public servants gather, generate, coordinate, and sieve data. Most of what department heads know about their area of responsibility comes from their subordinates and at their discretion, and subordinates mold information going up and orders coming down. In the ever-growing complexity of government, the legislature usually does not attempt to formulate details of enforcement, but leaves this to the respective department or ministry. Bureaucrats thus become secondary lawmakers.[28] For example, in the United States, the application of civil-rights legislation has been greatly expanded by civil servants, who were largely responsible for the "affirmative action" approach.

In modern democracies the civil service is characterized by entrance through impartial examination, regular career ladders under nonpolitical authorities, security of office during good behavior, and clearly demarcated duties and lines of responsibility. Professionalization of administration has been a major achievement of modernization, a long step toward efficiency in the West a century ago, still to be taken in much of the world today. But it greatly raises the power of the tenured public servants, who are not only enabled to defy, to some extent, political superiors but who also accumulate knowledge and expertise on which temporary chiefs must rely.

So far as it is competent and effective, the administrative apparatus is a major factor in the legitimation of government: official expertise is an important reason for acceptance of official policies. The bureaucracy represents, or should represent, the technocratic side of modern government—orderly, incorruptible, nonideological, and informed. It is intermediary between politicians who make laws and those affected by them and is sensitive to both. It is more influential in the long term than in crises, and it is largely responsible for the momentum of policies. For example, the Irish bureaucracy maintained and strengthened the policy of requiring fluency in the Irish language over a long period during which public interest greatly declined.[29]

In the United States, the bureaucracy is only partially under the control of the president.[30] In France, West Germany, and elsewhere, professional administrators are near the heart of government, performing tasks reserved for political figures in the United States; they are also free to take political office without loss of civil service status. There seems to be a trend in most democracies toward mixing bureaucratic and political careers.[31]

In Japan, the prestigious bureaucracy, recruited through a rigorous examination system, largely carries on the business of government. The democratic superstructure checks and guides the professional apparatus but seeks to direct the state only in regard to controversial issues. It mostly furnishes legitimacy for those who actually carry on the operations and mostly make the decisions. The Diet generally leaves untouched the budget drawn up by the bureaucrats. The latter also spread the bureaucratic influence when, having risen as far as they can on the promotion ladder, typically in their forties or fifties, they retire and enter business or electoral politics. A large majority of premiers and cabinet ministers have been former civil servants, and the long dominance of a single party has led to a symbiosis of administration and political organization. The competent and well-regulated civil service, practically dominant in the democratic framework, seems to have a good deal to do with the remarkable success of Japan in the postwar period. The Japanese are said to regard the bureaucracy as more attuned to their interests than the elected Diet or the cabinet.[32]

An efficient civil service aids stability, improves decision making, reduces the likelihood of foolish actions, and raises the prestige of government. A civil service is legalistic and antidictatorial; it may be lofty, but it is not arbitrary or tyrannical. It is a mainstay of constitutionalism, if not democracy, because it has an interest in defined procedures and regularized powers. Moreover, a well-ordered bureaucracy protects democracy because it removes much of the business of government from party strife, transferring issues from the political to the technical arena.[33]

In sum, power in a democracy is shared between a political apparatus formed by elections and an administrative apparatus selected supposedly by merit. The former rules legally supreme as the brain over the body; the latter provides the means of action and often sets limits, as the body does. The better the body can be trained and coordinated, the more effective the brain, or the sounder the democratic state.

## LEGAL ORDER

The democratic state may not bring social justice or come near representing the will of its citizens, but it can probably claim to act legally according to known rules fixed by an agreed procedure. One of its best-assured advantages is that it is minimally arbitrary in the treatment of its citizens.

Even a very authoritarian state probably proceeds rather predictably in a large majority of its relations with its people. But there is no guarantee of regularity when the interests of power holders are touched unless there is a recognized pluralism of offsetting powers. This seems, under contemporary conditions, to be possible only in the democratic system.

The principal institutions of democracy—freedom of expression, the election of governing powers, a strong legislative organ, and independent courts—all operate to hinder irregular use of state power. Conceivably, a democratic majority might act arbitrarily, and this was often argued when democratic ideas were being fashioned in the eighteenth and early nineteenth centuries. But the majority is rarely tyrannical, especially in large and diverse polities, in which a majority has to be a coalition. The democratic process is likely to be oppressive only if it yields to ethnic or racial prejudices, such as against Tamils in Sri Lanka, Catholics in Northern Ireland, or Blacks in the American South prior to the civil-rights movement.

If a majority were persuaded by emotions of crisis to sanction restrictions of the press, persecution of unpopular individuals, or the assumption of extraordinary powers by a popular savior of the state, rule of law should undemocratically restrict majority rule in the interests of the permanence and consistency of the political order that makes democracy possible. The rights of all persons should be protected because permitting the abuse of one would sanction the abuse of many. Judges are certainly aware of election returns but should not be led by them to abandon good law. It seems outwardly democratic for judges to be elected, but this is often regarded as improper.

The legal order must function within a stable framework, central to which is a constitution less subject to a temporary majority than ordinary law. Behind the document there must be, of course, a suitable political culture and basic agreement on values. For this reason, constitutions in the Third World have usually meant little. On the other hand, British democracy is secure although the "constitution" is unwritten and vague, lacks a bill of rights (although it would probably be useful for Britain to have a written constitution and a bill of rights for clarity), and is subject to amendment by simple legislation. But it is backed by a general sense of fairness and concern for freedom. If British political institutions were somehow dissolved, one may feel confident that something like the present system would be brought back—assuming continuity in British society—minus traditional features such as the House of Lords, which are kept because they have always been there.

### The Role of the Judiciary

A written constitution, spelling out in detail the understandings of the democratic state, sets forth the relative rights and duties of the more or less independent parts of the state and the manner in which sovereignty is divided between the executive and legislative organs. This is especially important for the inherently weakest part of the government, the courts. An independent judicial system should not only assure that laws are applied fairly but also check both executive and legislative branches. Ideally, it assures that governmental actions are within the law and that the laws are within the constitution (so far as the American invention of judicial review is copied elsewhere).

The United States has the strongest and politically most important court system. Although they are usually not answerable to the electorate, judges may represent the political conscience of the country. The U.S. Supreme Court has been in the forefront of democratization, such as in the reapportionment of electoral districts and the protection of civil rights, to an extent sometimes decried as contrary to the letter and intent of the constitution. The least democratic of the branches of the government has at times been the most forward in promoting democratic values.

The judiciary, with its professional training, is in a sense a protected autonomous branch of the administration; in most democratic countries it is closely allied with the civil service. The judges have to rely on the legislature for their monetary support and on the executive for the execution of their verdicts; much of their power rests on tradition, and their independence stems from irremovability and prestige. The boundaries between the judicial and executive branches are blurred as special courts or administrative tribunals are charged with dealing with various areas of controversy, and these are supplemented by many autonomous commissions or agencies, such as—in the United States—the General Accounting Office, the Federal Reserve Board, and the Federal Communications Commission. Typically, heads of such agencies are named by the executive but are not removable by him.

A semijudicial agency in the democratic spirit is the ombudsman, a Scandinavian invention which has been widely copied. This is a judge-like official with a small staff empowered to investigate citizen complaints against the government. The ombudsman can take no action except to require information and publicize findings; but in the well-ordered state, this is probably sufficient to bring redress.

Guarantees of the openness of the political order—the freedom of opposition and expression, pluralism, the division of power among governmental agencies, and the rule of law applied by an independent judiciary—rest on the general conviction that life is better in a more loosely structured society, that it is unjust to command without authorization from the community, that freedom rests on law, and that freedom is a value in itself.

## Notes

1. For this reason Dahl preferred the term "polyarchy." Robert A. Dahl, *Polyarchy: Participation and Opposition* (New Haven: Yale University Press, 1971).
2. Dahl, *Polyarchy*, pp. 2–3.
3. Carl Cohen, *Democracy* (Athens: University of Georgia Press, 1971), p. 245.
4. Thucydides, *The Peloponnesian War*, trans. B. Jowett (Oxford: Clarendon Press, 1881), vol. 2, 37–40.
5. G. Bingham Powell, *Contemporary Democracies: Participation, Stability, and Violence* (Cambridge: Harvard University Press, 1982), p. 175.
6. Arendt Lijphart, *Democracies: Patterns of Majoritarian and Consensus Government* (New Haven: Yale University Press, 1984), p. 4.
7. Verba and Gary R. Orren, *Equality in America: The View from the Top* (Cambridge: Harvard University Press, 1985), p. 368.
8. Robert Nisbet, *Conservatism: Dream and Reality* (Minneapolis: University of Minnesota Press, 1986), pp. 68–75.
9. Peter Calvert, *Politics, Power, and Revolution: An Introduction to Comparative Politics* (Brighton: Sussex Wheatsheaf Books, 1983), p. 74.
10. See Lijphart, *Democracies*.
11. Reinhard Bendix, "The Extension of Citizenship to the Lower Classes," in *Readings in Political Sociology*, ed. Richard G. Braungart (Englewood Cliffs, N.J.: Prentice-Hall, 1976), p. 85–86.
12. Harold Laski, *Politics* (London: J. B. Lippencott, 1931), p. 71.
13. Gabriel A. Almond and G. Bingham Powell, Jr., *Comparative Politics* (Boston: Little, Brown & Co., 1978), p. 235.
14. Robert A. Dahl, *Dilemmas of Pluralist Democracy: Autonomy or Control* (New Haven: Yale University Press, 1982), pp. 32–33.
15. Maurice Pinard, "Mass Society and Political Movements," in *Readings*, ed. Braungard, pp. 325–28.
16. Powell, *Contemporary Democracies*, p. 213.
17. Lijphart, *Democracies*, pp. 22–23.
18. On the relation of democracy and the market economy, see Charles E. Lindblom's *Politics and Markets: The World Political-Economic Systems* (New York: Basic Books, 1977), chap. 12.
19. Theodore J. Lowi, *The End of Liberalism: The Second Republic of the United States* (New York: W. W. Norton & Co., 1979), p. 33.
20. Tom Peters and Nancy Austin, "A Passion for Excellence," *Fortune*, May 13, 1985, pp. 26–28.
21. Donald Kagan, *The Great Dialogue: History of Greek Political Thought from Homer to Polybius* (New York: Free Press, 1965), p. 76.
22. Cohen, *Democracy*, p. 238.
23. Howard P. Kainz, *Democracy East and West: A Philosophical Overview* (London: Macmillan, 1984), p. 55.
24. Gregory Markus, "Pocketbook Voting," *Scientific American*, 225 (July 1986), 62.

25. G. Bingham Powell, *Contemporary Democracies: Participation, Stability and Violence* (Cambridge: Harvard University Press, 1982), pp. 213–14.
26. Seymour Martin Lipset, "Political Sociology," in *Readings*, ed. Braungart, p. 50.
27. Kenneth E. Boulding, *The World as a Total System* (Beverly Hills: Sage Publications, 1985), p. 116.
28. Joel D. Aberbach, Robert D. Putnam, and Bert A. Rockman, *Bureaucrats and Politicians in Western Democracies* (Cambridge: Harvard University Press, 1981), p. 245.
29. Cullen Murphy, "Language: The Irish Question," *Atlantic*, 256 (September 1985), 28–38.
30. Cf. William P. Browne, *Politics, Programs, and Bureaucrats* (Port Washington, N.Y.: Kennikat Press, 1980).
31. Aberbach and others *Bureaucrats and Politicians*, pp. 17–19.
32. Taketsuyu Tsurutani, "The Japanese Political System," in *Polities and Government: A Brief Introduction*, ed. Alex N. Dragnich, John T. Dorsey, Jr., and Taketsuyu Tsurutani (Chatham, N.J.: Chatham House, 1982), pp. 158–59.
33. Lipset, "Political Sociology," p. 52.

# The Problems of Democracy

7

Democracy conforms to much in human nature. It seems to accommodate and adjust the elements of cooperation and competition inherent in life better than an imposed order. It awakens spirit and energy and invites individual thought and action as well as social enterprise. It is more realistic than an authoritarian state because it is open to criticism, has little sacred dogma, and is based less on pretense. Democratic management is good for production and satisfaction in work. Self-determination on the job is more valued than a small increase of wages,[1] and people perform better when they have a sense of control over their circumstances.[2] On the one hand, the pluralistic open society has made possible, for better or worse, the rise of science and technological civilization. On the other hand, equality of rights is a long step toward the general equality and community most people seem to value.

Yet in a world of fallible people and flawed institutions, democracy suffers many problems and has sometimes failed, not only in the non-Western world but also in the classical West. People will often sacrifice freedom for security, or for what they believe to promise security. In Europe between the world wars, countries of more or less authoritarian background—Germany, Italy, Portugal, and many of Eastern Europe—shed the democratic clothing they had recently taken on; and the future of democracy seemed questionable even in France. Many believed that democracy had seen its day.

Although democratic institutions reinforce each other, there is no guarantee of stability if dissatisfaction should become general, as in the depression of the 1930s. Democracies are sometimes afflicted with malaise and purposelessness,[3] and serious frictions may obstruct the delicately balanced system. Excess pluralism leads to immobility. Democracy relies on the good sense of humans, whose rationality has been questioned. In the view of critics, democracy, by exalting individual self-seeking, defeats community goals; it gives real power to wealth, which governs the means of expression; and procedural politics rewards, and gives victory to, the stronger and less scrupulous.[4]

Holdovers from an authoritarian past—as in the Germany of the Weimar Republic—and present conditions—such as ethnic or racial conflict—both hinder the realization of democratic values. The greed of groups without thought of the community, lack of foresight or the unwillingness to defer desires, ignorance and the propensity to act blindly, the yen for easy solutions, clashes of values, the multiform misuse of authority, and many vices undermine the democratic state. Politicians preoccupied with popularity are perhaps compelled to superficiality, fearing to go deeper than the understanding of the average voter. Many have thought it necessary in the democracy to flatter popular prejudices. Democracy also suffers from the indifference of the majority, which is the opportunity of a few. For example, labor unions, democratically organized in theory, are often usurped by activist or self-serving minorities because few members bother to vote.

### Virtues Turned Faults

The virtues of democracy sometimes become faults. For example, the rule of law, the standing of the judiciary, and regard for individual rights and justice encourage litigation to an excessive degree, at least in the most legal-minded society, the United States. This means large outlays for deciding disputes in complex and protracted battles in which both sides lose because of delays and formalities and only lawyers win. The strength and independence of the courts in the United States have led to their assuming virtual legislative power, especially in extending constitutional rights, but also in regard to sundry other matters such as environmental protection and nuclear power. The courts may even take executive control, as many federal judges have administered school systems in the name of racial integration, a concept tenuously derived from the Constitution.

The democracy, sympathizing with victims of misfortune, overlooks the costs of legal liability. Large judgments for alleged malpractice may not so much improve the practice of medicine—the costs being covered by insurance—as raise the price of health care because of insurance costs and conceivably reduce its quality because compiling a record becomes more important than treating the ailment. Communities curtail recreation services because of the excessive insurance premiums brought by emotional judgments. Litigiousness accords with the pluralistic, democratic society, in which money is the chief measure of things, and the compassionate system would have the rich compensate the unfortunate. But it nourishes a very influential lawyer class with a vested interest in the quantity and complexity of law, not in simplicity, dispatch, and moderation in the handling of disputes; and the legal profession is greatly overrepresented in representative politics.

Rights of property clash with the ideal of racial equality, and the rights of criminals conflict with the right not to be victimized. The right to work contradicts the right of unionization and collective bargaining. Equal educational opportunity opposes freedom of choice of schools and community responsibility for them. Such conflicts are unresolvable, like the right of one homeowner to grow a shade tree and the right of a neighbor to enjoy sunshine; but the democratic society invites people to stake claims against one another. Groups and enterprises contend, sometimes ruinously; with some reason, authoritarians see the pluralistic society as given to mutual destruction.

Freedom of expression becomes license for salacious exploitation of the female body and for huckstering addictive substances. Violence is commercialized freely and to an exaggerated degree, with dubious effects on character, as though freedom elicits the antisocial in human nature. Freedom of speech is necessarily freedom both to criticize beyond warrant and to mislead (within limits of fraud). Criticism is more interesting than praise, and more useful, as praise only reinforces conduct but criticism may improve it. But there are incentives, in the condition of political opposition, for irresponsible criticism, for attacks beyond reason or justification on purely partisan grounds, confusing issues, raising distrust of the leadership, and reducing the capacity of government.

The democratic society is sometimes excessively self-critical not so much in regard to particular faults—which can be attended to—as in regard to general character. For reasons of sociology and psychology, most intellectuals are negative toward the status quo and tend to dislike power holders, or at least economic power holders, who are considered much worse than political power holders. Intellectuals who are fairly quiet and conformist under pressure become hypercritical and negative when dissent is invited.[5] The system is held guilty until proved innocent, and in some circles attacks on it are held admirable in principle even if unsupported. Writers seem to wish to feel repressed and to enjoy anger at the system that refuses to repress them. Intellectual elitists are antidemocratic in that they oppose the values of the majority in principle.

Critics attack democracy mostly for failure to fulfill economic and social rights. They advance claims of nonpolitical justice, which are called rights like political and civil rights but are really a different and more difficult category, including the right to work, to education, to medical care, and to a decent living. Such rights require not that the state exercise indiscriminate fairness but that it provide something to certain persons, which means taking something from others. It should be possible at some point to say that civil and political rights are adequately observed—indeed, in leading democracies there are few strong charges of violations of such rights—but economic and social rights are endlessly elastic. There is also a difference in that political rights should be judicially enforceable, whereas economic and social rights require administrative action.

In a very democratic and egalitarian society, as in some of the small countries of northern Europe, the idea of rights may reach very far. For example, in the Netherlands struggling painters unable to find appreciation have the right to sell their works to the state. Everyone has a right to a living; as a politician put it, "We believe you must give people a basic wage and let them choose whether or not to work"—an idea firmly rejected by Marxist-Leninist societies. A Dutch graduate, believing that "money shouldn't be tied to work" and seeing his social security "as a basic right," dedicated himself to helping people assert their rights against the police.[6]

The democracy could spend all its energy sorting out an infinity of contrary interests, inconsistent rights, and questions of authority and jurisdiction. Where many rights are precious, there are many ambiguities and conflicts. Democracy is saved by the willingness to compromise and the consensus or sense of community that values the democratic order as inherently desirable.

## COLLECTIVE SELF-SEEKING

The democracy faces difficult questions regarding the extent of freedom and the ability of groups, especially economic enterprises, to advance their interests. The basic policy might be to minimize state interference with private activities, on the presumption that the government in democracies (as in nondemocracies) is likely to control too much because persons with an interest in control usually have a share in determining its extent. But ordinary citizens need the state to protect them from a thousand dangers, deceits, and impositions. The state, moreover, faces the problem of the commons: if all parties maximize their benefits from the use of a shared resource, such as a pastureland or the oceans, they may destroy the resource—overgraze the pasture or overfish the ocean to barrenness. Or if there is freedom to use the atmosphere to carry away wastes, it is in the interest of any individual polluter to use it without restraint.

In conditions of excessive governmental interference, it is easy to see the removal of all trammels as the prerequisite to progress. Much of the rise of the West, it may be recalled, can be attributed to its release from feudal and mercantilist shackles, as brilliantly advocated by Adam Smith. But competition and free markets do not solve all problems, in part because markets, in the complexities of modern production and finance, are seldom really free and in part because the workings of competitive free enterprise are unsatisfactory. For example, it is regarded as desirable to ameliorate the effects of market forces on farmers. Labor unions create inequalities, distort prices, and perhaps increase unemployment; but they are widely viewed as desirable for equity, to equalize the bargaining power of workers and capitalists.

Many natural monopolies and oligopolies lend themselves to abuse. Only a single enterprise can economically provide electricity to any given neighborhood; and costs of development are such that even a large market, such as the United States, can apparently not sustain more than a small number of producers of, for example, automobiles. Deregulation of airlines means low fares between large cities, disproportionately high fares to small ones where there is no competition, and chaotic pricing.

### Interest Groups

Groups are not so energetic in driving for new privileges as in resisting the loss of acquired advantages, which become rights. Taxi drivers fight for the value of their licenses, and truckers protected by regulations protest deregulation. Corporations, having gained a special status of some kind, regard its loss as an unqualified injustice; and in the democracy they are likely to be able to protect it. The state subsidizes huge surpluses of agricultural commodities and forces consumers of many products to pay far more than world market prices; U.S. sugar producers, for example, enjoy what may be called a form of legalized corruption. The European Economic Community is even more irrational in this regard than the United States, providing butter, wine, and grain almost gratis to Arabs or Russians while forcing citizens of the community to pay dearly to keep farmers in business. This kind of agricultural policy has nearly bankrupted the community. Japan guarantees rice farmers about ten times the world price for the product of their tiny and uneconomic plots. The political clout of the farmers, supported by sentimental views, is too strong for the democratic polity.

Size of the self-seeking group is immaterial. Social Security having become accepted, its beneficiaries form a huge pressure group able to prevent even a gradual adjustment of retirement age for increased longevity. Only peanut farmers favor peanut price supports, which cost taxpayers and munchers, but the strong concern of a few outweighs the unconcern of many. The totally needless Teatasters' Board would never be created in modern conditions; being profitable for its members, it has sufficient influence that no one pushes hard enough to abolish it.[7] Networks of interest groups hinder reform and check competition. Even a newly elected, thoroughly legitimate new American administration can usually make major changes only in its first six to nine months, after which the "interests" have mobilized to protect themselves.[8]

More or less narrow groups, whose needs may be alien to those of the remainder of society, have a disproportionate influence.[9] A lobby is more effective as it concentrates, like the National Rifle Association, on a single objective. Groups engage in distributional struggle, politicize competition, and divert energies from production to division. An important reason for the extraordinary economic growth of postwar Germany and Japan seems to be the fact that defeat and occupation dissolved many of the cartelistic and semimonopolistic groups tying up their economies.[10]

Democratic politicians promise quick benefits with little regard for long-term costs, playing to the human disposition to think more of today than tomorrow. Rent control is pleasant for renters, who are more numerous than landlords, until it results in a shortage of housing. Preferring proximate pleasure at the cost of long-term damage to the economy has been part of the pathology of democracy in many countries. Although democratic participation stabilizes by enhancing legitimacy, it may destabilize by raising pressures on the state.[11] Political pressures for spending are more focused and concentrated and hence more effective than pressures to balance accounts. The problem of groups wanting more than their share of benefits and using political power to get it has no theoretical solution. There is only the hope that something not too far from a general interest will emerge from groups clashing and counterpoising each other.

Two principles of democracy conflict; that individuals should be left free so far as consonant with the well-being of others and that the interests or desires of the majority should prevail. To maximize freedom is to make life most fully human and to enlarge the sphere of discovery. Yet the complex modern society seems to require ever more detailed regulation. Since the democratic state can be roughly equated with the people, there is some presumption that its power is good and its intervention beneficent. This sentiment doubtless leads the state to undertake many things that might be more efficiently handled by nonstate agencies—for example, waste disposal.

Economic autonomy broadly accords with political autonomy, and acceptance of a large state role may threaten to lead toward acceptance of an authoritarian state. However, this has not been the road to serfdom.[12] Democracies have failed for various reasons, but there are no obvious examples of the gradual extinction of liberties through extension of the sphere of the state. Democracies with a very high share of the national product in the hands of the state (for example, Sweden, Denmark, and the Netherlands) do not seem the less democratic, whereas social conflict or economic troubles have been primarily responsible for opening the door to dictatorship in countries where the state assumed much less responsibility for the general welfare, as in Italy (1922), Poland (1926), Germany (1933), Brazil (1964), Chile (1973), India (1975), and Pakistan (1977).

## MONEY POWER

The strongest theoretical criticism of democracy is that it gives effective power to money. Even if there were no question of outright corruption, the control of the media and advertising influences not only consumer but political preferences. Television frankly promotes brands of deodorants or soap; sometimes less frankly, it gives wide publicity to certain views and ignores others, thereby influencing or even determining the direction of public attention and opinion. Newspapers, magazines, and broadcasting are big businesses, and they cannot be exempt from the vices of big business. They are increasingly monopolistic; in only a small minority of American cities is there real competition of local papers; and network television, which dominates the news, is a close oligopoly.

Especially because of the high cost and effectiveness of television, money looms large in democratic politics. In all modern countries—Europe and Japan as well as the United States—electoral campaigns require elaborate organization, a large staff, and, above all, political advertising. When it is more effective for a candidate to spend time raising funds for television spots than meeting voters, money cannot but play a large and not always ethical role; and well-financed groups have influence far beyond their popular representation. If there is to be freedom of expression, it is impossible to prevent the supporters of a candidate or a cause from using their resources to influence votes; but one cannot pretend that the representative nature of government is not distorted.

Happily, money is not all-powerful but is only one ingredient of electoral success, and it is no substitute for personal appeal. President Marcos found that Filipinos were willing to take bags of rice and vote for his opponent. In the commercialized society there is skepticism of advertising in general, and an excess of political messages may repel. Awareness that a candidate is backed by great wealth is very negative. Many multimillionaires have tried in vain to purchase political glory. But worthy candidates have also often failed for lack of funds.

Many corporate interests would also like to purchase favorable legislation; their ability to do so depends greatly on the publicity the subject receives. The saving fact is that particular interests are diverse and to a large extent neutralize one another. Not only do importers, for example, oppose producers seeking protection, but one corporation frequently is contrary to another. In matters of broad concern, such as taxation, legislators strive mightily to promote, or to seem to promote, the interests of the many.

The electoral power of wealth may be restricted by regulation of campaign expenditures, but it is impossible for the rules to be fully effective even if there should be a general desire to enforce them, as there is likely not to be. No way has been devised to exclude private financial support. It is possible, however, to place poorer and richer parties on a more equal footing by public funding of campaigns. This is commonly done in "advanced" democracies, although it tends to favor incumbent parties and persons, which have a large advantage in fund raising in any case.[13]

The democratic state inevitably has elements of plutocracy, representing economic interests as well as people. In a sense, this is a soft form of corruption. This is no special sin of democracies, however. Money gives political influence in nondemocratic systems as well, sometimes more amply and certainly more insidiously. And it is not clear that the influence of a nondemocratic political interest is more salutary than an economic interest.

In the nineteenth century it was common to limit the franchise to persons of certain wealth, or only to taxpayers, on the grounds that only they would deal responsibly with government expenditures. Although this no longer satisfies the prevalent sense of justice, there are probably not many democratic governments that are really prepared to accept a policy favored only by the poorer majority. Fortunately, however, people vote for many reasons other than material benefits or economic class, from patriotism to faith in leaders' judgments.[14]

The willingness to look to broader and longer-term advantages depends upon education and civic spirit and the reduction of class differences. Economic elites similarly, if they are wise, promote not only their own private gain but also sound basic economic policies of stability, investment, nondamaging taxation, and fiscal responsibility, and at the same time policies of reasonable social justice and reduction of differences and tensions—policies good in the long run for the producers as well as for the community.

The influence of wealth may realistically be considered a price for the firmness of democracy. Like other forms of government, democracy is sustained much more by an elite (in some cases, a rather broad elite) than by the support of the middle or of the poorer classes, who are usually too incoherent to offer much protection to a democracy under attack. But democracy is acceptable to the wealthy not only because of philosophic attachment to humanitarian principles but also because money has political influence, both in the electoral process and in the making of policy, and because a legal, constitutional government is the best guarantee of the security of persons and property. Economic elites have historically demanded rights for all while seeking rights for themselves, with some confidence that they would not thereby surrender superiority.

## INEQUALITY

The democratic society is intrinsically competitive-conflictual, and all manner of clashes arise between groups and institutions with incompatible or only partially compatible interests. The chief root of conflict is the eternal problem of dividing up limited resources—not only of material goods but of power, the gain of one side being the loss of the other. For the democracy to be successful, its conflicts must be resolved with minimal violence, preferably with minimal resentment and in ways that are broadly acceptable.

The extent to which this is possible depends above all on the sense of community and basic agreement, or the degree of dividedness of the society. This in part is a matter of extraneous conditions, such as race (as in South Africa) or religion (as in Lebanon) or ethnic background (as in Canada and Belgium). But the most basic question—and what gives explosive force to differences of race or religion—is inequality of possessions among groups or persons. The more inequality, the more difficult all political problems become.

Humans are unequal, by nature and even more by condition, both as groups and as individuals; the notion of equality is contrary to both reality and practice. Not only do people markedly differ in physique, talents, values, and drives; wherever they interact they settle into social inequalities. Like animal societies, they have, and perhaps need to have, their peck order. In a boys' gang, a school class, or a club, some lead and others follow, some are esteemed and others scorned, for reasons often unclear. This is not necessarily resented; some of those who stand below are satisfied with their less demanding condition or regard themselves as future leaders, just as some of the less affluent accept economic inequality cheerfully because they see themselves as potentially upper class. The sense of equality in the democratic society also runs counter to the stress on individualism and the respect for personal achievement.

The idea of equality is persuasive, however. The simplest and least controversial way to cut the cake is by equal shares, and the most appealing theory of government rests on a presumption of equal political rights. So far as all are reasonably level in condition and rewards, mutual understanding comes easily; as some advance and others fall behind, there is sure to be bitterness and dissatisfaction unless the inequality seems morally justified.

### Kinds of Inequality

Inequality has many aspects, such as differences of possessions, economic power, prestige, social standing, education, and access to political power. They tend to run together, but they do not necessarily coincide. Army officers are often powerful both as groups and as individuals without owning substantial property and perhaps without high social standing. Social divisions are as much a matter of a sense of superiority as of riches; impecunious aristocrats are likely to be snobbish. There can be fellow feeling among people of quite different wealth, as in a college fraternity, if it is accepted that belonging to the brotherhood is the essential matter. A kind of inequality built into the complex society and difficult to change is the difference of rewards and prestige of different occupations.[15]

There are many kinds of inequality: between races, sexes, religions, ages, and others.[16] The equality easiest to achieve is of rights (which people may not be in a condition, or have the will, to assert), such as the vote or free speech and press, or procedural guarantees if brought to trial—although one's access to the media or the quality of one's lawyer are as important as the formal right. The free-market economy is egalitarian in this sense because it treats all alike even though it allows some to build palaces and gives others equal freedom to sleep on the street.

Beyond this, one may wish equality of opportunity: that all be able to secure a good start in life, to step onto the ladder of success and climb to whatever height without unfair barriers or undue advantages. But opportunity can never be fully equalized. Children of parents who stress learning and achievement compete in school with those of no such background; equal classrooms which the state may provide cannot overcome unequal home environments. Some have very influential friends and relations, others have none, and no democracy is so legalistic that whom one knows does not matter.

Substantial formal equality, or equality of rights, is a magnificent achievement by the standard of history. It is a still greater accomplishment for the state to offer at least enough education that many of the bright and ambitious can ascend from humble conditions, so that a family can rise from bottom to top in a generation or two. The democratic state can further seek to prevent unjustifiable discriminations or unfair treatment from adding to inequalities, for example by banning racial discrimination in housing and employment. It can also reduce the penalties of falling behind by assuming responsibility for a minimum of subsistence and comfort for the neediest.

It may be further desired to seek equality of results, that all should enjoy more nearly equal shares of the goods of life. But equality of results is much more difficult to define as well as to achieve. Does it mean equal results regardless of unequal talents, the distribution of which by nature is unfair? Should there be equalization between the dull and the clever, the lazy and the industrious?

Equality of condition, however, hardly comes into question; the hope is only to moderate differences. Although there have been pendular swings toward and away from egalitarianism in the United States, few in this country (and probably other democracies) want radical redistribution of wealth.[17] The real demand is for a degree of equalizing and fair opportunities, as Henry Ward Beecher put it, not "that every man shall be on a level but that every man have liberty to be what God made him." Equality of opportunity justifies inequality of results,[18] making them the outcome of talent and effort.

For the ancient Greeks, democracy meant equal rights, not redistribution;[19] and the Athenians, despite attachment to equality, usually chose rich and well-born men for the important offices.[20] Idealists have sought to construct a perfect society by abolishing the inequality of property through communal sharing. Such efforts have never succeeded, even temporarily, unless the loss of individual ownership was compensated for by spiritual gain or a promise of salvation.[21]

### The Strength of Inequality

Equality collides with human nature. Social status—the sense of belonging to a higher category above the vulgar majority—is prized quite as much as material goods, and those who have a modicum of status fight against surrendering it.[22] A major reason for the desire for goods beyond necessity is the symbolism of superiority; consumption is the more enjoyable as it is the more conspicuous, just as diamonds are valued over equally refractive synthetic crystals because few can afford diamonds. Particularly in countries of traditional inequality, education is valued as title to status, and the school tie opens doors to elitehood. Race is also a subject of unequal pride. Until recently, even a small fraction of African ancestry carried low status in the United States unless outweighed by exceptional talents, as in sports or music. In Latin America, after the Spanish conquered and enserfed the native populations of the New World, to be of Spanish background (preferably born in Spain) conveyed automatic superiority; everything "Indian" was inferior. In Haiti and Liberia a tiny mulatto minority regards itself as inestimably better than the African-descended majority—sufficient reason that democracy is unlikely in those countries. Such feelings linger permanently.

Many who are deeply attached in theory to principles of equality uphold and esteem in practice their own distinctiveness. Reformers or radicals devoted to the cause of the poor commonly shrink from mingling socially with them, as though the disease of poverty were contagious. Leaders of communist parties are as elitist as leaders of conservative parties in their confidence in their right to guide the workers, with whom they may have little close contact.

Economic inequality is also a stubborn fact. Success of any kind can be compounded, and small advantages are converted into large differences. It is a tribute to social mobility if a few of the less privileged can climb to riches by entrepreneurship or good fortune; but having become rich, they probably adopt the values of the rich. Any organized group or sector of society that feels itself superior, as by race, inheritance, culture, or whatever, probably uses whatever advantages it may possess to affirm its position and exclude the less fortunate; and such differences are commonly reinforced by differences of wealth. The aristocrats' self-esteem is part of their being.

It is arguable that the structure of the modern society itself precludes equality and truly democratic management.[23] Complex organization implies hierarchy and the power of some over others. Position is allocated in many ways, some related to what might be called merits (talent and good performance), others to less relevant factors (familial and other relationships, wealth, aggressiveness, deceit, and so forth). The drive of socialism is dual; in part for the redistribution of wealth to benefit the poor and support the welfare state and in part toward the central or political direction of society. But the centralization of socialism increases effective inequality as it increases the organization of society, the hierarchization of its structures, and the status of a few.

### Values of Equality

There are many burdens of the inequality of the rich and the poor, the diplomaed and the unlettered, the respectable and the unclean, the fashionably dressed and the ragged, the powerful and the humble, the magnate and the serf. A high degree of separation of classes is the strongest cause of the unworkability of democracy in most of the world.[24] For example, it seems clear that the basic cause of the nondemocratic history of Argentina, as compared with other countries of abundant land, has been the tradition of social inequality from its Spanish background, incorporated in and reinforced by extremely large landholding—estates of hundreds of thousands of acres.

Democracy requires that people broadly share values and respect one another, but the classes that deem themselves superior have little respect for those whom they see as ignorant and dirty, if not immoral. Naturally, they resist the right of inferiors to an equal share in the choice of leadership. The upper classes also probably distrust politicians whom they regard as lower class, either coming out of the masses or speaking for them. The deprived, on the other hand, are subject to coercion and deception, even while they may be moved by envy.

The politically decisive division is not strictly between upper and lower economic classes but between the status-satisfied and the dissatisfied; many middle-class revolutionaries have been disappointed in conservative workers and peasants. In the unequal society, however, any political division may (so far as the masses participate) become an economic-class division, and labor disputes may become political quarrels. There is disagreement on a multitude of issues, such as the value of economic stability versus jobs or of property rights versus a multiform clamor for benefits.

Inequality lends passion to divisions. The antagonism of Protestants and Catholics in Northern Ireland, an incredibly irrational persistence of fierce religious bias in a modern society, owes much to the fact that the Catholics are generally much poorer than the Protestants. Asians have been persecuted in Africa not so much because they are alien as because they are richer.

Inequality makes for corruption, which increases inequality, as wealth is used to direct the benefits of the state to wealth. The more unequal the society, the more energies go into the maintenance of social hierarchy. The more artificial the superiority of a class, the more it focuses on its standing. Social status, aristocratic display, exclusiveness, and scorn for inferiors become central values, and cultivated hands should not be dirtied by doing any work that is for inferiors.

Equality makes more stimulating competition among individuals. It emphasizes knowledge and work as the means of distinction. Hence the scholastic race by the youth of such countries as Japan and Hong Kong leads them to frantic, perhaps excessive, intensity of studies, as their career depends heavily on ranking in the examinations. In conditions rewarding merit or achievement there may be rapid social differentiation.[25] But the ability to rise by effort and ability is commonly considered a chief attribute of democracy. The gross inequality of late nineteenth-century America was much mitigated by social fluidity, the possibility for the office boy to become corporation president; Horatio Alger was not entirely myth, and he had an effect on the national temper.

Part of the secular progress of civilization is the reduction of irrational discrimination. There is no reason in the modern world to treat people unequally except in response to their actions and needs. In the democratic society there must always be a presupposition in favor of inclusion in the community, and equal rights are to be denied only for powerful reasons, such as criminal character or mental incapacity;[26] and in return for equality of rights, the modern society can expect all to contribute. The French Revolution freed the serfs and struck off feudal chains; in compensation, it could require that all (men of military age) be subject to military duty in defense of what had become their nation; and the new egalitarian mass armies of France swept across Europe.

In conditions of equality, social controls are better accepted and more effective. Leaders or managers need information and ideas from below; but the greater the feeling of division is, the more slanted will the reports coming up be, the less inclined will the inferiors be to generate ideas or the superiors to listen to them, and, generally, the poorer will the motivation of subordinates be. Most high-growth economies have had relatively small income differentials; for example, Taiwan and Japan, are among the most egalitarian of nations. The managerial success of the Japanese owes something to the fact that the spread of pay between Japanese bosses and workers is less than half as great as in the United States, and Japanese executives are much more willing to consult with and listen to those on the shop floor and to eat in the same lunchroom. Workers are more productive when they share control over their world—for example, by having the power to halt assembly lines—and they are stimulated by the boss's interest.[27] Bringing executives closer to production workers and other bows to industrial democracy, such as classless parking lots, are as successful in the United States as in Japan.[28] Nearly equal-sized offices, workers' participation in corporate boards, and their great rights of information in Germany and Sweden help smooth industrial relations.[29]

In sum, equality, political as well as economic, is the essence of democracy. Yet the degree of effective equality differs among democracies. Some Third World countries with formal democratic institutions, citizens' rights, and election of leaders, have profound separation of rich and poor. These are better designated quasidemocracies and are considered in the following chapter. Among clearly democratic countries, France and Spain are relatively unequal, both socially and economically, bearing the heritage of authoritarian regimes of the past. The most egalitarian are small European nations, especially the Scandinavian countries, Switzerland, and the Netherlands. This may be the result of their century or more of democratic institutions, of smallness keeping the pyramid of organizational power low, and of their homogeneity. They have also profited from remaining almost wholly out of war.

The United States is more unequal in terms of income distribution than the small European democracies, perhaps mostly because of heterogeneity, with both racial and ethnic minorities and a continual influx from much poorer countries. It is also part of the American economic ethos that one is invited to get rich. A much larger proportion of Swedes than Americans want equalization of pay or a ceiling on earnings, and the disparity between top and bottom pay in industry is about six times greater in the United States than in Sweden.[30] Such differences are nearly permanent; the degree of inequality changes very slowly except in a situation of national catastrophe, such as the defeat and occupation of Japan, where the discrediting and improverishment of the elite made possible the democratization of a nonlegalistic, anti-individualist, and hierarchic society.

## THE PROBLEMS OF BUREAUCRACY

The most influential group in democratic societies is probably not the owners of productive capital [31]—a diverse and conflictual collection— but the apparatus of the state. Those charged with carrying out policies, who shape policies both by providing information and by the manner of execution, can be expected to exert influence on their own behalf, pursuing their own goals alongside, and sometimes ahead of, those of the state. For example, the intelligence agency of each of the American armed services makes estimates of Soviet capabilities to suit its own branch.[32]

The bureaucratic ethos is the opposite of the democratic, valuing unity, hierarchy, command, fixity in position, secrecy, and appointment from above over pluralism, equality, freedom, limited terms of office, and election from below.[33] Agencies are to a large extent closed and fond of secrecy; the U.S. penchant for "freedom of information" is not widespread even in democratic states. The apparatus, which is the least democratic aspect of the democratic state and the most legal-regularized aspect of the totalitarian state, is the area where the extremes are most alike.

Bureaucracies everywhere are notorious for slowness, indifference, pettifogging, immobility, formalism, and attachment to procedure. Bureaucracy promises security and presumably attracts persons more attached to guaranteed livelihood and formal status than to activity or innovation.[34] The setup discourages independent thinking, the making of waves, and perhaps even hard work, which may discomfit less dedicated colleagues. Accomplishment in any case is not proportional to hours spent.[35] The tendency is to maximize not productivity but personnel, as each head of a section wants to expand his or her little empire and increase its autonomy.

In any protected bureaucracy like the U.S. Civil Service, there is little incentive for efficiency or punishment for incompetence—which is usually safe from inquiry because investigation requires major and probably unrewarded exertions by superiors. Rank and size of budget are inevitably more important than performance, and bureaus commonly evaluate their own performance. Actions suitable for advancement diverge, often sharply, from those that best serve the overt purposes of the organization.[36] The aim of civil service rules is to reward merit, but the security of public servants from political dismissal becomes a virtual right not only to a job but to semiautomatic promotions. External political influences may be more or less eliminated, but appointment and advancement are subject to internal politics.

It is frequently accepted that the growth of public employment in recent decades has been brought about by the complexities of modern life, increased social consciousness, and the growing demand for governmental services, protection, and controls. This may be misleading, however. Public employment was a big problem for ancient Greek democracy.[37] The record-keeping functions of the state should have been much facilitated and simplified by modern labor-saving equipment, and the proportion of the work force on the public payroll bears no close relation to the modernity of the society. In Japan, for example, it is relatively low, although growing. It is extremely difficult to halt a program once underway, eliminate public jobs, or apply the standards of the private sector to civil-service pay scales. Bureaucratic organizations, once set up, are virtually immortal; and they never propose a decrease of expenditures. Economizing is taboo because saving money would mean that not so much was needed.

In both France and Japan, the administrative interests of the government tobacco monopoly, like tobacco manufacturers in the United States, have ignored the health hazards of smoking and found psychological virtues in cigarettes. The Kennedy administration was unable to build self-help into the welfare system because it threatened the positions of too many administrators. It seems probable that the complexity of the American welfare apparatus owes much to the fact that a large number of people have vested interests in maximizing the variety of services to the poor and dispensing them through a jungle of agencies.

In the United States, as in many countries, programs have grown relentlessly through administrations of different parties, through hard times and good; there is always more to be done by more employees. Typically, the governmental share of U.S. national output rose from 10 percent in 1929 to 32 percent in 1979 and 37 percent in 1984. The number of pages of federal regulations increased explosively from 10,000 pages in the early 1960s to 20,000 pages in 1970 and 77,500 pages in 1979,[38] regulations that add to the cost of government the billions of manhours spent in implementation. In Europe, the percentage of the national product taken by the state is even larger. Sweden headed the list, with government expenditures at 62 percent of the gross national product in 1984, followed by the Netherlands (58 percent), Denmark (58 percent), Belgium (54 percent), Italy (52 percent), and Ireland (51 percent). When such a large part of the national income flows through a semiunified organization (in the United States, the 37 percent is divided among the federal, state, and local governments), there is created a group that, so far as it has a sense of common interest in certain policies (such as the basic idea of state responsibility for welfare), is invincible in the political arena. Unhappily for efficiency, but happily for the political balance, agencies contend with one another more than they cooperate, as is evident, for example, in the notorious squabbles and failures of communication of branches of the American armed forces.

The overwhelming role of government in Sweden and other welfare-state democracies of northern Europe has seemed bearable until fairly recently. When Swedish moderate-conservatives were in power (from 1976 to 1982) they did not really try to shrink the state. At one time Sweden was praised as the "middle way," enjoying the benefits of statism and capitalism while minimizing the drawbacks of both. But the costs of protected labor have priced many Swedish goods out of world markets and the country has run up a heavy foreign debt. The tax on middle-class incomes is over 50 percent, youth seems bored with a protected existence, and much of the infrastructure is decayed. Freedoms are qualified as police keep full records on every citizen and detailed rules regulate trade.[39] Scandinavia is less egalitarian in practice than in theory, as standing in the political class is practically hereditary, and a relatively small number of persons strategically placed in leading organizations have disproportionate influence.[40]

### Bureaucracy and Politics

All countries face the problem of keeping the administrative corps subject to the political direction while maintaining a high level of expertise. Public servants exercise influence in many ways: by their ability to lobby with decision makers, by possession and selective transmission of information, by swamping their political superiors with a mass of data, and by unobtrusive noncooperation when they are opposed. It is seldom useful for a politician to press any measure opposed by a substantial sector of the apparatus.

In order to maximize the competence and objectivity of the public servants and to minimize the use of jobs for political ends, the elected authorities who fix priorities should have only general and impersonal control of the machinery. Administrators chosen on the basis of qualifications that can be appraised should be insulated from the political contest. In their professionalism they should be prepared to carry out orders without considering their own tastes or interests. But this is almost inhumanly difficult, and the reality is that a real attack on the power of the apparatus is almost impossible, in democratic as in communist countries; at best it can be whittled down. So far as the democratic bureaucracy is more flexible, rational, and dedicated to public service, it is the more invulnerable. To assault it is like hitting a mass of sticky jelly.

Nearly everyone is critical of the state apparatus, the very word *bureaucratic* being dyslogistic. In the common opinion, knowing the right people is the most important qualification for advancement in government service, whereas for success in business intelligence, hard work, and creativity are equally or more important.[41] In the bureaucracy it is more rewarding to serve the organization than the public interest, and it is much better to be wrong with the organization than right against it. The vices of the defense establishment—such as paying a hundred times the retail price for articles available in hardware stores, using nineteen pages to give specifications for a police whistle, or taking ten or twelve years to develop a weapons system—are the effects not of military purposes but of the size and insulation of the defense bureaucracy.

A possible remedy for some of the problems is a high level of training in order to inculcate not only skills but standards of conduct. France has gone furthest in this direction with its Ecole Nationale d'Administration, the graduates of which, called Énarques, are the elite of the French public service. Their training mixes academic work with practical experience, and some of them go into business instead of government. They form a network of understanding and shared values which facilitates cooperation within the administration and to some extent with corporate executives. The Énarques are an aristocracy, or a meritocracy, but the principle of climbing through education is egalitarian. All but the very poor have a reasonably good chance to be admitted, no tuition is ordinarily charged, and there is no shortcut for the wealthy. The values that graduates absorb are not those of an economic class but of a profession. But so far as the bureaucracy is more professional and efficient, it is more autonomous and removed from democratic guidance.

Large-scale management is inevitably flawed, and the bureaucracy can hardly be properly democratic and efficient at the same time. As the part of the state most alike in totalitarian and democratic states, it raises similar problems of responsibility, whether to an absolutist party leadership or to elected officers. It grows stale, like the authoritarian apparatus, and to keep efficient needs periodic shake-ups, which are difficult to carry out. In the administrative state, the regulations of the apparatus take the place of the laws of the political authorities, and the role of the sovereign people is replaced by the discretion of appointed officials. Democracy compromises with practical necessity.

## THE CAPACITY OF THE STATE

There is something of a contest for survival among political forms, and the one that makes the most effective state—not necessarily the one most pleasing to the mass of citizens—may be expected to prevail. In this trial, the democratic polity comes out well. Even though the democracies are only a small minority among sovereignties, the preponderance of wealth and power is theirs; and they have the advantage of greater innovativeness when high technology is determinant of military strength. But the assets of authoritarianism make the outcome of the duel unpredictable.

### Foreign Policy

The state has two basic functions: relations with other states and internal governance. In regard to foreign affairs, it has traditionally been held that the democracy is handicapped, if not hamstrung, by the inability to decide and act quickly and secretly. In diplomacy it is undeniably negative for the adversary to know much more about one's purposes and conditions than vice versa. The monocratic state has the advantage that it can more freely adopt or discard positions for purposes of bargaining or influencing opinion. It also can dedicate a larger share of its resources to military power.

On the other hand, deliberation and open discussion bring about better-informed decision making. In the long run this probably more than offsets whatever advantages the less responsible government may have. Seldom is much really to be gained by surprise actions (except in military operations), and it may be useful that other powers, friendly or not, have an understanding of the reasons behind policies. The American negotiator is beset by a thousand voices, urging, clamoring, and questioning; the Soviet negotiator has only a claque. But in many, perhaps most, cases, more is lost by poorly considered actions than by delay or inaction; on balance it seems to the benefit of the nation if a Congress or public opinion checks a possibly impetuous Executive. It is a long-term benefit that the democracy finds it difficult to be aggressive. Democracies have been engaged in many conflicts and have undertaken countless punitive actions, but they have never, for a century or more, initiated major wars.

The problem of the democracy in foreign policy is rather that it lacks definite purpose and is subject to numerous, sometimes emotional pressures in contrary directions. Foreign policy is more or less geared to domestic politics. In the United States, ethnic demands are prominent; not only are congressmen attentive to the needs of Israel, but policy toward Greece and Turkey, for example, is much influenced by the respective lobbies. The looseness of the government and the openness of the media to differing views make it hard to mobilize the nation behind any purpose unless the need is very convincing. A coherent pluralist foreign policy is almost a contradiction in terms. An authoritarian state probably has fairly definite goals that it pursues steadily; the democracy acts only in response to an acute need. As long as a troubled situation raises no immediate threat, the democratic regime probably ignores it; the United States, for example, pays little heed to Latin America unless there is political violence or what may be seen as a communist threat.

### The Economy

Ultimately more important is the ability of the democracy in internal management, which not only affects the well-being of the people but promotes the national strength—keeping good order, adjusting conflicts of interests and values, and guiding the economy for justice, stability, and productivity, all of which enable it to hold its own in a competitive world.

Questions of economic management include the official or market guidance of investment, the admittance or exclusion of foreign competition and capital, the support for ailing industries or their abandonment, priority for investment or producer goods, centralization versus decentralization, amalgamation versus competition, military versus civilian production, control versus decontrol of markets, monetary regulation, and taxation. This is all too complex for skillful handling by any government. The democratic powers have the advantage that they do not try to decide so much as does the authoritarian state, although they can and must intervene extensively, mostly indirectly, in the management of the economy. The inability of the state to manage a modern economy in detail is attested by the fact that 10 to 20 percent of the economy is in "parallel" markets in both the Soviet Union and Eastern Europe and in Western democracies.

The democratic state has similar handicaps and advantages in social and economic policy as in foreign affairs. The authoritarian government can act with little consideration of public opinion (although it must reckon with bureaucratic resistance). It can decree the closing of vodka shops, have television programs carry a moral message, and dedicate more resources to what it believes contributes to national strength, less to consumerist frivolities. The democracy admits much more obvious anarchy, trusts that voluntary commitment is more effective, and relies on the not well proved proposition that people left to themselves will generally act for the better.

It is sometimes claimed that a strong leadership, whether a military dictatorship or a Marxist-Leninist totalitarianism, with no need to fear the next election can adopt immediately painful but ultimately salutary economic measures impossible for a democratic leadership. This alleged superiority of authoritarianism is hardly confirmed by the record. An opposite argument can be made, that people in a democracy, if they understand the need, accept hardships they would strongly oppose if inflicted by a less legitimate and less trusted government. Several new Latin American democracies—including Argentina, Bolivia, Brazil, and Peru—have imposed rigorous anti-inflationary programs seemingly beyond the capacity of the previous militocracy; and their peoples have shown remarkable willingness to accept sacrifices required by legitimate governments.

Both authoritarian, or controlled, and pluralist, or liberal, economies suffer severe problems, but they are mostly different: on the one hand, inefficiency, rigidity, difficulty of innovation, misallocation of resources, and corruption; on the other, instability, unemployment, inflation, financial irresponsibility, and protection for special interests. Overall, the pluralists seem to come out ahead, if only because the modern economy is too complex for the controllers.

## THE QUALITY OF DEMOCRACY

From the point of view of the anarchist, all government is bad. No large state is free of serious flaws and arbitrary, even oppressive, elements. Defects in the American democracy, surely among the better, are familiar.

Japanese democracy, in some ways a model, is quite imperfect: xenophobia is strong and minorities are stigmatized; the long tenure of one party makes for a cozy personalized relationship between government and business; the civil service is not far from being an unelected government; the vote of a rural inhabitant is worth several times as much as that of a city dweller. Japan is rather effectively but not quite democratically governed by a network of business and government leaders and high civil servants, chiefly alumni of Tokyo University.

One can find in most democracies examples of the faults of totalitarian regimes: police brutality and harassment of political dissidents occur; pressure is exerted, albeit quietly and with variable success, against press criticism; election results deviate from ballots actually cast; officials act beyond the letter of the law; the scales of justice are weighted unequally; officials profit from positions; there is official support for a set of beliefs; force is used to secure foreign aims; and so forth.

The Marxist-Leninists harshly criticize the United States and other Western powers for all these failures and others, and the criticisms have much effect on world opinion. The critics do not need to invent the evils. The misdeeds of a democratic government, however, are relatively marginal, usually hesitant and mild, and subject to criticism and to correction. Although the difference between the pluralistic-open society and the totalitarian-closed society is only a matter of degree, the degree is large.

This is the meaning of the Churchillian saying that democracy is the worst form of government except all the others. Democracy can be best understood not as something totally different and distinct but as authoritarian government modified or softened by restricting power and adding elements (not utterly absent in most authoritarianisms) of freedom and responsibility. In the monistic state there is a group who use the government to make the country more or less their property and to impose their will on the whole people. In the best democracy, likewise, some in positions of influence—appointed officials, elected magistrates, or other wielders of political power—will misuse their standing. But the means available to the democratic elite are feeble indeed by comparison with the instruments of totalitarianism, and the politically privileged group is undefinable and open. Hence there is a large space of freedom, and anyone on the outside can aspire to join the insiders. Democracy is not government by the people but a balance between government and people. We have democracy less because of love for truth, freedom, and justice than because it is a tolerably workable way of managing the state.

Democracy has historically arisen, not from an ungoverned people deciding to organize or from the masses demanding rights, but from the decay or weakening of monarchy. For example, Greek kings of Homeric times were restricted to short terms of office or reduced to priests as first aristocrats and then ordinary citizens asserted themselves. European monarchs of early modern times had to turn to the estates of the realm for money, and it became difficult or impossible to govern without their concurrence. The opinion grew that good government should be fair and equal, the arbitrary right of kings became hard to defend, and thinkers of the upper classes joined with discontented leaders of newer classes to demand more suitable procedures. The success of representative government, particularly in England, led to the spread of fundamentally similar institutions to the United States and elsewhere and encouraged people in many lands to demand rights for themselves.

Democracy, then, is basically monarchy or autocracy reformed and modified for practical reasons (chiefly to secure the cooperation of different classes and to benefit the economy) and for ideal reasons (chiefly the sense of human equality and individual worth, and the repugnance for arbitrary action). This does not mean that all the reforms, or democratic aspects, are necessarily good (however goodness be defined) or that the more authoritarian systems are wholly weak or bad. But it may reasonably be assumed that the democratic states are, generally speaking, more modern, more enlightened, and probably better vehicles to the human future.

### Notes

1. Eric S. Einhorn and John Logue, eds., *Democracy on the Shop Floor: An American Look at Employee Influence in Scandinavia Today* (Kent, Ohio: Kent Popular Press, 1982), p. 13.
2. Tom Peters and Nancy Austin, "A Passion for Excellence," *Fortune*, May 13, 1985, p. 26.
3. Michel Crozier, Samuel P. Huntington, and Jori Watamuki, *The Crisis of Democracy* (New York: New York University Press, 1975).
4. Larry M. Preston and Royse J. Smith, "An Alternative to Liberal Pedagogy," *Teaching Political Science*, 13 (Winter 1985–86).
5. As noted of the Germans by Walter Laqueur in *Germany Today* (Boston: Little, Brown & Company, 1985), p. 199.
6. Richard Reeves, "The Permissive Dutch," *New York Times Magazine*, October 20, 1985, pp. 32, 34, 101.
7. Rose and Milton Friedman, *The Tyranny of the Status Quo* (San Diego: Harcourt Brace Jovanovich, 1984), p. 51.
8. Friedman, *Tyranny*, pp. 3, 165.
9. Mancur Olson, *The Rise and Decline of Nations* (New Haven: Yale University Press, 1983).
10. Cf. Olson, *Rise and Decline*.
11. Bingham Powell, Jr., *Contemporary Democracy: Participation, Stability, and Violence* (Cambridge: Harvard University Press, 1982).
12. As contended by Frederich Hayek. Cf. Calvin M. Hay, *A Philosophy of Individual Freedom: The Political Thought of F. A. Hayek* (Westport, Conn.: Greenwood Press, 1984).
13. David Nachmias and David H. Rosenbloom, *Bureaucratic Government USA* (New York: St. Martin's Press, 1980), p. 202.
14. Dennis H. Wrong, *Power: Its Forms, Bases, and Uses* (New York: Harper & Row Publishers, 1979), p. 203.

15. John Plamenatz, *Democracy and Illusion* (London: Longmans, 1973), p. 50.
16. Sidney Verba and Gary R. Orren, "The Meaning of Equality in America," *Political Science Quarterly*, 100 (Fall 1985), 375.
17. Ibid., pp. 370, 376.
18. Sidney Verba and Gary R. Orren, *Equality in America: The View from the Top* (Cambridge: Harvard University Press, 1985), p. 28.
19. Donald Kagan, *The Great Dialogue: History of Greek Political Thought from Homer to Polybius* (New York: Free Press, 1965), pp. 77, 84.
20. Dorothy Pickles, *Democracy* (New York: Penguin Books, 1970), p. 37.
21. Robert Wesson, *Soviet Communes* (New Brunswick, N.J.: Rutgers University Press, 1963), chap. 2.
22. Bill Saporito, "The Revolt Against Working Smarter," *Fortune*, July 21, 1986, pp. 58–60.
23. Plamenatz, *Democracy*, p. 31.
24. Robert D. Dahl, *Modern Political Analysis* (Englewood Cliffs, N.J.: Prentice-Hall, 1976), p. 96.
25. Susan L. Shirk, *Competitive Comrades: Career Incentives and Student Strategies in China* (Berkeley: University of California Press, 1982), pp. 188–90.
26. Carl Cohen, *Democracy* (Athens: University of Georgia Press, 1971), p. 51.
27. Tom Peters and Nancy Austin, "A Passion for Excellence," *Fortune*, May 25, 1985, pp. 20–29.
28. *U.S. News and World Report*, May 6, 1985, pp. 75–76.
29. Einhorn and Logue, *Democracy on the Shop Floor*, p. 20.
30. Verba and Orren, "Equality in America," p. 378.
31. As contended by Charles E. Lindblom in *Politics and Markets: The World Political-Economic Systems* (New York: Basic Books, 1977).
32. Stansfield Turner, "No Joke: Military Intelligence Really Is an Oxymoron," *Christian Science Monitor*, January 29, 1986, p. 12.
33. Nachmias and Rosenbloom, *Bureaucratic Government*, p. 31.
34. Joel D. Aberbach, Robert D. Pittnam, and Bert A. Rockman, *Bureaucrats and Politicians in Western Democracies* (Cambridge: Harvard University Press, 1981), p. 257.
35. Stephan Michelson, "The Working Bureaucrat and the Nonworking Bureaucracy," in *Making Bureaucracies Work*, ed. Carol H. Weiss and Allen H. Barton (Beverly Hills: Sage Publications, 1980), p. 175.
36. Gordon Tullock, *The Politics of Bureaucracy* (Washington, D.C.: Public Affairs Press, 1965), p. 21.
37. C. Northcote Parkinson, *The Evolution of Political Thought* (Boston: Houghton Mifflin, 1958), p. 174.
38. *Time*, April 21, 1980, p. 42.
39. *Christian Science Monitor*, September 21, 1982, p. 6.
40. Michael Roskin, *Other Governments of Europe: Sweden, Spain, Italy, Yugoslavia, and East Germany* (Englewood Cliffs, N.J.: Prentice-Hall, 1977), p. 33.
41. *Washington Post National Weekly*, February 24, 1986, p. 37.

# Quasidemocracy

## 8

The nations of Western and Northern Europe, those of British colonization, and Japan are stable democracies in which free elections are decisive, civil liberties and political rights are taken for granted, and no one contemplates a military coup under any conditions. Many other nations, especially in Latin America and Southern Asia, also have democratic institutions. But their elections, although they may be fair, are more subject to management; liberties and rights are less firm; and intervention by the military, which almost everywhere exercises great influence, is always possible if the government should meet serious trouble. Their democracy is a political, but hardly a social, reality.

This shallowness of democratic institutions is natural or inevitable because they have been grafted onto societies lacking the historical development of the Western state system, and nowhere else have they been so firmly and effectively imposed as in Japan. Democratization has been mostly hesitant, managed primarily by elites that had much to lose if it were deep and thorough. They have wanted to make their societies workable and modern, not wholly to transform them, much less to surrender their status. Their democracy has consequently remained inegalitarian and distrustful of the popular will—something reasonably called quasidemocracy.

The ideas of representative and constitutional government have been spreading irregularly and fitfully in the world since they took their modern shape in the American and French Revolutions of the late eighteenth century. In the first decades of the nineteenth century, most of Spanish America was throwing off colonial domination in the name of freedom and republicanism, and the new emergent nations adopted constitutions after the U.S. model. There was a constitutionalist movement in Russia as early as 1825. More strongly, since the mid-nineteenth century the material and political expansion of the West has been generating, especially in the educated youth of non-Western societies, the desire to adopt basic Western patterns of government, partly because they were seen as more just than traditional empires and sultanates and partly because they were associated with power and prosperity. The profoundly autocratic Ottoman (Turkish) Empire introduced local elections in the 1860s, adopted a constitution in 1876, and elected a legislature, which was prorogued a year later.[1] Subsequent decades saw moves for representative government in Iran, China, Thailand, and elsewhere.

The aspiration to democracy rose greatly with the First World War, in which the Allies fighting in the name of freedom and popular government were victorious over the more militaristic-authoritarian powers of Wilhelmian Germany and its allies. The Second World War and the victory of the side proclaiming freedom and human rights as its cause made democracy (possibly in the Soviet version) the way to the future;

and the subsequent dissolution of colonial empires seemed the opportunity to put its principles into effect around the world.

In recent decades the enormous expansion of international trade, travel, and communications and the growth of cities and industry have given a better material base for democratization in many lands. In the modernizing society the development of journalism and broadcasting means the growth of a class of people interested in freedom of expression, desirous of making the most of their professional possibilities, and impatient with regimentation. In a complex modern society there will be lawyers interested in legality, businessmen wanting freedom of economic activities and the security of the rule of law, and a growing middle class desirous of securing channels of influence not available in the traditional society. Modernization has brought in rationalism and Western culture, discredited traditional authority, and created a demand for legal, secular, representative government and for civil and political rights.

### Incomplete Democracy

But it was too much to expect that older societies on which the West impinged would simply shift over to the alien way of organizing power. The market economy may not work well, for many of the reasons that impede basic reform in Marxist-Leninist countries; and excessive unemployment, often over 20 percent, undermines democracy not only because it provides a clientele for extremists but also because it makes government jobs all too valuable. Large differences in values mean differences in the content of politics. People accustomed to a hierarchic society expect decisive leadership. Conflicts are sure to arise, and if Western political vocabulary and institutions are partly adopted, older ways and social relations do not simply disappear. In many languages there is no word for "opposition," the nearest equivalent being "enemy." At best, democracy is an ideal, always less in fact than in appearances and claims even in relatively democratic countries such as the United States and Japan. It would be miraculous if the victory of democratic forms in the non-Western world were not generally superficial.

Democracy in the Third World, so far as it exists formally, is a garb for decidedly unequal or quite elitist societies, in which democratic institutions are insecure and subject to negation if they threaten the undemocratic power structure. Elites have no intention of surrendering basic power because of democratic theory. If persons who could move with the international set prefer to live in less developed countries, it may be because of attachment to the motherland or the climate. It is equally likely that they enjoy being bigger fish among the many minnows and have servants and conspicuous social standing they would lack in New

York or Paris, without having to work so hard—all of which would be lost in a truly democratic society.

The quasidemocracies differ from pseudodemocracies intended to disguise totalitarianism in that the former have considerable respect for legal forms and institutions for real political contestation. Pseudodemocracy is only a screen to make controls more efficient. Quasidemocracies differ from full democracies in that the masses share real power only conditionally or equivocally, and there is little idea that political democracy might have to do with social and economic equality. Quasidemocracy may be understood as a set of concessions made by the elite for the sake of legitimization, modernization, and social peace. Sometimes democratic institutions in undemocratic countries are reminiscent of the British-style wigs worn by African judges.

Third World democracy is quasidemocracy almost by definition, because popular democracy is hardly practical under Third World conditions, and if a country could really make itself democratic, it would probably soon cease to be counted a Third World nation.

Quasidemocracy has some resemblance to the condition of Britain or Sweden prior to the extension of suffrage to the masses in the nineteenth century, and partial democracies of today may be moving likewise toward full democracy. However, they cannot closely replicate the historical experience of Europe, and it is not certain that they are progressing in that direction. In most countries there has recently been no evidence of a trend toward the decrease of socioeconomic inequality, the primary condition for a thoroughly democratic order. To the contrary, the interaction of richer and poorer societies, while forwarding pseudodemocracy, is in various ways adverse to real democracy. The cultural and economic gap between classes may have grown, as modern world-oriented elites leave traditional ways farther behind. Chiefs and followers had more in common.

There are fundamental differences between the quasidemocratic and the predemocratic state. In the former, suffrage is universal, probably even for illiterates; and institutions are ordinarily quite democratic in form, except perhaps for such limitations as the granting of very broad powers to the president or provision in the constitution for the suspension of rights in an emergency. The failure of the quasidemocracy to be fully democratic is hardly a matter of forms and institutions or of laws and constitutions but rather of how they are applied. To the contrary, the predemocratic state in Europe had many overt limitations of the popular power, such as highly restricted suffrage, the role of feudal institutions like the British House of Lords, and the power of the monarch in Bismarckian Germany.

Nonetheless, many persons of influence desire to have a democratic order and may bring it about. From the time of the Magna Carta, when the barons demanding rights for themselves forced King John to concede rights for all, elites have often rejected arbitrary and repressive rulerships. Dictatorship is unintelligent, unmodern, and probably unprofitable except for a narrow clique around the dictator; it creates insecurity and gives power to the organs of repression. Elites feel that democracy, the way of the rich, strong states, will help their countries to progress, that it protects against arbitrary actions, that the opening of democratic liberties relieves pressures, and that in the name of democracy their government gains respect. Traveling abroad, they feel better carrying the passport of a democratic, rather than a dictatorial, state. To have a constitutional state is good for credit and foreign trade and for world standing. The ideal is a modern, that is, democratic, state, however unprepared the nation.[2]

A democratic constitutional order is made possible by the conviction on the part of opinion leaders, magistrates, officers, and magnates that it is right.[3] Democracy can come to a decidedly unequal country if, and only if, elites are convinced of the need for it, as occurred in Spain after Franco, with help from masses who press for change without raising too much fear of revolution.[4]

Quasidemocracy has much value. Constitutional forms, even without much content of popular will, make for an orderly political system. Democratic processes are interesting and educational for elites as well as masses. Freedom of criticism reduces corruption; the uncovering of scandals is so attractive to journalists that it is difficult for informal controls to be fully effective. The rule of law largely dispels the atmosphere of fear that weighs upon dictatorships. People released from a tyranny to an imperfect democracy feel they can breathe easily, and they acquire a new self-respect.

Many people strongly desire decency, openness, respect for individuals, national community, and freedom. This is especially true of the liberal professionals, for whom it is an essential of self-fulfillment. Ordinary people like the democratic order, at least in principle. Theoretical support for political rights has been found to be nearly as high in Mexico as in New York.[5] Poor Jamaicans express pride in the right to vote, and they find in the political parties their only channel for influence, however modest.[6] A qualified democracy is a satisfaction where thorough democracy is impractical.

## THE QUASIDEMOCRATIC SYSTEM

A list of quasidemocracies, subject to change according to events, might include Argentina, Brazil, Bolivia, Botswana, Colombia, the Dominican Republic, Ecuador, El Salvador, Gambia, perhaps Greece, Guatemala,

Honduras, India, Jamaica, Malaysia, Mexico, Panama, Peru, Papua New Guinea, Singapore, Sri Lanka, Sudan, Turkey, Uruguay, and Venezuela. By the democratic end of the group one might place Costa Rica. Countries such as Senegal and Thailand would be around the authoritarian extreme, along with what have been called "tutelary democracies," supposedly preparing for the genuine article. Sundry other countries, such as Pakistan and Bangladesh, have democratic elements that may grow; nearly all countries find it desirable to have a constitution, which invariably has some democratic forms.

The category covers a range from states where there is much open political contestation to those where there is little, and institutions are correspondingly varied. Some are one-party dominant (as Botswana, India, and Mexico); in others, parties compete normally (as in Colombia and Venezuela), although competition remains essentially intraelite. In some, the armed forces are very influential; in others, less so. Some have a socialistic bent, and others are market oriented.

It is typical of quasidemocracy that attachment to rights is more theoretical than binding; for example, the press is legally free but in practice more or less controlled, and broadcasting is probably largely or entirely in official hands. Politics are mostly of and by the upper classes, assisted by the middle classes, although the masses also probably enjoy the electoral campaigns, the only time anyone pays much attention to them. Some shallowness of democracy is also shown in frequent indifference to it in foreign policy; for example, many quasidemocracies are much more inclined to criticize the United States than the Soviet Union. Such countries as India, Sri Lanka, Botswana, and Latin American democracies vote against the United States in the United Nations as regularly as nondemocratic Third World states and states of the Soviet bloc.[7] Latin American nations, such as Brazil and Argentina, are generally pleased to develop relations with communist countries as an offset to U.S. dominance; so far as they hang back, it is more from fear of subversion than from repugnance for the totalitarian system. Unequal Third World nations are less repelled by the Soviet violations of human rights, which are less dramatic than those of many Third World nations, than by revolutionism, so far as this still figures in the Soviet outlook.

The political reality of quasidemocracy is more pluralistic than democratic: groups or sectors in effect agree on a formal framework for coexistence, which in modern conditions has to be constitutional-democratic. Democratic institutions are not intended to decide power or give a voice to influential sectors. Not going very deep, they are often unstable; and military coups do not much alter the tenor of life. On the other hand, a military regime may call elections and walk away without trauma or turmoil, leaving the country to be run more or less as before, as in

Guatemala in 1986. The benefits of elections are usually deemed worth the risk of uncomfortable results. They are the stamp of legitimacy: it was notable how, after the fall of Marcos in the Philippines, mayors and governors retained some standing by virtue of having been elected, however fraudulently. Dictatorship is dangerous and unmodern, and military government is unappealing. Best is a government that is as legitimate and constitutional as can be arranged without much opening doors to popular demands.

In the variable fusion of mass and elite politics, there is much more of the latter except at election time. Consultation and participation are mixed with repression, co-optation, and exploitation. There are many ways in which nominal democracy is prevented from becoming popular democracy, from selective application of the laws to informal control of information media, controlled organization of the people, and electoral fraud, much as dictators try to get a little legitimacy without risk by holding plebiscites.[8] Expanding the electorate does not so much deepen democracy as bring in larger numbers whose votes may be influenced. Electoral campaigns are expensive, the more costly as modern methods are used to reach the masses, and are virtually limited to those with large resources.

The constitution is more declaratory than mandatory. Most "legislation" is decreed by the executive with minimal consultation. The government is paternalistic and patriarchal; the lower classes petition it as they would a colonial overlord.[9] Leaders are interested in democracy mostly for themselves; the loyalty to it of powerful sectors is equivocal, although they may accept it as long as they are not troubled. Chile formerly seemed to be one of the more democratic countries in the world;[10] yet in a time of trouble and threats of revolutionary violence, it, like the outwardly very democratic Weimar Republic, succumbed to exceptionally harsh dictatorship.

Party competition is part of the system in such countries as India, Costa Rica, Jamaica, Venezuela, and Colombia, but it is not to be allowed to get out of hand. Changes of party tend to defuse discontent and encourage hope that a new set of politicians replacing the failed ones of the previous administration will bring a better life. Mexico is exceptional in regularly changing the top personality without a change of parties; the new presidency brings a large upper-level turnover and a new tone, at least for a time, in the administration. The competition of small opposition parties is accepted and useful, and it invigorates the system without endangering it. A Mexican specialty is to co-opt opposition leaders by offering them a place in the system; if they decline and remain disagreeable, they may be in some danger. Despite official denials, in the 1970s hundreds of persons quietly "disappeared."[11] Opposition parties receive a fourth of the seats in the Chamber of Deputies regardless of the total votes credited to them; they can speak in the legislature without detriment to control by the PRI.

Freedom of opposition in many quasidemocratic countries is circumscribed by repression or potential repression. Violence however, makes everyone uncomfortable. It should be unnecessary in the well-ordered quasidemocracy, and gross transgressions of human rights are the less necessary because there are extensive levers over the economy and forms of penetration in national life sanctioned by the democratic ethos of serving the people.

There are numerous more or less state-controlled groups and organizations, such as producer boards for leading commodities; many that would be pressure groups in a more thoroughly democratic society become agents of centralization. Influence flows both from state to private or semiprivate organizations and vice versa. Trade unions and many professional groups require government approval and can assist their members mostly by the grace of the corresponding ministry. The labor unions often keep workers divided, basically powerless, and dependent on the government.[12]

### Corporatism

The mode of managed group participation and the political use of semiprivate organizations is *corporatism*. A monopoly may be given in return for subordination to the state, which probably subsidizes the group and influences the selection of leadership. The tendency is traditionally rightist; the idea of the corporatist state, with participation of economic interests, was much promoted by Mussolini and Italian fascism. However, if the corporatist idea were carried to an extreme, it would not be easy to distinguish it from the party-controlled Marxist-Leninist state, which likewise works through controlled unions, professional societies, peasant collectives, and so forth down to the league of elementary school children, all under the aegis of the ruling party elite.

Corporatism in the Third World is part of the tendency of the state to intervene in the economy. Almost anything may be regulated, and urbanization has greatly increased the burdens, opportunities, and capacities of the state. Ideological tendencies—leftist and rightist—have little meaning. For example, the rightist military government of Brazil expanded and multiplied state enterprises to a near-dominant position in the economy and undertook to plan production in considerable detail by requiring permits for almost any policy. The succeeding civilian government of José Sarney declared by fiat a broad economic policy, including fixing of all prices. Corporations in Brazil may be ordered to buy, sell, or produce particular goods, or do virtually whatever authorities desire.

State control of basic industry, utilities, and most credit and investment is general in the Third World, as is command of broadcasting facilities. There are scores or hundreds of state enterprises in most Third World countries, democratic or not, and domestic capital must cooperate with the state in order to prosper. Venezuela, for example, in 1980 had 226 public or mixed enterprises, and the public sector accounted for 44 percent of the GNP.[13]

The idea that the state was to be the locomotive of progress was strong in the 1960s because of the impression that economic planning was carrying the Soviet Union to victory in its race with the West. As stated at a time when this thesis was losing cogency, "Most scholars clearly agree that the state or government will have to assume a much more direct role than in the past in the planning and implementation of developmental programs in all areas of society."[14] But the Soviet Union has ceased to be a persuasive model, and many countries that developed a large socialist sector of industry and agriculture have reaped disappointment. Their losses have contributed heavily to the deficits and inflation that have plagued the Third World, democratic as well as authoritarian.

If state management of the economy is difficult for advanced Western countries, it is triply so for countries lacking a competent administrative apparatus. The importance of the state as chief provider of jobs and advantages and as the determiner of economic success and failure is a major hindrance to the full realization of democracy. Many proposals for privatization of public enterprises, however, have had little success. It is much easier to scramble than unscramble eggs and economies. Despite the poor record of statist production, only a few countries—none of them democracies or quasidemocracies—have resolutely rejected interventionism. They have included Pinochet's Chile (for a few years, until overtaken by economic crisis), in reaction to the Marxist episode of Allende that terrified the middle classes, and Taiwan, in its semi-war with Communist China.

The chief motivation for a retreat from economic statism is that the elites need to keep the economic pie growing; expanding resources for distribution are the best remedy for instability. Singapore, Sri Lanka, Mexico, Jamaica, Venezuela, for example, have delivered benefits to very many people; and they have tried to build enough of a welfare state to provide minimum needs and reduce insecurity. But elites are much more responsive to elite needs,[15] and the commitment to popular welfare is not very effective. Such countries as India, Venezuela, Colombia, and even Costa Rica have a high degree of economic inequality, which does not seem to become less. In Mexico, with a tradition of popular revolution,

two of the three sectors of the ruling PRI party are for workers and peasants; and the party continually proclaims its dedication to the underprivi-
leged. Yet inequality is excessive even by Third World standards, and
there has been little gain in the material well-being of the poor since
the revolution began in 1910. In part, continuing inequality and poverty
are due to population growth. In the case of Mexico, for example, this
has defeated extensive confiscatory land reform and left most of the peasants as impoverished as ever. But the supposedly popular-revolutionary
state has failed to spread the benefits of modern productivity.

Quasidemocracy is unstable, fairly easily installed (because it
permits broader participation than a dictatorship but does not really
change the prevalent order), and in most countries fairly easily set aside
if it ceases to function well. Well-crafted absolutist, that is, communist,
states seem, like well-ordered democratic states, to be immune to overthrow (except where nationalism collides with communism). But those
midway between extremes waver uncertainly.

## QUASIDEMOCRACY IN PRACTICE

Latin America is the region most given to quasidemocracy. It rejected
the authoritarian model in fighting for independence, has long been under
the influence of U.S. (and to a smaller extent British and French) ideals,
and has developed its economy and society much beyond levels in most
parts of the Third World. There is a good deal of quasidemocracy in
Southern Asia, not only in India (with a population double all of Latin
America) but also in Sri Lanka and, in more embryonic conditions, in
such countries as Pakistan and Bangladesh. In the Near East and Africa
it is weak.

### Asia

A British-educated elite provided the backbone of democracy in
India during the first generation after independence. There were limited
local elections in colonial times, and provincial and national parliaments
have functioned regularly for some forty years. Many persons, from Prime
Minister Rajiv Gandhi down, have demonstrated a strong desire for orderly constitutional procedures. But the Congress party and the family
of Jawaharlal Nehru have been on top except for a few years (which
tended to discredit the ineffective opposition), ever since the country
gained independence in 1947. As political leadership has slipped from
elite hands and politicians and legislators are drawn from the less educated strata, politics has become cruder and more venal.[16]

The low status of Indian women is underlined by the practices of female infanticide and bride burning.[17] The undiminished prevalence of violence between religious groups, ethnic groups, and castes attests to the incapacity of the political process. If democracy requires consensus, India cannot be democratic. India is of all countries the most riven by social barriers, formalized by castes. Paradoxically, these assist the maintenance of democratic forms by stabilizing society. But they cannot possibly promote a spirit of free and egalitarian community.

The government generally follows the constitutional rules. However, it has large, virtually dictatorial powers, such as that of preventive detention, that could be exercised at any time. Elected state governments are freely and frequently removed by the central authorities, on an average of two per year. When political rights were suppressed by Indira Gandhi's emergency of 1975, there was no solid protest, and there would probably be none if the government should again assert full powers.

Sri Lanka, formerly Ceylon, at one time was one of the most promising Third World democracies. Becoming independent in 1948 after 150 years of British rule, it enjoyed a decade of fair tranquillity but was gradually torn apart by violence between the majority Sinhalese and the Tamils. In 1978 a new constitution established a strong presidency. The judiciary has lost independence, and the parliament has been reduced to a rubber stamp; the president has undated letters of resignation from all deputies of the majority party.[18]

In Thailand, which has never been under colonial rule, there have been moves toward democracy since the 1880s. A constitution adopted in 1932 was put on exhibit for the public to come and bow to it. Since then the form of government has shifted between democratic, semidemocratic, and authoritarian a dozen times. Real power has remained with the civilian-military bureaucracy, but elections have been held regularly since 1978. Democracy consists in having an elected assembly to bargain, along with other pressure groups, with the bureaucracy.[19]

The Philippines had the benefit of U.S. overlordship from 1898 to 1942, U.S. sponsorship of the new republic established in 1946, and very close ties for years thereafter. There was active competitive politics through the 1950s and 1960s, despite violence, corruption, oligarchy, extreme inequality, and economic problems. But chronic disorder led to the declaration of martial law by President Ferdinand Marcos in 1972 and rationalized his continuing in office, by one device or another, until he ventured an election in February 1986. The Filipinos, angered by the scale of official and semiofficial thievery, then demonstrated much more devotion to democracy than they had shown when they had more of it, and they thwarted Marcos's effort to reelect himself. It was dissident military leaders who gave the victory to "people power," but only the exceptional leadership of Corazon Aquino prevented a descent to anarchy or return to dictatorship in 1986.

In many countries, such as Singapore and Malaysia, governments try to rule by consensus politics, allowing opposition parties to enjoy considerable political freedom but not to offer serious competition. When a new Malaysian party won an upset victory in a state election, it immediately petitioned to join the ruling National Front. In Singapore, the governing party uses censorship, preventive detention, and controlled unions to keep minor parties in check.[20] The prospective heir to Lee Kuan Yew, who has governed almost unchallenged since 1959, spoke of the need for "a stabilizer to steady the ship against waves of popular demands."[21]

### Africa

In Africa, no government (aside from racist South Africa) has ever transferred power by election. Botswana is nearest to a functioning democracy, having held regular and reasonably honest elections since 1965. There is genuine competition for popular favor, but the opposition is subject to harassment, and the press is subsidized and pressured; the dominant party receives over two-thirds of the seats and votes. Candidates for office must be literate in English, which excludes all but a small minority. There are many Europeans in the civil service, which effectively guides the nation. In other African countries, such as Kenya, Tanzania, Zambia, and Ivory Coast, there are strongly contested intraparty elections, which give legitimacy, permit representation of minorities, and renew cadres but do not affect power at the top.[22]

The most promising African democracy until late 1983 was federal Nigeria. It had a democratic structure from 1960 to 1966; this broke down in ethnic violence and was replaced by military dictatorship until 1979. Elections were held under a carefully drafted constitution, and the country enjoyed a boom because of high oil prices. But there was growing party violence, massive corruption, waste, and political conflict. Elections in 1983 were disorderly and fraud ridden, although U.S. firms were hired to manage the campaign.[23] As the economy sank with lowered oil revenues, the people generally welcomed a military coup at the end of that year.[24] More characteristic is Ghana, which was "democratic" in 1957 to 1960, 1961 to 1972, and 1979 to 1981, the government having been turned out each time for no particular reason. Not much was changed by transition either to a military or to an electoral regime.

### Latin America

Quasidemocracy comes naturally to Latin America. The general structure of colonial society (large landholding, deep class differences, corrupt and bureaucratized government, and statist habits) continued after the winning of independence early in the nineteenth century; at the same time, the new national authorities, repelled by the old monarchic-colonial power, turned to the examples of the American and French revolutions and the successful new democracy of the United States. Constitutions were drafted after the American model; but when elections were held, mostly to validate dictatorship, only 1 to 3 percent of the population were permitted to vote, and whoever commanded the most force became president. Democratic institutions gained ground after the latter part of the nineteenth century, and mass politics have come to the fore on occasion; but many a coup has cast down constitutional governments. In recent years the tide toward democracy has flowed faster than ever, and it is very broad, touching nearly every country of the hemisphere. Its depth is less certain; much of the colonial social structure and mentality continues in various countries to this day. Formally democratic institutions in various Latin American countries, such as Guatemala, Colombia, and El Salvador, coexist with, and perhaps are sustained by, the so-called security forces' frequent use of murder as a means of political action.

Argentina in 1983 celebrated the end of a harsh militocracy. Because of terrorism plus the loss of the foolish Falklands War, the generals were discredited as never before, and Raul Alfonsín apparently has a good chance to complete his six-year term in 1989. If he does so, he will be the first president to leave office constitutionally since 1928. Yet Argentina has had quasidemocracy since 1853. In 1912, the landholding elite, complacent with decades of extraordinary economic growth, changed the electoral law to permit genuine, instead of fake, elections in order to modernize the country and defuse political protest. But the result was to bring the opposition into office; as the depression of the 1930s struck, the concession was revoked as too dangerous. The military came to the fore, and for the next half century the country was subjected to electoral fraud, Perónist demagoguery, interludes of ineffective democracy, and military dictatorship. The receptivity of the elite to democracy was weakened by the pressure of the large educated middle and working classes for effectively popular government; it was also lessened by national antagonism to Britain, viewed as an economic exploiter, and to the United States, seen as the bar to natural Argentine leadership in Latin America.[25]

On the other hand, Colombia, with much less favorable conditions for democracy than Argentina (heterogeneous population, small middle class, lower economic level, higher illiteracy) has had a regular constitutional succession of civilian presidencies since 1904, except for an interlude of dictatorship from 1953 to 1957. The elites of the two parties shift power from time to time, and sometimes there has been considerable violence, but the people who count usually play by the rules of the game. Quasidemocracy was formalized by the National Front agreement of 1957, whereby the parties, chastened by the years of sometimes demagogic dictatorship, agreed to alternate the presidency and share offices for six-teen years. Something of this arrangement has been continued.

Ordinary people count for more in Venezuela. Lively electoral campaigns arouse much enthusiasm, and they have usually brought a change of ruling party. But there is not much connection between political rhetoric and government policies. Voters choose only parties, not candidates, in the selection of whom they have no share; for the most part, they do not even know who the candidates are. There are few active party members and little popular mobilization, and representation is through the leading multiclass parties only. They function not only as aggregators but as the means of control of unions and other popular organizations. They are managed from the top; their democratic apparatus of assemblies and membership representation serves rather to applaud than to decide.[26]

The leading Venezuelan parties have agreed to avoid the radicalism and disorder that might provoke military intervention. Agrarian reform, which is more symbolic than effective, is designed for party purposes and is carried out not by peasant but by party action. Political careers are made in the capital, not by advancing local interests. Parties are primarily promoters of individual careers and dispensers of patronage, and they seek to avoid deep partisan or ideological antagonisms. Much power rests with business groups and the inflated bureaucracy.[27] Over-critical journalists may be subject to arrest, and the security police may occasionally resort to murder.[28]

The Dominican Republic, which has been subject to considerable U.S. intervention, has had regular constitutional government since 1978, when the United States insisted that ballots should actually be counted. The government is somewhat responsive to popular needs but more so to demands for public jobs. Their number swells after each election, and they are a way to improve one's material condition despite low pay. The congress has ceased to be a rubber stamp, and may be effectively obstructive, but members usually remain for only one term and have little understanding of their role. The judiciary is starved for support, and the military continues to exercise much weight.[29]

*Costa Rica*    Costa Rica is perhaps the country where quasidemocracy works best, as it is at once quite democratic and more than a little elitist; a few people are important and the large majority lack influence except at elections once in four years. Local government is feeble, dominated by a few families. The courts are independent, and the laws are generally fair, but they are to a considerable degree applied according to the category of persons involved.[30] Despite the lively press, corruption has increased in the last decade; there is a common expectation that high leaders will profit by their office, although much less than in other

Latin American countries. Most "laws" are presidential decrees, and the stronger presidents stretch the constitution freely.[31] Organized labor, except for public servants and banana workers, is very weak. Strikes, to be legal, must be authorized, and they seldom are; workers' rights and benefits are regulated by code and the ministry. Landholding is only a little less concentrated than in neighboring countries. There has been some effort to distribute small properties, but three-fourths of rural workers are landless.[32] Unreliable statistics show that inequality is nearly as great as in many less democratic Latin American countries. A few leading families dominated politics for many generations;[33] their hegemony has faded, but it is fair to say that the country is governed by an alliance of the economic elite and the bureaucracy. Yet Costa Rican democracy is real. There are extensive welfare benefits, an effective social-security–health-care system, and an ambitious educational system. Honest and impartial elections excite much enthusiasm. There is a turnover of high office; the incumbent party has usually lost the election. There is no military political influence, as the guard forces are staffed by patronage and there is no professional officers' corps. Not least, the national character shows the effects of democracy. The level of literacy is very high, people discuss affairs of their nation with much interest, the press is informative, bookstores are numerous and well stocked (in contrast to their near absence or triviality in other Central American countries), and there are numerous well-informed experts on the politics and economics of the country.

The most important reason that Costa Rica has developed more democratically than its neighbors is the lack of a considerable Indian population and hence of an enserfed subclass, as in Guatemala. Costa Rica has had much more sense of community, nourished by the feelings of superiority of a largely Spanish population in a region of mostly mestizo-Indian nations. Legality and democracy became the hallmark of Costa Rican superiority over states irregularly ruled by usually unpleasant military-dominated dictatorships. The democratic order is the national pride. There is no large alienated sector threatening to turn political power into social revolution, and the Costa Rican elite has been willing to make concessions for social peace.

Nonetheless, Costa Rican democracy had had problems when intraelite dissension led to mobilizing the masses politically and to a populist movement frightening for the upper classes. In 1940 Rafael Angel Calderón Guardia was elected president, presumably as a creature of the conservative oligarchy. However, probably mostly for reasons of conscience, he undertook a mission of social reform, including an income tax and a social-security system. As his upper- and middle-class backing fell away, he sought allies on the Left, including the Communists. Social conflict intensified through political complications to a civil war in 1948 in which the opposition was led not by conservatives but by social democrats. The victory of the latter reaffirmed the democratic system and led to the abolition of the small armed forces (which had supported the leftist government). The result was to preempt radical politics by a non-Marxist welfare state.

## POLITICS OF QUASIDEMOCRACY

### Clientelism

Quasidemocracy, implying keeping control with the few but recognizing rights of the many, is characterized by vertical structures rather than class polarization, by a joining of political and personal or social bonds, and by fluid relations among elites.[34]

The commonest political mode, not only of quasidemocracy but of Third World politics in general, may be summed up as *clientelism*, whereby a few persons, perhaps numbered in dozens, attach themselves to a leader or boss. They give loyalty, deference, and support, in return for which he turns official favors their way, especially jobs; and members of a clique probably advance together. Leaders of cliques form higher cliques, pyramiding up to the boss of the party or chief of the state. It is not entirely different from the machine politics of American cities of an earlier day, in which bosses organized electoral support in return for favors to the needy. But clientelism runs much deeper and influences the whole character of life, being not an incidental but a primary structure of society. It is irregular and informal feudalism, patrons and clients being loosely like the lords and vassals of an earlier time.

Clientelism goes from bottom to top of the social scale. Its power structure reflects the social structure more than it serves as an electoral device; it follows the pattern of the hacienda extended to urban politics, as those below look up to their superiors.[35] It rests on inequality and the need of some for material help, of others for services, with obligations in both directions. The coin of clientelism is influence with the state and its agencies, to be traded, bartered, or cashed according to need.

Clientelism differs from ethnic or communal politics, also common in the Third World, especially in Asia; from charismatic politics, based on the personality of a leader; and from class politics, with its Marxist tone. Patron-client relations group people at all levels, across class and often ethnic lines. They are the stronger as the legal order is ineffective and unreliable.[36] They are usually stable, because of the value placed on loyalty, although there may be restructuring when the top leader changes, as in Mexico with each new presidency.[37] Kinship, friendship, school ties, and social dependency mingle with straightforward mutual advantage.[38]

Position depends on nearness to the leader; factions vie for standing with him, and jockeying near the top is replicated below. The contest is much less for support at the base than for gaining influence above; a following is mostly a lever to bargain for leadership positions. The network links the poor to the upper classes and provides ladders of upward movement, while it co-opts potential leaders from the ranks of the poor.[39]

Much, but by no means all, clientelistic politics goes on in the framework of a political party, whether monopolistic or competitive. Parties are more or less authoritarian in spirit and structure, more agencies of ambitions than representatives of the people. They are generally patronage based, not programmatic; if they were strongly programmatic, the democratic institutions could be in trouble. Essentially controlled by a few, if not by one, they may serve to keep the citizenry in line under political overlords by means both of incentives provided by the state and coercion to repress dissent.[40] There is probably not much internal criticism or free-flowing debate. The professionals are in charge, and decision making is usually wrapped in secrecy, a common trait in quasidemocracy.

Parties are sometimes transient and usually poorly organized and financed, with few engaged members. Even leftist parties commonly have little mass organization and are more parts of the system than movements to change it.[41] Although theoretically lower-class oriented, they are led by persons of middle- or upper-class background and are seldom a threat to the status quo.

The clientelistic polity holds authority close to the center; leaders want the maximum of benefits to disburse. This means enfeeblement of local endeavors without effective direction from the central powers, who are unable to attend to many matters, reach decisions without adequate information, and are unable to implement policies disliked by the locals. Clientelism reduces autonomy without giving effective strength.

### Corruption

It is the essence of clientelism to use governmental powers for private benefit. The bosses can be bosses only because they use or disregard laws and procedures to reward their followers and themselves.[42] Many varied goods are to be obtained, from innocent social distinctions and invitations to official functions through travel at government expense, furnishing of inside information, and jobs for unqualified persons, to advantageous contracts, graft, and outright stealing. Many transactions can be understood as an extension in the monetary society of traditional gift giving. However, they are to be summarized as corruption.

The extent of corruption is not closely related to the democracy or authoritarianism of the state. Although it is more visible in the opener system, the checks of public exposure have limited effect. Corruption, even where moderated, provides the cement that holds the clientelistic system together and makes it function. It is part of the blending of the pretenses of the legal state with the realities of the arbitrary state. It goes with low respect for the law in general. It is a major cause of inefficiency in government, both because officials bend the rules for improper reasons and because their motivation is perverted.

Corruption undermines taxation. On the one hand, awareness of the misuse of government funds is reason for reluctance to pay; on the other, nonfulfillment of tax obligations is perhaps the most generalized form of corruption. In Argentina, for example, only about 25 percent of taxable income is declared,[43] and in most Third World countries the proportion is probably even less. The government consequently relies mostly on indirect taxes, chiefly import duties. But smuggling is big business in many countries. It is carried on with the connivance of the authorities, and one reason for high tariffs is their usefulness for both customs officials and smugglers. Corruption makes it harder to check spending and deficits, as every program and contract is an opportunity for a rake-off. It multiplies, as one wants to get what others get, and corruption is the chief defense of the gains of corruption. In the Philippines, it is more a part of life than taxation, and President Aquino despite the best intentions was able to do little about it. A contractor even sued the mayor of Manila when a gift was not followed by a lucrative contract.[44]

All this does not quite mean that corruption is morally approved. Many are uncomfortable with it, because it has a bad odor in the world and bespeaks disorder. The 1979 Nigerian constitution had strong provisions for coping with corruption, but they were ignored. Mexicans know what honesty is; the foreign ministry, the Bank of Mexico, and the finance ministry have a reputation for rectitude. There is a feeling that corruption should not be too flagrant; and there is resentment that some are luxuriously enriched while most people are very poor—Mexicans do not have the Soviet style of hiding the conspicuous consumption of the powerful. In the Mexican case, new presidents regularly express an apparently sincere desire to halt or at least restrain corruption; but after punishing a few notorious malefactors of the preceding administration, they find themselves caught up in the system, which can hardly be changed without a revolution. Miguel de la Madrid, entering in 1982, pushed harder than most for "moral renovation," but he could only reduce the blatancy of the corruption, jail a handful of culprits, and let the rest go on as before.

The expected benefits of corruption make it difficult to surrender office because of electoral figures, which are, of course, falsifiable. The high stakes of politics, by virtue of state ownership or regulation, make the democratic processes the more subject to fraud. Growing opposition means more need for tampering of various kinds. In July 1985 it seemed that the opposition PAN party might win in some northern states of Mexico; in the official results, PAN was credited with more votes where it was less threatening. In the 1986 elections the PRI showed even more clearly that it was prepared to announce electoral results to suit itself.

The freedom of the press is subject to the same manipulation. The means of control include giving or withdrawing government advertising (a large part of all advertising, perhaps most of the revenue of weak papers) and payments to editors and reporters, who, like police, are underpaid and dependent on the government for access to news as well as livelihood. Although papers often assert partisanship and may make or threaten exposés unless bought off,[45] the press becomes to a large extent a tool of the state, carrying the desired messages to the people and politicians.

### Who Rules

Many kinds of persons are influential in the politics of quasidemocracies, including business and financial magnates, landowners, politicians, generals, journalists, and highly placed bureaucrats, or technocrats. But landowners cannot swing much weight unless they have a political following and make themselves felt in political circles or through a producers' association, and business leaders wield influence mostly as supporters for political leaders or collaborators in economic planning and management. Where a large part of the economy—probably a third, as in Jamaica and Costa Rica, or two-thirds, as in Mexico—is in the hands of the state and the remainder is subject to an indefinite degree of regulation of markets, credits, wages, and production, the capitalist class is relatively weak compared with those who have political standing. These include traders in electoral politics, or the political class, as it is sometimes called; high officials of various state organs; leading bureau-technocrats; military leaders; and so forth—those at or near the center of political and politico-economic power.

The political-bureaucratic upper class roughly corresponds, informally, to the upper party apparatus of communist countries. They more than anyone else determine which policies prevail and which enterprises flourish. Their superiority is exemplified by the general addiction to overvaluation of the national currency. This obviously hurts exports, subsidizes imports and foreign travel, and facilitates capital flight. It has again and again been economically ruinous, yet countries resist allowing exchange rates to fall in step with the rate of inflation. In business-oriented countries, where producers are very influential, the tendency is the opposite, to push exchange rates down in order to promote exports. The quasidemocratic elite—and governments of the Third World generally—have good reason to hold rates high: to levy a tax on exports that is rather easily collectible (although cheating on invoicing is unavoidable), to permit cheap luxury imports, to have the power of allocating a valuable resource (foreign exchange sold at unrealistic rates), to be able to send assets to security abroad, and to favor urbanites (by subsidization of imports) over the less influential rural population.

If the political-bureaucratic ruling sector comprises the officer corps of the state, the troops are the civil service (with which may be included some political professionals not strictly in the government). If the bureaucracy is the single biggest pressure group in the United States and other Western countries (including Japan), it is much more so where capitalism is less well developed and government is the chief reliance. Generally speaking, the governmental apparatus is personalistic, with irregular career patterns, nepotistic, uncoordinated, routine and red-tape bound, and insecure, and for these reasons the more involved in politics. In the way of quasidemocracy, the bureaucracy may be a force for order but not for broad sharing of power. Its interest lies in maximization of the role of the state and in corruption. India's public sector employs more than twice as many as private industry, and it has something approaching a veto over reform.[46]

The bureaucracy in non-Western countries is ordinarily the best paid and probably best organized sector of the labor force. It is a prime means of upward mobility and usually the chief employer of recipients of diplomas, especially in prestigious but not very productive subjects such as law and the social sciences. Higher education is divorced from the labor market, and a dominant purpose of the university is to qualify for the bureaucracy. The expansion of higher education increases pressures for employment, and the rulership accepts the obligation of providing a suitable living for the educated.

The political-bureaucratic class suffers the basic contradiction of quasidemocracy. It desires the legitimation and regularity of the democratic order, within which it operates comfortably, yet it cannot desire wholehearted democracy, and the importance of jobs and opportunities for gain is such that turning the state over to an opposition party is inadmissible unless the competing parties have a level of understanding that is seldom possible. A happy compromise is to leave the office holders of the vanquished party in place and create new positions for the hungry victors.

One sector of the public service has a special role; namely, the armed forces. They have the capacity to remove civilian leadership in almost all civilian-ruled Third World countries, quasidemocratic or dictatorial, but they are not well equipped to administer the nation. For them, the more desirable situation is to watch over the civilian administration without assuming responsibility for policy, especially economic, and escaping the blame for failures. They are to be consulted, and they exercise a mostly silent veto. If they command the police, as they do in many countries, the independence of the judiciary is tenuous.[47] Most Latin American nations might be called civilian-military coalitions in which the military stands behind, and keeps order for, the civilians at the front of the state. In fact, the military is often seen as the guarantor of the constitution and hence of the democratic order; it has been called the "moderating power" in Brazilian parlance. They frequently favor the democratic state for its legality and order. The generals may be better supporters of the constitution than civilian politicians because the former, who already hold office in a sense, are more secure. For example, the president of Honduras, Roberto Suazo Córdoba, tried to change the constitution to extend his presidency; but the military insisted on proper elections.[48]

Usually military power is conservative, as is to be expected of an organization dedicated to hierarchy and order. Sometimes, as in Peru from 1968 to 1975, the army sees the old elite as an obstacle to development and undertakes a program of social change. Even then, however, the military did not want to militarize society or to mobilize mass action. When Latin American military men have gone over to mass mobilization, as did Jacobo Arbenz of Guatemala and Juan Perón of Argentina, they have alienated themselves from their fellow officers.

Although a military coup places a new layer at the top, most of the elite remain in place, administering the state and the economy. Aside from effects of reaction by the military to a previous leftist regime, the recent economic policies of democratic and authoritarian governments in Latin America have been indistinguishable. Both kinds have made the same errors and fallen into the same traps.[49]

Those of a middling economic level are not much of a political force in quasidemocracy. The middle class is largely dependent on the state, and is much divided. It generally seeks to join the privileged rather than trying to displace them[50] and has no desire to give power to the masses. The poor are politically active only under the guidance of superior strata. They demand much less of the state than the middle sectors, and are mostly happy to be left alone. Communication is downward only, and the poor are much divided, the interests of the urban masses being at odds with those of the rural masses and those of organized labor with those of the unorganized. The upper classes regard them with ignorance, disdain, and fear; and few leaders try to use them as an important political resource. Even communist parties hesitate to mobilize them.[51]

### Populism

Political and opinion leaders, including military leaders desirous of broadening their following, may begin taking more seriously the tenets of popular democracy and politics based on the voice, or the rising clamor, of the organized or organizable masses. There is a feeling, especially among intellectuals and leaders of popular groups, such as labor unions, of a new dawning of equality; the sufferings of the masses no longer seem inevitable. A popular power base grows in the burgeoning cities, as urbanizing peasants leave traditional bonds behind; and rootlessness and confusion of new needs make many clients for ambitious leadership.

Populism is an effort to gain political advantage by securing the backing of the masses (generally urban) by promising benefits (not revolution) and redistribution (to the neglect and probably the detriment of economic growth).[52] Whether paternalistic or charismatic, it is more personalist and elitist led than ideological or mass based, not for the "working class" but for the "people" in general. It emerges at any level of development,[53] but it becomes attractive in the weakening of traditional bonds, especially owner-peasant relations, when rural-to-urban migration offers a ready clientele for ambitious politicians. It represents an effort to use the lower classes politically when power has not gone to the middle class.[54]

Giving a mass electorate powers of economic decision is problematic anywhere; in a highly unequal society it is an invitation to disaster, as the urge to turn political rights into economic improvement leads to a politics of envy.[55] So far as raising the hopes of the poor is more politically rewarding than trying to reconcile the capitalists to reform, politicians will promise benefits, which seem a hope of long deferred justice to the reformers but to the affluent appear to be demagoguery or vote buying at the expense of the better off. Even in a settled and prosperous country like the United States, enlarging the electorate changes the political balance and disturbs the status quo. In a Third World country, it is not easy for populist movements to avoid moving toward extremism if leaders compete for a mass following and moderates feel compelled to preempt the radicals. They are impatient for quick payoffs, and, aware of unscrupulous powers against them, they are probably unscrupulous.[56] As Aristotle said, "When laws are not supreme, demagogues spring up."

The obvious way to help the masses is redistribution of wealth; a small percentage of the income of the upper classes could do much to relieve the misery of the poorest. But any effort to spread wealth is complicated at best, probably irregular, wasteful, and ineffective because of the incapacity of the politicians and the state apparatus.[57] Redistributive policies, of course, frighten the possessors, and they are successful (to a degree) only when a considerable fraction of the upper classes concur. This is likely to occur only when there seems to be no threat of Marxist-Leninist radicalism, as in Perónist Argentina or Costa Rica after the 1948 defeat of the communists. Taxpayers see benefits going more to dangerous politicians and hangers-on than to improvement of the well-being of the people—as is perhaps unavoidable in view of the difficulty of assuring the proper expenditure of funds. Moreover, inequality is not only economic and political but social and cultural, very likely racial.

Nonetheless, the obvious cause of the failure of social democratization in developing countries has been less the direct resistance of the wealthy than the failure of the economy. Economic troubles are accompanied by resentment of more or less corrupt and abusive manipulators and fear of radical revolution—cause enough for economic and hence political failure. Inflation is a seemingly inevitable outcome of the effort to use the state for political purposes. Needs, wholly justified in terms of democratic-egalitarian values, are infinite; and spending—less for welfare than for the political apparatus—grows, while the ability of the state to raise revenues shrinks as the wealthy withdraw support. Popular parties want not only to promote welfare programs but also to make jobs and industrialize, and this is inevitably costly and probably inefficient. They also come to the rescue of failing industries for the benefit of politicians as well as workers, with prospects of indefinite losses.

Populist politics calls for such benefits as raising wages, security of employment, extra pay and vacations, easy credit at low interest rates, controlled or subsidized prices of necessities, and public works. Artificial exchange rates for the national currency should be maintained to keep down the cost of imported goods, and there is pressure to protect and support, and perhaps to nationalize, uneconomic industries. Politicians need ever more jobs, and bureaucrats demand tenure. So far as the government is responsive, the result is deficits, sometimes amounting to half of government expenditures. Deficits may be financed to some extent by foreign borrowing, which at best postpones problems a little and increases them as payments come due, or by domestic borrowing, which is limited not only by the feeble capital market but by the atmosphere of uncertainty. The shortfall is covered in the easy way—perhaps the only way open to the populist state—by printing money.

Despite indexation, inflation disturbs the economy, maldistributes wealth, and reduces most persons' stake in the existent order. Together with mismanagement, protectionism, uncertainty, and hostility to wealth (and by extension, to production) it sets the economy on a downhill course, and troubles compound each other. There is disinvestment, and capital flees the country. Many of the upper and middle classes may take their skills abroad also, as occurred in Uruguay in the 1960s and in Jamaica in the 1970s.[58] Demoralization sets in. Inflation spirals. Corruption grows, especially as the salaries of bureaucrats (the backbone of the political organization) shrink, and both the old apparatus men and the new politicians strive to make up their losses.

Efforts to compensate by additional benefits and more protection worsen the situation. Once a populist government has gotten on the slippery slope of catering to itself and its clientele, it is very hard to reverse its course. Moderate reforms do not work, needs increase, tempers rise, and it becomes more necessary to promise great change in order to hold the loyalty of the followers, who find their hoped-for gains evaporating. Popular democracy easily turns extremist, and violence comes to the fore. A disappointed populist movement may turn revolutionary, or the privileged classes fear that it may do so. They know that there is even less respect for legality and constitutionalism on the part of the uneducated than the educated. By radical concepts of rights, the privileged have no rights: the old rules of the social order and probably the constitution itself are viewed as part of the oppressive system. The populist leaders, not prepared to admit their course was wrong, blame the reactionaries' hostility to reform and feel justified in stronger measures.

Landowners, industrialists, bankers, and merchants cannot themselves overthrow a state they fear and dislike, but they can sabotage it by withdrawing cooperation and supporting opposition activity of various kinds. The military forces, who can change the government, probably sympathize with the governing classes and hear their pleas for action. But they mostly act on their own behalf, fearful of the effects of radical politics in their own organizations.[59]

Ordinarily the course has been rather brief and sharp. Uruguay, however, is an example of nonrevolutionary chronic populism. Long hailed as the model democracy of Latin America, land of freedom, civic virtues, and social programs, with an educated, relatively homogeneous population and good agricultural resources, it prospered until the 1950s.[60] But Uruguay tried to provide a better life for the city population to the neglect of agriculture and tied up the economy in a web of protective measures, from all manner of labor laws to subsidies for noncompetitive industries. Real incomes declined rather steadily for a generation under many presidents. Inflation mounted as benefits for the many and the few caused chronic deficits. The economy was increasingly demoralized, and livestock raising, the sole source of exports, was stagnant for many decades. Elections became a means of sharing positions in the bureaucracy among the factions of the principal parties. Most people assumed that the democratically elected government was corrupt and responsible for the ills of the country.[61]

During the 1960s about a sixth of the population departed to seek a better life elsewhere. Some who remained, seeing no hope in the stagnant democratic system, decided revolution was the answer and began an urban guerrilla campaign. In the polarization, the electoral system also became corrupted,[62] subject to both demagoguery and vote buying. The president, unable to cope with the terrorists, called on the army to help. It stepped in and crushed the radicals. The generals, instead of letting the politicians resume the old game, stayed on and imposed a severe dictatorship from 1973 to 1985 intended to remake the nation.

Populism in the Third World is something between a new garb for the old politics and an effort to break the mold of the old politics. The masses, in fact, have little to say about it but listen to middle class or more or less elite leaders. Populism claims to promote democratic goals, but it fails because the society cannot really be changed by a few laws.

This scenario has been fully played out thus far only in Latin America, probably in large part because ideas of democracy have penetrated more strongly to the lower classes and have had more effect in Latin America than elsewhere in the Third World. Moreover, in the African and Asian spheres ethnic and religious cleavages often complicate or override economic class decisions. But something like it is probably unavoidable in very many countries if the basis of democracy is much broadened.

## THE MOVEMENT TOWARD DEMOCRACY

Whether partly democratic states are likely to move toward fuller democracy is unanswerable. The experience of the past half century is only moderately encouraging. It would be difficult to say that Mexico, after sixty years of experience with democratic forms, is much less firmly controlled by the "revolutionary family" and the ruling PRI party. They are obviously resolved to continue in the enjoyment of the state, as was shown by the shameless fraud in the 1985 and 1986 elections, accompanied by growls about the impossibility of the PRI's surrendering power.[63] In some ways, the country is better prepared for democracy—better educated, ampler means of communication, larger numbers of professionals, and so forth. In others it is less prepared: inequality, corruption, state control of the economy, and the size of the bureaucracy and its dominance have increased markedly. Power has shifted from the local chiefs, not to the masses, but to the federal bureaucrats and managers, from the bosses to the ministries. Democracy in India is not apparently firmer or more real than it was several decades ago; in Sri Lanka, it is much less so. On the other hand, there has been visible movement toward democratic institutions in many countries of Latin America and Southern Asia. If quasidemocracy is not becoming much more democratic, it is spreading more widely.

It is probably also becoming more sophisticated and civilized, improving formal institutions and making elite controls more refined. It is not necessarily deepening. The experience of quasidemocracy accustoms people to its mixture of democratic form and oligarchic substance, and the existence of functioning democratic institutions partly satisfies the demand for democratization. If appearances are improved, realities do not have to change.

Many Third World countries seem to be virtually trapped in that the dominance of the state and the interests of those who use it are strong enough to negate both economic development and political reform. Corruption becomes a vested interest, and retreat from economic intervention is very difficult. Yet it can hardly be hoped that elections will shift power as long as the economy is politically at stake. In other words, democracy would seem to await the growth of a dominant private sector, which the most influential groups do not favor. The apparent reason that Botswana can be relatively democratic is that wealth is more based on ownership of cattle and less on political position than in other African states. If the private sector is allowed to grow in other African countries, there should be a parallel effect. Alternatively, institutions might be developed to insulate management of state enterprises from politics. Democracy in Austria and other Western European countries is not much injured by public ownership of basic sectors of the economy. But any development severely reducing the privileges of present beneficiaries of the state is problematic in most of the world.

There has sometimes been sufficient motivation to make substantial changes at the expense of elites. The Nationalists on Taiwan, in intense antagonism to the communist government of Mainland China, not only created favorable conditions for private production but also carried out land reform, inaugurated many social services, instituted a strong educational system, promoted labor-intensive industry, and established a progressive system of taxation.[64] Thus far, however, they have not been persuaded to surrender much political power to democratic institutions. The South Korean military government has similarly been moved by its cold war with North Korea to create favorable conditions for business but not to admit an open electoral contest.

A possible hope for the quasidemocracy is that apprehensions of radicalism may be left behind, as they have been in the growth of democracy in the West, by gradual change. If there is no threat of total upheaval and if reform is justified by humanitarian values instead of by extremist rhetoric or the Marxist theory of class struggle, elite rule may be made more civilized and just, and ultimately less elitist. A more democratic and law-bound politics should also raise business confidence and encourage investment and production, reduce antieconomic corruption, broaden participation, minimize political violence, and over a long run foster character traits favorable for democracy, such as directness, openness, and the work ethic. It is easier to check the rapacity of the state, strengthen the legal order, regularize the replacement of leaders, and protect civil rights than to transfer much power to the lower classes; but everyone benefits from the improvement of standards of government. Opening the political system can overcome apathy and resentment without directly assaulting the comfortable world of the elite. Development of the economy should ease fears of redistribution by satisfying basic needs and hence reduce middle- and upper-class distrust of mass politics, while generating broad demands for greater political participation.

Much of the pressure for or against democratization comes from abroad, as elites and intellectuals look for models in more powerful countries. In the 1930s, Italian and German authoritarianisms persuaded many persons in Latin America, especially but not only in the armed forces, that democracy was a wave of the past. This idea was killed by the Second World War, but both the Soviet Union and Maoist China seemed to show that there was a stronger kind of party-managed "democracy." The sclerosis and de-utopianization of the Soviet Union and the repudiation of Maoism by China have left the authoritarians without good models.

The West, on the other hand, has been notably prosperous and correspondingly attractive; and the democratic states play an active role, just as the American and French revolutions broadcast their messages of liberation and Britain was a model of constitutional rule in the eighteenth century. The broad swing toward democratic government in Latin America since 1978 would not have been possible without the pressure, usually mild, of the United States. Quasidemocracy is the political system of basically authoritarian societies much influenced by the democratic West, and that influence can increase.

## MILITARY TUTELAGE FOR DEMOCRACY

Democratization must deal with and, if possible, make use of present forces in less developed societies. Chief of these are the soldiers, the strongest single political factor in most countries of the Third World. In some places, they are rapacious, acting virtually like gangsters holding a gun over the people, as in several African nations and, less crudely, in countries like Guatemala and El Salvador until recently. But a trained and professionalized military may play a positive political role—happily, because democracy in the Third World can come only with the assent of the military.

Military training, which necessarily looks abroad for models, is a prime channel for modern thinking. The resultant professionalism, which implies discipline, respect for rules, and character training, seems to generate reformist, if not democratic, currents, at least among the junior officers, who are less corrupted than their seniors by the fruits of power. For example, during many years when the Salvadoran army was supporting a narrow oligarchic regime, liberal-reformist officers would press strongly for a more progressive approach, including land redistribution; they had the upper hand briefly in 1979. The Peruvians in 1968 tried to institute a virtually revolutionary program, and young officer groups in

Thailand, Turkey, and elsewhere have attacked traditional corruption. The downfall of the Marcos government in the Philippines was possible because a military reform movement turned away from the abuses ruining the nation.

In Latin America, military governments, even when directly in power, have taken only a modest share of the national product, usually under 1 percent; and officers, while profiting in many ways, especially from positions in state enterprises, have not sequestered huge amounts like dictators such as Duvalier of Haiti, Mobutu of Zaire, or Marcos of the Philippines. In many cases, a genuine military government would be a big improvement over crude personal dictatorship, as in Zaire or Paraguay.

The military are not usually greedy for political power. If they were, they would directly run nearly all Third World countries instead of mostly looking over the shoulders of the civilian leadership. The hierarchic and rule-bound military organization is ill equipped to handle political questions of clashing interests, especially economic. The military mentality is neither economically oriented nor geared to compromise, adjustment, and practical answers, but to command and clear-cut decisions; the unity the officers cherish is jeopardized by the need to weigh conflicting demands.

A civilian gang running a country cannot voluntarily give up power. They pretend to correspond to the will of the people and cannot admit it is a lie. Worse, if they lose political position, they lose everything and are even likely to be prosecuted for their malfeasance. But a military rulership without democratic pretenses can withdraw to the barracks, retaining status, perquisites, and the ability to reassert themselves subsequently if they should feel the need. Consequently, military governors have many times yielded without violence, sponsored honest elections, and permitted civilians to replace them at the helm of the state. The military probably leave behind a correctly democratic state, as recently in Argentina, Peru, Venezuela, Colombia, Ecuador, and Bolivia. The step-by-step shuffling of the Brazilian generals from dictatorship to democracy in 1974 to 1984, with the measured development of free institutions, was a model transition.

The military out of power may exercise an informal restraining role that makes quasidemocracy possible, deterring the politicians from extremism and disorder. The leading parties in Venezuela, for example, understand that the inability to manage effectively and to contain their quarrels, political violence of any kind, or outrageous corruption would be likely to bring intervention. The military commonly regard themselves as guardians of the constitution; any gross violation of it by a civilian president might serve as a pretext for the generals to remove him. All Brazilian constitutions have charged the armed forces with assuring the normal functioning of the powers of the state, although no means other than the coup has been provided for exercising this function.

The army may serve informally as moderator of politics and watchdog of constitutionality, but it would do better in a defined role. In particular, it would be helpful for Third World democracy if the military could guarantee the regularity and purity of elections through an organization not subject to political interference. Constituting or supporting an unchallengeable electoral tribunal would satisfy some of the urge of the officers to protect the nation from the misdeeds of civilian politicians and to assert their guardianship, in fulfillment of their ethos. Elections could be much more effective if carried out under the aegis of a nonpolitical institution without a direct stake in the outcome. The military see themselves as defining the national interest; a regularized role for them would much decrease the temptation to intervene irregularly, especially against a government certified as duly elected by a military-backed agency.

It should be possible also to reduce burdens on the democratic process if the military were to assume a protectorate over other functions, such as the enforcement of decisions of an independent judiciary, which needs strong backing in order to guard against violations of the constitution. Or the military might directly or indirectly monitor corruption, especially at high levels. In a quasidemocracy the press and other normal control agencies, such as opposition spokesmen and police, are likely to be themselves corrupt and hence ineffective in checking misuse of office. The military are by no means exempt, but so far as they are professionally trained and brought to accept a mission of national strength—patriotism being their strong point—they are somewhat less susceptible to temptations than the civilians whose sole interest is the business of the state. Military-backed surveillance from outside should be able at least to reduce the magnitude of corruption.[65]

The military profession has no special virtue, of course, but in Third World societies it often represents a higher level of training and regular professionalism than any other politically significant group. Disciplined character and purposefulness may be lacking in the organization charged with the national defense, but they are more likely to be found there than in ordinary politics. Whatever the failings of the soldiers, they may represent the best prospect for an essentially nonpolitical control institution in less-developed countries.

The value of a force for guardianship over the political game must rest primarily on values inculcated by education and professional dedication; people get satisfaction from doing what they are trained and equipped to do. Just as doctors like to cure, military chiefs usually like to act for the security of the nation, which includes the soundness of its basic institutions. The military can make itself felt in any case, and it is better that it do so in defined and proper ways. Unless the military can be enlisted in democratization by helping to regularize the state, prospects for genuine improvement in the large majority of Third World countries are very dim.

In a more general way, countries that are not prepared to move quickly to popular democracy would do well to undertake constitutional engineering suitable for their societies. Political forces and mores are quite different in Latin American countries—not to speak of African— from those in North America or Western Europe; and it is absurd to copy constitutions from the latter with minor modifications. The aspiration to democracy is laudable, but it should be recognized that the democracy in less-developed and inegalitarian nations needs special protection to enable it to ripen. If a country is not yet in a position to be fully democratic, it should seek institutions appropriate for evolving quasidemocracy.

## THE ENCOURAGEMENT OF DEMOCRACY

The Western powers have generally recognized that they have an interest in assisting, or even an obligation to assist, the peoples of the Third World. All major industrial democracies have foreign aid programs. They are not large, but they are a novelty in history. Although in bygone days a number of earnest persons worked to save heathen souls, before World War II it would have seemed ridiculous to suggest that taxpayers should be called upon to contribute to health programs in Africa or agricultural extension in Bangladesh. But direct economic assistance is of uncertain long-term value; the greater contribution of the Western powers to political development must be the fostering of a world environment increasingly inhospitable to ascriptive or self-imposed rulership.

The first principle might be simply to stand firmly for democratic ideals. Foreign policy makers in Washington have frequently believed that security interests are best served by fidelity to rulers, whatever their character, who most firmly pledge themselves to anticommunism and military cooperation with the United States. It is easy to prefer assured and unconditional allies, albeit dictatorial, to uncertain and probably critical democratic ones. Unhappily, a really popular movement in the Third World is likely to be anti-Western because the privileged classes share in the Western-dominated world economy and because the interests and values of less-developed countries diverge from those of the modernized West.

Collaborating with dictatorships has turned disastrous, however, when such governments have become excessively unpopular and have been replaced by movements blaming the United States for all the evils of misgovernment, as occurred in Iran and Nicaragua in 1979. The value of withdrawing support from a tyrant, to the contrary, was demonstrated in the Philippines in 1986. But the debate about how to weigh interest in democratization against strategic utility is undecidable, and the temptation to seek a short-term advantage is strong.

Foreign support, even though only verbal, gives confidence to either democratic or antidemocratic forces. Anything less than a legitimate constitutional order must be held disreputable, as it is in the modern philosophic view. Violation of human rights is shameful, and it should be treated as such to the disgrace of the violators, regardless of their disposition. Countries should be encouraged to take pride in the justice of their constitutions; perhaps they can be led to emulate in the application of democracy, just as they emulate in Olympic Games. Indians are rightfully proud that theirs is a democratic state unique in the Afro-Asian world.

The value of democracy can be underlined by economic favors for countries moving toward it; the attractiveness of democracy to the elite will rise sharply if it is perceived as materially advantageous. More broadly, the fostering of world exchanges in general, along with better management of problems of currency exchange and international financial flows, would promote open economies congenial for democratic politics. Simplest and of no real cost to the industrial country would be to open markets to non-Western exports, with or without compensating concessions. Foreign trade, export orientation, and making production world-competitive should help countries to climb out of the political ownership trap, and the best promotion of democracy is the maximum of contacts with the outside world.

The enlargement of international cultural exchanges would be equally beneficial. This should include encouraging cultural exports of the less-developed world—which can be more productive of cultural than material goods—as well as making Western achievements more abundantly available everywhere. Maximum participation in world cultural flow should both help the creativity of less developed nations and give them the maximum benefit of world culture. Worldwide television is probably on the way, despite the horror of many states, and the democracies should be prepared to make it a positive force for better understanding. An incidental contribution might be the propagation of the international language, which happens to be English. This has left competitors far behind; it is the language of half the world's newspapers, most international business, and at least 80 percent of computer software. The more readily elites everywhere can communicate in a shared language and through it familiarize themselves with all the world's ideas and learning, the more manageable differences should be.

Part of the cultural achievement the West could share to a much greater extent is knowledge of the ways, institutions, strengths, weaknesses, and values of democracy, the legal order, administrative practices, and procedures of popular government. Elections are more practical if people are familiar with their procedures and less falsifiable if the proper mechanisms are in place. U.S.-sponsored Salvadoran elections, for example, benefited by a mechanized registry of voters. A helpful institution for democratization is an independent and impartial authority to conduct elections—a Third World invention not needed in thoroughly democratic societies. Such an agency, with full authority over all aspects of the electoral process, has helped Costa Rica to hold regular and unchallenged elections since 1949. Even more remarkable, the Brazilian electoral tribunal during two decades of military government regularly conducted elections that were accepted as fair, at least in access to the polls and the counting of the ballots.

### The Social Factor

Real democratization, however, must rest on the better integration of society, chiefly the reduction of economic and social inequality. If this is not achieved, electoral mechanisms are of little avail, and democratic institutions may bring negative as well as positive results. Improvement of the social structure involves many things, from education for citizenship to the development of voluntary, economic, professional, cooperative, and other organizations, which should serve as intermediaries between individuals, political movements, and the state. Above all, however, it is requisite to reduce the gap between the upper and lower classes.

Modernization and industrialization outmode old sources of status and open new ways for people to climb by skills and training. But they cause new inequalities because some sectors of the society are raised by higher productivity, while others fail to improve or may even find themselves worse off because their skills are no longer in demand. Capital-intensive industry and agriculture make few jobs. At a certain level, however, perhaps when a nation passes the middle tier of modernization or when more than half of the population is brought into the modernizing sector, inequality probably declines.[66]

Although the initial effect of modernization is to promote centralization, its long-term impact may be toward pluralism by virtue of the growth of independent classes and organizations.[67] It also equalizes by raising the importance of technical qualifications, more attainable by brains and ambition than by wealth. In the technological age, racial and other discriminations make no sense, just as it is impractical to have different rules for different classes of drivers on the road. The rapidly changing technological society, moreover, is continually churning and creating new opportunities; and it can hardly be doubted that rising income levels make it easier for a semiauthoritarian government to move toward democracy if it desires.

The affluent society is sure to have more communication and contacts with the outside world, and as long as the richest and most advanced nations are democratic, elites will associate democracy with high material standards. Increasing numbers of elites and nonelites are exposed to the Western world both through trade and tourism, which have increased enormously in the past generation, and by increasingly internationalized media. Western pop culture may not be uplifting, but it is antitraditional and antiaristocratic.

Social structures can be improved, however, and inequality decreased in advance of the slow and somewhat uncertain effects of modernization. Most useful would be to make people more valuable and hence more esteemed. Unlike redistribution of wealth, this need not arouse anxieties. To attack the waste of human resources associated with poverty is unacceptable only to the narrowest of the privileged. The principal means is education oriented mostly to economic utility.[68] The best long-term investment is in human capital.[69] Professional abilities override artificial differences; trained people with useful skills are respected. Aristocrats are readier to accept the company of the educated, although they be of humble origin; education has been a prime criterion of status almost everywhere and always. The outstanding educational systems of Taiwan and Japan, producing total literacy (in difficult languages) and many highly qualified graduates, deserve much credit both for the phenomenal growth of these societies and for their relative egalitarianism.

It would be simple and unobjectionable to enable many more, especially of the less-affluent sectors, to come to schools and universities in the advanced democracies. The Soviet Union provides several times as many scholarships to the Third World as does the United States, despite the disparity of resources. Likewise the establishment of numerous subsidized schools in Third World countries, both secondary and higher-technical, would be a salutary token of the American faith in education and should have returns for the long-term security of the United States far beyond a comparable military expenditure. A network of business schools would do far more to raise the economy of a Third World country than a huge infusion of money.

Better schooling would be especially appropriate for the improvement and professionalization of the bureaucracy. This would help to remove the public service from the political contest. Many Third World countries have largely excluded politics from one sector of the government, the military, basing promotions more or less systematically on education and qualifications, at least up to the higher ranks; the diplomatic service is sometimes similarly professionalized. Hardly anything would improve the political picture more than regularization of the public service.

Education promotes not only productivity but health. The two go together; the sickly or poorly nourished are not likely to stay in school or to learn much if they do. It may be reasonably guessed that over half the population of the Third World is physically and mentally below its potential because of childhood malnutrition. Yet expenditure for child health is as unobjectionable as schooling, and costs are slight in comparison with eventual returns. Educational and health programs would also make democracy more practicable in countries of great inequality by reducing social tensions and giving the masses a stake in the social order.

Education and health, however, cannot do much to bring economic improvement and equality as long as people crowd into the cities unable to absorb them. Cairo has swollen from 2.5 million in 1955 to 14 million in 1985, and most other Third World cities, especially capitals, have similarly outgrown both employment opportunities and facilities. The masses are driven by poverty from the farms, there being ten Egyptians for each tillable acre; but in the city they find no proper work and exist only by the bread provided nearly gratis by the state. Democracy is hardly in question, as people rather feel that modernization—or what they see of it—has failed, and they revert to the veil and Islamic law.

If labor shortage is good for democracy, a surplus of hands devalues workers. Rapid swelling of the population negates economic growth, burdens the government with providing ever more services and infrastructure, and creates a mass of unemployed for whom no government can make jobs. It fills the political arena with unsteady youth with no stake in legal order, who are the militia for confrontation. Many countries have recognized the problem, but it has hardly been diminished.

No less negative in the long term is the unequalizing effect of differences in fertility of economic groups. The reproductive rate of uneducated urban women is commonly many times higher than that of women who have received at least a secondary education. For example, in Brazil in 1980, urban women of no schooling had 5.5 times as many children as those with thirteen years or more; [70] and average intelligence declines rather sharply with family size.[71] The effects on the capacities of the next generations must be great, even if one assumes that the genetic endowments of the two groups are equal. Inequality is increased so far as the ability of parents to give their children proper nourishment, education, and a good start decreases with their number. On the other hand, if the possessing classes were persuaded to have more children, their estates would be divided and the advantages they furnish their offspring would be spread out. Differential birthrates contribute to economic and political inequality of both classes and nations.

Since the yearning for security in old age is a major reason for desiring large families, a benign way to foster population control is general pensions, especially for the aged childless. This would also represent justice, that is, compensation for the fact that those who have no or few children have not burdened the state with the costs of education and other services and have not swollen the ranks of the unemployed. Support for the elderly would even more than health care give the poor a stake in society. Extensive programs for social improvement would cost the Western powers only a small fraction of the amounts generously disbursed as foreign loans in the late 1970s and early 1980s with little prospect of repayment and should give very large economic and political returns.

The outlook is not entirely bleak. With favorable conditions, democracy should spread by propinquity, as it did to Spain and Portugal, which seem to have joined the ranks of genuine democracy. For example, it may mature in Turkey, where it is well fixed in the political culture.[72] If the United States lends its support to democracy in Latin America, reversion to military government or old-style dictatorships seems unlikely; but deepening of democracy requires a difficult reversal of the present trend toward greater inequality. Prospects for Africa, the Near East, southern Asia, and China are problematic. But if democracy is more and more evidently the mode of the advanced sector of the world, it will be increasingly imitated, at least superficially, and frank dictatorship may come to be regarded as barbaric.

### Notes

1. Frank Tachau, Turkey: The Politics of Authority, Democracy, and Development (New York: Praeger Publishers, 1984), p. 36.
2. As African nationalists felt at the time of independence. Robert H. Jackson and Carl G. Rosberg, "Popular Legitimacy in African Multi-Ethnic States," Journal of Modern African Studies, 22, no. 2 (June 1984), p. 186.
3. I. Roland Pennock, Democratic Political Theory (Princeton: Princeton University Press, 1979), p. 518.
4. Cf. Donald Share, The Making of Spanish Democracy (New York: Praeger Publishers, 1986).
5. John A. Booth and Mitchell A. Seligson, "The Political Culture of Authoritarianism in Mexico: A Reexamination," Latin American Research Review, 19, no. 1 (1984), 106–24.
6. Carl Stone, Class, State, and Democracy in Jamaica (New York: Praeger Publishers, 1986), pp. 49–50.
7. Report to Congress on Voting Practices in the United Nations, Department of State (Washington, D.C.: 1985); and Jeane J. Kirkpatrick, "The U.S. Leads; Who Follows?" Washington Post, June 9, 1986, p. 21.
8. Robert H. Jackson and Carl G. Rosberg, Personal Rule in Black Africa: Prince, Autocrat, Prophet, Tyrant (Berkeley: University of California Press, 1982), p. 269.
9. James C. Scott, Comparative Political Corruption (Englewood Cliffs, N.J.: Prentice-Hall, 1972), p. 15.
10. Arturo Valenzuela, "Los origenes de la democracia chilena," Estudios Públicos, 12 (Spring 1983), 12–14.

11. Alan Riding, *Distant Neighbors: A Portrait of the Mexicans* (New York: Alfred A. Knopf, 1985), p. 103.

12. John W. Sloan, *Public Policy in Latin America: A Comparative Survey* (Pittsburgh: University of Pittsburgh Press, 1984), p. 164–65.

13. David E. Blank, *Venezuela: Politics in a Petroleum Republic* (New York: Praeger Publishers, 1984), pp. 50, 124.

14. Edward G. Stockwell and Karen A. Laidlaw, *Third World Development: Problems and Prospects* (Chicago: Nelson-Hall, 1981), p. 251.

15. For Jamaica, see Carl Stone's *Democracy and Clientelism in Jamaica* (New Brunswick, N.J.: Transaction Books, 1983), pp. 55, 83, 186.

16. Ved Mehta, "Letter from New Delhi," *New Yorker*, August 3, 1981, p. 52.

17. *Wall Street Journal*, August 21, 1986, p. 1.

18. Urmila Phadnis, "Democracy in Sri Lanka: Crises of Legitimacy and Integration" (paper, Conference on Democracy in Developing Nations, Hoover Institution, December 19–21, 1985).

19. Chai-Anan Samudavanija, "Democracy in Thailand: A Case of a Stable Semi-democratic Regime" (conference, Hoover Institution, Stanford University, December 19–21, 1985).

20. Heng Chee Chan, *The Dynamics of One Party Dominance: The PAP at the Grass-Roots* (Singapore: Singapore University Press, 1976), pp. 202–5.

21. *New York Times*, August 14, 1985, p. 8.

22. Robert H. Jackson and Carl G. Rosberg, "Popular Legitimacy in African Multi-Ethnic States," *Journal of Modern African Studies*, 22 (June 1984), 190.

23. Sanford Ungar, *Africa* (New York: Simon & Schuster, 1985), p. 145.

24. Larry Diamond, "Democracy in Nigeria: Failure and Promise" (conference, Stanford, Conn., December 19–21, 1985).

25. Carlos H. Waisman, "Development and Democracy: The Case of Argentina" (conference, Stanford, Conn., December 19–21, 1985).

26. Ricardo Combellas Lares, *Copei: Ideologia y Liderazgo* (Caracas: Ariel, 1985), pp. 18–19, 312–13.

27. Blank, *Venezuela*, pp. 47, 49, 131, 189–90, 192.

28. *South*, 69 (July 1986), p. 59.

29. Richard C. Kearney, "Dominican Update: Can Politics Contain the Economic Crisis," *Caribbean Review*, 14, no. 4, 13–14.

30. Charles Ameringer, *Democracy in Costa Rica* (New York: Praeger Publishers, 1982), pp. 53–4.

31. Richard Biesanz, Karen Biesanz, and Mavis Biesanz, *The Costa Ricans* (Englewood Cliffs, N.J.: Prentice-Hall, 1982), p. 193.

32. Ameringer, *Democracy*, pp. 75, 100.

33. Samuel Stone, *La dinastia de los conquistadores* (San Jose: Editorial Universidad Centroamericana, 1975).

34. Douglas A. Chalmers, "Parties and Society in Latin America," in *Friends, Followers, and Factions: A Reader in Political Clientalism*, ed. Steffen W. Schmidt, Laura Guasti, Carl H. Lande and James C. Scott (Berkeley: University of California Press, 1977), p. 403.

35. Carl Stone, *Democracy and Clientelism in Jamaica* (New Brunswick, N.J.: Transaction Books, 1983), p. 96.

36. James C. Scott, "Clientelistic Relations and Policy Change in Southeast Asia," in *Friends, Followers, and Factions*, pp. 123–4, 139.

37. Susan Purcell, "Mexico," in *Political Clientelism, Patronage and Development*, ed. S. N. Eisenstadt and Rene Lemarchand (Beverly Hills: Sage Publications, 1981), pp. 202–4.

38. Rene Lemarchand and Keith Legg, "Political Clientelism and Development," in *Analyzing the Third World*, ed. Norman Provizer (Cambridge, Mass.: Schenkman Publishing, 1978), p. 123.

39. Joan M. Nelson, *Access to Power: Politics and the Urban Poor in Developing Nations* (Princeton: Princeton University Press, 1979), p. 383.

40. As in Jamaica; see Stone, *Class*, p. 53.

41. As in Mexico; see Alan Riding, *Distant Neighbors: A Portrait of the Mexicans* (New York: Alfred A. Knopf, 1985), p. 105.
42. Stone, *Democracy*, p. 101.
43. As stated by Gary Wynia and cited by John W. Sloan in *Public Policy in Latin America: A Comparative Survey* (Pittsburgh: University of Pittsburgh Press, 1984), p. 64.
44. *The New York Times*, October 30, 1986, p. 6.
45. Riding, *Distant Neighbors*, pp. 106, 124.
46. *Wall Street Journal*, November 7, 1986, p. 25.
47. Raymond D. Gastil, *Freedom in the World: Political Rights and Civil Liberties, 1984–1985* (Westport, Conn.: Greenwood Press, 1985), p. 253.
48. *New York Times*, November 13, 1985, p. 4.
49. Robert Wesson, "Conclusion," in *Politics, Policies, and Economic Development in Latin America* (Stanford: Hoover Institution Press, 1984), p. 236.
50. Dennis H. Wrong, *Power: Its Forms, Bases and Uses* (New York: Harper & Row Publishers, 1979), p. 202.
51. Nelson, *Access to Power*, pp. 320–24, 387–97.
52. Sloan, *Public Policy*, p. 183.
53. Robert Dix, "Populism: Authoritarian and Democratic," *Latin American Research Review*, 20, no. 2 (1985).
54. Gastil, *Freedom*, p. 237.
55. John W. Sloan, "Comparative Public Policy Choice and Public Policy in Latin America," *Journal of Developing Areas*, 16 (April 1982), 427.
56. Gary W. Wynia, *The Politics of Latin American Political Development* (New York: Cambridge University Press, 1978), p. 139.
57. Sloan, "Public Policy in Latin America" pp. 430–31.
58. Edy Kaufman, *Uruguay in Transition: From Civilian to Military Rule* (New York: Transaction Books, 1979), p. 206.
59. For discussion of this sequence see Robert Wesson's *Democracy in Latin America* (New York: Praeger Publishers, 1982), pp. 138–85.
60. Russell H. Fitzgibbon, *Uruguay: Portrait of a Democracy* (New Brunswick, N.J.: Rutgers University Press, 1954).
61. Kaufman, *Uruguay*, pp. 42, 66.
62. Martin Weinstein, *Uruguay: The Politics of Failure* (Westport, Conn.: Greenwood Press, 1975), p. 126.
63. Jose Fernandez, "Mexico: From Hope to Frustration," *Freedom at Issue*, September-October 1985, p. 20.
64. Hung-cha-Tai, "The KMT and Modernization in Taiwan," in *Authoritarian Politics in Modern Society: The Dynamics of Established One-Party Systems* ed. Samuel P. Huntington and Clement H. Moore (New York: Basic Books, 1970), pp. 427–28; and William H. Overholt, "The Moderation of Politics," *The Pacific Basin: New Challenge for the United States*, Academy of Political Science, (New York: 1986), James W. Morley, ed.
65. As suggested by Diamond in *Democracy*, pp. 88–90.
66. Erich Weede and Horst Tiefenback, "Some Recent Explanations of Income Inequality," in *The Gap Between Rich and Poor: Contending Perspectives on the Political Economy of Development*, ed. Mitchell A. Seligson (Boulder: Westview, 1984), p. 248; and Irma Adelman, "A Poverty-Focused Approach to Development Strategy," in *Development Strategies Reconsidered*, ed. John P. Lewis and Valeriana Kallab (New Brunswick, N.J.: Transaction Books, 1986), p. 51.
67. Samuel P. Huntington, "Social and Institutional Dynamics of One-Party Systems," in *Authoritarian Politics in Modern Society: The Dynamics of Established One-Party Systems*, ed. Samuel P. Huntington and Clement H. Moore (New York: Basic Books, 1970), p. 7.
68. John W. Sloan, *Public Policy in Latin America: A Comparative Survey* (Pittsburgh: University of Pittsburgh Press, 1984), p. 91.
69. Kim Carney, "Development Aid: An Economist's Perception," *International Journal on Peace*, 2, (July-September 1985), 15.

70. Peter T. Knight and Richard Moran, *Brazil: Poverty and Basic Needs Series* (Washington D.C.: World Bank, 1981), p. 15.
71. *Science News*, April 17, 1976, p. 245.
72. Frank Tachau, *Turkey: The Politics of Authority, Democracy, and Development* (New York: Praeger Publishers, 1984), p. 8.

# Superpower Rivalry

## ANTAGONISM

Ours is an era of relative freedom and representative government, exuberant cultural ferment, and considerable material prosperity. This means that we live in a system of independent competitive sovereignties. The freedom of independent states—competing but not destroying one another, usually engaging in mutually beneficial exchanges although capable of murderous conflict, and sharing something of a common culture—seems to be essential today, as it has been in the past, for the existence of pluralistic societies, constitutional republican or democratic states, and innovative culture. International freedom of states opens political and intellectual space for freedom at all levels. It is conceivable that a world authority could guarantee a modicum of order, like a confederal government, leaving individual states adequate autonomy; but it is difficult to envisage how this could come about except by the worldwide victory of one power, which would mean world empire.

The community of sovereign states interacting politically and economically is parallel to the pluralistic society with its autonomous groups and powers. On the world level, the central authority of the democratic state is missing, of course; but there is a certain acceptance of international law in peacetime, or at least habits and conventions that make it possible for independent entities to coexist and have useful relations with one another. There must be some rules of the game, and violence must ordinarily be excluded. This comity is parallel to the consensus that is necessary for the cohesion of democratic states.

The pressure of rivalries in the open international system is invigorating, as the less advanced seek to catch up and the more advanced to get or stay ahead, for security, power, prestige, and prosperity. The principle of competition is at least as vital for nations as it is for corporations. An antagonist is essential for group integrity and serves as both excuse for failures and spur to improvement.[1] The technical-economic contest between the United States and Japan has been enormously stimulating for both, as the Japanese have striven to compensate economically for political losses, and the United States has been startled by Japanese successes into studying seriously the methods of another nation, from industrial management to the school system, for the first time since the United States became an industrial power. Competition between the United States and the Soviet Union, for both of whom slackness might mean unbearable loss, was most potent when the United States was shocked by Soviet space firsts to upgrade American education, but the determination to check the growth of Soviet power continues to keep America from going to sleep in satisfaction. On the other hand, the lack of international competition is deadening for many African states, which are relieved of the penalties of mismanagement.[2]

The most vigorous and compelling form of international competition, war, is no longer admissible for major powers; but the need to keep pace economically impels nations to dedication and rationality, just as competition in the marketplace drives firms to efficiency and excellence. The need to advance economically is the best argument for reform in China and Eastern Europe. Competition among nations also brings elites and masses closer together, generating common values without which democracy would be problematic. In the rivalry of states, it is necessary to secure the loyalty of the people, joining team spirit, or patriotism, with humane idealism.

The sharpest aspect of international competition, the condition of superpowers glaring at one another, may seem, at first view, to be an accident of world history. But something like it is probably inevitable in any free international system. States measure themselves by their power in relation to others or by the influence they can exercise. Standing in the world is enormously important for leadership and people alike—for pride, even if no material advantages are to be had—and the great game is inordinately costly. Competitive-aggressive instincts bring men to the top in the political contest; having achieved the highest ambition within the nation, they can hardly refrain from turning to the contest of sovereignties. The strongest of human organizations, the powers that envision themselves as world leaders, are correspondingly strongly driven to self-assertion. By the dynamics of political interaction, the two leading powers are thus inevitably at odds.

Nothing in human behavior has changed so little since the beginnings of civilization as the character of relations between sovereign powers. The Hittites and Egyptians contended in much the same fashion as modern states. The principle of antithesis of power was old twenty-four hundred years ago, when the Corinthians pointed to the power of Athens and urged, "Let us attack and subdue her, that we may live safely for the future." [3] The two supreme states can never establish a dyarchy to exercise joint hegemony, because for each the other is the chief impediment to full dominion and the main obstacle to fulfillment of its will; and only one can be at the summit of prestige and potency. The United States and the Soviet Union, as the two most powerful by a wide margin, are each the only political-military threat to the other. They have to be antagonists.

### The Ideological Confrontation

A sharp difference in political ideals and complexion also exacerbates tensions. Just as the workings of a pluralistic democracy are made difficult by unbridgeable ideological differences and the presence of a strong antidemocratic party, the international system is strained by a great power of imperial mode, hostile to the values of pluralism both domestically and internationally, opposed in principle to nationalism (other than its own), economic freedom, political autonomy, and "bourgeois" democracy.

Ideological antagonism also follows from power rivalry. Political opposition has to be rationalized, and the contenders for supremacy must be ideally contradictory. Each has to assert its claim to superiority and sees its national goals as universal values. For the most part, the prizes in the U.S.-Soviet rivalry are intrinsically unimportant; but both sides have to see them as part of the struggle for ALL.

Although the United States and the Soviet Union did not become different originally because of the conflict of ideals, this serves to maintain their political distance and makes hateful to both of them the idea of "convergence," which has seemed to sociologists the logical result of modernization. Each side sees the other as not only adversary but evil, and the spirit of antagonism confirms each in its ideological position. Hostility may rise or fall at times because of circumstances, but it cannot cease. Foreign policy is at best subject to ignorance and irrationality; in it decision makers are much less subjected to the checks of realism than in domestic affairs. In attitudes toward the global rival, emotions have full play, and the contest of great powers is the supreme game.

A secondary factor in the ideological repulsion of the superpowers is the difference of economic level: the United States can extol the fruits of its liberal economy and the consumer society and look down on Soviet poverty, adding economic incompetence to the sins of the Soviet system. Self-respect requires the Soviet leadership to exalt moral-political values of order and dedication not free from envy of American abundance; and it imputes to the United States anarchic materialism and inequality. America has money but no ideals. Intelligent people, even more detached and sincere than national leaders usually are, see the world in very different colors. Understanding becomes the more difficult because the leaders on both sides not only have different values and political perceptions but they project their mentality on the other side. Americans are disappointed that Soviet officials do not behave more or less the way that Americans are expected to behave; because Soviet journalists function as spies, the Soviets expect American journalists to do likewise.

The mutual ideological repugnance of contending powers is a general principle. If Japan, for example, should acquire strength comparable to that of the United States, it would doubtless feel freer to press interests, both economic and political, contradicting those of the United States, asserting strictly Japanese values. A rising Japanese nationalism, born of economic success and unburdened by war guilt, already tends to identify with the Third World and sees Americanization as a betrayal of the nation.[4] The Japanese-American rivalry has a different temper because of the absence of physical (military) threat, but the United States resents Japanese assertiveness, when the Japanese economy is only half the American. Although both countries are open and democratic and have had much experience in dealings, they often seem to talk past one another. Unions and politicians blame Japan for American economic woes and suspect the Japanese of villainy even as they smile.

The mingling of ideological and power antagonisms was apparent in the great confrontation of the mid-1930s to 1945. Two major authoritarian powers on opposite sides of the globe, Germany and Japan, faced Britain, France, and the United States, with the Soviet Union playing a secondary and ambiguous role until the invasion of June 1941. Germany, then the nation of greatest industrial capacity in Europe, and Japan, the dominant power of the western Pacific, undertook their reach toward world power in the name of fiercely antiliberal doctrines and ideologies of militarism and hypernationalism, in opposition both to Soviet communism and to what they regarded as the decadent democracies standing selfishly in their way. In the ensuing war it was the Nazis who, as antidemocrats, vehemently denounced capitalism and "plutocracy" along with Jews and Bolshevism.

The same pattern of ideological or political-social polarization joined to power antagonism has reappeared repeatedly in history. The bloody desperation of World War I was not mere capricious madness but arose from the fact that the two coalitions represented contrary outlooks: relatively libertarian Britain and France, joined by the United States (autocratic Russia being rather far away), fought against monarchic Prussian-led Germany, imbued with militaristic virtues, alongside Austria-Hungary, striving to preserve an outmoded multinational empire. If the antithesis in the first round of world war was less total than in the second, it was because the sides were not so well defined and because there still existed in 1914 some of the old tolerant European spirit of the balance of power.

Earlier, the wars of the French Revolution pitted a radical disruptive France against conservative Europe, although relatively liberal but nonrevolutionary England was on the same side as Austria in defense of the traditional order. Napoleon's effort to make a revolutionary-authoritarian empire was slightly parallel to the Leninists drive for revolution. In the seventeenth century, the imperial France of the Sun King battled against the most liberal powers of the day, England and the Netherlands. Before him, the contest was between the republican Netherlands and autocratic Spain, leader of Europe's conservative forces. England and Spain likewise found themselves in this same political-ideological opposition.

This classic confrontation is also enshrined in ancient history. The free Greek cities fought off the great despotic empire of the day,

Persia, in a prolonged duel. Shortly after Persia had been repelled, a contest arose between Athens, the leading Greek democracy, and Sparta, the foremost Greek exponent of militarism, oligarchy, discipline, conformism, and repression. This led to the twenty-seven-year Peloponnesian War, which was bitter and uncompromising beyond the traditional quarrels of the Greek city-states.

The ideological contrariety also coincides with the fact that one contender for world supremacy (the more commercially minded) is sure to be more the defender of the prevalent world order; the other (the more militaristic), the beneficiary of discontents. The one is in this sense conservative; the other, the more frustrated and dissatisfied power, is more aggressive and ideological, more disruptive or, as commonly stated, revolutionary. To be opposed in principle and philosophy to autonomy, as the Soviets are, is to be opposed to the free international system. Even if the Soviets did not concretely support revolution and terrorism, their opposition to the prevalent system encourages revolutionaries and terrorists.

The antithesis may also be expressed in a different way: the United States stands for the "free world," that is, the pluralist, capitalist West that has grown out of the European nation-state system. The Soviet Union spearheads the reaction of the non-West, defending "socialism," that is, the principle of political management and authority against the corrosive onslaught of Western ways. It is not mere opportunism that the Soviet Union regularly sides with Third World countries in North-South controversies; in a real sense, they have a common cause. In the Arab-Israeli aspect of the East-West confrontation, the Soviets have sided with the Arabs with exceptional vehemence, doubtless not only because of political calculation but from a feeling that the Arabs' resistance to the intrusion of Zionism in their world is akin to Soviet rejection of Western values. This also suggests that the Soviet Union is politically the conservative power, despite its claim to revolution and its hostility toward the Western-oriented international order. The Soviet Union is fundamentally uncomfortable with modernization, whereas the more fluid pluralist, even anarchic, society of the West opens the way to indefinite change through uncontrolled modernization.

### The Primacy of Power

The antithesis of power is nonetheless primary. When the Soviet Union was weak, it and the United States each had a distaste for the other, but there was no special antagonism. The United States did not seek to strangle the new Soviet state when this was tottering during the civil war. A small force was sent to Siberia more to check Japanese ambitions than to trouble the Leninists, and when the Soviets were afflicted by famine in 1921 to 1922, the United States generously sent food without political conditions. In the 1920s and early 1930s Moscow was relatively friendly toward the United States; its bugaboos were Britain and France. In the hectic industrialization of the First Five Year Plan, the Stalinists preferred American engineers. During the Second World War, Americans found the Russians heroic and thought they saw sprouts of Soviet democracy beneath the autocratic surface of Stalinism; the Soviets accepted the capitalist powers as real allies as their mentality swung toward pragmatism and a realistic world view. Stalin made peace with the church, forgot about class struggle and proletarianism, accepted the legitimacy of the international system, and called on the people to fight for Mother Russia.

But as soon as Hitler, Mussolini, and the Japanese militarists were vanquished, the United States found itself alone—Britain and France no longer being able to carry the burden of world power—facing a formidable antagonist in Stalinist Russia with its huge victorious army and its newly acquired empire. At first there were hopes of settling differences and keeping the peace through the United Nations. But by 1947 it was evident that Stalin meant to Sovietize Eastern Europe permanently (as was unavoidable in the philosophy of Leninism), and apprehension at Soviet or Soviet-sponsored communist expansion in Greece and Turkey caused feelings to shift to general hostility. The Truman Doctrine (1947) promised assistance to peoples threatened by communism anywhere, and the cold war was under way.

This polarity has dominated world politics ever since, mixing ideology with patriotism. All major forceful actions of the United States abroad have been essentially anti-Soviet, motivated by fears of expansion by the Soviet Union directly or through surrogates. From the Korean War and the Vietnam War through the Dominican intervention (1965), the occupation of Grenada (1983), and support for Nicaraguan anti-Sandinistas, virtually the entirety of U.S. political foreign policy has aimed, directly or indirectly, against Soviet influence or pro-Soviet radicalism. The only purpose of the astronomical amounts spent on defense has been to counter the communist, that is, Soviet, threat.

Soviet behavior has been similarly guided by anti-Americanism. In the normal course of affairs, one would expect that the revolutionary ideal of social change would long since have been dropped; and it surely would have been if it did not correspond to power needs. A revolutionary movement normally lasts several years, not seven decades. Russia emerged from World War II imperially sated by ordinary standards, and the Soviet ruling class has long since settled down to enjoyment of its station. But the Soviets began reasserting an ideological stance as soon as their armies crossed the frontiers in pursuit of the Nazis and occupied most of Eastern and Central Europe. They have since kept up their worldwide support for communist parties, despite the political liabilities, and have spent on arms at least double the American percentage of the national product, regardless of their dire need for capital. The apparent purpose of their military machine is only to oppose the United States, both as a world power and as the bearer of anti-Soviet subversion, as in Hungary, Czechoslovakia, and Afghanistan. The great evil in the Soviet political vocabulary is "imperialism," a synonym for the power and influence of the United States; and to support "liberation movements" is to combat "imperialism."

The rivals for world leadership have necessarily to emphasize their special virtues and the faults of the antagonist, stressing their ideal right as justification of the exercise of power and using the vices and the threat of the other both as an explanation for difficulties and as a cause for the loyalty and dedication of their own citizens. In a typical expression of Gorbachev, "[U.S.] imperialism is impelled by its mainsprings and its very social and economic essence to translate the competition of the two systems [capitalism and socialism] into the language of military confrontation. Because of its social nature, imperialism continually generates aggressive, adventuristic policies." [5] The Soviets are probably sincere in seeing the hand of the United States in their troubles in Poland and Afghanistan, much as Washington sees Soviet-Cuban meddling as the chief cause of disorder in Central America. By extension, the Soviets seem willing to embrace almost any regime, such as that of Qaddafi in Libya, that is anti-American.

On the other side, the United States is quite willing to treat with and help communist states opposed to the Soviet Union. The United States came to the rescue of Tito's Yugoslavia when it was menaced by Stalin, and in the last decade has increasingly regarded Communist China as a potential ally against the Soviet Union, turning its back on ideologically more congenial Nationalist China to placate frankly communist Beijing. The crudely oppressive Romanian regime is viewed fairly sympathetically because of its glimmers of anti-Sovietism.

The antitheses of capitalism and socialism, religious belief (or tolerance) and atheism, upper- or non-class values and proletarianism (or Right versus Left), and traditional and revolutionary causes all have validity; but the real issue is, are you with us against the enemy? "Are you resolved to strike against communism in (for example) Central America?"—for which it is not necessary to know anything about Central America or communism but the horror of a Soviet presence within the American sphere. Or "Will you cooperate with the party against capitalism and imperialism?"—a question which has little to do with the rights of the workers. Ideology marks the sides and defines who is one of "us", just as the controversy of the Eucharist did in fifteenth century Europe.

Theory deals with institutions, however, and the ideological quarrel is mostly a commitment to limited versus unlimited government. In other words, the contenders for world leadership stand near opposite ends of the spectrum running from the democratic or pluralistic to the authoritarian or monistic. Ideology thus concerns the basic structure of society and the vision of the ideal order. The spread of democracy and the development of free-enterprise economies are basic to the American dream of an ever more prosperous world free of serious conflict. Similarly, for the Soviets true peace means the triumph of socialism and the universal mission of the Russians as bringers of order and peace to the world. The very great powers, regarding their ways as valid for all humanity, are inspired by, and filled with a sense of, righteous destiny, the hindrance to which is the contrary power.

Each superpower is the greatest danger to the stability, or even political existence, of the other, and for many persons the essence of patriotism is to combat the designs of the opposite superpower. On both sides, the more traditionally and conservatively minded are more inclined to stress the "us" versus "them" view of foreign relations, and they lead the fight for a stern approach to the global rival, with few concessions to neutrals or allies. The most truculent on the Soviet side are the "leftists," or neo-Stalinists; whereas in the United States, the "rightists" take the lead in pointing to the Soviet danger. The element of sporting rivalry is not absent, as leaders play a sort of game with the highest possible stakes, free from the restraints of domestic policy. On both sides there are strong sectors with an interest in maximum tensions short of war. The most uncompromising anticommunists or anticapitalists are not those most deeply enamored of freedom or socialism but those most involved with the spirit of superpower rivalry or most interested in the confrontation; and clear-cut victories of confrontation are much preferable to the gradual growth of influence.

### The Ideological View

Although each side sees itself as virtuous and patient and regards the other as evil and aggressive, the opener society is far more self-critical. The more authoritarian power is the more self-righteous because of its closure and the lack of criticism of self-serving views; and the rulership, strongly desiring to mobilize the people psychologically, reindoctrinates itself. The Soviet people, aware of propaganda, seem to reject obviously false contentions, such as that Americans are impoverished; but they apparently accept broad ideas not rebutted by visible fact and confirmed by many facts as seen through Soviet lenses, such as that theirs is the superior, more orderly government and way of life, threatened by a vicious selfish "imperialism." They like to think of the United States as a land of immorality and repression, a society without a soul, even while they display exaggerated fondness for American and other Western styles in all realms and love American popular music and literature. As they have virtually given up the dream of catching up materially with the United States and the West, it becomes the more necessary for ideologues to engage in, and for people to believe, all manner of vilification.[6] They are probably sincere in attributing to the United States the vices of the police state, among others, because they see the world in such terms. Despite the Soviet economic slowdown, they continue to insist on the imminent demise of capitalism. In self-justification, they make acceptance of necessity into freedom when they regard the rule of the party and its strong government as necessary if not virtuous.[7]

Recent years have seen a reassertion of Soviet ideological fundamentalism, as the people have been summoned to reject even more strongly "ideological coexistence." General Secretary Gorbachev, in a sense of siege,[8] seems much more set in his world view than Khrushchev was, accepting the strict Marxist-Leninist interpretation that the United States, under the rule of a rich few (like the communist party elite) and suffering skyrocketing unemployment and urban strife, is on the border of economic collapse. Moreover, he has shown no curiosity to learn anything different about the country.[9] An anti-U.S. line, moreover, is useful cover. Gorbachev, speaking to the party congress, had to dwell on the greater evils of capitalism before attacking the shortcomings of the Soviet economy and proposing semicapitalistic remedies of incentives, enterprise autonomy, and attention to market needs.[10]

American attitudes toward the Soviet Union are more diverse, as sources of information are more varied. There are books, papers, and broadcast programs friendly as well as hostile to the Soviets. Many persons, especially intellectuals, are inclined to be critical of their own country and concomitantly kind toward the Soviet way or at least the Soviet people. They make great efforts to be fair, balancing American and Soviet faults and individual American and official Soviet views. But anti-Sovietism has grown in the folk culture; and in the common mind the Russians are associated with poverty, slavery, deceit, and militarism, along with images melded with those of the Nazis. Views have varied somewhat, but they have been hardened by Soviet assertions of power, the arms build-up, and the war on Afghanistan. Anti-Soviet feeling had much to do with the triumph in the United States of the conservative, most anticommunist wing of the Republican party, accompanied by a revival of deeply anticommunist religious fundamentalism.

There is no end of ideology. Happily, it does not dictate conflict, and ideology tells both the United States and the Soviet Union that time is on their side. But it underlines the confrontation of power.

## SUPERPOWERS AND LESSER POWERS

The superpowers cannot refrain from exercising their influence where they can and working to extend their sway. Each dominant power treats clients and allies as part of its projection in the world, especially in the sphere within which it feels responsible, and seeks to lead others into or toward its camp. Prestige and self-respect as a superpower are assuredly more important than any economic motivation in the desire to swing an uncommitted nation or in the vexation at a loss to the other side; if the Soviet Union has become less Marxist, it has not become any less anti-Western in its foreign policy. In the age of intercontinental missiles and submarine deterrents, the psychological rewards or losses are also probably more significant than strategic positions, despite the utility of bases in the vicinity of the adversary.

The attractiveness of colonial holdings has doubtless decreased for the Russians as it has for the Western European powers that cheerfully surrendered their overseas empires. Yet the Soviet Union would find loss of dominion in Eastern Europe unbearable not because it profits economically—the region may cost more than it returns—or because there might be a new German invasion across it but because the loss would be morally and ideologically shattering. Without it, the rulers of Moscow would appear as only secondary actors in world affairs; the claims of special historic destiny would be belied; the loyalty to Moscow of minority peoples, forming half the Soviet population, might become questionable; and the whole idea of a Soviet-led socialist movement would be wounded, perhaps mortally. The expression of this feeling is the Brezhnev Doctrine; that the "socialist" states are responsible to their fellow "socialist" states, in effect, to the Soviet Union, that they have an overriding common interest in the Soviet-led order, that they cannot leave the community, and that the hegemonic power is the sole judge of their conduct.[11]

For the United States, it is vital to support and promote pluralist societies, partly to make a congenial world but even more to keep them free of Soviet domination or influence. It is especially important to check Soviet penetration in the area of most immediate and symbolic significance for the United States, Latin America, particularly Central America and the Caribbean. It is asked, "If we can't stand up to communism in our own backyard, how can we defend freedom anywhere?"

In some ways the relations of the United States and the Soviet Union to weaker powers are parallel. Each has a sphere within which it is dominant, although the United States nowhere approaches the fullness of control exercised by the Soviets in their bloc, where they have forces on the ground or surrounding the country. Out of respect for nuclear arsenals, each keeps hands fairly well off the sphere of the other, without recognizing its legitimacy—indeed, while affirming the universal applicability of freedom or Soviet socialism. Rebellious groups on either side look to the support of the superpower on the opposite side, as Castro's government and the Nicaraguan Sandinistas have done in seeking aid and protection from the Soviet Union, and as Poland's Solidarity movement did in looking to the United States for help. But the support has mostly been moral. The United States has given little beyond verbal assistance to Hungarians, Czechs, and Poles. The Soviet Union, having given large amounts of economic aid to Cuba, has refrained from a formal commitment to its defense, and it has left helping the Sandinistas mostly to Cubans and Eastern Europeans.

But those who would work to change or weaken the Soviet domination of their homeland receive their greatest moral nourishment from the knowledge that the West, especially the United States, is watching and approving; and they keep informed through Western radio and other media. Similarly or to a higher degree, the Soviet Union plays on discontents in the American sphere, furnishing political and financial help to communist and near-communist parties and guerrilla movements, which are not admirers of the Soviet system but protesters against Western or American dominance. It would be far more difficult for any of those in the area of U.S. hegemony to think of going against the regnant system if they did not know that a supportive superpower is ready to give some, albeit limited, assistance, to help organize the movement, to give it an international presence, and to assure them that the future will be theirs.

Any anti-Western movement is naturally anti-pluralist or authoritarian and looks to the backing of those disadvantaged in the prevalent economic order, partly to strengthen its authoritarianism and partly because it opposes the classes benefiting from the status quo. It consequently tends to align itself with the great power hostile to the prevalent order. Concomitantly, U.S. leaders suspect that any movement stressing the lower classes and social change is congenitally anti-U.S. The expectation of hostility is self-fulfilling as leaders of the discontented see their ideology confirmed by the unsympathetic attitude of the great power, which supports the status quo and perhaps prefers a clear-cut anticommunist dictatorship to a more ambiguous democracy.

There is a parallel psychology of dependence in both subordinate spheres. Most people seem to accept the inevitability of the present power structure, and their options are limited by it. Elites look to their hegemon for political guidance, at least to see what assistance they can procure. They also tend to rely on the hegemonic power for security, which means pleasing it so far as this is not too costly in terms of popularity at home; and the more they can rely on foreign support the less they have to take account of the needs and wishes of the people. Communist rulerships of Eastern Europe, aware that their well-being rests on the Soviet Union, are consequently obedient, although they may make some small gestures of independence (as in the case of East Germany's reaching in 1984 toward accommodation with the Federal Republic) or pursue mildly variant policies (as in the case of Hungary's New Economic Model) or seek legitimacy by emphasizing nationalism without deviating from basic Soviet patterns (as in the case of Romania).

Likewise, political elites of the American sphere, whether dictatorial or democratic, have generally been conformist. Really to break away has implied a revolutionary upheaval, as in the cases of Cuba, Grenada, and Nicaragua, possible only under exceptional conditions and at large material sacrifices. The charge most persistently and effectively leveled at rulerships in the American as in the Soviet sphere is that they are puppets of a foreign imperialism. For example, the principal battle cry of the Salvadoran guerrillas is denunciation not of the iniquities of the army or landowners but of the alleged domination and exploitation of the nation by the United States. The Polish regime of General Jaruzelski might be popular if it were not seen as the creature of the Soviet Union.

Although political elites of dependent countries look to their patron for support and guidance, their political interests are by no means identical. The cause is of the superpowers; the dependents go along partly because they have to and partly for concrete advantages, but seldom with enthusiasm. They are definitely not desirous of the worldwide victory of their superpower, which would mean loss of whatever autonomy they retain. In fact they probably do not care for it to become stronger, unless they feel directly threatened by the other side, as they usually do not. They might well be happy to see it somewhat weaker, in order to permit them more freedom of action and to make their cooperation more needed.

Thus Latin American nations are generally unconcerned with the U.S.-Soviet balance. They mostly perceive little danger from communism or Soviet power but considerable pressure against their autonomy from the United States. So far as their independence is in question, the threat they envisage is from the United States, which to them is much the more potent presence. The existence and power of the Soviet Union rather open up more latitude for them.[12] Hence South American nations, such as Brazil and Argentina, regret the attention the United States has given to fighting communism in Central America and cultivate commercial relations with the Soviet Union despite lack of ideological sympathies. If there were a real strategic danger, however, they would probably leap to the support of the United States, as they did in the Second World War and in the Cuban missile crisis—just as did de Gaulle, who had been working to reduce the U.S. presence in Europe.

It is doubtful that any Eastern European state has much enthusiasm for the spreading of Marxism-Leninism except perhaps to earn credits with the Soviet Union. The communist ideology is in general feebler in them than in the Soviet Union (although the less secure regimes, especially Cuba and East Germany, assert more strongly the ideological mission). This is shown, for example, in the somewhat livelier press and the more relaxed economic policies of most of the Comecon states. Hungary seems to have gone about as far toward market socialism as permitted by the Soviet overlordship; and even Bulgaria, the most friendly toward Moscow, has permitted considerable privatization of agriculture. Romania has put nationalism in place of Marxism. Nations that do not have the responsibility of leadership of their camp can be more flexible and ideologically relaxed.

The Soviet Union presses its satellites in vain to increase military spending, but they spend a smaller fraction of their income on defense. Ardent anticommunists in the United States are annoyed by the nonchalance of Europeans in regard to the Soviet menace. Other NATO members are more directly threatened than the United States, as is Japan, but none pays its proportionate share of the cost of the collective umbrella.

The relations of the Soviet Union with its dependents are quite different, however, from those of the United States, in the measure that the ideologically opposite powers are different. The Soviet sphere consists of countries that fell under Soviet military domination (primarily Eastern Europe) plus some outlying powers dependent on Soviet military support (Vietnam, Cuba, Ethiopia, and Angola, in particular). In addition, a number of dictatorial regimes look to Soviet support in holding power. Cuban detachments serve as palace guards in some twenty countries to protect sympathetic rulers. A major form of assistance to Soviet clients is the training and helping of the political police, sometimes by East German experts.

The Soviet sphere is very much a politico-military structure, just as is the Soviet state at home, with relatively tight bonds. The Soviet sphere in the narrower sense—the members of the Warsaw pact—is something between an empire and a confederation. Countries that are militarily held are, of course, not free to break away, whereas for others the loss of Soviet backing would probably mean overthrow of the regime. Since the heady days of Khrushchev's evangelism, the Soviet Union has largely given up the effort to win new clients in the Third World except by military means. It concentrates rather on holding those it has.[13] A corollary is that the Soviet Union has vassals and clients but does not have and cannot have a real ally. Its only alliance, with China, broke up in bitterness after little more than a decade.

The United States, being economically stronger, has much broader means of influence; and a majority of countries may be considered affiliated with it or at least economically dependent on the Western system led by the United States. Only a few—China, India, and some African, Near Eastern and Southeast Asian countries—can really be considered nonaligned. In contrast to the Soviet sphere, the U.S. sphere is primarily commercial; and bonds are not merely or primarily with the political leadership (as in the Soviet case) but with the economic elite.

The United States, not insisting on much conformity, has not only clients but allies, chiefly Japan and the European democracies. It also follows that the U.S. sphere is much looser; the United States exports an ideology of pluralism, which includes freedom to attack the United States. The chief bar to breaking away is economic cost and the inability of the Soviet Union to supply the needs of more countries. When client governments become abusive and corrupt, the United States lacks the means of putting them in order. Consequently the rotting of pro-U.S. dictatorships, as in Iran and Nicaragua, has given power to anti-U.S. movements. It has been fairly easy for the Soviets to install new absolutist regimes to their liking; the United States meets great difficulty in imposing democracy where societies are not hospitable.

It may be that the system of clientage or spheres of influence reduces U.S.-Soviet frictions by placing certain regions off limits. So far as each superpower renounces, in effect, the right of intervention in the area tacitly recognized as pertaining to the other, the world is that much less dangerous. On the other hand, local problems tend to escalate into confrontations of the patrons. What might be purely domestic difficulties in Central America or southern Africa become or are made into skirmishes of the global contest, and the superpowers are set at odds by the effort to satisfy clients. It is difficult for the United States or the Soviet Union to be accommodating when accused of selling out supporters, whether governments, such as El Salvador or Syria, or movements, such as anti-Castro Cubans or anti-Israeli Arabs.[14]

### Advantages and Disadvantages of Both Sides

In this competition for influence, adherents, and power, each side has advantages corresponding to those of authoritarianism and democracy. The Soviet Union profits not only from military bonds but from the fear of war, both by casting a military shadow and by appealing to the fear of nuclear catastrophe. It is also attractive as a model for strong rule and support for those who turn to it to help maintain full power in their societies. If this means turning to some extent away from the modern world, intellectually, politically, and economically, this is for some governments an acceptable price for security and totality of rule.

The authoritarian camp also suffers grave disadvantages. The most serious is that military strength, like civilian productivity, requires extremely refined techniques and engineering; and it is difficult to keep well up technologically without the flexibility and innovativeness of a relatively free society. It is impossible fully to compensate for the shortcomings of the planning mechanism by licit or illicit borrowing. The Soviet Union increasingly lags in productivity and loses the capacity to support clients. The Soviet Union also lacks cultural appeal. For such reasons only very poor states, especially of Africa, seem prepared to follow the Soviet example; and some of these, such as Mozambique, Guinea, and Guyana are drawn to improve relations with the Western powers for economic needs. The Soviet Union, with all the advantages of proximity, could not bring Afghanistan into its orbit without a large-scale invasion, which has been only partially successful.

The same shortcomings have considerably eroded Soviet control in Eastern Europe. Instability calls for aid, but this only raises the need for more.[15] Material dissatisfaction was the primary cause behind the 1980 to 1982 Polish insurgency and the continued unpopularity of the Soviet-dominated government. Other countries, led by Hungary, have increasingly departed from the Soviet politico-economic model in the direction of incentives and some freedom of economic enterprise. This does not imply political deviation, however. The respective governments would like to modernize their economies and alleviate the shortcomings of the control system without sacrificing the security of the Soviet connection.

The Soviet Union is also unable to reduce its commitment to military strength, although to do so would probably bring more strength in the long run by making available needed investment funds. It is politically impossible because of the centrality of military power in sustaining or expanding the Soviet domain. It is psychologically impossible because military power is what makes Soviet leaders tall on the world stage as rulers of a superpower. In terms of participation in the world economy, the Soviet Union is a secondary power; culturally it has even less to offer. But the world listens when the general secretary speaks from a platform held up by tanks, planes, and nuclear warheads.

The United States has advantages in laying stakes on economic free enterprise, human rights, and participatory politics. Elites generally favor democracy as long as it implies no important sacrifices, because they prefer to belong to the modern world and because authoritarianism, except of the extreme variety, often brings insecurity. There is little real radicalism in the Third World except in the upheaval of war; the idea of progress by revolution is moribund because too many clamorous revolutions have brought more distress than progress. Communist parties have not prospered in competitive politics except where they have been rather moderate, as in India. However poor the masses, they are seldom given to violence. With the continual growth of international exchanges, the needs of modernization pull all countries toward economic openness and, by implication, the loosening of political structures. The tide of recent years has been away from state enterprise almost everywhere, and the claims of Marxism-Leninism to high productivity are better fulfilled by capitalism and trade.

The West also gains from the forces bringing the world culturally together with the consequent political effects. More and more people travel internationally; although few are missionaries of political improvement, many carry or are exposed to different modes of life and thought corrosive of the authoritarian mentality. If a society is defined by density of communication, the world is becoming a single society, and there is no more cultural autonomy.

The interaction of independent sovereignties of itself is corrosive of authoritarianism. The intellectual poverty and low creativity of the authoritarian society is a major weakness, as the influence of the United States and of the West in general on styles, entertainment, and culture, popular and highbrow, goes almost everywhere, even widely across the Soviet sphere; and modern technology makes it harder to seal borders. The importance of the rise of English as the world's lingua franca is seldom recognized. To be really educated today, it is necessary to know English; and the language of leading democratic powers not only conveys television comedy but opens to pluralistic attitudes.

It is a consequential cost of the open society that it has countless swirling currents and is far less dedicated to power. Pluralism is more disorderly; authoritarianism appeals to the yearning for order and simplicity. Moreover, the looser society is blamed beyond its demerits. Well-intentioned people consider it their duty to criticize their own country and its actions; the Soviet press fills its columns with anti-U.S. propaganda by quoting the American press. For good or ill, attention is called to defects of American society that would be ignored in the Soviet Union. American foreign policy also lacks the freedom of the Soviets to engage in realpolitik, that is, supposedly advantageous actions contrary to legal or moral standards.

Yet the openness of the democratic society to sometimes destructive criticism carries a promise of long-term success. The more relaxed and undirected order is more flexible and not subject to the decadence, or to the same kind of decadence, that threatens the absolutist order, which slowly becomes sclerotic. The democracy has elections; the highly controlled state can renew itself or shift power from one group to another only haphazardly or by revolution. Unless the imperial order can make its military strength rather rapidly effective, its expansion comes to a halt, and to halt means to decay.

The competition between the democratic and authoritarian principles on the world stage must go on in variable form and intensity as long as there is a system of diverse independent sovereignties. Authoritarianism is fundamentally unmodern, but it is no more outmoded than inequality.

## DÉTENTE

The helmsmen of American policy, opposing a power of alien motives and attitudes, face difficult choices: to what extent to confront the Soviet Union with frank hostility or to try to soften its leaders by mildness and meeting their fears, improving the international atmosphere and giving the Soviet Union a greater stake in the open international system; to what extent to oppose everyone friendly to the Soviet Union or to conciliate neutrals and Soviet client or dependent states, making it easier for them to distance themselves from the Soviet Union; to pressure the Soviet Union to modify its policies or to lead it to change by relaxation; to trade with the Soviets for mutual gain or to restrict trade to hamper Soviet military production. Behind these dilemmas is an even more crucial one: how to reduce the dangers of an utterly catastrophic war between the two nuclear antagonists, while assuring the defense of the United States and democratic institutions from Soviet encroachment and potential destruction.

The Soviet Union faces similar dilemmas: to assert positions against the United States as dictated by ideology or to try to soften its opposition by minor concessions; to woo U.S. allies or to try to drive them from the alliance by fear of war; to court governments in the Third World or to back revolutionary movements; to maintain high principles of socialist struggle or to compromise with capitalism for profit; to seek self-sufficiency at a high cost or to accept dependency on foreign suppliers. The Soviet Union likewise has to decide whether to devote scarce resources to military strength to impress the world, or to invest in the future at the risk of near-term military inferiority.

The greatest reason for moderation on both sides is fear of nuclear war, along with the burdens of overpreparing for conflict by piling up vastly redundant force. Many persons in the United States quite without sympathies for the Soviet system plead for more careful diplomacy or more forthcoming approaches because the dangers are obvious and compelling. The impetus for the 1985 Reagan-Gorbachev summit, like other meetings of the superpower chiefs, came from the nuclear worry. It is objectionable to call the Soviet Union an evil empire not because of the possible falsity of that designation (it is hard to deny that, according to prevalent American values, the Soviet Union is an "evil empire," just as the United States is the equivalent in Soviet terms) but because it is dangerous to treat such a powerful country like an evil thing, and a negative characterization contradicts hopes of accommodation. It is highly unlikely that sane persons will engage hostilities against a nuclear power except in a condition of the most extreme desperation, and the idea of a possible nuclear attack is more sobering than ice water. The superpowers have consequently many times drawn back from a collision course and have engaged millions of man-hours in disarmament or arms control negotiations. But desperation and error are not inconceivable, and a small chance of a nuclear war is very grave. No one has any idea what might happen if a missile of unknown nationality came onto radar screens or even if surveillance satellites were suddenly shot down.

The nuclear preoccupation restrains the intensity of confrontation. But when the superpowers, worried by the nuclear cloud, open negotiations, or as soon as they reach sufficient understanding to lessen slightly their fear of war, they encounter concrete differences and conflicts of interest in how specifically to reduce arms and in how to handle contrary claims in a hundred areas. If the big issue is partly laid aside, smaller issues crowd to the fore to upset relations.

It would be no gain, moreover, if the superpowers, freed of fear of the ultimate horror, were thereby led to risk conventional war. This could prove ultimately as totally destructive as a war that was nuclear from the outset—if only because both powers, having renounced nuclear weapons, would immediately begin manufacturing them under the pressure of war. If nuclear exchanges began in the heat of a conventional war, emotional pressures would make it harder to stop than if the world woke up one morning horrified by the annihilation of a few cities. The real imperative is not to avoid nuclear war but to avoid any war between the superpowers. In this technological age, any violent fight for life or death between very great powers would be excessively calamitous. Modern science and engineering are as potent for destruction as for creation.

### Shared Values

More hopeful than disarmament negotiations is the modification of attitudes by the common engagement and interests of the rivals. Convergence is not entirely mythical; as Soviet revolutionism fades into the mists of history, and as both societies become more bureaucratic, their temperaments become less dissimilar. War between modern powers would be insane. A century or so ago, territorial aggrandizement seemed automatically to increase national power and was seen as a sign of vigor; for this age, a mass of unwilling subjects is probably a burden and certainly not faintly worth risking a conflict, even nonnuclear. The idea of annexation seems to have faded; no major state has added formally to its territory since the aftermath of World War II; and hegemony, as in the spheres of influence, brings few benefits except to pride.

In various ways, of course, U.S. and Soviet interests are not opposite but similar; and the tendency is for the similar interests to grow as the world becomes more integrated. Many world problems call for U.S.-Soviet collaboration, especially in relation to Third World needs; cooperation has not been totally frustrated by contrary purposes. International agreement to strictly limit whaling demonstrates the reality of cooperation in a minor matter.

Elements of condominium exist. For example, the United States and the Soviet Union joined in promoting the postwar dissolution of European colonial empires. They worked together for the Nuclear Non-Proliferation Treaty (1970) and share an interest in limiting the spread of nuclear weapons. They agree on keeping Germany divided and nonnuclear, and both probably favor the status quo in Europe over any likely alternative.[16] The Soviets, like the United States, applauded the inauguration of a civilian president in Guatemala in January 1986.[17] The two powers also share material interests in many areas, from environmental concerns to drug trafficking. The Soviet nuclear disaster at Chernobyl in April 1986, spreading radioactivity over most of Europe, was a reminder that nations are not alone; and the Soviets showed some inclination to accept responsibility.

Trade does not guarantee friendship, but it gives a stake in nonantagonistic relations and promotes the habit of regarding the other side as commercial partner rather than political rival. One of the major developments of the postwar era has been the internationalization of the world economy, and the Soviet bloc has not been excluded. The Soviet Union is an important market for U.S. grain, and the United States and its close allies are the Soviets' chief source of technology. Eagerness for business pushes farmers and industrialists toward accommodation with the Soviets, and there must be parallel effects on the other side. It is decidedly non-Leninist for the Soviet Union to want observer status in GATT, the organization of free trading countries, and to move to allow foreign participation in Soviet enterprises.[18] It is a retreat from principle to honor tsarist bonds to improve the Soviet credit rating. Trade also gives many influential individuals a stake in good, or at least correct relations, and it exposes them to the realities and values of the other side. It is significant that foreign trade has been a steadily growing share of the Soviet national product since the death of Stalin. It is, of course, to the advantage of the United States that competition be commercial rather than military.

Broadly speaking, travel and an ever-growing volume of international communication make something of a world cultural community. In the main Russian cities under half of the films shown are Soviet-made.[19] Russians make a big business of copying and selling recordings of Western shows, even advertising their wares publicly.[20] The importance of video and direct reception of foreign broadcasts can only grow.

Democracy is not so easily transmissible as melodrama and porn, but there is created something of a world political culture. The values of peace, human rights, popular government, and freedom carry some weight everywhere, however the words are reinterpreted or misinterpreted; we are far from the 1930s, when the fascists boasted of trampling on freedom. The Soviets bow to generally accepted values by accusing the United States of censorship, government by a small minority, human rights violations, and such recognized political sins. It is considered proper for the world to concern itself with the internal affairs of sovereign nations—the way they treat their people—and there is no self-proclaimed despotism in the modern world. Gestures made toward democratic institutions—such as fake elections or empty promises of civil liberties—are not wholly without effect. As long as they cannot rule the world but recognize that other lands are richer than their own, Soviet leaders will measure themselves to some extent by world opinion. Soviet leaders seem frequently to listen to Western broadcasts, and the district where they weekend is reportedly spared jamming.[21]

International organizations, the United Nations, its subsidiaries, and a host of others must have some effect on the mentality of the Soviets. Although they will do nothing for the sake of the United Nations, they find these and other bodies useful. But international organizations are pluralism incarnate, and their central objectives—peace and voluntary cooperation, implying respect for separate wills—are the opposite of absolutism.

All such influences contribute at least a little to realistic awareness. The system that talks loudly to itself and hears what it chooses to hear may act out of ignorance as well as malice. It is difficult enough for the democratic leaders to keep impartially informed; for the absolutist ruler, it is impossible. Visits and conferences are consequently valuable, at least so far as they involve people with input to decision making. Most important is a meeting of the heads of the two governments, which humanizes the other side to both leaders and people. No one is expected to change basic views, but both can learn. When Nikita Khrushchev visited the United States in 1959, he not only talked with Eisenhower but saw a great deal of the enemy nation and was impressed with it. Back home, he told his people that the American government was not merely the creature of the monopolists but was supported by its people, that Eisenhower was a man of peace, and that they should plant corn like Iowa farmers.

Both Reagan and Gorbachev left Geneva in November 1985 speaking differently about their counterpart. Soviet television gave a decidedly positive image of President Reagan,[22] and a majority of Americans were optimistic about relations with the Soviets and thought Gorbachev an improvement over previous Soviet leaders.[23] A few months of politics as usual brought relations back about to their presummit low, although disarmament negotiations were continued with some vigor. The October 1986 "minisummit" in Iceland left more acrimony, but the two sides spoke of the most far-reaching disarmament and were prepared to consider considerable expansion of exchanges, including radio and television broadcasts.[24]

It is possible, then, within the limits of political realities on both sides, to promote moderation, better understanding, and the preference for negotiation over confrontation. This is essentially in the democratic way, and the United States has an interest in the strength and breadth of democracy even greater than the Soviet interest in the propagation of Marxist-Leninist authoritarianism, not only to deprive the Soviet Union of potential adherents but to reduce the dangers of war. Democratic states are less likely to be bellicose and to raise international tempers. Mutually beneficial economic relations flourish among pluralistic states; and the international system, including Marxist-Leninist countries, prospers as states take advantage of the open world order and turn their economies toward the world marketplace, in which each has an interest in the prosperity of the others. A pluralistic international order also facilitates cooperative approaches to many modern problems, such as disease control, narcotics traffic, and environmental pollution; and so far as nations of all political complexions are brought into such relations, the world should be safer.

The advance of pluralism in the Soviet Union itself would most ease world strains. The only promising way in which the threat of nuclear holocaust can be much reduced is by the evolution of the Soviet Union toward more moderate politics, less dogmatism, less emphasis on power and military strength, and easier interactions with the outside world—in effect, movement in the direction of a more democratic, or at least less regimented, order.

Unhappily, it is least feasible for the Western powers to attempt to influence the countries of the Soviet bloc, because they are most determined not to be influenced. There is not much to be done beyond a general easing of strains and tensions, but many actions might slightly help to open Soviet society, from more broadcasting and wider exchange programs to moral and political support for pluralist tendencies within the Soviet bloc.[25]

Most important is the prosperity and free order of the United States and other democratic countries. If they stumble and fall back, extremism may well surge up as it did in the 1930s but with even more disastrous results. Although the two leading powers have to occupy opposite ends of the political spectrum, the world average can be moved in either direction.

The enmity or opposition of the two strongest powers is inevitable and enduring. The long-term tendency, however, is toward its moderation, as both the United States and the Soviet Union see their relative power in the world and in their respective spheres slowly slipping in the measure that their shares of the world economy edge downward. Both increasingly have to plead instead of command; it is difficult for either to do much to punish powers that displease it. Politics are consequently softened, and the ideological antithesis is dulled. One day, no doubt, other powers, such as Japan and China, will become political giants and bring about an ideological realignment. Meanwhile, the contest of the present superpowers has to be kept in bounds, as the safety of the world depends on the mitigation of an essentially primitive contest in a world of perhaps too potent technology.

## Notes

1. Howard F. Stein, "Psychological Complementarity in Soviet-American Relations," *Political Psychology*, 6, no. 2 (1985), 253–54.
2. Robert H. Jackson, "Sovereignty and Underdevelopment: Juridical Statehood in the African Crisis" (paper for International Political Science Association, World Congress, July 1985, Paris).
3. Thucydides, *The Pelopennesian War*, trans. B. Jowett (Oxford: Clarendon Press, 1881), vol. 1, 124.
4. *Christian Science Monitor*, March 24, 1986, p. 12.
5. "Political Report of the CPSU Central Committee to the 27th Congress of the Communist Party of the Soviet Union," *Pravda* and *Izvestia*, February 26, 1986, pp. 2–10; and *The Current Digest of the Soviet Press*, 38 (March 26), 4–40.
6. *Christian Science Monitor*, April 8, 1986, p. 21.
7. David K. Shipler, "The View from America," *New York Times Magazine*, November 10, 1985, p. 82.
8. Philip D. Stewart, "Gorbachev and Obstacles Toward Detente," *Political Science Quarterly*, 101, no. 1 (1986).
9. *Washington Post National Weekly Edition*, December 16, 1985, p. 16.
10. *New York Times*, February 23, 1986, p. 4.
11. Michael Handel, *Weak States in the International System* (London: Frank Carr, 1981), p. 189.
12. Robert Wesson and Heraldo Munoz, eds., *Latin American Views of U.S. Policy* (New York: Praeger Publishers, 1986), p. 151.
13. Francis Fukuyama, "Gorbachev and the Third World," *Foreign Affairs*, 64, no. 4 (1986).
14. Stewart, "Gorbachev," pp. 18–19.
15. Valerie Bunce, "The Empire Strikes Back: The Evolution of the Soviet Bloc from a Soviet Asset to a Soviet Liability," *International Organization*, 39 (Winter 1985), 44.
16. Hedley Bull, *The Anarchical Society: A Study of Order in World Politics* (London: Macmillan, 1977), p. 226.
17. *Pravda*, January 17, 1986, p. 5; and *Current Digest*, 38 (February 19, 1986), 17.
18. *Wall Street Journal*, September 12, 1986, p. 28; and *New York Times*, April 7, 1986, p. 24.
19. *Sovetskaya Rossia*, July 18, 1985, p. 2; and *Current Digest*, 37 (October 30, 1985), p. 18.
20. *Izvestia*, July 18, 1985, p. 3; and *Current Digest*, 37 (August 14, 1985), 9.
21. Vladimir Solovyov and Elena Klepikova, "Where the Kremlin Gets the News and How," *Christian Science Monitor*, June 19, 1986, p. 15.

22. *New York Times*, November 23, 1985, p. 4.
23. *Wall Street Journal*, November 26, 1985, p. 62.
24. *The New York Times*, October 26, 1986, p. 6.
25. George Weigel, "Beyond Containment or Detente: Pluralizing the Soviet Union," *Freedom at Issue*, 88 (November-December 1985), pp. 3–6.

# The Future of Politics

## 10

## THE NEW WORLD

This book has thus far been history, dealing with the past of a world in rapid change. Much of it should continue to be valid because human institutions do not change rapidly. But material change is ever more rapid, directions are new, and humanity faces problems of new dimensions in a new framework.

A new era is overtaking the world. It does not come with the suddenness of the opening of the Great War in August 1914; but if we look back a few years, it is remarkable how much concerns have changed. Such issues as terrorism, foreign debt, narcotics traffic, and illegal immigration, hardly noticed a half-dozen years ago, have come to the fore; the concept of national sovereignty has been altered and eroded; and the role of government in the economy is questioned as it had not been for generations.

Two fundamental facts operate to alter the nature of politics. One is technological development, in communications, transportation, information, and production. Moderns are increasingly aware of events in South Africa or the Near East almost as though they happened in their own country. No modern nation can cut itself off from cosmopolitan modes and currents of ideas. Corporations look for business everywhere, not only selling but producing thousands of miles from headquarters, often in partnership with foreign enterprises. Industry surges in Korea or Brazil, and disappears where it seemed fixed. New techniques and products appear so rapidly that any nation has to race to escape falling behind.

Another fundamental fact transforming our condition is that there has been no big war, no conflict of great powers, for over forty years, nearly as long as the period of peace preceding the First World War. The monstrous massacre-conflicts of 1914 to 1918 and of 1939 to 1945, with the worst of world depressions between them, deeply burned human consciousness, shook faith in everything, loosened morals, and made violence the mode. The years 1914 to 1945 were practically a prolonged depression for the world economy, with much slower growth than in decades before and since.[1] The time of troubles created moods of disorder and radicalism and brought the great political aberrations of modern times, communism and fascism.

Nearly two generations later, the world is recovering from that tragic turmoil and finally forgetting much of the nightmare. It slips into the jumble of the past, wonderful material for television drama, but not much more relevant than the Victorian age. The last cohorts of those into whose character the great war was burned are leaving the stage. Those who take charge have never felt that the world was at stake and their country was in danger.

The First World War and the great depression gave rise to Leninist communism in Russia and fascism in Italy, Germany, and Japan, and to dictatorships in a host of other countries, especially Eastern and Central Europe. But the big political sicknesses engendered by crisis and wars are dead or waning. Fascism, crushed by defeat, remains as little more than an eccentricity. There are still spiritual fascists, but they have no place in the modern world. Communism, to the contrary, came out victorious in 1945; and it expanded broadly. But the emotions driving it have been worn out, and it is exhausted and in retreat. Its dynamism and utopianism have been killed by the solidification of a parasitic new ruling class and the failure of what was to bring paradise on earth even to keep up with the modern world. The second superpower fights a rearguard action against obvious and probably irreversible decline. Once-flourishing communist movements have nearly everywhere become insignificant, as in Western Europe and Latin America. The very idea of class conflict has lost most of its appeal in the complex new service-oriented economies, where declining unions may prefer a wage cut to a strike.

Such violent radicalism as still prospers no longer has much connection with Leninism except so far as Leninists opportunistically try to take advantage of it. In the weakness of revolutionism, traditional beliefs resurge. The most forceful ideological movement of our day, Islamic fundamentalism, is deeply reactionary. This is the only new political movement that has received much attention from the United States since the preoccupation with communism began in 1947, as it has brought problems with Iran and Libya. Yet the dynamism of Islamic fundamentalism, boiling up in the Iranian revolution of 1979, seems already to be waning.

The wave of socialism, the idea that economic problems were to be solved by turning them over to the state, was also a product of the time of the wars, when government necessarily commanded production and made business its tool. A decade or so ago socialist parties were powerful in many countries of Western Europe, and it was taken for granted that the state should be the locomotive of modernization in the Third World, even at a sacrifice of liberties. Socialism was also a nativist reaction to capitalist colonialism. But this sentiment, too, is worn out, and hardly anyone still believes that nationalization of industries is a panacea or that the state can bring rapid development by planning. Destatization is the mode in the West and the Third World (where resistance is very strong); even communist states tend to relax economic planning. Countries rather compete to draw foreign investment and reduce taxes to make themselves attractive to entrepreneurs. The radicals of Western Europe are more preoccupied with the arms race and nuclear energy than with nationalizing more corporations.

In the weakness of ideological politics, recent "isms," not only fascism and Marxism but conservatism, socialism, corporatism, and libertarianism, are intellectually barren. No political theory gives a coherent or persuasive outline of the good society to be built in place of the old. There are discontents enough, but they are not intellectually focused. The idea of remaking the political order has largely faded away.

The world has grown in many ways more conservative, contrary to the dizzy pace of material change. Ceremony is back in style. Most people, including the young, accommodate to existing conditions and seek to improve not society but their own condition. Those few who are unable to accept the present way of things go over to mindless bombings. Many terrorist groups, from West Germany or Italy to the Peruvian Shining Path, seem to have virtually no idea except the violent destruction of what they hate. The chief broad and appealing scheme with a mild hope for general improvement is the competitive free-market economy, or what was formerly called the liberal state, than which nothing could be further from violent revolution. The decades of relative tranquillity since World War II have brought the world in certain respects back near where it was around the beginning of this century.

### New Problems

If there is little theory, there is an abundance of problems, largely arising from the technological transformation of the world. Electronics, computer technology, medicine, genetic engineering, and many related fields advance explosively. Not only does science keep making new discoveries; it increases the store of knowledge at an ever rising rate, and knowledge of things becomes knowledge of how to do things and continually alters the conditions of life. At the same time, the effects of technology accumulate: the human situation would continue being altered even if all scientists went on permanent vacation, in ways such as growth of population, the shift of manufacturing to low-wage areas, the deforestation in the tropics, or the accumulation of carbon dioxide in the air.

Material, social, and psychological needs raise ever new demands, and humans have collectively to solve a hundred problems that seem beyond the present capacities of the community. For example, there is no way to decide how to apportion ever more costly medical care and what value is to be placed on human life. If every failing heart is to be replaced by an artificial one, in time all the resources of society would be dedicated to making heart substitutions and taking care of the invalids thus kept alive. An ever-increasing share of the social product in modern countries goes to the elderly, and there is no limit on how much could be spent for the prolongation of senility. Ultimately it must be recognized that what is given to some must be taken from others, and that there is no right to life, only a right not to be wrongly deprived of life.

In a different way, it cannot be decided how far the state is to deny people substances that they desire but that are deemed bad for them; or the decision cannot, in a more or less free society, be made effective. Cocaine and marijuana are ineffectually prohibited, whereas alcohol and tobacco are not; and commerce in the banned substances overburdens law enforcement in the industrial countries and undermines the whole fabric of society in numerous Third World countries.

Major problems arise from the difficulty of reconciling short- and long-term needs. It is not easy to weigh the convenience of burning fossil fuels against the foreseeable effect on another generation of warming climate by the greenhouse effect, causing the melting of polar ice and the flooding of vast lowland areas. Similarly, it may be advantageous, locally and temporarily, to cut down tropical forests, regardless of the possible damage to the global climate. Human reproduction has been largely released from the controls of nature, leading to rates of population growth many times higher than even a century ago. Ironically, in the wealthier countries that could better afford more population growth, the birthrate is far below the replacement level. In both conditions, there must be long-term effects of the gravest moment. But they are beyond the normal horizon of political leadership, and it does not seem possible to cope effectively with them.

Problems are certain to become increasingly global, as humans become technologically more and more proficient and operate on a larger scale, with effects far beyond national boundaries. It would seem indispensable one day to establish international cooperation capable of checking or requiring actions of the sovereign states, just as national governments control the behavior of groups within their boundaries. The success of the eighteen nations bordering the Mediterranean in checking pollution of that beautiful inland sea shows what can be achieved by politically disparate governments with a common interest.[2] International regulation may be necessary in many areas, such as narcotics and nuclear energy: safety precautions may seem uneconomic for a small state, but a meltdown could be murderous for states downwind. There is no apparent way to set up any compulsory international jurisdiction until the nations become much more brotherly than they have ever been, but it is conceivable that in the not-distant future strong nations will be able to persuade, if not compel, weaker ones to desist from detrimental actions. If the release of chlorofluorocarbons threatens the world's ozone layer, national sovereignty is likely to be set aside.

National sovereignty is also being set aside by the ever-growing powers of annihilation. Not only does the nuclear potential of the leading powers grow astronomically, but the dangers of chemical or biological weapons are sure to increase. It may well be, moreover, that nations of the second rank will be able to hold a threat of unacceptable damage over the strongest. The world is increasingly hostage to madness on the part of any person or party controlling an industrially advanced nation.

All such problems, from the narcotics trade to the arms race, are related to the division of the world into rich and poor or—what is roughly equivalent—into West and non-West.

## THE DISPARATE WORLD AND DISPARATE SOCIETIES

In both there are contrary trends. The political antagonism of East and West is made more dangerous by the technological arms race, in which both sides feel driven to push ahead because they cannot be sure what the other might invent and deploy. Technology drives the arms race; if it came to a halt it might become possible to negotiate a standstill where more destructive power is close to madness. At the same time, the contrary trend of modernity is toward world integration, interdependence, and cultural uniformity. Thus far this tendency seems to have kept pace, approximately, with the rising dangers of the arms race, and no one can say whether the world is more at risk now than twenty years ago or will be twenty years from now.

The world confrontation is dangerous mostly because of the economic division between the beneficiaries and the nonbeneficiaries of the Western technological and industrial development. If all countries were roughly at the level of Western Europe and the United States, temptations to foreign expansiveness and the consequent dangers of escalating confrontation would be minimal. Most countries of the Third World are fearfully weak militarily and perhaps politically, and both the United States and the Soviet Union see an opportunity, if not an obligation, to spread their influence in political near-vacuums. For the Soviet Union, the peoples of the South are or should be natural allies in its contest with the hostile West.

Here again the effects of the technological revolution have been, and will probably continue to be, equivocal. On the positive side, for many years productivity and standards of living have risen not only in the industrialized countries but also in most of the less-developed world, and global trade has grown phenomenally. The result has been optimism and a substantial spread and deepening of institutions of popular government. As eighty years ago, it would be pleasant to project the trends of the recent past into the indefinite future and to assume that humanity is on the way to a new era of political enlightenment and general happiness.

It is not certain, however, that the democratization of Third World countries today has a very much sounder basis than the constitutionalism of Iran and Turkey prior to World War I, although it certainly has spread far more widely and has reached very many more people. Most of the world is very far from having well-functioning governments or reasonably productive economies. The failure of natively capable and intelligent people to use their capacities is such that their income, in terms of salable goods, may be a tenth to a hundredth of that of the average inhabitant of the United States, Western European countries, or Japan; and they lack not only shiny gadgets but good diets, health care, and cultural opportunities.

The gap between average income levels of the First and Third Worlds has increased from 1950 to the present, and the widening of the gap is understated because the higher prices of manufactured goods and the growth of the market at the expense of the informal economy cause the economic growth of the Third World to be overstated. As trade, travel, and communications force the world more and more into a single complex, problems of migration, mostly illegal, of narcotics, and of financial imbalance grow and defy hesitant efforts at solution. Many countries have become hopelessly dependent on imports of foodstuffs, for which they lack the means to pay. Not long ago it seemed possible that a fair number of Third World countries might achieve an economic level comparable to that of the Western world within a generation. This is no longer conceivable. On the contrary, the technological gap grows. Hardly any Third World country can reasonably aspire to high-tech industry, except as planted there from outside to use cheap labor or to gain market access. Since 1982, moreover, much of the Third World has been plunged into depression by financial dependence.

The advanced industrial world has a strong negative impact on Third World societies. The modern sector tends to separate from the premodern, not only economically but culturally, as the elite become more or less assimilated to world culture, devaluing things native. The insignificance of most Third World countries is ever more patent, as their televisions are graced by foreign soaps. Condemned to permanent poverty, with little to raise national pride, they have ever less basis for patriotism. As movement becomes easier, many of the more capable and enterprising persons, especially of countries wracked by violence or oppression, depart for more promising lands. It is a little like the decay of the inner cities of the United States, from which persons of education and ambition move to the suburbs, leaving the more demoralized behind.

In sum, the political and economic inequalities of nations are made more acute by the very modernization that may promise eventually to reduce them. There is no obvious solution within either the democratic or the authoritarian framework. Yet solutions must be found if civilization is to stabilize itself or rise to a higher level of humanity.

## THE IMPROVEMENT OF DEMOCRACY

The advanced countries can hope to lead and assist the majority of the human race only if they can cope with their own needs and meet the rising challenges of the technological age. In the United States, Western Europe, and Japan, the government functions passably well, at least avoiding serious violent confrontations and managing rationally enough to preside over slowly rising standards of living. But it could do much better in the present and is far from adequate for the needs of the future. The United States particularly lags in such significant matters as the literacy rate, the scientific-technical education of the masses, the percentage of national product directed to research, and the savings ratio. It, like other advanced nations, has largely failed to convert the fabulous wealth of technology into greater productivity, much less human welfare.

Within the United States and other advanced nations the swirl of modern development has effects parallel to the separation of the sectors of the world community. Income inequality tends to grow as some profit from the cornucopia of opportunities of the technological revolution and others are left behind and demoralized. The distance from the stagnant north and the prosperous south of Britain is far greater than appears on the map, and it does not decrease. To go from the slums of New York or Chicago, or depressed Appalachia, to Silicon Valley is a bit like going from Honduras to the United States. Sectoral inequality maintains or increases itself, like the inequality among nations, as money, brains, and technology are drawn to favored areas.

If the modern society is divided between those riding the knowledge revolution and those left drifting, the government largely belongs to the backward category. Aside from such superficialities as office automation, the ways of government in the United States and other Western nations have been improved only slightly for many decades. Institutional innovation and adaptation have been minimal; the same structures that came out of World War II have to cope with the complex problems of the waning of the century. It is with reason that *politician* and *bureaucrat* are pejorative, and most people in the best governed countries have some distrust for the government. If its purpose is to convert the wisdom of the nation into action for the common benefit, it fails as much as it succeeds. It is obviously wasteful, inefficient, seems incapable of managing its finances, and cannot provide anything like full employment. If the inadequacy of political institutions is a chief cause of poverty in the Third World, it is also a reason for the failure of advanced democracies to satisfy better the aspirations of the people.

In many ways, to be sure, standards have improved in the developed countries over a long period, and especially since World War II, with better observance of civil rights, greater responsibility of the state, and better informed electorates. Political understanding has become much more sophisticated. But complexity outgrows understanding; needs expand more rapidly than capacities, and unless institutions are continually improved they gradually become less adequate. Yet purposeful reform of political institutions is very difficult. People are normally conservative, feel comfortable with the known, and are rightly distrustful of the untried. The legitimacy and in part the effectiveness of authority, in democratic as well as in nondemocratic societies, rest heavily on custom. Moves for change—at least deeper change—are fueled by violence, and violence is inacceptable in the modern world.

All political systems, moreover, carry inertia because those to whom power is allocated are ipso facto beneficiaries of the given arrangements and sure to be skeptical of changes possibly detrimental, even slightly, to their own position. This holds strongly where the political system totally dominates society, as in the absolutist states; it is less emphatically true of the democracies, where the structure of power is less coherent and influential people outside the political system can press for change. Short of a breakdown of authority, changes of political institutions have to be acceptable to those whom present institutions place on top. For example, an elected body can rarely be persuaded to change the rules for its election.

### Political Reforms in American Government

Dissatisfaction with major political institutions has increased in recent years, however, and various reforms may conceivably be adopted to meet criticisms and make the state more effective. For example, there is a strong drive in the United States to compel balancing of the budget by law. A slightly more radical move for this country would be to adopt the near-universal practice of other democracies and deprive the legislative organ of the power to increase expenditures beyond the budget proposed by the executive. The Congress itself might be strengthened by extending the term of representatives from two to four years. This might be balanced by limiting the number of terms senators and representatives can serve in order to offset the advantages of incumbency.

Nearly everyone agrees that the means of choosing the American president is highly defective, as it virtually excludes persons actively engaged in public service unless, perhaps, they can combine current duties with a compulsion to become president. It is a dilemma of democracy that the people are entitled to choose, but the qualifications for winning their favor are not the same as those for best service to the state. Similarly, it could be required that the candidates for president have served in some high capacity—for example, in the Senate—in order to assure relevant experience.

Many have urged that presidents should have a nonrenewable six-year term in the hope that, with a single term of reasonable length to try out their stock of ideas, they could think more of their legacy and less of their popularity. It is contended that the people should be free to elect or reelect whomever they please, and that presidents should always follow the wishes of the people. But incumbency makes a dubious contest in which sitting presidents are burdened with responsibility for events beyond their control or are credited with benefits they have not brought. They have advantages of publicity, and they may do much to make themselves seem indispensable.[3]

One reason to limit the presidential term is that the office is impossible: one person is supposed to be representative of the nation, party leader, chief executive, manager, and guide or at least supreme judge of foreign, economic, and social policy. The burden might be a little relieved, and the executive officer made more effective, by delegating ceremonial duties and some residual powers to a formal chief of state, like the British monarch or the German president, who stands behind the chancellor. The U.S. Constitution was drawn up at a time when parliamentary government was incompletely evolved; if it had been drafted fifty years later, the Constitution would doubtless have incorporated more responsibility of the executive to the legislative body.

It would also seem appropriate to make the former chief executive a member of a high advisory or constitutional council for a number of years or for life, at least if, after leaving office, he were judged to have served well. This would give the nation greater benefit of the experience of persons best acquainted with the needs of the state; it would also somewhat reduce the acrimony of the political struggle. The high council might be a body somewhat like the Roman Senate, a group of experienced former officials and military leaders who by sage and disinterested judgment greatly helped the Roman republic on its way to world empire.

The presidency might also be eased if more decision making were shifted to qualified nonpolitical groups, permanent or ad hoc, in the Japanese way of making permanent civil servants responsible for much policy formation or as the American president is relieved in nuclear matters by the Nuclear Regulatory Commission. It is a sound principle that elected authorities name suitable persons to head departments and turn over to them the direction of most affairs, especially technical and economic, under general guidance of the political sovereign. This would be in the manner of local governments hiring professional city managers, under the scrutiny, but not direct control, of the elected mayor or council.

On the other hand, the workings of the apparatus are quite as defective as the institutions of political leadership. Much might be done to raise the standards of the bureaucracy by more specialized training. More important, the bureaucracy needs to be made more responsible and less of an independent and self-serving segment of society with its own bureaucratic mentality. There have been irregular moves in this direction by contracting out services, including rather high-level studies, to private persons and organizations. Some of the alienation of public servants from civil society arises from making government service a lifetime career, with which the individual may be expected to identify. The principle of limited terms of political office is broadly appropriate; for example, it is argued that leading corporate executives should shift after five or six years.[4]

It would democratize the civil service to abandon the principle of permanent tenure in favor of term appointments to responsible positions: after a certain number of years, an official would have to compete for a new appointment or go back to the private sector. This would make possible more rapid advancement and more responsibility for young persons. It would avoid the rigidity and staleness that come from people staying too long in comfortable ruts, building up cozy relations, and turning responsibility into routine. It would facilitate the emergence of new ideas and bring government and unofficial society closer as people moved in and out of official service. By giving more civil servants experience in the private sector, and private managers experience in government, the qualifications of both would be improved. Such a reform could also reduce the bureaucratic esprit de corps that leads civil servants to favor their organizational interests over those of the community. It would undercut the perennial drive of the fixed bureaucracy to inflate itself, the budget, and the state, and to serve itself.

### Extending Equality

Whatever the value of patching institutions, however, most improvement of government in the West, as in the Third World, can come from the development of equality. If government in Japan is exceptionally effective, this may be due not so much to specific institutions as to the broadly egalitarian mentality of the nation. Taiwan has an authoritarian regime but a competent government; this may be due in good part to the relatively high degree of equality on the island. The more equality, the more manageable political problems become and the easier it is to adapt the state to changing conditions. So far as the community is joined in basic values, the government can be closely responsible and responsive to the needs of the citizenry, and political differences are less threatening to anyone's vital concerns.

As in the Third World, redistribution is difficult, problematic, and of doubtful efficacy. But inequality can be attacked by making people more productive and—especially in the United States where opportunities are often more available than used—motivating backward groups to self-realization and bringing them more fully into the broader community. The ethnic and racial diversity of the United States and the large influx from poorer countries markedly increase inequality, but it could be the American goal that no one have to sleep in the street and that all enjoy a decent subsistence, as is claimed of Scandinavia.[5]

### The Need for Order

The centrality of equality and community does not mean, however, that more responsive equals more responsible. It cannot be assumed that the more closely the state is geared to the wishes of the citizens the better. There is justice in the criticism that democracy lends itself to chaos and that liberty becomes license. Those who claim to act on behalf of the people, even if contrary to the momentary desires of the majority, are not necessarily wrong. People desire not only freedom but direction and order, a political will expressing community purpose, and assurance that matters beyond their competence are in good hands. Government has to become more technocratic and specialized. Democracy is incomplete not only because people have not gotten around to making it complete but also because it is inevitably qualified by the contradictions of the individual and social sides of human nature and needs. There is no solid philosophical basis for total democracy, because it is only partially true that individuals know what is best for them and act for the common good while following their own impulses. Society has to guide itself in many ways, and for coherence it must have authoritarian elements along with responsibility to prevent misuse of power.

Democratic institutions are by no means a full answer. Great Britain has hardly been seriously faulted for lack of democracy, and since World War II it has been more politically (although not socially) egalitarian than before. Yet in the past generation it has fallen from being one of the richest of the industrial nations into the ranks of the poorer. It has suffered chronic regional depression and excessive unemployment for many years; British industry lags; and living standards have climbed only modestly through decades of technological change. The rich have gotten richer, but the poor have stayed poor. The nation suffers a deep malaise.

On the other hand, if Japan has been hugely successful by all historic standards, democratic institutions cannot claim full credit. Economically, Japan performed quite well under the old quasidemocracy. The Japanese bureaucracy, which has contributed greatly to economic guidance, is directly descended from the imperial bureaucracy.[6] It is in the national character to see virtue in obedience to law, but this is as much a feudal inheritance as a democratic adaptation. Something of the Japanese performance may be ascribable to the survival of authoritarian discipline and the subordination of the individual to the group. Directness and openness are frequently associated with democracy, but Japanese manners are the opposite.

Purposeful national leadership, as in Japan, may be at least as important for the prosperity of a country as representative institutions. The problem of government is not strictly to secure a maximum of freedom and democracy but to join freedom and equality with order and leadership for the maximum of well-being. Political reform has to combine or balance more direct influence of the people with greater effectiveness of authority.

Most observers would probably agree that the state should be predictable or nonarbitrary and responsible to its citizens, and that it should permit freedom of expression and criticism. It should encourage readiness for social growth and change, the increase of useful information, a respect for human dignity, and adherence to law, all of which are elements of modernization.[7] The problem of government is that of managing a large organization that happens to be involuntary and peculiarly powerful. Its principles are in many ways those of a social club or of a corporation. The leadership should be responsible to the members or stockholders, who should be able to remove executives and board at designated times, and there should be clear rules defining procedures and powers, permitting rational decisions promoting the interests of the member-stockholders.

The state is the nearest thing to the incarnation of the large community, and we want it not only to be just but to be strong, at least in relation to other states, not only to defend and lead but to do a thousand things for us that we cannot or will not do for ourselves.

## POLITICAL DEVELOPMENT

Causes and effects in deeper political issues are unclear. The character of the state clearly is vital; but no one can say, for example, how much of the success by world standards of the United States or Sweden or Switzerland is ascribable to political forms and how much to less tangible national traits such as industriousness and respect for law. In Scandinavia, it is awkward to arrive five minutes late for appointments; in parts of Latin America, an hour's tardiness is standard. How this may be related to the Scandinavian sense of community responsibility, high productivity, and the welfare state has not been clarified. Likewise, we do not know how to weigh freedom against security, opportunity against equality, morality against indulgence, relaxation against material production, or the present against the future. If it is hard for moderns to find purpose in personal life, it is harder for the state to do more than respond to the multitude of pressures brought on it.

However inadequate the state, to engineer its improvement seems impossible except in conditions of violence, not only because of the overwhelming influence of the status quo but also because the discontented cannot agree on new blueprints. There will be change, but it will doubtless continue to be—absent disastrous conflict—mostly by gradual reinterpretation and changes of values and usage. For example, the powers of the American presidency have been enlarged far beyond the imagination of the writers of the Constitution, although none of the twenty-six amendments explicitly adds to its authority. Similarly, without change of constitutional structures, the American government has undertaken responsibility for securing nondiscrimination on grounds of race and sex to an extent that would have seemed utopian a generation ago.

It is the duty of the state to protect both the autonomy of individuals, with their rights to an equal voice, and the broader needs and longer view of the community, finding the proper balance between public and private needs and rights. The separate intelligences of these semisocial creatures must be induced to work independently for the common, as well as the individual, good and to use their initiative in harmony with collective purposes. To join and adjust the individual and social sides of human nature, opposites must be brought into concord: there should be stability and openness to change, and appropriate rewards for work or merit without too much injury to equality. Personal values have to be balanced by community values, and independence by cooperation; pluralism has to be reconciled with collectivism.

The future order of society requires not that all be regulated by the state but that all, or a sufficiently large majority, be motivated toward the well-being of the community and a livable world. Freedom can be sustainable only if people voluntarily subordinate personal interests to a high degree, that is, take pleasure in doing what they understand needs to be done. Freedom has to be restricted, but it is best restricted informally and nonpolitically, in ways that give no individual the means of exploiting others. The needs of the good society should be a useful guide for conduct, just as under natural conditions biological urges are a good guide to fulfilling the needs of the body.

This implies goals of generally recognized justice and full equality of opportunity, with inequality of results tempered by compassion and the realization that fortune is unfair. It also implies competition, perhaps very intense, among nations, organizations, groups, and individuals—a competition, not in destructive, but constructive capacities. For nations, for example, competition is appropriate in science and the arts of production; it might well be also in social reform and the ability to handle the problems of vertiginous modernization. In this regard, the Japanese may take the lead, but others will no doubt be stimulated to follow. The Japanese also are leaders in competitive learning, at least for getting ahead on the educational ladder. Whereas in some ways, such as dedication to the corporation, they are apparently softening, their contest for scholastic excellence seems to be losing none of its intensity.

The principle of competition is close to the principle of freedom and the opposite of monopoly, which is the essence of tyranny. The competition for political position should be as open as possible, just as the competition for economic advantage or wealth should be unbiased, thereby giving maximum flexibility and realism. This should be the purpose of political institutions, if they are to meet the challenge of the future; to integrate the individual and social natures of humans to give maximum effect to human capacities.

The state must either become something much better or have no future. Civilization seems to become too complex too rapidly for human self-rule to keep pace, and problems of which we have no inkling may prove ultimately unsolvable within the parameters of organized society. If that occurs and democratic government fails by suicide through technology, humankind cannot go back to a simpler culture without biological disaster. It would probably see a radical reduction of the earth's population and reversion to a primitivism as of the isolated Indian village, reliant only on its own resources—a primitivism from which the climb back to the technology of gene splicing and production by robots might be impossible. We know that the universe has to be such as to make possible the development of intelligent beings such as ourselves who observe it, and from this "anthropic principle" physicists make interesting deductions. But whether or not the level of humanity can rise much higher or to endure much longer depends on us.

### Notes

1. Lloyd G. Reynolds, "The Spread of Economic Growth to the Third World," *Journal of Economic Literature*, 21 (September 1983), p. 961.
2. *The New York Times*, October 21, 1986, p. 21.
3. Griffin D. Bell, "One-Term Six-Year Presidency," and Arthur Schlesinger, Jr., "Against a One-Term Six-Year Presidency," *New York Times*, December 31, 1985, p. 21 and January 10, 1986, p. 27, respectively.
4. Robert Townsend, *Up the Organization* (New York: Alfred A. Knopf, 1984), p. 197.
5. Michael Roskin, *Other Governments of Europe: Sweden, Spain, Italy, Yugoslavia, and East Germany* (Englewood Cliffs, N.J.: Prentice-Hall, 1977), p. 35.
6. Chalmers Johnson, *MITI and the Japanese Miracle* (Stanford: Stanford University Press, 1982), chap. 3.
7. Alex Inkeles and David K. Smith, *Becoming Modern: Industrial Change in Six Developing Countries* (Cambridge: Harvard University Press, 1974), pp. 19–25.

# Index

Absolute state:
 communication control, 120
 establishment of support, 117–18
 evolutionary course, 88
 fear of change, 120
 isolation, 120
 leadership characteristics, 87–88, 117
 oligarchic form, 86–87
 population control, 106
 power distribution, 120
 supporter, corruption of, 117–18
Acton, Lord, 159
Adams, John, 155, 162
Adenauer, Konrad, 71
Administrative staff, 167. See also Bureaucracy; Civil Service
Advanced democracies. See Democracies
Advertising, influence, 183
Aerospatiale (France), 157
Afghanistan, 246
 invasion of, 248, 254
Africa:
 ethnic persecutions, 189
 grain production, 60
 and Western ideals, 50
"Africanism," Zaire, 50
Africans, 9
Afrikaaners, 9
Agricultural subsidies, 182
Agriculture, Russia, 45–46
Akkadian Empire, 29
Albania, 108, 134
 divergence from Soviet path, 90
Alexander the Great, 31
Alphonsin, Raúl, 213
Allende, Salvador, 88–89
Allies, Western, 230–31
Alma-Ata riots, 142
American Motors, 157
American Revolution, 35
Amin, Idi, 62, 67–68, 137
Andropov, Yuri, 87, 116
Angola, 90
Anti-Sandinista support, 245
Aquino, Corazon, 170, 211, 218
Arab countries:
 democracies, 49
 fundamentalism in, 49
 Soviet support of, 244
Arabs, 9

Arbenz, Jacobo, 221
Argentina, 61, 62, 77, 78, 87, 222
 austerity measures of, 197
 church influence in, 89
  governability of, 52
 military regime of, 139, 213, 228
 19th century dictatorship of, 92
 quasidemocracy elite, 213
 social inequity, 189
 tax evasion, 218
 upper class, 89
Aristotle, 6, 12, 30
 on law, 222
 on the state, 86
Armed Forces, quasidemocracy:
 role of, 220–21
 in Uruguay, 224. See also Military
Arms limitation, 257
Asian, 9
Assyrian Empire, 29
Athens, 244
 democracy, 30, 150
Australia, federalism, 154
Austro-Hungarian Empire, 37
Authoritarianism:
 brutality, 68
 concessions to democracy, 134
 and corruption, 122
 necessary elements, 90
 as role model, 122
 social mobility, 90
Authoritarian leaders, 135
Authoritarian societies, 255
Authoritarian state:
 character, 10, 11, 21, 67–69, 70
 claims to legitimacy, 69, 83, 140
 continuity problem, 73, 141
 control within, 69–70
 dissension, 119
 economy, 67
 and human nature, 66
 judicial system, 70
 personal basis of, 68
 political control, 67–68
 political orientation, 69
 rigidity, 119, 140
 role of, 125
 success areas, 134
 variety of, 69

Authority, role, 66
Autocratic government:
 character of, 114–15
 innovations, 20

Balance of power, 33, 36
 intermediate organizations, 153
 Europe, 38
 and representative governments, 153
Balts, 90
Batista, Fulgencio, 80
"Bay of Pigs" incursion, 89
Beecher, Henry Ward, 187
Belgium:
 bureaucracy, 192
 ethnic division, 54, 186
Birthrate, Third World, 234
Black market, 127
Blacks, 9
Bolivia:
 austerity measures, 197
 military dictatorship, 228
Bolivian Revolution of 1952, 62
Bolshevism, 38
 ideological synthesis, 45
 establishment, 95
Botswana:
 democracy, 212
 economy, 226
Bourgeoisie, 55, 98
Brazil, 56, 61, 77, 79, 168, 183
 austerity measures, 197
 civil government, 208
 corporatism, 208–9
 economy, 135
 elections, 232
 federalism, 154
 role of military, 228–29
 state enterprises, 208
Brest-Litovsk, Treaty of, 95
Brezhnev, Leonid, 87, 115
 death, 118–19
 and reform, 131
Brezhnev Doctrine, 249
Bribes. See Corruption
Britain:
 and Argentina, 213
 democracy of, 20
 empire of, 36
 and influence on India, 49
 institutions, 54. See also England; Great Britain; United Kingdom
British institutions, Ireland, 54